Data Warehouse Performance

W.H. Inmon

Ken Rudin

Christopher K. Buss

Ryan Sousa

D1633760

W_____ _____ _____SHING

John Wiley & Sons, Inc.

New York • Chichester • Weinheim • Brisbane • Singapore • Toronto

Publisher: Robert Ipsen
Editor: Robert Elliott
Assistant Editor: Pam Sobotka
Managing Editor: Micheline Frederick
Text Design & Composition: Publishers' Design and Production Services, Inc.

Designations used by companies to distinguish their products are often claimed as trademarks. In all instances where John Wiley & Sons, Inc., is aware of a claim, the product names appear in initial capital or ALL CAPITAL LETTERS. Readers, however, should contact the appropriate companies for more complete information regarding trademarks and registration.

This book is printed on acid-free paper. ⊗

Published by John Wiley & Sons, Inc.

Published simultaneously in Canada.

This publication is designed to provide accurate and authoritative information in regard to the subject matter covered. It is sold with the understanding that the publisher is not engaged in professional services. If professional advice or other expert assistance is required, the services of a competent professional person should be sought.

Library of Congress Cataloging-in-Publication Data:

Data warehouse performance / W. H. Inmon . . . [et al.].
    p.   cm.
  Includes index.
  ISBN 0-471-29808-5 (pbk. : alk. paper)
  1. Data warehousing. I. Inmon, William H.
QA76.9.D37D39 1998
658.4'038'0285574—dc21   98-35004
                         CIP

Printed in the United States of America.

10 9 8 7 6 5 4 3 2 1

Contents

Chapter Nine **Building a High-Performance Platform** **197**

Acknowledgments

The authors wish to express thanks to the many colleagues who have contributed to our understanding of what it takes to plan, build and manage a high-performance data warehouse environment. No such book would be possible without the support of such a talented group of people.

Bob Barthelow—Hewlett-Packard Co.
Bruce Jenks—Hewlett-Packard Co.
Claudia Imhoff—Intelligent Solutions, Inc.
Corinne Jullian—Bristol-Myers Squibb
Debra Colombona—Pine Cone Systems
Dennis McCann—Pine Cone Systems
Dhamodhar Ramanathan—Hewlett-Packard Co.
Doug McBride—Hewlett-Packard Co.
Greg Battas—Tandem Computers
Greg Blair—Bristol-Myers Squibb
Jim Meyerson—Hewlett-Packard Co.
JD Welch—Datawing Consulting
Joe Reese—Cornerstone Concepts, Inc.
Joel Cyr—MCI Communications, Inc.
John Geiger—Intelligent Solutions, Inc.
John Michael Dunn, Jr.—FMG Marketing
John Zachman—Zachman International

Joyce Norris-Montanari—Intelligent Solutions, Inc.
Ken Jacobs—Oracle Corporation
Ken Richardson—Pine Cone Systems
Kevin Waugh—MCI Communications
Lowell Fryman—Intelligent Solutions, Inc.
Lynne Uyehara—Hewlett-Packard Co.
Marc Weinberg—Pacific Bell
Mark Mays—Arrowhead Consulting
Mark Sturdevant—Hewlett-Packard Co.
Martin Haworth—Hewlett-Packard Co.
Pam Munsch—Hewlett-Packard Co.
Pete Simcox—Informix
Roger Geiwitz—Pine Cone Systems
Ron Patterson—MCI Communications, Inc.
Tom Connolly—S3 Consulting
warehouseMCI team—MCI Communications

We would also like to extend a special thanks to our parents, wives and children who provided us with encouragement to begin such an endeavor and who shared in our sacrifice, trials and tribulations along the way. Finally, we would like to thank Bill Inmon for his undying contributions and leadership toward the cause of data warehousing. He is a mentor and friend, and helped us realized that one can write a book, have a career and still have time for friends and family.

Preface

Data warehousing has evolved from theory to conventional wisdom in a very short amount of time. In the early years of information processing, data was stored and organized in a manner that was optimal for collection and storage. Early structures that were optimal for this were hierarchical structures, networked structures, and inverted list structures. These early operational structures were good for the basic needs of gathering and storing data, but were hardly optimal for the access and analysis of data. As a result, the marketing, sales, and finance departments had nowhere to turn to access the data they knew was in the corporate collection of systems to support their need for business intelligence. They were continually being rebuffed and shunned aside by the information systems (IS) department who had their hands full running systems to support the day-to-day business. Eventually marketing, sales, and finance took matters in their own hands and built their own stores of data. These early stores of data were refined into what is today called the data warehouse.

The data warehouse unlocks the data jailed in the corporate bowels and allows easy and unfettered access. The appeal of data warehousing is equally strong to the business person as it is to the technician. Both communities have much to gain by building and maintaining a data warehouse. There are some very good reasons why data warehousing has become a permanent fixture in the halls and walls of the corporation.

The world of data warehousing is fundamentally different from the classical operational, transaction processing world. In many regards data warehousing turns the world of operational systems upside down:

The development approaches are different. The operational world relies on a disciplined waterfall approach to systems development. The world of data warehousing requires a circular, spiral approach to systems development, where results are produced in short, fast iterations. One of the most alluring aspect of data warehousing is that the end user does not have to wait for lengthy periods of time in order to be able to see results.

Transactions are completely different. An operational transaction operates in two to three seconds on a consistent basis and demonstrates a fairly predictable pattern of access. In contrast, a data warehouse transaction operates in thirty seconds to five minutes to an hour to as much as three to four days and demonstrates a fairly unpredictable pattern of access.

The operational world serves the clerical and business administration community. The data warehouse world serves the managerial and business planning community.

The decisions made coming out of the operational world are very short term. The decisions made coming out of the data warehouse world are long term and strategic.

The amount of data accessed by an operational transaction is small—a few rows or records at a time. The amount of data accessed by a data warehouse transaction may be hundreds of thousands of records or even millions of records at a time, and so forth.

There are then many significant differences between the worlds of operational processing and data warehousing. So as you might expect, the concepts, techniques and technologies used in building and administering the data warehouse are very different (in their form and application) than those that once applied. An entirely new discipline must be learned in order to be successful. This book is about the most important of disciplines needed to deliver and manage a high-performance data warehouse environment.

Performance in the data warehouse environment first becomes an issue when the volumes of data start to mount in the data warehouse. As long as there is only a small amount of data, it is easy to overwhelm the environment with hardware resources and achieve very good query response time for all users. It is only when the amounts of data start to accumulate that the issue of performance even begins to arise. But once the volumes of data start to rise, performance concerns rise in equal measure. Soon the data warehouse administrator finds himself/herself beset with unhappy users. It is at this point that the data warehouse administrator takes a hard look at optimizing performance.

However, query response time is not the only measurement of performance. No sooner does the data warehouse administrator get query performance under control, than he begins to realize that this is just one of a variety of measurements needed to be factored into the performance equation. In addition to query performance, such factors as availability, data quality, data currency, and throughput must be considered in measuring performance of the data warehouse environment (perhaps even before query response time).

Suffice to say a high-performance data warehouse environment is one that supports the immediate expectations (i.e., needs) of the business and is an environment that will scale (i.e., grow) to support these needs as they evolve. A number of factors must be considered in defining and delivering on these performance objectives.

This book addresses performance by first acknowledging that a high-performance data warehouse is not a single architectural construct based on some exotic design technique and technology running on a piece of hardware (though this may suffice initially). Rather a high-performance data warehouse is an environment that contains a variety of architectural constructs, techniques, and technologies that are carefully combined to arrive at a balance solution that delivers on the diverse analytical needs of the user community. Sound complex? It is. However, this book will help you through these complexities to arrive at a data warehouse environment that not only meets the initial needs of the user community but scales to support these needs over time.

This book is organized into three parts. The first part is an introduction that provides the basis for the issues facing designers, implementors, and administrators of a high-performance data warehouse environment. Following the introduction we cover what it takes to build and maintain a high-performance data warehouse environment from several very important perspectives as depicted in Figure P.1.

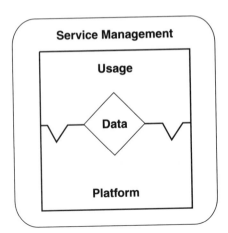

FIGURE P.1

Elements of a high-performancing data warehouse environment.

These perspectives are covered in detail in the chapters that follow and are organized into four Parts. The first Part—*Usage, Data and Performance*—focuses on building the high-performance data warehouse environment from the perspectives of usage and data since these layers fundamentally shape the landscape of this environment. The second Part—*Platform and Performance*—focuses on constructing the platform on which the usage and data reside. This is an important perspective because if the platform is not constructed properly, the data warehouse environment will *not* scale to support the evolving needs of the business. The third Part—*Service Management and Performance*—focuses on the "pearl" of the high-performance data warehouse environment, service management. In contrast to the perspectives of data, usage, and platform which focus on the delivery of business capabilities, the perspective of service management focuses on ensuring that these capabilities meet customer expectations as they evolve.

Finally we wrap-up the book with a Part—*Piecing Together the Elements*—that puts all these perspectives of a high-performance data warehouse environment to work.

Some of the important issues addressed by this book include:

❑ *The user community*—farmers and explorers—who they are, what their habits are, how they are relevant to performance.

❑ *Dormant data*—what it is, how it can be managed.

❏ *Service Management Contract*—what a data warehouse service management contract looks like and how it can be used to manage performance.

❏ *Hardware architectures*—MPP, SMP, NUMA—what they are and how they can be used as a basis for understanding performance.

❏ *Data warehouse monitors*—what a warehouse monitor is, how it can be used, and what its limitations are.

❏ *Parallelism and data warehousing.*

❏ *Scalability and data warehouses.*

❏ *Star schemas and ER modelling*—where to use them.

❏ *Data warehouses and data marts,* and plenty more.

This book is for data warehouse designers and developers who must build data warehouse environments. Data warehouse administrators who must manage these environments once they are built will also find this book useful. In addition, system architects who must understand the underlying hardware platforms and DBMS software will find this book to be invaluable. And finally, students of information systems technology will find this book most useful because it approaches performance from an extremely nonconventional perspective.

Introduction to Data Warehouse Performance

In the beginning, successful data warehouse environments were relatively small given suggested industry practice was to build them in an iterative fashion so that business value could be realized quickly and incrementally. As a result, performance was not much of an issue. There were few users, small amounts of data, and plenty of hardware on which to run queries and conduct analysis. Under these conditions, it was unusual for performance to be an issue. But these conditions were to disappear very, very quickly. The success of data warehousing was such that the volumes of data began to mount rapidly. Where once there were small amounts of data, there soon appeared massive amounts of data. And where there were only a few users in the data warehouse environment, there appeared many users. The result was increasingly poorer and poorer performance for the end-user community in terms of query response time, availability, data quality, etc.

To understand how performance becomes an issue, let's take a look at the progression through the eyes of the end user. On day one, the end user discovers data warehousing as a discipline. The end user writes a query and sends it into execution. On that day, the query operates in a few seconds. The end user simply does not notice performance at all. However, six months later the end user notices that the same query now operates in a few minutes. The end user starts to notice performance but does not complain, hoping that things will get better. Unfortunately, as time passes, end-user response time gets worse. Six months later the same query operates in an hour's time. The end user is perplexed. The end user has not changed a thing about the query, not even a single line of SQL, yet response time just keeps getting worse and worse.

What has happened is that the query has not changed, but the environment in which the query operates has changed dramatically. The end user is correct in pointing out that nothing about the query has changed. Instead the query is operating against more and more data and is competing for resources with more and more users. Just at the moment in time when the end user is getting the maximum benefit from the data warehouse environment, the environment lets the end user down by operating so slowly and unreliably that the end user is turned off.

MEASURING PERFORMANCE

The basis for measuring query performance in the data warehouse environment is the time from the submission of a query to the moment the results of the query are returned. In this regard query performance is measured the same as performance for an OLTP (OnLine Transaction Processing) query. But there are some important differences between OLTP query performance and data warehouse query performance. The most notable difference is that an OLTP query typically operates in two to three seconds while a data warehouse query can take 30 seconds to 5 minutes to even 24 hours or more to complete. A data warehouse query is designed to perform a very different function than an OLTP query. For example, an OLTP query is more characteristic of an administration function. An example of this would be a service representative who is making changes to a customer's account while the customer is on the phone. In this environment there is a strong correlation between productivity and customer satisfaction, and the timeliness of a query. In contrast, a data warehouse query is more characteristic of a user who is responsible for making more long-term, strategic decisions versus up-to-the-second decisions. For this type of end user, depth and breath of data becomes more important to effective decision making than a one- or two-second query response time.

There is another important difference between an OLTP query and data warehouse query in terms of how response time is measured. For an OLTP query, measurement takes place from the moment of submission to the moment when data is first returned to the end user. In contrast, the data warehouse query has not one, but two important measurements:

❑ The length of time from the moment of the submission of the query to the time when the first row/record is returned to the end user

❑ The length of time from the submission of the query until the row is returned

In a data warehouse world, a query may request many, many rows of data. For this reason, response time needs to be measured for the return of the first and the last row of the data. By contrast, in the OLTP world each query only accesses a limited number of rows. As a result, there is little if any difference between the return of the first and the last row of data. For example, in the OLTP world you are probably interested in information about a particular customer or account. As a result, only a few rows are returned. In the data warehouse world you are likely to be interested in comparing and contrasting customers or customer accounts. As a result, many, many rows are returned.

PRODUCTIVITY AND PERFORMANCE

Just because data warehouse query response time characteristics are different from OLTP query response time characteristics does not mean that performance in the data warehouse environment is not important. Indeed, it is very important to the analyst, but in a different way. There is a most interesting indirect relationship between the productivity of the data warehouse analyst and performance. To illustrate this relationship, consider two data warehouse analysts—Ann and Bob. Ann submits her query and receives a response in 30 minutes. Bob submits his query and receives a reply a day later. The performance of the system has a great impact on the way that Ann and Bob work. Because Ann gets good performance, Ann can make and test hypotheses with impunity. Ann has the luxury of being able to be experimental. Ann tries first one thing then another. If one hypothesis proves to be untrue, then Ann tries another. Ann does not feel constrained by her environment and as a result is quite productive and creative.

On the other hand, Bob has fewer opportunities to experiment. Because his query response time is nearly 24 hours, Bob gets very few opportunities to do iterations of analysis. For this reason, Bob must carefully formulate what can and cannot be tested with each iteration of analysis. As a result, Bob has much less opportunity to be creative and experimental than does Ann. In addition, Bob has yet another constraint. By the time Bob receives an answer to his question, he may have forgotten the reason for the question or the question may be outdated. For these reasons, Bob's productivity and ability to use his intuition is much less than Ann's simply because of the performance that each enjoys. There is then a powerful but indirect relationship between performance and productivity in the data warehouse environment.

DATA VOLUMES AND PERFORMANCE

One key challenge to performance in the data warehouse environment is the ability to manage and tune access to a relatively large amount of data. Figure 1.1 shows the very significant volumes of data that accrue within the data warehouse environment.

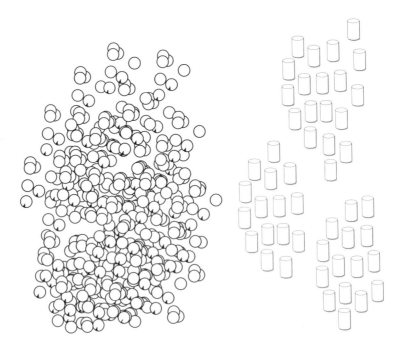

FIGURE 1.1

The key to performance in the data warehouse environment is the ability to manage large volumes of data.

The data warehouse environment attracts volumes of data that have never before been experienced in the information processing milieu. In previous environments, volumes of data were measured in the thousands (kilobytes) and millions (megabytes) of bytes of data. In the data warehouse environment volumes of data are measured in gigabytes and terabytes of data. There are of course many orders of magnitude of difference between these measurements.

Why the Growth of Data?

There are several reasons for the massive growth of volumes of data in the data warehouse environment:

Data warehouses collect historical data. Previous systems looked at only current data. As such, earlier systems operated on only limited amounts of data. But where 5 to 10 years of data are collected in a data warehouse, there simply is no way to avoid amassing huge amounts of data.

Data warehouses involve the collection of data to satisfy unknown requirements. The database designer must accommodate both known requirements *and* unknown requirements. In order to do this the database designer incorporates extraneous and nonobvious data into the data warehouse. This need to accommodate unknown or potential requirements leads to the storage of large amounts of data, some of which will be used and some of which will not be used.

Data warehouses include data at both the very detailed and the summary level. The need to accommodate both detail and summary data leads to the accumulation of large amounts of data.

Data warehouses contain external data as well (e.g., demographic, psychographic, etc.). Significant amounts of external data are collected to support a variety of predictive data mining activities. For example, data mining tools would use this external data to predict who is likely to be a good customer or how certain companies are likely to perform in the marketplace.

There are undoubtedly many other reasons why data warehouses attract massive amounts of data. However, these reasons alone mandate that a data warehouse will contain more data than the data processing professional has ever had to deal with before.

Data Gets in the Way

Why is it that volumes of data have such an impact on performance in the data warehouse environment? The answer is simple. Volumes of data get in the way of finding selected rows of data that the analyst wishes to see. In the OLTP environment, the OLTP user wishes to see only one or two units of data per query. As long as the data can be indexed or partitioned in an optimal manner, then the OLTP user can quickly find the relevant data regardless of how much data there is. But in the data warehouse environment, the user normally wishes to see many rows of data—in some cases many, many rows of data. The desire to look at many rows of data means that a simple index or an efficient data partitioning scheme by itself will not suffice to yield good performance.

Furthermore, optimizing data structures in the data warehouse environment is difficult because many different sets of requirements must be satisfied all at once. One analyst wishes to query the data warehouse one way, another analyst wishes to query the data warehouse another way, and yet another analyst wishes to query the data warehouse another way. At the end of the day the data warehouse can be physically optimized in only one way. There cannot be multiple physical arrangements of the same database. This is one reason for the use of data marts as an extension to the data warehouse. Data marts allow customized views of the data warehouse to support varying analytical needs (e.g., Multidimensional analysis, data mining). Therefore great care must be taken in the physical organization of the data in the warehouse because data can physically be optimized in only one way.

Finding Hidden Data

How is it that large volumes of data hide the data the analyst wishes to see? Figure 1.2 shows that the analyst wishes to find a row of data.

In order to find a row of data that is of interest, the analyst must first wade through many occurrences (i.e., rows) of data in a physical block that are not relevant to the task. Even when the rows can be processed at very high speeds within memory, scan-

A physical block of data

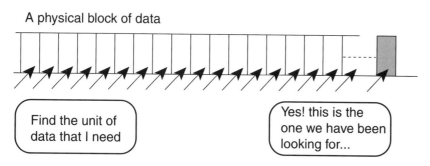

Find the unit of data that I need

Yes! this is the one we have been looking for...

FIGURE 1.2
In order to find the unit of data that is needed, much data that is not needed must first be processed.

ning through these unneeded rows can cost performance. There are a number of tuning techniques that the data warehouse administrator can employ that improve query performance by reducing the time needed to retrieve hidden data. These techniques include

❑ Denormalization

❑ Indexing

❑ Parallelism

❑ Archiving

In Chapter 3, we discuss these techniques in terms of how they support different types of end users (explorers and farmers). In Chapter 9, we discuss these techniques in terms of how they are deployed as part of the data warehouse platform. To familiarize ourselves with these techniques, let's take a brief look at each.

DENORMALIZATION Denormalization is the process of introducing controlled data redundancy in a relational database. The purpose of this redundancy is to improve query performance by reducing frequent joins, aggregations, and derivations. This technique improves query performance through optimal physical placement of data in the same physical block and through pre-deriving and pre-calculating frequently requested attributes. By exploiting these techniques, the data warehouse administrator can minimize the total amount of data and I/O needed to support query processing.

There are some important considerations that must be made, however, before denormalization of data can be used effectively.

The first consideration is that the data can be optimized for only one user or class of users. Upon choosing the one physical design that is optimal, all other uses of the data will not be optimal. This strongly suggests that denormalization of data applies only to data warehouse analysts that can be described as farmers, since it is farmers that have an idea of how they want to use data before they do their processing. Explorers do not know how they want to do processing, so it is very, very difficult to imagine how data should be physically organized in order to optimize the performance of the explorer. The second consideration of denormalization is that it often causes the data to take awkward and brittle shapes. As a rule, the more denormalized the data, the more arcane and difficult the structure of the data and the more complexity and effort involved in its management. The use of denormalization must be considered very carefully and used judiciously because of the effect denormalization has on the structure of the data and because denormalization optimizes processing for only one class of user.

There are four frequently used approaches to denormalization, which are discussed in detail in Chapter 3, "Farmers and Explorers," and Chapter 9, "Building a High-Performance Platform." The approaches are preaggregation, column replication, prejoin, and array.

INDEXING   The argument can be made that the data that needs to be searched can be indexed, thereby bypassing the need to look at extraneous data. Indeed, indexing can greatly enhance performance. Figure 1.3 shows the creation of an index.

The index bypasses the need to physically search nonrelevant rows of data, as seen in Figure 1.2. In such a manner, performance is improved. But there are some good reasons why simply saying that the creation of an index will not suffice to improve performance on an overall basis. The reasons why an index cannot be created to enhance performance as a general purpose solution to the problems of performance in the data warehouse environment are

> **The creation of an index requires overhead and resources.** If the data warehouse administrator specifies too many indexes, the overhead of building and maintaining the index becomes very onerous, and the effect of this overhead on performance becomes unacceptable.
>
> **Indexes do not suffice to solve every problem related to performance.** There is the case of the few valued domain,

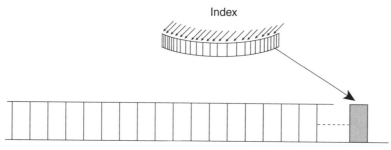

A physical block of data

Of course indexes can be created that bypass the need for a
sequential search of data within the physical block but...
❏ The indexes must be loaded.
❏ Indexes require their own data management.
❏ Indexes require volumes of data on their own.
❏ Indexes require maintenance.
❏ Not all values can/should be indexed.
❏ If the index is large enough, considerable time may
be required in doing processing within the index.

FIGURE 1.3

An index has been created.

where it is easier to scan the database than use an index, and
the case of the multivariable index, where multiple indexes
must be created and coordinated to index a single logical
occurrence of data.

**Unknown requirements cannot be addressed by the cre-
ation of an index.** The very essence of an index is that the
index organizes data according to a known set of requirements. If you do not know how you need to access data, you
cannot logically and optimally define an index. An index presupposes that the requirements for access are known. In the
case of the data warehouse environment, in many cases the
requirements for access will not be known until the data is
actually needed. When that is the case, it is faster to access the
data than it is to stop and create an index and then access the
data.

For these reasons then, it is clear that indexes only address
some of the problems of performance in the data warehouse environment. In general, indexes can address the needs of the farmers
given the selectivity and predictability of their work. Unfortunately
indexes infrequently address the needs of the explorers given the
unpredictable nature of their workload.

PARALLELISM   One of the architectural approaches to the management of huge amounts of data is to use a hardware architecture that is parallelized. In a parallel hardware machine, multiple processors are brought to bear on a unit of processing. Instead of having one processor sequentially churn through a collection of data, multiple parallel processors attack different parts of the collection of data. The total amount of processing needed to access the collection of data is the same, but the elapsed time required to do the processing is reduced linearly by the number of processors doing the processing. Given the volume of data in the data warehouse environment, the issue is not whether parallel processing is required, but what form of parallel processing is most appropriate. There are four scalable hardware architectures, which are discussed in Chapter 9: "Building a High Performance Platform."

- ❑ Symmetric multiprocessors (SMPs)
- ❑ Clusters
- ❑ Massively parallel processors (MPP)
- ❑ Nonuniform memory access (NUMA)

In addition, this section details the different types of parallelism and approaches for spreading data across CPUs and disks in a scalable hardware machine.

ARCHIVING   As a rule, when it comes to managing large amounts of data, the database designer wants to keep only data that has a reasonable probability of access in the data warehouse environment. Eliminating data that has zero or a very low probability of access from the data warehouse environment is the single best thing a designer can do to enhance performance. This type of data is known as dormant data and is discussed in detail in chapter 5, "Dormant Data."

USER EXPECTATIONS AND PERFORMANCE

Possibly the most important factor to consider in arriving at a high-performance data warehouse environment is that of end-user expectations. Unless end-user needs are understood and met, terabytes of data will mean no more to the business than kilobytes of data. These expectations represent unambiguous objectives that provide direction for performance tuning and capacity planning

activities within the data warehouse environment. These objectives
are generally derived as a result of collaboration between the user
and the data warehouse administrator, and are documented in a
Service Management Contract (SMC). The SMC provides a basis
for measuring performance quantitatively. With an SMC the measurement of performance is objective rather than subjective. Trying
to performance tune without such a document would be like sail-
ing a ship without a destination. In Part 3, "Service Management
and Performance" we will discuss:

- ❏ The critical importance of the SMC in creating a high-
  performance data warehouse environment
- ❏ The steps to follow in creating an SMC
- ❏ The sections contained within an SMC and the types of
  metrics used to assess performance
- ❏ The ongoing management of and tracking performance
  relative to the SMC

Although there are a variety of ways to assess performance in
an SMC (e.g., data quality, availability, recoverability, number of
users supported, etc.), probably the most elusive is query response
time. As discussed previously, measuring query response time in
the data warehouse environment is very different from measuring
query response time in the OLTP environment. To complicate matters further, measuring query response time varies with the type of
end user. To illustrate, lets take a look at query response expectations for three types of users in the data warehouse environment—
farmers, explorers, and a variation of the farmer, the operator. The
response time for farmers is measured in a few minutes to maybe an
hour. The response time for explorers is measured in terms of hours
and perhaps days, depending on the work the explorer is doing and
the load on the system at the time the explorer is doing her analysis.
The response time demands for the operator are similar to those of
the farmer; however, as time goes on, the demand for faster
response time increases as does the demand for data currency, content, and availability. This is because the operator is either a system
(e.g., fraud detection, campaign management) or user (e.g., service
representative) that is very much part of the daily operations of the
business. Given this, the data warehouse administrator needs to
begin to question whether performance is best achieved by moving
some or all of the operator's workload to an operational data store.
But this is a subject for another book. For our purpose, query perfor-

mance for the operator is viewed as similar to that of the farmer. In Chapter 2, "User Community and Performance," we discuss the issue of performance and the end user. In Chapter 3, "Farmers and Explorers," we discuss techniques for tuning query performance for the different types of end users.

EDUCATION AND PERFORMANCE

Yet another challenge to overcome in achieving a high-performance data warehouse environment is that of education. Regardless of whether the end user is a farmer or an explorer, there is one way to achieve very significant performance gains for the absolute least amount of money. That approach is to provide each end user—farmer or explorer—with adequate training before the end user starts on the data warehouse adventure. There are at least two types of training the end user needs:

Tool familiarization. What does the tool do? What are some of its pitfalls? What does the tool not do well? What needs to be avoided?

Data warehouse familiarization. What is in the warehouse? How do you access what is there? What will be coming in the future?

The first type of training is generic to the tool set employed within the data warehouse environment. The vendor of the tool set is the logical place to seek this type of training. The second type of training is peculiar to each shop. In-house trainers or database administrators are probably the most likely sources for this type of training. It is worth repeating that *both* types of training are necessary if the end user is not to inadvertently make serious mistakes.

There are, of course, other kinds of training that can be used. If the end user desires to become a power user, the end user can investigate

❑ General systems courses

❑ DBMS

❑ Operating systems

❑ Analytical tool operation and internals

❑ Data mining techniques

❏ General pattern analysis
❏ Actuarial analysis
❏ Statistical analysis

Perhaps no other technique or approach has the same impact for the dollars spent when it comes to improving performance across the entire data warehouse environment.

ACHIEVING PERFORMANCE

In order to overcome the challenges and achieve long-term satisfactory performance in the data warehouse environment, the data warehouse administrator needs to carefully and proactively plan and manage four elements of the data warehouse environment critical to optimizing performance as depicted in Figure 1.4.

All four of these elements are required to achieve optimal and long-term performance in a data warehouse environment. If any one of these elements is not present and/or adequately accounted for, then performance is sure to be an issue.

WHEN SHOULD PERFORMANCE BE CONSIDERED?

In most organizations the performance of the data warehouse environment is not considered until performance deteriorates. By this time the database has been designed, the programs have been

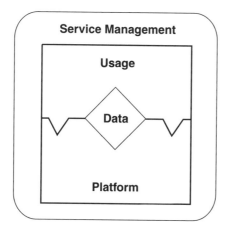

FIGURE 1.4

Elements of a high-performance data warehouse environment.

written, the hardware and software platforms have been selected and installed, data has been collected, and so forth. In a word, all the major and important decisions that affect performance have already been made. While it is possible to make small improvements in performance once an organization arrives at this state, it is not possible to make major improvements in performance without significant investment in time and money. About the best the organization can hope for at this point is a marginal improvement in performance.

In the ideal case the organization has been thinking about performance from the inception of the data warehouse environment. Following are things to consider (in the approximate order in which they will occur) when building a high-performance data warehouse platform:

❏ Base level architecture—hardware and software.

❏ Does the hardware platform support the volume of data, the types of users, types of workload, and the number of requests that will be run against it?

❏ Does the software platform organize and manage the data in an efficient and optimal manner?

❏ Has the growth of the system—data and processes—been anticipated?

After the base level technologies have been selected, then comes the design and implementation of the data warehouse platform based on usage and data:

❏ Database design. Have the elements of data that will be accessed been identified? Have those elements of data been organized so that there is efficient access to them? Have the different elements of data been profiled so that the occurrences of data that will exist for each entity are roughly approximated?

❏ Have the users of the data been identified? Have the profiles of the users been categorized? Does the database design take into account the predicted and/or known usage of the data?

After the database design is done and data starts to enter the system, the next event is the creation of the programs and configuration of tools that will make use of the data (many times this will happen before the database is built so as to provide input into what data is needed).

❏ Have the programs that will access the data warehouse been profiled? Have the number of programs been anticipated? the rate at which the programs are run? the amount of data accessed by each program? the priority at which the programs expect to be run?

❏ Who is writing the programs? Are they aware of proper design practices? Are the programs periodically reviewed?

After programs are written and the data warehouse is being populated, the ongoing system utilization needs to be monitored and system guidelines—service management contracts—need to be established.

❏ Is the system being monitored? at what level of granularity? how often?

❏ Are service management contracts in place?

❏ Is the data warehouse platform performing to the level specified in the service management contract?

If an organization follows these guidelines and carefully considers performance at each appropriate point in time, the organization will arrive at a point in time where performance is truly optimal. Note, however, that to arrive at that place and time, the considerations of performance need to have been made from the very inception of the data warehouse experience.

SUMMARY

As the organization matures in the data warehouse experience, performance inevitably becomes an issue. Data warehouse performance is significantly different from OLTP performance. Data warehouse performance is measured in terms of terms of minutes and hours. OLTP performance is measured in terms of seconds. In addition, data warehouse performance is measured in terms of the time it takes for the first row to be returned as well as the time it takes for the last row to be returned. Performance is important to the analyst because there is an important relationship between performance and productivity. The faster the turnaround an analyst can get, the more productive that analyst can be.

In addition to this query response time perspective to performance, the success of a high-performing data warehouse environment will also be measured in terms of reliability (e.g., data quality, availability, etc.).

There are a number of challenges to overcome in building a high-performance data warehouse environment. These challenges include tuning access to volumes of data based on user (farmer and explorer) workload and their expectations, understanding and tracking performance relative to user expectations, and educating the user community. To overcome these challenges, the data warehouse administrator needs to carefully and proactively plan and manage four elements of the data warehouse environment critical to optimizing performance usage, data, platform, and service management.

Usage, Data, and Perforr

This section focuses on the two components of the data warehouse environment that fundamentally shape the platform on which services are delivered and managed; usage and data. In the first two chapters we talk about the types of end users, their usage and techniques for optimizing performance. In Chapter 4, we talk about the role of the data mart in supporting these end users. In Chapter 5 we talk about the impact of dormant data on query performance, and steps for identifying and archiving dormant data. In Chapter 6 we change gears a bit and focus on another aspect of performance in the data warehouse environment, data cleanliness. Finally we wrap up our discussion on usage and data by talking about the monitors needed to capture metrics about the performance of these elements which is used to plan and optimize the platform, balance the workload, and assess whether service levels are meeting user expectations.

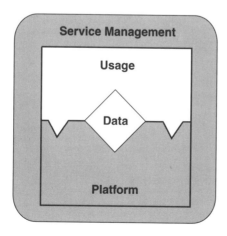

2

User Community and Performance

The factor that has the most profound influence on the complexion of the data warehouse environment is the end-user community. From the standpoint of the diversity of the community, the data warehouse environment is perhaps more diverse than any other. There are several different kinds of end users in this community. Each type of end user has his own unique characteristics and requirements for the usage of the data warehouse. In order to achieve optimal performance, the data warehouse administrator needs to understand a great deal about the different end users because the end users cannot be managed as if they are a homogeneous group of people. There are different considerations of performance for each type of end user. In this chapter we will talk about the different types of end users. In the following chapter we will discuss the different techniques that are used to tune the data warehouse platform to support these different types of end users.

KNOW YOUR END USERS: FARMERS AND EXPLORERS

The world of decision support and data warehouses can be very confusing. There are many different techniques and approaches that can be used to enhance and improve performance. Unfortunately many of these techniques are at odds with each other, with one technique enhancing performance at the expense of another technique. What is needed is a broad framework that allows the different approaches to performance in the data warehouse environment to be understood in a comprehensive manner. At the heart of that framework is the notion that the world of decision support and data warehouses is made up of two essentially different types of end users. Those end users are explorers and farmers, as illustrated in Figure 2.1

Farmers are those users who use the data warehouse platform in a predictable, repetitive manner. Farmers know what they want before they set out to query the system and seldom fail to find what they want. However, farmers find only tiny flakes of gold upon completion of their query. In their transactions, farmers

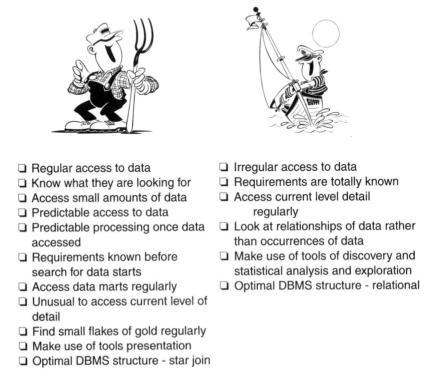

Farmers

Explorers

❑ Regular access to data
❑ Know what they are looking for
❑ Access small amounts of data
❑ Predictable access to data
❑ Predictable processing once data accessed
❑ Requirements known before search for data starts
❑ Access data marts regularly
❑ Unusual to access current level of detail
❑ Find small flakes of gold regularly
❑ Make use of tools presentation
❑ Optimal DBMS structure - star join

❑ Irregular access to data
❑ Requirements are totally known
❑ Access current level detail regularly
❑ Look at relationships of data rather than occurrences of data
❑ Make use of tools of discovery and statistical analysis and exploration
❑ Optimal DBMS structure - relational

FIGURE 2.1

End users of the data warehouse enviroment.

look at relatively small amounts of data. Often, because the analytical focus of the farmer is predictable, farmers look at summarized or aggregated data. Farmers make little use of metadata since farmers repeat the same type of activity, day in and day out. As a matter of fact, it is said that metadata can even get in the way.

Farmers are the bulk of the users in the data warehouse environment and they demonstrate a fairly predicable pattern of usage. That is, farmers generally look at trends in the same business dimensions (i.e., product, customer, time) and metrics (i.e., revenue, cost) over time. The only thing that might change is the way in which they report on the trends. In addition, farmers typically look at fairly current data. Given the relative tactical nature of their work, the return on investment for farmers is measured daily in many small units of information at a time.

Explorers are very different from farmers. Explorers have a very unpredictable, nonrepetitive pattern of data usage. Explorers sometimes go six months without ever touching their computers. Then, in the seventh month, they unleash huge amounts of analytical processing all at once. The explorer does not know what she wants when the analysis is created. The explorer has the attitude that "I will know what I want when I see it." The explorer operates in an almost purely heuristic manner. The explorer looks at massive amounts of data, typically at a detailed level. Summary data gets in the way of the kind of analysis the explorer wishes to do. Explorers often look at historical data, going back in time much further than do farmers. Explorers look at relationships between different types of data and patterns of different occurrences of the same data type. In this way, the explorer can uncover such things as

❏ What products sell well together?
❏ What business transactions are likely to be fraudulent?
❏ What do high-value customers have in common?

The explorer often finds nothing as a result of her analysis. But occasionally the explorer discovers invaluable and unexpected information—huge nuggets of information. On these occasions the explorer more than pays back the cost of the data warehouse environment. For example, being able to identify what characterizes a high-value customer or a customer who is likely to leave (i.e., churn), a company can quickly recover the cost of the data warehouse environment by reducing customer acquisition costs and costs associated with reacquiring customers lost to the competition.

The World of the Explorer

The explorer endeavors to understand what makes the wheels of the corporation turn. To this end, the explorer looks for hidden meaning in corporate data and strives to predict the outcome of future decisions based on past events.

Another way of viewing the role of the explorer is that the explorer is trying to determine betters ways of doing business in the future based on past successes and failures. For example, what promotions have done well in the past? Of those that did well, what characterizes the customers that responded favorably? What other customers match these characteristics (i.e., model), as they are likely respond favorably as well?

There are four fundamental types of work that the explorer performs:

❑ Profiling
❑ Extracting
❑ Modeling
❑ Classifying

PROFOUND DIFFERENCES

From these descriptions of farmers and explorers it can be seen that there are many profound differences between the two communities and their expectations. When it comes to performance, the first thing that must be done is to qualify which audience is being considered because

The design approaches for farmers are diametrically opposed to the approaches that apply to explorers.

In order to understand why the difference between the two environments is so important from a performance perspective, consider the environment in which each of the communities operates.

We'll discuss each so you can become familiar with this primary end user.

PROFILING   Profiling is a fairly common activity performed by the explorer and is generally the first step in his analytical process. During this activity, the explorer begins to gain insights into the complexion of data within the data warehouse in terms of its completeness and accuracy (i.e., quality). In addition, profiling is used to assess whether a sufficient sample size exists and to create the criteria for the sample. This sample is then used as input for the extraction activity. This step is critical to ensuring that the data quality is sufficient before too much time is spent extracting, modeling, and classifying. The types of questions typically asked include

❏ How many different gender codes exist and what are they?
❏ How sparsely is household income populated?
❏ How many account statuses exist and what are they?
❏ How many accounts exist with monthly invoicing greater than $20? How many accounts exist with monthly invoicing less than or equal to $20?
❏ How many customers have more than two kids and live in an urban area?

Profiling queries are fairly complex though they generally return small result sets sometimes consisting of simple row counts. In addition, profiling queries are fairly unpredictable in terms of their use of data and their frequency of execution. As a result, it is nearly impossible to commit to any query response time guarantee in a Service Management Contract (SMC)—more on the SMC in Chapters 11 and 12. A query may run only a few minutes or perhaps as long as several hours.

EXTRACTING   Once the complexion of data is understood (i.e., profiling is complete), the next step for the explorer is to create a data extract that is used for off-line analysis activities (i.e., modeling). The profile of data to be selected is generally developed during profiling activities. The role of extracting is to extract the specified data from the data warehouse and to organize it into the desired format for analysis. The output is then loaded into a data mart or exploration warehouse where it is used to support the analytical activities of the explorer.

In general, these extracting activities are very resource intensive given the breath of data being extracted and the work being performed to prepare the data. Fortunately, this activity is fairly infrequent relative to other explorer activities performed within the data warehouse environment. In addition, this activity is fairly predictable and can be scheduled so as to not impact ad hoc workloads (e.g., profiling) within the data warehouse. As with profiling, it is nearly impossible to commit to any response time guarantee in the SMC given the unpredictable nature of the request. However, if the request is run on a repeated basis, the data warehouse administrator can begin to assess actual run times (if a usage monitor is in place) and make response time commits.

MODELING   Modeling is probably at the heart of what an explorer wants to do. Up to this point, most of the explorers time has been spent understanding the data (i.e., profiling) and preparing the data (i.e., extracting). Now it is time to analyze the data. Modeling is the process of developing a pattern that describes the observation of an entity (i.e., customer, product, channel) such that a prediction can be made. From the resulting model, entities in the data warehouse can be classified based on their affinity to the model, and future outcomes can be predicted. For example, let's take a look at how modeling would be used to identify customers who are likely to be late paying their phone bill.

❑ First, a model would be built—based on demographic and behavioral characteristics—that characterizes customers who have been late paying their phone bill. This model is developed using such data mining techniques as statistical analysis and/or machine learning.

❑ This model is then used to classify all customers relative to their affinity to the model, thus providing some degree of prediction as to the likelihood of who is and is not going to pay their phone bill.

❑ A marketing program promoting early payment of bills is then targeted at those customers who show the strongest affinity to the model.

Some of the models that are common in many corporations include

❑ Customer segmentation
❑ Next product
❑ Fraud detection
❑ Channel response (e.g., telemarketing, direct mail)
❑ Vulnerability
❑ Credit risk
❑ Customer lifetime value
❑ Promotion response

The process of modeling is fairly predictable and supported by a platform (e.g., data mart or exploration data warehouse) that is tailored to the needs of the analyst. As a result, some degree of predictability can be expected in terms of query response time. As a rule, query response time is measured in terms of a percent of some end goal. For example, the SMC could state that the query response time must be less than three minutes, 70% of the time.

CLASSIFYING   This is the final activity in the analysis life cycle of the explorer. As has been discussed, the explorer first profiles the data warehouse to understand the complexion of the data and to prepare a profile of the data to be extracted. Next the explorer extracts and formats the desired data and loads it into a data mart or exploration warehouse. Then the explorer develops a model that predicts some characteristic of an entity (e.g., likelihood that a customer will pay a bill late). Finally, the explorer classifies other entities in the data warehouse based on their match to the model.

Classifying is generally a single process—per entity—that runs against the data warehouse on a weekly or monthly basis. The execution of this activity generally depends on the refreshment of data within the data warehouse. For example, it wouldn't make sense to reclassify the data weekly when the data used in the classification is refreshed monthly. In addition, classifying is commonly done using several models with a single pass through the data. Query response time for the classifying activity is documented in the SMC in terms of a completion date following the refreshment of data to be classified. For example, if we were classifying using demographic data, we might state in the SMC that classification would be completed the Sunday following refreshment of the demographic data.

Profile of Execution

The explorer operates in an environment that in most ways is the opposite of that of the farmer. The explorers profile of execution is shown in Figure 2.2.

Explorer transactions are usually large affairs, where the transaction submitted by the explorer looks at lots of data. The explorer may look at three or four orders of magnitude more data than the farmer does (and by any measurement, that is a large difference). However, the explorer does not create and execute very many of these requests (thankfully!). The explorer has the attitude that the system will finish with the request when it is finished. On occasion 24 hours may pass from the moment the transaction is submitted until the request is completed. Occasionally the explorer's response time is even slower, but this does not bother the explorer. The kinds of decisions that rest on the results of the explorer's analysis are not the kind that are immediate.

Tuning the environment and documenting SMCs can be a bit challenging when one is addressing an explorer. This is primarily

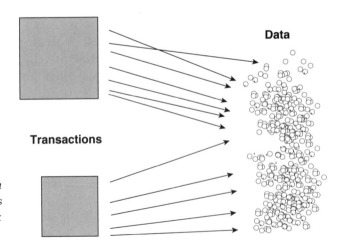

FIGURE 2.2

The explorers' transaction profile: many transactions and transactions that look at limited units of data.

because the explorer's workload is a mix of predictable and unpredictable activities. For example, profiling and extracting have a very unpredictable frequency of execution and query complexity. As a result, it is nearly impossible to guarantee a query response time measurement in the SMC. On the other hand, modeling and classifying activities are fairly predictable in terms of frequency of access and query complexity. As a result, the establishment of query response time guarantees in the SMC is a must.

Whether query response time guarantees can or cannot be made in the SMC for the explorer, it is important to remember that query response time is only one category used in measuring the level of service. An effective SMC contains other categories of service that apply to both the explorer and farmer. These categories include

- ❏ Data storage limits
- ❏ User concurrency
- ❏ System availability
- ❏ Data quality
- ❏ Data currency

Each of these categories, and others, are detailed in Chapters 11 and 12 where we discuss creating and managing a winning Service Management Contract or SMC.

World of the Farmer

Whereas the explorer is trying to derive intelligence to help direct what the business should be doing strategically, the farmer is monitoring the effect of those decisions tactically. For example, let's say that a business determines that their biggest problem is customer retention. As a matter of fact, the company is currently losing more customers than they are retaining according to reports produced by the farmer community. As a result, the explorer embarks on a journey to discover why the company is losing so many customers. From that the explorer will work with the business groups to derive retention strategies that will endeavor to identify and retain high-value customers who are likely to leave. Once these strategies are deployed, it is the role of the farmer to continue observing customer retention and to report on how well these strategies performed and to what degree they matched expectations. These reports are fed back into the explorer's analysis process as input to refine or retire the strategies. This life cycle of analysis is referred to as the virtuous life cycle. Figure 2.3 shows the virtuous life cycle as discussed in Michael J. A. Berry's and Gordon Linoff's book *Data Mining Techniques for Marketing, Sales and Customer Support*.

As was previously discussed, the explorer endeavors to understand what makes the wheels of the corporation turn. In contrast, the farmer monitors the effect of decisions on the wheels of the corporation. To that end the farmer tracks key performance metrics that report on the health of the corporation and provides the explorer with feedback on the effectiveness of the recommended strategies.

Given the nature of the work, the farmer performs limited profiling and is drawn toward tools and technologies that support multidimensional analysis. By using these tools, the farmer can

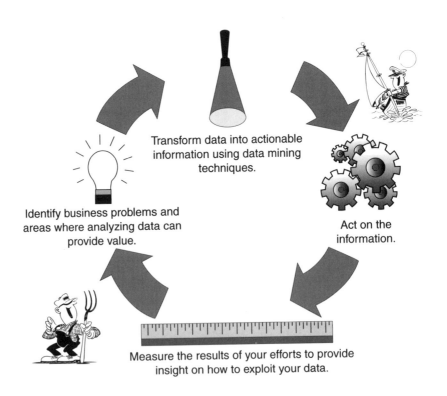

Transform data into actionable information using data mining techniques.

Identify business problems and areas where analyzing data can provide value.

Act on the information.

Measure the results of your efforts to provide insight on how to exploit your data.

FIGURE 2.3
The virtuous life cycle.

effectively monitor and communicate the status of key performance metrics used to assess the health of the enterprise. Some of the metrics that are typically monitored include

❏ Install and disconnect rates

❏ Inventory and product movement

❏ Call center average sales per hour

❏ Call center average "talk time"

❏ Campaign performance

❏ Customer segment lifetime value

❏ Peak network volumes

❏ Uncollected receivables

❏ Customer satisfaction

❏ Fraud trends

❏ Profitability tracking

❏ Market segment penetration versus potential

Very much like modeling activities performed by the explorer, multidimensional analysis activities performed by the farmer are relatively predictable in terms of business dimensions and metrics. Business metrics consist of measurements that are of interest to the business (e.g., revenue, costs), whereas dimensions represent constraints or headings (e.g., product, location, customer segment) used in reporting the metrics. Because of the similar workload between modeling and multidimensional analysis activities, query response time can be defined in the SMC in a similar fashion.

PROFILE OF EXECUTION   Figure 2.4 shows that the processing profile of the farmer is one where there are many small transactions. Each transaction looks at a (relatively) small amount of data. The pattern in which the transactions are executed is fairly predictable in terms of

❏ The hour of the day transactions are sent into execution

❏ The day of the week transactions are sent to the system

❏ The week of the month when transactions are sent

Transactions

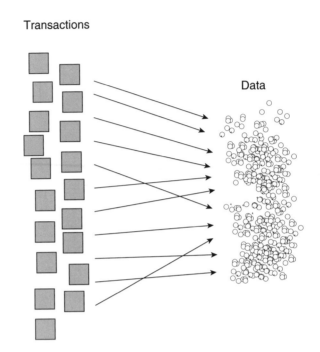

Data

FIGURE 2.4
*The farmer's day-to-day
transaction processing
profile.*

Service Management Contracts for performance can be made
for farmers because of the predictability of their processing. In the
same vein, because there is predictability of processing, data structures and database designs can be optimized for the farmer as
well.

TYPING THE FARMER AND THE EXPLORER

Farmers and explorers have an affinity with the different classifications of processing. In general, farmers are those analysts who are
clerical in nature, are casual users, use predefined queries, operate
at a summary level, and do simple processing. Explorers are those
analysts who are managerial or are creating reports for management, are power users, do ad hoc queries, operate at a complex
level, and do complex processing.

There are, of course, exceptions to the rule. It is possible to
find a farmer doing managerial work, and it is possible to find an
explorer at the clerical level. But the general classifications of data

fit farmers and explorers rather consistently. However, organizing end users into the broad categories of farmers and explorers is not the only useful way to categorize them. There are other classifications that are important as well.

Clerical versus Management

Another way of segmenting the community in the data warehouse environment is by clerical and management use of the data. The clerical community runs the day-to-day detailed activities of the business. Their analytical queries are relatively short and are targeted at answering specific questions. The managerial community does long- and midrange planning for the business. Their analytical queries look over lots of data over time.

The primary domain for the queries of the clerical community is the operational environment. However, there are cases where the clerical community will use the data warehouse environment. One such case is when a query has just been established and the clerical community is experimenting with its inclusion as part of the repertoire of activities available to the end user. Another case is when the end user occasionally needs to know information—usually historical—that is contained in the data warehouse. In any case, the data warehouse environment serves the needs of the clerical community well as long as there are only a limited number of queries submitted and the expectation for response time and availability is casual.

In the eventuality that the end user needs to submit many queries and the expectation is for two- to three-second response time, then the query belongs outside the domain of the data warehouse environment. As long as the expectations are set properly and as long as the platform has been properly established, clerical queries are the least damaging to performance of all the communities who submit queries.

Management's queries against the data warehouse environment range from queries that look at a few rows of data to queries that access many, many rows of data. Given that management is making long-term decisions based on the results of the queries, response time is relaxed. The queries submitted by management are usually the most resource intensive queries that exist. Management's queries have the potential to do real damage to the performance characteristics of the system.

Casual versus Power

Another classification of user access is by casual user versus power user. The casual user is one that has a very tenuous relationship with the computer. He accesses the data warehouse platform only infrequently and has many learning curves of technology in front of him. The casual user expects information to be presented to him with little or no effort and merely wants to get on the computer and have the information magically appear with no great amount of effort or thought. He also does no great amount of analytical processing. From a performance perspective, the casual user is very dangerous because he is not acquainted enough with the tools of the environment to appreciate the difference between a potentially dangerous query and one that is not.

The power user is the opposite of the casual user. The power user is very computer literate and possesses the technological skills to conduct detailed and sophisticated analysis of the data. He knows the structures of the data as well as the tools that are required to access and analyze that data and is quite comfortable creating an analysis from scratch. The power user is always aware of the impact of the query that is being submitted on performance. Because of the background of the power user, he is the "safest animal in the forest." However, on occasion the power user turns into a performance problem when the power user experiments with new parts of the technology or goes to parts of the database not regularly traversed.

Predefined versus Ad Hoc

Another important criteria distinguishing users is whether the user submits predefined queries or ad hoc queries. A predefined query is one where the query is established long before the query is sent into execution. In order to create a predefined query, the requirements for processing and the structure and content of the data must be known before the processing is to occur. As a rule, predefined queries are not performance problems because the nature of the query and the structure and content of the data are anticipated as part of the process of the definition of the query. Performance can become a problem when the environment changes significantly from when the query was formulated until the query is executed.

An ad hoc query is one that is created "on the fly," as part of an iterative analysis. The query may not have any real purpose other than to set the stage for what the next query will address. The ad hoc query is dangerous from the standpoint of performance in that it is very easy to submit a query that will consume many resources.

Summary versus Detailed

Yet another category of queries is that of queries that operate at a summarized level and queries that operate at a detailed level. When queries are submitted at a query level, the efficiency of operation is at a peak. Summarization of the data at a previous point in time permits very efficient access of the data. From a performance standpoint, very little can compete with accessing summary data. However, there are several drawbacks to summary data. The first drawback is that the summary data is created under a set of assumptions—what data will be summarized, how will it be summarized, when will it be summarized, and so forth. If the data that has been summarized meets the criteria of the analyst, then much time and energy will be saved. But if the summarization does not meet the needs of the analyst, then the summary data is of no use whatsoever. The second drawback to summary data is that, of necessity, detail is lost in the process of summarization. If the analyst needs to see the detail that has been lost in summarization, then the summary data is of no use. The third drawback to summary data is that summary data carries with it a need for documentation that no other data carries. Because summary data is calculated, for the analyst to effectively use the summary data, the analyst must know how the summarization has been conducted. In other words, with summary data it is not sufficient for the analyst to merely look at the data. The analyst must also know about the calculations that were made. Unfortunately, this documentation is often lost and is never captured in a systematic manner.

Detailed data is at the heart of the data warehouse environment. The analytical process starts with detailed data. Summarization starts with detailed data. Data marts start with detailed data. Reconciliation starts with detailed data. In short, detailed data is the basic unit of atomicity that drives the data warehouse environment. However, there are dire performance considerations that go hand in hand with detailed data. In every case, if performance is to be optimal, it must be conducted as far away from detailed data as possible. Stated differently, performance improves with every step we take away from the detail data. When end users first discover the data warehouse, they typically fall in love with the detailed data that resides there. The end users immediately attach themselves to the detailed data and use it as their security blanket. But as time passes and a summary infrastructure appears, the end users need to be weaned away from the detail because as long as detailed data forms the basis of every process they do, then performance will always be poor. It is the job of the data warehouse administrator to encourage the end user to do as much processing as possible at as low a level of detail as possible.

Simple versus Complex

Still another way to categorize end users is by simple and complex processes. Simple processes are those that access a small amount of data in a straightforward manner and quickly analyze and present the data. Complex processes are those that access lots of data, access data in a Byzantine manner, and/or access many types of data, and/or merge, relate, and aggregate the data, or analyze the data in a sophisticated or awkward manner.

SUMMARY

One of the keys to achieving good long-term performance in the data warehouse environment is to understand the community of users that help shape the complexion of the environment (along with data). The user community is quite diverse, and different segments have quite different expectations for performance.

The major dividing line between users of the data warehouse environment is between farmers and explorers. Farmers are those people who do repetitive activities, looking for small amounts of data. Farmers know what they are looking for before they use the data warehouse platform. Explorers are those people who do not know what they are looking for. Explorers are those people who look at massive amounts of data, looking at associations, relationships, and patterns. Explorers often find nothing. Occasionally explorers find huge unexpected nuggets of information. Put another way, the explorer endeavors to understand what makes the wheels of the corporation turn and strive to develop strategies that reduce cost and increase revenue, whereas the farmer monitors the effect of these strategies on the wheels of the corporation (i.e., did the strategy reduce cost and/or increase revenue).

The distinction between the world of the explorer and the world of the farmer is best characterized by the analytical activities (i.e., workload) they perform. The explorer typically performs activities such as profiling, extracting, modeling, classifying, and multidimensional analysis (to a limited degree). In contrast, the farmer typically performs multidimensional analysis and profiling (to a limited degree).

In addition to contrasting explorers and farmers, the type of analysis performed is very important because some activities demonstrate a degree of predictability that can be used to tune the environment and define query response time measurements in the SMC. Activities that fall within this category include modeling, classifying, and multidimensional analysis. Other activities are very unpredictable and make tuning and the establishment of objective query response time service level measurement nearly impossible. Activities in this category include profiling and extracting.

Other ways to characterize the end user in the data warehouse environment include clerical versus management, casual versus power, predefined versus ad hoc, summary versus detailed user, and simple versus complex.

Now that we have described the different types of users and their respective workloads, let's take a look in the next chapter at the different tuning techniques that can be employed to optimize the data warehouse platform based on these types of usage to support their needs.

3

Farmers and Explorers

As discussed in the previous chapter, the users of the data warehouse platform can be divided between farmers and explorers. Each of these communities has distinctive habits, characteristics, and expectations in terms of performance. Because of the profound differences between the processing profile of the explorer and the farmer, there is a natural gravitation toward different architectural components in the data warehouse platform. Figure 3.1 shows this affinity.

In Figure 3.1, farmers are attracted to the data mart environment to support their multidimensional analysis. In contrast, ex-

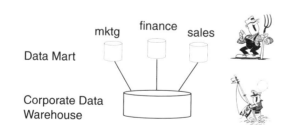

FIGURE 3.1

There is a natural affinity of farmers toward the data mart and an affinity of explorers toward the data warehouse.

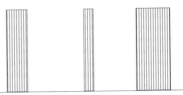

FIGURE 3.2
*System utilization of the
farmer and explorer.*

The pattern of system
utilization over time for the
farmer community.

The pattern of system
utilization over time for the
explorer community.

plorers are attracted to the data warehouse to support profiling,
extracting, classifying, and modeling activities. The primary reason
for this is that the data warehouse contains the needed depth and
breadth of data. However, explorers prefer to do their modeling
activities against the data mart when a representative sample or
subset of data is sufficient. In general, the two different user communities operate at a different level of detail in the data warehouse
environment.

Another perspective of the processing profile highlights the
dissimilarities between the explorer and the farmer. Figure 3.2
shows that from the standpoint of transaction arrival predictability, explorers and farmers have a very different pattern of activity.
Throughout the day, the farmer has a reasonably predictable pattern of request submissions. More transactions are submitted between 9:30 A.M. and 11:30 A.M., with another peak between 2:00 P.M.
and 4:30 P.M. Day in and day out the farmer's workload profile can
be characterized.

Now contrast the predictability of the farmer's profile with
the lack of predictability that characterizes the processing profile of
the explorer. The explorer operates in essentially a binary mode.
At any one point in time, the explorer has nothing going on in the
system or the explorer is consuming every system resource there
is. There is no pattern of predictability as to when requests are
submitted by the explorer. This lack of predictability makes capacity planning and system performance optimization for the explorer
almost impossible.

OPTIMIZING FOR THE EXPLORER

Explorers are the community of users who look for unusual and useful patterns in the business operation. Explorers operate on a whimsical, unpredictable, random basis. Most of the time explorers find nothing for their efforts. Occasionally explorers find previously unknown and unsuspected nuggets of information. Optimizing a database for performance for an explorer is difficult because the random nature of the explorers business prevents anything from being done prior to the actual exploration. The best that can be done for the explorer is to capture, cleanse, document, and roughly organize the data on which the explorer can operate. When there is no foreknowledge of the way a database will be used, any design is as good as any other design. The best the designer can do is to guess about the common relationships that will be analyzed.

The explorer typically looks at two things: detail and history. In most cases, the explorer looks at relationships between different types and/or occurrences of data. In order to discover these patterns, the explorer uses statistical inference made from observations of many occurrences of data. The explorer is essentially the classic data miner. The problem with the explorer and the data warehouse platform is that

❑ The explorer needs to look at massive amounts of data

❑ The explorer does not know precisely what needs to be analyzed

❑ The explorer looks at relationships of data and sets of data that have never before been correlated

In order to accomplish these analytical processes, the explorer creates queries that consume huge amounts of resources. The transactions created by the explorer may be three to four orders of magnitude larger than a query created by a farmer. Putting an explorer's query in the queue with farmers' queries for standard data warehouse processing is a prescription for disaster. When the transactions from the explorer are mixed with the transactions from farmers, what happens is that the system operates at a snail's pace and all the farmers, who have come to expect reasonable response times, start to complain. Only after the explorer's query has been purged from the system does response time for the farmers (who are the day-to-day users of the data warehouse) return to its normal state. In short, it is a big mistake to simply throw an explorer's request into the data warehouse work queue and hope for the best.

One approach to solving the problem of intermixing the workload from the farmer and the explorer is to require the explorer to use the system only during off-hours—on the weekend or in the wee hours of the morning. But there are problems with this approach:

❏ The explorer wants regular working hours just as everyone else does.

❏ Some requests the explorer submits may run right through the slack hours that have been allocated, thereby impacting regular operating hours for the farmers. In addition, there often are other batch and long-running processes that need to be run which may be preempted by the explorer.

Another approach to satisfy the needs of the explorer and to keep performance adequate is to allow the explorer to do only small browsing (i.e., profiling) activities on the data warehouse. These browsing activities can be done very quickly on a small scale and can serve to stimulate the imagination of the explorer. However, these limited browsing activities do not suffice to serve the fully mature needs of the explorer.

Subsetting and Removing Data

As you can see, the worst thing for performance is to simply turn the explorer loose against the data warehouse, as seen in Figure 3.3.

As a general approach, the explorer has her needs best satisfied by removing whole sections of data from the data warehouse and moving the data off to a separate set of processors. In Figure 3.3, the explorer is trying to do modeling activities against the data warehouse but finds that the restrictions are simply too binding. The explorer does some profiling and then selects a likely subset of data on which to operate and extracts that subset of data to a separate set of processors (i.e., data mart). Once the data has been extracted and placed on a separate set of processors, the explorer can do as much modeling as desired with no impact on the

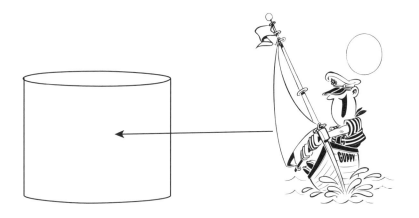

FIGURE 3.3
The explorer accessing the data warehouse.

performance of the data warehouse. The farmers have no idea that any exploration is occurring.

ACCESSING NEAR-LINE AND ARCHIVAL STORAGE The explorer can also choose data from near-line storage, as seen in Figure 3.4, or from off-line archival storage, as seen in Figure 3.5. While the data that comes from near-line or archival storage is perfectly fine for the analytical processing of the explorer (and indeed may be the only source of the data), the explorer has some things to consider. One consideration is that the data found in near-line or archival storage may not have been subjected to the rigor of the data found in the data warehouse. Near-line and archival data may be terribly unintegrated. In addition, near-line and archival data may be incomplete. Either some data was not put onto near-line storage or

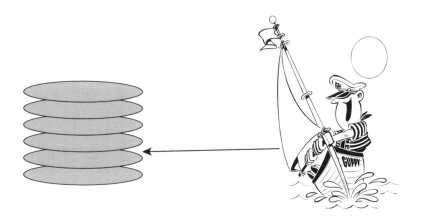

FIGURE 3.4
The explorer accessing near-line storage.

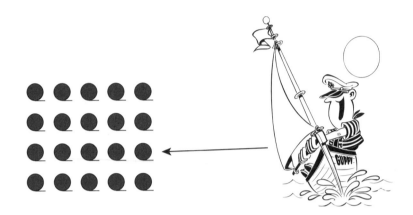

FIGURE 3.5
The explorer accessing archival data.

archival storage, or data was put on those types of storage and was lost to the imperfections of the medium. Or perhaps the data was placed on near-line storage or archival storage and has since been lost.

The explorer must be careful in assuming that data found in near-line storage and archival storage is of the same caliber as the data found in the data warehouse.

MERGING NEAR-LINE AND ARCHIVAL STORAGE   A powerful option the explorer has is to merge data from near-line and archival storage, as shown in Figure 3.6. There is no reason why the explorer cannot bring data from the data warehouse, from near-line storage, and from archival storage for the purpose of analysis. Of course, the explorer must make sure the data is compatible in terms of structure, keys, and definitions.

Creating a Living Sample

In the case where an explorer wishes to do statistical analysis, there is an alternative that can save huge amounts of resources and still produce the analysis needed by the analyst. In order to achieve this, a unique environment must be created. The environment is called the "living sample" environment. The living sample environment is a subset of the data warehouse (and type of data mart) where the analyst can do statistical analysis on a selected subset of data. The living sample environment is one that is permanent rather than temporary. Figure 3.7 depicts the living sample database.

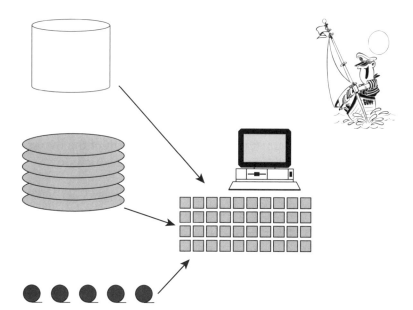

FIGURE 3.6
The explorer retrieving a subset of data from one of the sites where historical data is located.

The living sample environment is created by selecting a small subset of data that is representative of the data warehouse. The living sample database is periodically refreshed from the data warehouse or other sources. Typically the living sample database

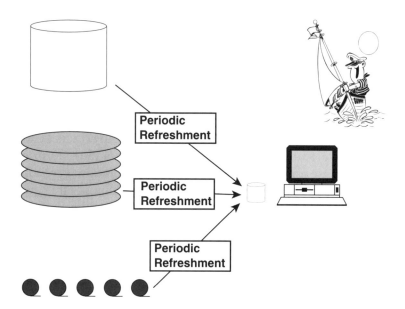

FIGURE 3.7
Creating a living sample database.

contains only a fraction of the data found in the originating source. By using the living sample analysis database for statistical processing, the analyst saves huge amounts of resources at the cost of some data replication. The living sample database is good for doing modeling and profiling. Often it is much more efficient to do analysis on a living sample database than it is to do the analysis against the data warehouse.

There are many considerations in the creation of the living sample environment. Some of these considerations include

❑ How frequently is the living sample database populated?

❑ What data is selected for the living sample database (i.e., what sample size is statistically valid)? Typically judgment samples are chosen or purely random samples are created.

❑ How large is the living sample database to be?

❑ What bias is there in the data that has been collected in the living sample database?

In the instance of truly large amounts of data, the explorer can do much statistical analysis very efficiently using a living sample database. One of the best uses of the living sample database is doing iterative analysis and query formulation. Once the explorer thinks that the heuristic processing is complete, then the final pass is done against the complete database (i.e., data warehouse). In this way the explorer gets to do iterative analysis very efficiently and attains the accuracy of processing using the entire database.

Exploration Warehouse

There is another architectural structure that greatly benefits the explorer called the "exploration warehouse." The exploration warehouse supplements data warehouse processing. In its general usage, the exploration warehouse is "rolled off" of the enterprise data warehouse for special analyses. Some exploration warehouses live for less than an hour; other exploration warehouses live quite a bit longer. Data is placed on a wholesale basis into the exploration warehouse. There is no incremental update into the exploration warehouse. The sole purpose of the exploration warehouse is to serve the explorer.

EVOLUTION OF THE EXPLORATION WAREHOUSE   The exploration warehouse, like all forms of data warehouse constructs, was shaped out of need. Consider the organization with an enterprise data warehouse. The enterprise data warehouse contains much detailed data and deep history. The enterprise data warehouse serves many purposes—as a clearinghouse for feeding data marts, as a basis for farmer queries, as a source of reconciliation, as a historical repository of data. Because of the volume of data, the cost of the processor that the enterprise data warehouse resides on, and the volume of data flowing into and out of the enterprise data warehouse, resources are always scarce.

It is into this world that the explorer enters. The explorer needs to look at large amounts of data in a random manner operating in a random, nonrepetitive mode. When the explorer embarks on an analytical quest trying to use the enterprise data warehouse, the explorer is pushed away. The volume of data the explorer requires, the unusual and unpredictable ways in which the explorer wishes to look at the data, and the time frame the explorer wishes to look at never fit easily with the enterprise data warehouse. A very convenient way to accommodate the needs of the explorer is by the creation of a separate exploration warehouse. By creating an exploration warehouse, the explorer achieves optimal performance at no expense to the regular users of the enterprise data warehouse.

But there is a second very important reason why having an exploration warehouse separate and apart from an enterprise warehouse makes sense, and that reason is that the exploration warehouse is built on a foundation of technology that is optimal for exploration. The foundation that exploration warehouses are built on is called "token"-based technology. Token-based technology allows the economics of an exploration warehouse to be very favorable. In addition, token-based technology provides performance for the explorer that cannot be achieved from the technology typically used to support the enterprise data warehouse. Token-based technology allows data to be condensed to the point that it can be placed in memory (fully or to a large degree). Once placed in memory, the speed of analysis and retrieval is a fraction of the speed that can be obtained using standard enterprise data warehouse technology.

**WHY HAVE EXPLORATION
WAREHOUSES EVOLVED?**

There are some powerful reasons why exploration
warehouses have evolved:

❏ The displacement of expensive machine cycles that the
   enterprise data warehouse resides on.
❏ An awkward fit between the needs of the explorer and
   the structure and technology of data residing on the
   enterprise warehouse.
❏ The speed and economy of processing that can be
   achieved by creating an exploration warehouse with
   technology that is most appropriate for the needs of the
   explorers.

POPULAR FORMS OF THE EXPLORATION WAREHOUSE   As its name implies,
the exploration warehouse is a structure useful for dealing with
the unknown in a data warehouse environment. The exploration
warehouse is a component of the data warehouse platform whose
purpose is to provide a safe haven for exploratory processing and
move ad hoc processes away from the primary enterprise data
warehouse.

The exploration warehouse can take one of two basic forms
depending on its usage. The first way the exploration warehouse
can be used is as a front end to the enterprise warehouse during the
development process. But the most popular way the exploration
warehouse can be used is as a "roll-off" database copied from the
enterprise data warehouse for the purpose of exploratory processing. When the exploration warehouse is used as a basis for
exploratory processing for data that already exists, the exploration
warehouse is fed directly and only from the enterprise data warehouse. When the exploration warehouse is refreshed, it is simply
reloaded from the freshest data found in the enterprise data warehouse. But when the exploration warehouse is used in the mode of
providing a "what if" foundation for the initial building from the
enterprise data warehouse, the exploration warehouse is fed directly from the legacy systems environment. When used in this
manner, the exploratory processing done by the end user forms
the basis for designing the enterprise data warehouse.

In any case, the exploration warehouse is of a temporary, transitory nature. An exploration warehouse may have a life of several months or a life as short as a half hour. The very nature of the exploration warehouse is constant construction and reconstruction. It is very likely that once built, an exploration warehouse may never be built again with the same form or content. And it is unusual for an exploration warehouse to physically exist in a single state for more than a few weeks. The exploration warehouse serves the purpose of satisfying the need for very unstructured processing within the data warehouse environment. The exploration warehouse is for the explorer who is mining data and the initial designer of the warehouse who is unsure of the requirements for the data warehouse environment and wishes to create a database "straw man."

DATA MINING AND THE EXPLORATION WAREHOUSE   The explorer is an end user who looks at data in a random, nonrepetitive manner. The explorer often looks at very large amounts of data because the explorer needs to work with detail and history. The level of detail that the explorer examines and the length of time that history is spread over conspire to make the queries done by the explorer very large. Furthermore, the queries done by the explorer are very heuristic and iterative. There is no pattern of repetition in the queries submitted by the explorer. In some cases the explorer is looking for patterns of data. In other cases the explorer is looking for associations and relationships that are hidden in the bulk of the data. In yet other cases the explorer is looking at the quality and consistency of data that is being entered into the data warehouse. Because of the very random nature of explorer processing, data is highly indexed in the exploration warehouse. Indeed, because of token-based technology, all columns and all rows are indexed as a byproduct of how the technology stores and manages data.

INITIAL DEVELOPMENT AND THE EXPLORATION WAREHOUSE   When the exploration warehouse is used as a "trial balloon" for the testing of the initial design of the data warehouse, the explorer is more interested in examining and probing what data and what relationships are in (or are going to be in) the data warehouse. The nature of the exploration warehouse in this mode is one that allows an enterprise warehouse to be constructed and reconstructed quickly when the explorer finds data that is not quite right or where there are relationships that just don't add up. Used in this mode, the exploration warehouse has a flavor of being very much like a prototype warehouse.

A very real case can be made for the exploration warehouse being used as the first iteration of development of the enterprise data warehouse. As data becomes integrated, it is often unclear exactly how the enterprise data warehouse should be shaped. Using the exploration warehouse as a precursor to the data warehouse allows design to be done very quickly. The mistakes in design (which are a fact of life with every data warehouse) can be done in miniature and on a small and inexpensive scale. Once the early iterations of development have been created, the full-fledged enterprise data warehouse can be created. When the exploration warehouse is used in this mode, it is mandatory that data be integrated before being placed into the exploration warehouse. Merely copying or replicating data into an exploration warehouse creates (and proliferates) the problem of the lack of integration of the legacy, operational environment. Therefore merely copying data into an exploration warehouse without integration is a exceedingly poor idea.

THROWAWAY EXPLORATION WAREHOUSES   One of the appealing aspects of the exploration warehouse is that because of the ease of development and because of the often transitory nature of the data residing in the data warehouse, the exploratory warehouse can be considered to be "throwaway." Indeed, for an analyst studying a problem that will change a week from now, it does not make sense to create a special structure that will stand forever yet be used only once or twice. The cost of creating and operating an exploration warehouse is such that a throwaway database is a real possibility. Under these circumstances—which coincide very nicely with the needs of an explorer—throwaway exploration warehouses make sense. However, there is nothing to say that you have to throw away an exploration warehouse. Circumstances will arise where a body of data will be needed indefinitely. There is then the possibility of a long-term exploration warehouse.

A BRIDGE TO DATA MINING   There is another role played by the exploration warehouse and that is as a bridge to the world of data mining. The question can be raised, why do we need another warehouse for data mining? The answer is that data mining can be done on the enterprise data warehouse, but there are many reasons why a separate database makes sense.

The first reason why a separate exploration warehouse makes sense is that performance in the enterprise data warehouse is not affected when the explorer builds an exploration warehouse and does the exploration against it. Consider what happens when there is no exploration warehouse. The explorer sends very large queries to the enterprise data warehouse. Each of the exploration queries executes and in doing so consumes a large number of resources. Performance for everything but the explorers processing comes to a halt in the enterprise data warehouse. The cessation of predictable service by the enterprise data warehouse is not a good thing as the enterprise data warehouse serves many purposes. If the explorer executes only a few transactions operating only against a reasonably small amount of data, then the resource load against the enterprise data warehouse may not be too bad. But in the face of the explorer who wants to run an unlimited amount of processes against an unlimited amount of data in an unpredictable manner, then the enterprise data warehouse does not serve as a viable foundation for corporate exploration. It is under these circumstances that the exploration warehouse works exceedingly well.

HOUSING THE EXPLORATION WAREHOUSE   At least in theory, the exploration warehouse can be housed in standard DBMS technology. But standard database technology is very expensive when used in this manner. A much better alternative is for the exploration warehouse to be housed in token-based technology. This differs radically from relational database technology. In relational database technology, when a record is added to the system, a physical representation of the data is appended onto disk. Consider the few simple records that might be found in a standard database management system:

Record 1	James Johnson 459-070-1872 Dallas, TX	1000.00
Record 2	Tom Swanson 498-998-1097 El Paso, TX	550.00
Record 3	James Thomas 349-550-1093 Waco, TX	1000.00
Record 4	Tom Inmon 109-338-1097 Dallas, TX	275.00
Record 5	Bill Johnson 187-550-1082 El Paso, TX	300.00

Record 6	Terry Thomas 398-220-9832 Dallas, TX
Record 7	James Swanson 187-220-2987 El Paso, TX
Record 8	Bill Wilson 498-209-1098 Dallas, TX
Record 9	John Thompson 187-207-1108 El Paso, TX
Record 10	John Thomas 108-207-2008 Waco, TX

With amounts: Record 6 — 1000.00; Record 7 — 575.00; Record 8 — 1000.00; Record 9 — 550.00; Record 10 — 1000.00.

Each time a transaction is completed, a new record is added to the standard database. The scaling of data is said to be linear because the volume of data is a function of how many records there are. But look at the records of data in the small and simple database above. There is redundancy of data throughout the database. The name "James" appears three times. The number "1000.00" appears five times. The state "Texas" appears 10 times. There is significant physical redundancy in the database.

Consider the possibility of creating a token for each entry in the database. "James" would have a token of 01 for a first name. "Texas" would have a token of 01 for state name. "El Paso" might have a token of 02 for city name. The above database could be reduced to a series of tokens that could be represented like:

First name		Last name		City		State		Amount		Area Code		Exchange	
James	01	Johnson	01	Dallas	01	TX	01	1000.00	01	459	01	070	01
Tom	02	Swanson	02	El Paso	02			550.00	02	498	02	998	02
Bill	03	Thomas	03	Waco	03			275.00	03	349	03	550	03
Terry	04	Inmon	04					300.00	04	109	04	338	04
John	05	Wilson	05					575.00	05	187	05	220	05
Thompson	06									398	06	209	06
										498	07	207	07
										187	08		
										108	09		

Once the tokens have been established, the database can be reduced to the following:

Record 1   01,01,01-01-1872,01,01,01

Record 2   02,02,02-02-1097,02,01,02

Record 3   01,03,03-03-1093,03,01,01

Record 4   02,04,04-04-1097,01,01,03

Record 5   03,01,05-03-1082,02,01,04

Record 6   04,03,06-05-9832,01,01,01

Record 7   01,02,07-05-2987,02,01,05

Record 8   03,05,02-06-1098,01,01,01

Record 9   05,06,08-07-1108,02,01,02

Record 10   05,03,09-07-2008,03,01,01

Once the records have been reduced to tokens, the space required for storing those records shrinks dramatically. Furthermore, the larger the amount of data (i.e., the greater the number of records), the greater the difference in storage requirements for a standard linearly scalable database and a token database. Stated differently, the greater the number of records, the greater the advantage of a token-based database. In token database technology, several very beneficial things happen:

❏ Data is greatly condensed.
❏ The more data there is, the more favorable the ratio between token data and standard record-based data.
❏ Because data is greatly condensed, entire databases can be placed in memory.
❏ All rows and all columns are indexed.

Once token-based databases are placed in memory, the speed of processing is greatly accelerated. Depending on the particulars, the acceleration of a query may be two or three orders (or even more) of magnitude. Once the speed of processing is greatly accelerated, many possibilities become manifested. For example, very high speed in memory processing allows the analyst to employ techniques for heuristic analysis that otherwise would not be feasible. The analyst can submit queries that scan entire databases with impunity.

Another major benefit of the gross shrinkage of data is the possibility of indexing all attributes. Once all attributes are indexed, heuristic analysis by the explorer is unlimited. The analyst can look at any field in any manner desired. The speed of the query is such that if the analyst wants to refine the results, a new query can be reformulated and rerun. All the reformulation and recalculation can be done in a fraction of the time that would have been required if the database had been built in a standard record-based technology. In truth, the efficacy of the exploration warehouse depends on the existence and economies of token-based database technology. Using standard database technology, it is questionable whether exploration warehouse structures can ever become a standard part of the platform.

DESIGNING THE EXPLORATION WAREHOUSE   The database structure commonly deployed in an exploration warehouse is the normalized structure. The normalized structure is optimal because the exploration warehouse is servicing people who do not know what they want. If there happens to be a pattern of data access that is used by everyone, then the structure of the exploration warehouse may start to resemble a star-join. But creating star-joins in an exploration warehouse presupposes that we have some idea of how the data is going to be used in terms of business dimensions (e.g., product, client, time) and metrics (e.g., revenue, costs). This supposition goes against the grain of the explorer, who by definition does not know what will be examined or how it will be examined.

The explorer can take an entire enterprise data warehouse and condense it into a token-based exploration warehouse. Or the explorer can choose a subset of the enterprise data warehouse and use that as a basis for condensation. For example, the enterprise data warehouse may have five years of history in the database and the explorer may choose three years for the exploration warehouse. Because of token-based technology, there are very few restrictions as to the data that can be selected for the population of the exploration warehouse. In addition, more than one explorer can build an exploration warehouse. A financial explorer can build one exploration warehouse; a marketing explorer can build another exploration warehouse. As long as the different exploration warehouses have the same foundation enterprise data warehouse, there is always a single point of reconciliation.

OLAP AND THE EXPLORATION WAREHOUSE   One of the questions that can be asked is whether OLAP/multidimensional (i.e., "cube") technology can be used as a basis for doing exploration warehouse processing rather than token-based technology. The answer is that superficially cube technology can be used. But there are some severe restrictions that greatly limit cube as a basis for exploration warehouse processing. The essence of cube technology is that all possible outcomes are calculated in a cube before the user starts processing. By precalculating the questions that might be asked, cube technology can provide very quick response time. The problem is that there are only so many possible outcomes that can be imagined before any processing starts to occur. The explorer will always have more ways to look at the data than can be predetermined by the design of any cube. And when the cube has to go back and try to calculate what the explorer wanted but which did not exist in the cube, performance suffers.

Another implication of the approach of precalculation is that only so much detailed data can be managed. When there are many dimensions to the cube, there is a limitation on what detailed data can go into the dimensions. While there are limitations on token-based technology, it is fair to say that since token-based technology does not try to precalculate every possible permutation, far more detailed data can go into a token-based exploration warehouse than a cube-based exploration warehouse.

REFRESHMENT AND THE EXPLORATION WAREHOUSE   One of the benefits of an exploration warehouse is that the data is stable once loaded. No updates are done to the exploration warehouse until the exploration warehouse is completely recast. This provides a very solid foundation for heuristic analysis. When an analyst runs an analysis, then reformulates the analysis and runs it again, the analyst knows that any differences achieved are due to reformulation, not to changing data. In other words, if data were to be updated between one iteration of analysis and another, then when the analyst compared the results of analysis, the analyst would never know whether the difference in results was due to a change in data or a change in analysis formulation.

The use of token-based technology for exploration warehouse processing is especially appropriate in the face of the need for periodic reformulation of the entire database. When data can be condensed into memory-sized databases, it is possible to construct one version of a database, examine it, decide that it is not quite properly structured, then reconstruct the database all within a half-hour's time. The load time alone precludes this sort of reformulation of a standard record-based implementation of an exploration warehouse.

METADATA AND THE EXPLORATION WAREHOUSE   Metadata plays an important role in all parts of the data warehouse environment, and the exploration warehouse environment is no exception. Because explorers are looking at the exploration warehouse in many ways, not a few of which have never been examined before, metadata plays an especially important role. In order for there to be effective metadata at the exploration warehouse, there needs to be an effective metadata layer at the enterprise data warehouse. That layer needs to be able to be transported to the exploration warehouse environment every time there is a reconstruction of the exploration warehouse.

OPTIMIZING FOR THE FARMER

Farmers in the data warehouse environment have a different measure of response time than do explorers. Farmers operate in a mode of relative predictability. The queries submitted by the farmer operate on a uniform and reasonably small amount of data. For these reasons farmers enjoy good response time. The practices that can be used to enhance performance in the data warehouse environment for farmers can be divided into three classes—strategic, tactical, and operational—as shown in Figure 3.8.

Strategic practices are those that can yield up to several orders of magnitude of improvement in performance. Tactical practices are those that can yield up to an order of magnitude of performance improvement. Operational practices are those that can yield up to 50% gain in performance. The data warehouse administrator needs to be aware of these categories because if the administrator is facing a problem that requires a huge performance increase, then the administrator is not going to get it by using an

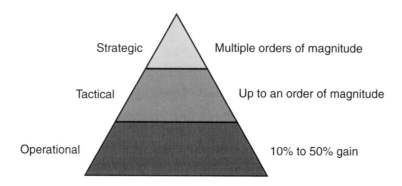

FIGURE 3.8
The approaches to improving data warehouse performance.

operational approach to performance improvement. If only a minor performance increase is desired, the administrator is wise to not choose the expense and complexity associated with a strategic improvement in performance.

Strategic Approaches to Performance

Although several techniques exist to improve performance from a strategic perspective, the two most important are archiving of dormant data and star-join schemas. Let's take a quick look at each of these approaches.

ARCHIVING DORMANT DATA   The most strategic approach to the improvement of performance the data warehouse administrator can take is to archive data that does not belong in the data warehouse. Figure 3.9 shows the volumes of data that are behind this most basic activity of data warehouse administration.

As discussed in Chapter 1, removing unneeded data from the data warehouse brings data that is needed out in the open. When data that is unneeded is left in the data warehouse, the data that is useful "hides" behind unneeded data, slowing performance. We will discuss dormant data and performance in further detail in Chapter 5.

STAR-JOIN SCHEMAS   The essence of farmers is that their usage is predictable and that they are organized into departments. From a department's perspective, there is a "right way" and a "wrong way" in which to organize data for the department. The right way to

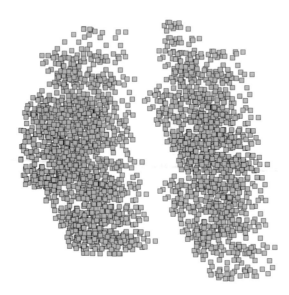

FIGURE 3.9
Volumes of data are the primary impediment to performance.

organize data is in accordance with the way that most people in the department perceive the data to be structured. Because there is a consensus of opinion as to how the data ought to be organized, the high-level database design approach that can be employed for optimal farmer/departmental design of the database can be called a "star-join." Figure 3.10 shows a simple case of a star-join.

There are several related tables in Figure 3.10. At the center of the structure is the sales table. The sales table is called a fact table and is so designated because it contains a very large number of occurrences of data containing facts or measurements that are of interest to the business. Each occurrence contains a "fact" or measurement that is at the intersection of a dimension. For example, a measurement might be revenue at the intersection of "product" and "customer." The fact table shares a relationship with other outlying tables called dimension tables. The dimension tables are (in this example) time, promotion, market, and product tables. The data that resides in the dimension tables is far less voluminous than the data in the fact table. This organization of data is optimal for one set of farmers. It is very efficient for the farmer to go into the fact table and extract and analyze data.

It is important to note that each department will have its own rendition of the star-join and it is unlikely that the data structure that is optimal for one department will be the same structure that

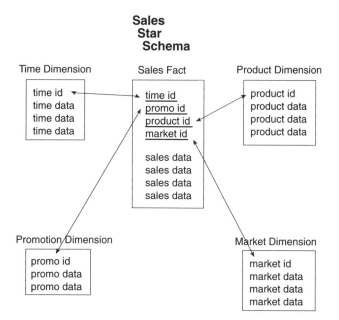

**Sales
Star
Schema**

FIGURE 3.10
*A star-join with a fact
table and dimensions.*

is optimal for another department. Star-joins are a strategic approach to the improvement of performance and can greatly minimize the amount of resources needed to optimize query performance in a data warehouse environment. Because of its affinity toward addressing the performance needs of a department, this design approach is best suited for the data mart component of the data warehouse platform.

The star-join structure, pioneered by Ralph Kimball, is optimal for the farmers of the organization. For more information on creating a star schema design, see Ralph's book *The Data Warehouse Toolkit*.

Tactical Approaches to Performance

There are a variety of tactical approaches to support the performance needs of the farmer community. Some of the more popular approaches include

- ❏ Denormalization
- ❏ Clustering data
- ❏ Compacting data
- ❏ Colocating data

Although we cover the implementation of these techniques in more detail when we discuss building the high-performance platform in Chapter 9, let's take a quick look at each from the perspective of the farmer.

DENORMALIZATION   The effect of data modeling and normalization is that of producing a design where data is perfectly nonredundant. The only redundancy in a normalized design is for the purpose of foreign key relationships and referential integrity of the data. Other than that there is no redundancy of data. However, on infrequent occasions, it makes sense to introduce some limited redundancy of data into the data warehouse design. Figure 3.11 shows such a case.

At the top of Figure 3.11 the designer has created a perfectly nonredundant design. At the bottom, the designer has reconsidered and has taken the column "desc" and has placed that data in several tables where the data is regularly accessed. In doing so, the designer has optimized the access of the data at the expense of the update of the data and the volume of data in the database. Since data in the data warehouse is never updated once entered, update is no problem. What is a problem is the space that is required for the multiple occurrences of the data. Data warehouses are most sensitive to space. Adding data deliberately must be done very carefully and judiciously. When used properly, however, a significant amount of machine resources can be saved. Now that we have taken a look at one form of denormalization (i.e., column replication), let's take a look at several others:

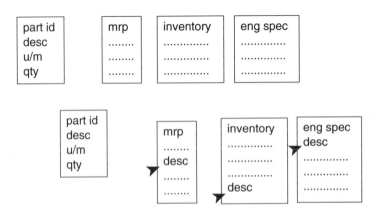

FIGURE 3.11

Selectively introducing redundancy.

1. Creating arrays of data
2. Prejoining tables
3. Preaggregating data

Creating Arrays of Data While normalization accomplished some worthy goals (in the eyes of the explorers, at least), normalization did not enhance performance for farmers. One of the techniques of normalization is the separation of different related types of data from each other. This is called the "first normal form." Experienced data warehouse administrators have found that when related types of data are used together frequently, it makes sense to store those units of data together. Figure 3.12 shows an example.

In the top of Figure 3.12, data is normalized and separated. In this case the months of the year are located in very different physical locations. When a query wishes to see the data for January, February, March, April, etc., the system is forced to look in many different locations. An alternative organization of data is the creation of arrays of data in which related data types are physically placed in the same location. In the bottom of Figure 3.12, the months of the year have been placed in a physically contiguous location. Now when the system wishes to see the data for January, February, March, April, etc., only one physical access into the system is required because the data has been optimally located to accommodate such a request. Note that if there is no recognized and regular need to see the months of the year together, this technique does not optimize performance. However, in the case of farmers, where there is a predictable and regular use of the data, such a technique works quite well.

There are several ways to accomplish the loading of data in an array. In some cases, the database allows such an organization of data (see the section on clustering of data). In other cases, the data warehouse administrator must specify a single row of data in which different column types correspond to the entries into the array. There are design trade-offs no matter how the creation and update of arrays is accomplished.

Prejoining Tables One of the most potent techniques for the saving of machine resources is that of merging tables together based on a common key and based on common usage. Figure 3.13 depicts this technique.

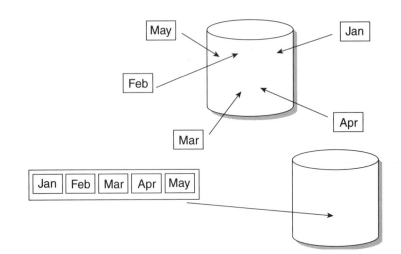

FIGURE 3.12
Using arrays of data in order to physically juxtapose related records of date to minimize the amount of I/O needed to access and analyze the data.

The result of data modeling and normalization typically is the specification of many tables. The data warehouse administrator can cause each of the normalized tables to be turned into a physical table. Or if there is a common key shared among two or more

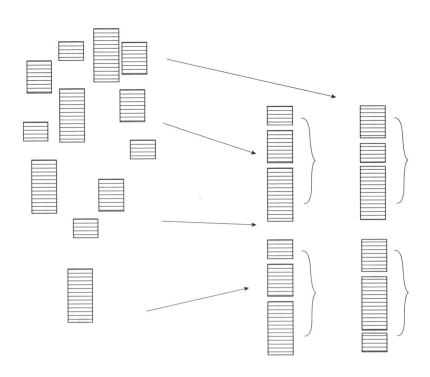

FIGURE 3.13
Prejoining tables.

tables and common and regular usage of the tables, then it makes sense to merge the tables physically into a single table. In doing so, the access of data is greatly streamlined.

Preaggregating Data   A very useful technique for structuring data for optimal access is to organize the data according to a "rolling summary" structure, as shown in Figure 3.14. As data enters the data warehouse it is stored on an hourly basis. At the end of the day, the hourly data is stored on a daily basis. At the end of the week, the daily data is stored on a weekly basis. At the end of the month, the data is stored on a monthly basis. By organizing data this way, the designer has greatly reduced the amount of space required to house the data and has potentially greatly increased performance. Of course, the designer has forfeited the right to look at detailed data that has aged. The older data gets, the less detail is retained. However, many types of data are amenable to this treatment. Sales, production, and marketing data are all able to be rolled up with little or no loss of efficacy.

CLUSTERING DATA   Not only can arrays of data be created and physically colocated into the same vicinity of data inside the data warehouse, but different types of data can be physically colocated as well. Figure 3.15 shows one such common technique for the placement of different records of data into the same location based on common information.

In the case of Figure 3.15, four different records have been physically placed into the database based on some common unit of information inside the records. The common unit of data may be a key, but it does not have to be. The net effect is that when the end user wants to see all four records, they will be sitting there waiting in the same location. It is very efficient for the system to pick up all

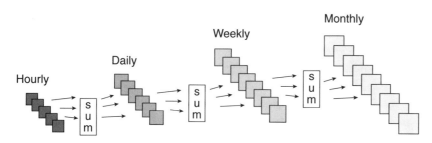

FIGURE 3.14
Rolling summary data.

FIGURE 3.15
Clustering data in order to optimize access.

four records at the same time. Note that the strategy for the placement of data into the same location based on clustering depends on the predictability of usage and the regularity of usage. If usage is not both predictable and regular, then clustering of data makes no sense. Clustering in one database may be quite different from the clustering in another. Careful attention needs to be paid to exactly how a given database handles clustering.

COMPACTING DATA   A simple yet very effective technique for the optimization of performance is the compaction of data. Figure 3.16 illustrates this technique.

Compaction saves resources because it optimizes the amount of data that is retrieved when the system accesses a physical block of data. In such a manner, compaction makes the reading of data an extremely rich and robust experience. There are, however, some considerations for the best application of compaction. Compaction requires CPU resources at the moment of writing and at the moment of reading. But more importantly, compaction requires that data not be changed (i.e., rewritten or updated, once written). In order to illustrate why compacted data is not easily updated, consider a field of 60 bytes that is written in a compacted format. One

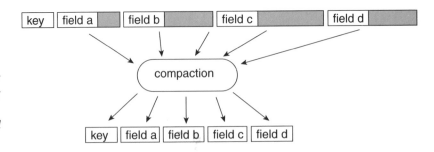

FIGURE 3.16
Compaction optimizes the access of data because any given I/O gets more data than if no compaction had occurred.

day the user decides to change the data. The 60-byte occurrence of data is changed into a 62-byte occurrence of data. Because the data is initially compacted, there is no room to accommodate the 2-byte difference. The simple change from 60 bytes to 62 bytes causes the entire record to be recompacted. In the worst case, the original record spills over into two records. The implication is that very tight compaction of data must be used only when data is not updated and when the pattern of usage of the data is very predictable. These two requirements fit very nicely with database design for farmers inside the data warehouse.

COLOCATING DATA Two types of physical colocation of data within the data warehouse have already been discussed—the creation of arrays inside the data warehouse and the use of clustering. But in truth there are many forms of physical colocation of data inside the data warehouse, as suggested by Figure 3.17.

One way the programmer has of effecting the physical colocation of data inside the data warehouse is at the moment of initial load. Many databases physically load the data in the order in which it is sequenced at load time. By taking advantage of this, the data warehouse administrator can cause the data to be loaded in the order that is most propitious.

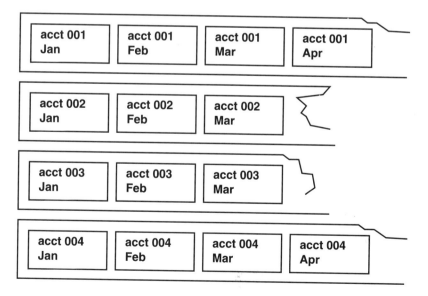

FIGURE 3.17
Physical colocation of data by the programmer.

Operational Approaches to Performance

Now that we have looked at approaches to address the performance needs of the farmer from a strategic and tactical perspective, let's look at the performance needs operationally. Some of the more popular approaches to improving performance from an operational perspective include

❑ Perform inserts, deletes, and updates off-line
❑ Sequence insertions before execution
❑ Use third-party utilities
❑ Index after loading
❑ Purge the warehouse regularly
❑ Monitor activity
❑ Consolidate queries
❑ Source from log tapes
❑ Chargeback usage

Let's take a look at each one of these operational techniques in a bit of detail.

PERFORM INSERTS, DELETES, AND UPDATES OFF-LINE   Under no circumstances does it make sense for regular update activity to be done online in the middle of the DSS analysts processing day. Instead, necessary insert, delete, and update processing should be done during off hours, as shown in Figure 3.18.

There is no impact on the analytical processing done on the data warehouse. Performance is enhanced in two ways:

❑ The actual activity of insert, delete, and update is done when the analyst is not using the system heavily.
❑ The database data integrity mechanism does not have to be turned on during the day, waiting for the possibility of an activity which will require COMMIT processing.

The assertion has been made that updates are not done on a database in a data warehouse environment. An explanation is in order.

No updates should ever be done during the day. Indeed, if updating is done at all, it should be done after hours. And even in

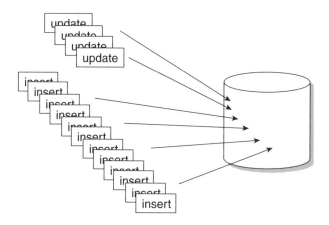

FIGURE 3.18
All offline insert, delete, and update processing is done after hours.

the case of after hours updates, they should be done only for the correction and amendment of data. If updating is done at all, it should be done on an exception basis on small amounts of data, and only for the purpose of correcting data that has been placed in the data warehouse incorrectly. Doing updates destroys the integrity of the reports and analysis that have come out of the data warehouse. When a unit of data is changed, for whatever reason, an analyst that has used the data for an analysis can never re-create the analysis or reconcile her reports. For this reason, updates should not be a regular and normal part of the data warehouse workload.

SEQUENCE INSERTIONS BEFORE EXECUTION   A really simple (but potentially very effective) idea is to make sure that data is sequenced properly (if in fact there is a proper order) prior to insertion into the data warehouse. In the case of hashed data, this option will not apply. But in the case of nonhashed data, presequencing the data may save significant machine cycles. Figure 3.19 shows the presequencing of data prior to insertion. The value of presequencing data prior to insertion is that the presequencing can be done on an available, inexpensive processor during slack hours, and the data "slides" into the data warehouse server in the sequence that the data would otherwise be placed in were it not sequenced.

USE OF THIRD-PARTY UTILITIES   At first glance it would seem that the utilities provided by the vendor with the database software would be the most efficient in their operation, and in some cases that is true. However, in many cases third-party software performs signif-

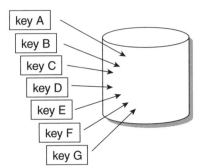

FIGURE 3.19
Sequencing insertions before execution.

icantly faster than vendor-supplied software. Figure 3.20 shows a load utility supplied by a third party.

Just because the database vendor supplies the utilities does not necessarily mean that those utilities run in an optimal fashion. The data warehouse administrator should be alert to the opportunities afforded by non-vendor-supplied utilities.

INDEX AFTER LOADING   When loading data into the data warehouse, there is the need to create indexes. In some cases, depending on the database, the amount of data being loaded, and whether the database is being completely or partially loaded, it makes sense to delay the creation of indexes until after hours when massive amounts of machine cycles are available. Figure 3.21 describes this option.

Of course, when the indexes are delayed, the data that has been loaded can only be accessed by means of a sequential search. If there is an immediate need to find the data, then this may prove to be an inviable option.

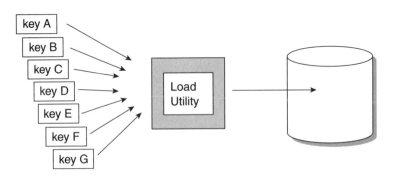

FIGURE 3.20
Third-party utilities.

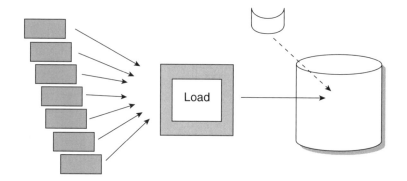

FIGURE 3.21
Delay indexing until after hours.

PURGE DATA REGULARLY   Data does not enter the data warehouse in a continuous fashion (although at times that may seem to be the case). Data has a regular life cycle inside the data warehouse and needs to be purged according to a regular schedule. Figure 3.22 shows the need for purging (or archiving) unneeded data from the data warehouse. By removing unneeded data from the data warehouse, the database administrator enhances performance for everyone. There is no single act that is more beneficial for the data warehouse than the removal of unneeded data.

MONITOR ACTIVITY   As is discussed in Chapter 7, monitoring data warehouse activity has greatly beneficial effects (see Figure 3.23).

CONSOLIDATE QUERIES   Some queries are spontaneous and ad hoc and are unable to be managed with any predictability. But other queries are run regularly. You can save tremendous amounts of machine resources by combining queries against the same table when the queries are regularly scheduled. Figure 3.24 shows the combining of queries.

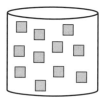

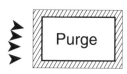

FIGURE 3.22
Purging the data warehouse.

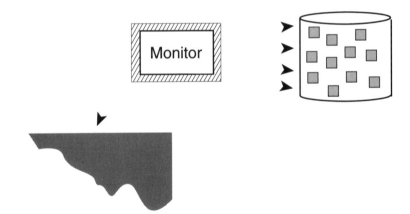

FIGURE 3.23
Regular monitoring of the data warehouse.

When the queries are consolidated, there is the need for only one pass of the data warehouse table. Each row in the table is accessed and if the row qualifies for one of the queries that has been submitted, then the relevant data is taken from the row. At the end of the consolidated query processing, the data that has been collected for each query is passed to the query as a result set. The effect of query consolidation is to minimize the number of passes through the data warehouse table.

The query consolidation facility is not a general purpose facility. It is not designed to suit every need in every organization. Instead, it is designed to suit the needs of many organizations for some, but not all, of their query processing. The conditions under which the query consolidation facility operates are

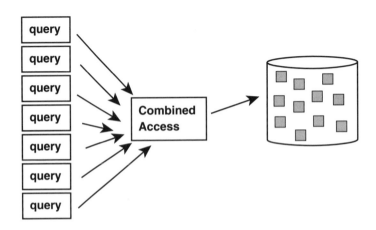

FIGURE 3.24
Combined access for multiple queries.

❏ When there are multiple queries going against the same table

❏ Where the table being accessed is a large table

❏ Where the queries are run on a predictable, regular basis

❏ Where the joins done in the queries are done on a row-by-row basis, not on a wholesale table basis

❏ Where the execution of the query is not terribly time sensitive

These are admittedly stringent conditions. There will be many queries and circumstances that will not fit within these parameters. When that is the case, the query consolidation facility offers no advantage. However, there will be many queries and circumstances that will fit within the guidelines of the query consolidation facility; for those queries, there will be savings that are significant.

When the query consolidation facility applies, how does it work? The data warehouse administrator collects all the query requirements into a single large pool. The queries focus on one table—the prime table. The queries can look at other tables as part of the query process as long as the connection to the secondary tables is through a one-row join. The query requirements are collected and consolidated. The pass against the primary table commences, and each row is accessed. If the row qualifies for selection for any of the selection criteria for any of the queries, it is kept for analysis. Otherwise processing continues to the next row. Once a row is qualified as being one that is of interest, the data that is requested is written to a work file. If more than one query has requested the same data, then the result set is tagged with multiple queries. If the row participates in a join, the join is made and the results set is created and tagged. Again, if more than one query has requested the join, then the result set is tagged with more than one query.

Processing continues until all rows in the primary table have been serviced. At the end of the processing, the dataset that has been created is scanned. The scan then passes the data to the appropriate query as its result set. The query consolidation facility optimizes resource utilization around the passing of a file one time. Were it not for the query consolidation facility, the primary file would have to be passed in its entirety (or at least for major subsets of the file) for each query. Under the right conditions, the query consolidation facility can save very large amounts of resources.

SOURCE FROM LOG TAPES   Most data warehouse administrators assume that the proper source for refreshment of data into the data warehouse is the native source system (i.e., legacy) database. Without thinking, the administrator assumes that reading the native legacy databases is the proper way to find data for refreshment. But in most cases, extracting data from the native legacy database is a very expensive proposition. Consider the following set of very normal circumstances. Suppose a data warehouse administrator has the following set of circumstances:

- ❏ A large file.
- ❏ The file is in a traditionally operational database, such as IMS.
- ❏ The file is very stable containing customer data.
- ❏ In a weeks time less than 1% of the customers' data changes.

Suppose the data warehouse administrator wishes to refresh the data warehouse weekly. What happens when the data warehouse administrator goes back and reads the customer file each week? The following scenario occurs:

- ❏ Jan 1—100% of file read, 1% of reads result in refreshment
- ❏ Jan 8—100% of file read, 1% of reads result in refreshment
- ❏ Jan 15—100% of file read, 1% of reads result in refreshment
- ❏ Jan 22—100% of file read, 1% of reads result in refreshment
- ❏ Jan 29—100% of file read, 1% of reads result in refreshment

At the end of the year, 99% of the reads against the legacy data have been a total waste because from week to week there has been no change in the data. Furthermore, the reads have occurred on the most expensive processor the shop owns. And to top things off, the online DBMS (in this case IMS) has had to be up and active during the reads. Operations groans every week when it comes time to pass the entire file once again because the online window is already full.

For these reasons then, it is worthwhile investigating alternatives because the practice of simply going and reading legacy databases is an extremely costly way to proceed. A much better alternative is that of using the log tape as the source of data that goes into the refreshment process. Figure 3.25 shows this alternative.

In Figure 3.25 the log tape flows into a utility which reads the log tape data and processes it prior to going into the data warehouse weekly refreshment process. There are some very significant advantages to using the log tape as a source:

❏ The log tape contains only the changes that have occurred since the last refreshment. There is no need to pass the many records that have not changed since the last refreshment.

❏ The log tape can be processed on a stand-alone server. There is no need to use expensive mainframe machine cycles.

❏ There is no need to keep the online system up and running while the log tape is being processed. Operations can operate the online DBMS independent of any processing being done to the log tape.

In order to make log tape processing a reality, it is necessary to use a utility to pull the data from the log tape so that it can be processed in a normal manner. The use of a log tape as a source can cut in half the total processing costs of making the data warehouse work.

CHARGEBACK USAGE   In order to instill a sense of responsible usage of system resources, many organizations use chargeback processing in the data warehouse environment (see Figure 3.26).

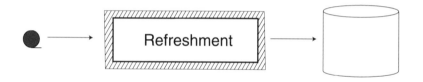

Refreshment

FIGURE 3.25
Log tapes as a source of refreshment.

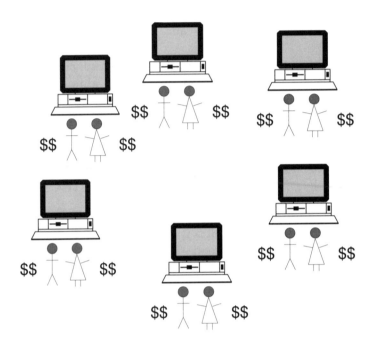

FIGURE 3.26
Chargeback makes the analyst aware of resources that are being used.

Chargeback processing is based on the individual activities of the users of the data warehouse environment. Such measurements of activity as number of rows accessed, time of day of submission of the request, number of requests made, and so forth can be incorporated into the chargeback algorithm. Chargeback is peculiar in that where it is used, no real money changes hands (usually!). In this regard, chargeback is merely a psychological mechanism to get the organization to become aware of the resources that are being consumed. But even when chargeback is measured in "funny money," there is the heightened awareness of the cost of resources consumed by the end user. And once the end user becomes aware of the cost of resource consumption, better performance is the result.

SUMMARY

There are many approaches to the enhancement of performance. Some approaches are simple and yield good results. Other approaches are complex and can be applied only in certain circumstances. The data warehouse administrator needs to be aware of all

Strategic Approaches ± multiple orders of magnitude	Parallel shared nothing hardware. DW specific DBMS. Altering granularity of data. Living sample data. Departmental (OLAP) processing. Strategic use of metadata. Star joins.
Tactical Approaches ± up to an order of magnitude	Indexing data. • standard indexes • specialized indexes Prejoined data. Arrays of data for physical colocation. Clustering data by DBMS. Data compaction. Programmer physical colocation of data. Merging tables together. Selective redundacy. Rolling summary data.
Operational Approaches ± 10% to 20% improvement	Offline insertions, updates. Sequencing insertions before update. Third-party load utilities. Delayed indexing. Regular DW purge. Monitoring of the DW. Separating explorers and farmers. Combined access for multiple queries. Log tapes for refreshment. Chargeback.

FIGURE 3.27
A summary of the different performance enhancement techniques.

the approaches to the enhancement of performance. Figure 3.27 outlines some of the approaches that have been discussed and classifies whether those approaches are strategic, tactical, or operational.

In this chapter we discussed a number of techniques that can be used to optimize performance for the farmer and explorer. Implementation of many of these techniques is discussed in detail in Chapter 9 as we discuss building a high-performance data warehouse platform. In the next chapter, we will take a closer look at an architectural component of the platform used to support the query performance needs of the farmer and explorer, the data mart.

4

Data Marts

The most notable component of the data warehouse platform is the data warehouse itself. The atomic, granular data found in the data warehouse is at the center of the data warehouse environment. The data warehouse contains integrated, historical data that is common to the entire corporation. In addition, the data warehouse contains both summarized and detailed data. An essential component of the data warehouse is metadata that describes the contents and source of the data that flows into the data warehouse. But for all of the benefits derived from a data warehouse, there are other components needed to balance the data warehouse platform. One of those components is the exploration warehouse (discussed in Chapter 3) and the other is the data mart.

WHAT IS A DATA MART?

From the data warehouse, atomic data flows to various departments for their customized usage. These departmental databases are called data marts. A data mart is a body of data for a department that has an architectural foundation of a data warehouse. Figure 4.1 shows data marts as they emanate from the data warehouse.

In Figure 4.1 the data that resides in the data warehouse is at a very granular level and the data in the data mart is at a refined (usually summarized) level. The data marts that house data for various departments contain different combinations and selections

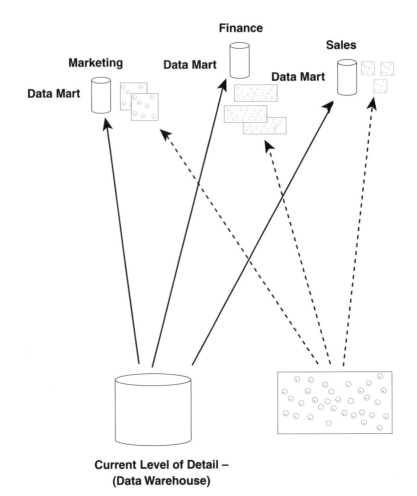

FIGURE 4.1

Data is held at the most granular level in the current level of detail. That detail is reshaped by each data mart to meet its own particular needs.

of the same detailed data found at the data warehouse. In some cases one data mart selects detailed data other than that found in other data marts. In other cases, the same data warehouse detailed data is added or calculated differently across the different data marts. In other cases, a data mart will structure detailed data differently from other data marts. However, in every case the data warehouse provides the granular foundation for all of the data found in all of the data marts. Because a data warehouse provides a foundation for all data marts, data marts have a common heritage and are able to be reconciled at the most basic level. There is, in fact, a single version of the "truth" in the data warehouse. In addition, Figure 4.1 shows that different departments will have their own data marts (though functional data marts could be shared across departments to report on such things as customer churn or sales).

Data marts are known by many names including

❑ Reporting databases
❑ Departmental DSS databases
❑ OLAP databases
❑ Multidimensional databases (MDDBMS)
❑ Lightly summarized databases

Different operating departments within the organization generally want their own data marts. The departments that typically have their own data marts include finance, marketing, sales, and accounting. Of course, any department can have its own data mart. In addition, a data mart can serve several departments. For example, if sales and marketing both have a need to do profitability analysis, you can build a single data mart to do profitability analysis that is used by both departments.

Data Mart Community

The user of the data mart environment can be called the departmental analyst. The departmental analyst is an individual who does decision making with a departmental bias. The departmental analyst is not a technician but is a businessperson first and foremost. The decisions the analyst makes are mid- to long-term, strategic decisions. Farmers and explorers are both found at the data mart level. However, farmers are much more commonly found in the data mart than explorers. Because the farmers' perspective of data can be predicted and the explorers' cannot, farmers find the data mart to be much more attractive than explorers do.

Data Mart Appeal

What is the appeal of the data mart? Why do departments find it convenient to do their decision support processing in their own data mart? What is wrong with the data warehouse as a basis for standard decision support processing? There are several factors leading to the popularity of the data mart.

As long as the data warehouse doesn't contain much data, then the data warehouse may serve the needs of different departments as a basis for decision support processing. But data warehouses do not stay small very long. As data warehouses grow, the motivation for data marts increases. As data warehouses grow

❑ The competition to get inside the data warehouse grows fierce. More and more departmental decision support processing is done inside the data warehouse to the point where resource consumption becomes a real problem.

❑ Data becomes harder to customize. In the face of a small amount of data in a data warehouse, the analyst can afford to customize and summarize data every time an analysis is done. But in the face of lots of data in a data warehouse, the analyst does not have the time and resources to summarize and customize the data.

❑ The cost of doing processing in the data warehouse increases as the volume of data increases.

❑ The software that is available for accessing and analyzing large amounts of data (typical of the data warehouse) is not nearly as elegant as the software that can process smaller amounts of data (typical of the data mart).

But perhaps the single most important reason why data marts grow in popularity is because of performance. Once the data warehouse grows large and many users want to access data inside the data warehouse, the end user finds that performance suffers. It is a natural step to go to data marts, where good performance can be easily achieved. A much improved transaction response time is one of the main motivating factors for going to a data mart. Other reasons why data marts are attractive include

❑ When a department has its own data mart, it can customize the data as the data flows into the data mart from the data warehouse. The data in the data mart does not have to serve the entire corporation. Therefore, the department can summarize, sort, select, structure, etc., its own data without consideration for any other department.

❑ The amount of historical data that is needed is a function of the department, not the corporation. The department can select a much smaller amount of historical data than that found in the data warehouse.

❑ The department can do whatever decision support processing it wants whenever it wants without considering the impact of resource utilization on other departments.

❑ The department can build the data mart on its own budget, thereby making all the technological decisions it wants.

❑ The department can select analytical software as it wishes. There is a wealth of access and analysis software at the level of the processor that houses the data mart.

❑ The unit cost of processing and storage on the size machine that is appropriate to the data mart is significantly less than the unit cost of processing and storage on the machine that houses the data warehouse.

There are many reasons then why the data mart becomes attractive as the data warehouse grows in volume. There are organizational, technological, and economic reasons why the data mart is so beguiling and is a natural outgrowth of the data warehouse.

Data Mart Source

The proper source of data for the data mart is the data warehouse. Figure 4.2 shows that under normal conditions the source of data that flows into the data mart is the current level detail, or the data warehouse.

Detailed data is customized, selected, and summarized as it is placed in the data mart. In addition, the data mart can be fed data from external sources. The programs that interface the data mart and the data warehouse become an important part of the documentation and metaprocess infrastructure. Note that Figure 4.2 does not show data coming from the operational or legacy environment as a legitimate source for data mart data. Of course, the operational environment can be used as a basis for the building of a data mart. However, using the operational environment as the basis for the data mart is a mistake. There are many reasons why the operational environment is not the proper foundation for the data mart. When the operational environment is used as a basis for the data mart environment:

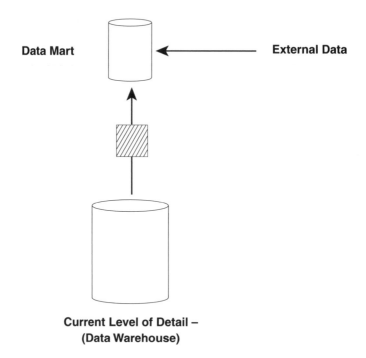

Data Mart　　　　　　　　　　　　　　　　**External Data**

FIGURE 4.2
Data is fed into the data mart from either the data warehouse or external sources.

**Current Level of Detail –
(Data Warehouse)**

❏ There is no integrated source of data.

❏ Many interface programs are required—at least one interface program from each data mart to each operational application must be written, maintained, and executed.

❏ There is no final point of reconciliation—no single point of truth—for corporate data.

❏ There is a massive amount of redundant data. Each data mart captures, stores, and maintains some of the same detailed data as every other data mart (e.g., product reference table).

BUILDING THE DATA MART FIRST

Because the operational environment is never a legitimate source for data feeding directly into the data mart, the implication is that the data warehouse should be built before the data mart (see Figure 4.3).

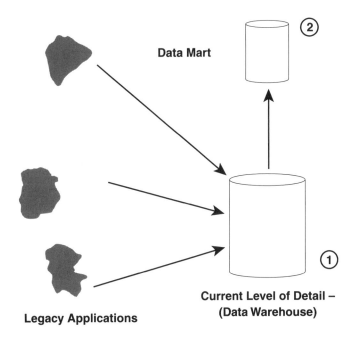

FIGURE 4.3
The order in which the data mart and the data warehouse should be built.

Different Kinds of Data Marts

There are different kinds of data marts. Figure 4.4 shows some of the more interesting data marts.

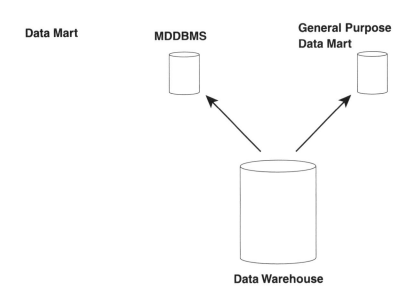

FIGURE 4.4
There are different types of data marts: MDDBMS, RCLAP, and general purpose.

One type of data mart is the MDDBMS (multidimensional database) data mart. The MDDBMS data mart is one that is used for slicing and dicing numeric data in a free-form fashion (i.e., free-form within the framework of the database that holds the multidimensional data). MDDBMS supports management's ability to analytically look at the same data in different ways. Some of the characteristics of the MDDBMS are

❑ Sparsely populated matrices
❑ Numeric data
❑ Rigid structure of data once the data enters the MDDBMS framework
❑ Consistently fast response time

Another type of data mart is one that can be called the general purpose data mart. General purpose data marts contain both numeric and textual data. General purpose data marts serve a much wider audience than their MDDBMS counterparts. Unlike MDDBMS, which are supported by specialized database management systems, general purpose data marts are supported by relational technology. Some of the characteristics of the database that support a general purpose data mart are

❑ The support of numeric, textual, and other forms of data
❑ The support of general purpose analysis
❑ The support of freely structured data
❑ The ability to have numerous indexes
❑ Support of star schemas

General purpose data marts can have both disciplined and ad hoc uses. Some of the processing in the general purpose data mart environment is very predictable. Other processing in the general purpose data mart environment is very unpredictable. The general purpose data mart environment contains both detailed and summarized data.

Loading the Data Mart

The data mart is properly loaded from the data warehouse by means of a load program. Figure 4.5 shows a load program from

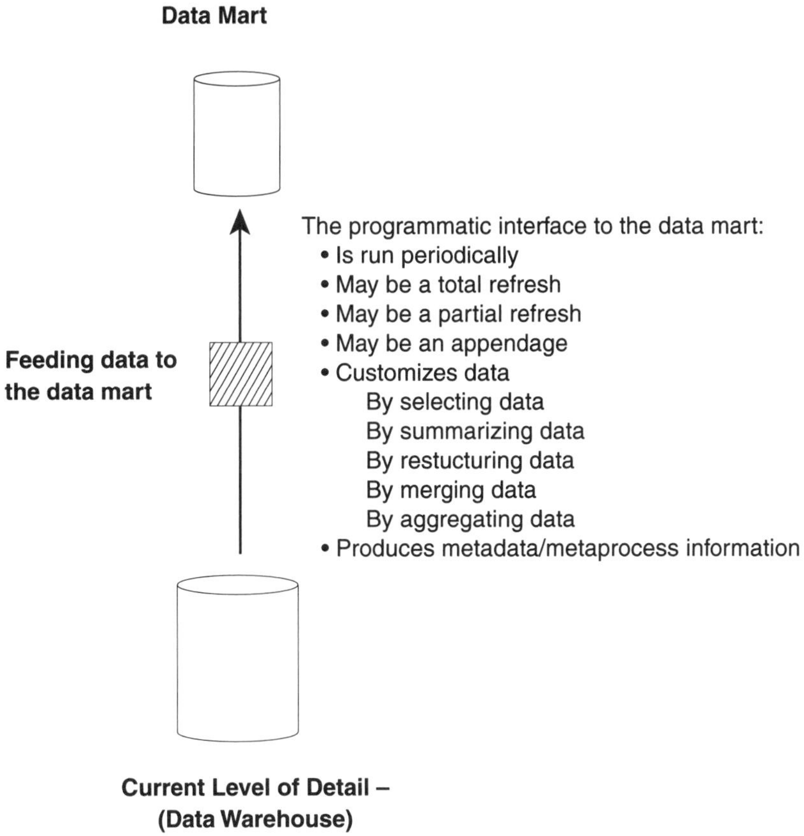

Data Mart

The programmatic interface to the data mart:
- Is run periodically
- May be a total refresh
- May be a partial refresh
- May be an appendage
- Customizes data
    By selecting data
    By summarizing data
    By restucturing data
    By merging data
    By aggregating data
- Produces metadata/metaprocess information

**Feeding data to
the data mart**

**Current Level of Detail –
(Data Warehouse)**

FIGURE 4.5
*A load program from the
data warehouse to the data
mart.*

the data warehouse to the data mart. Some of the factors considered by the load program include

❏ The schedule of loading

❏ How frequently the program is run

❏ Total or partial refreshment

❏ Whether the data mart table is to be refreshed in its entirety or only added to

❏ Customization of data warehouse data

❏ Selection, resequencing, merging, aggregation, and summarization of data

❏ Efficiency of execution—how quickly can the loading be accomplished

❏ Integrity of the data—integrity of relationships, integrity of data domain

❏ Production of metadata describing the load process itself

Metadata in the Data Mart

One of the most important components of the data mart is that of metadata. Figure 4.6 depicts metadata in the data mart environment. Metadata in the data mart environment serves the same purpose as metadata in the data warehouse. Data mart metadata allows the data mart analyst to find out where data is in the

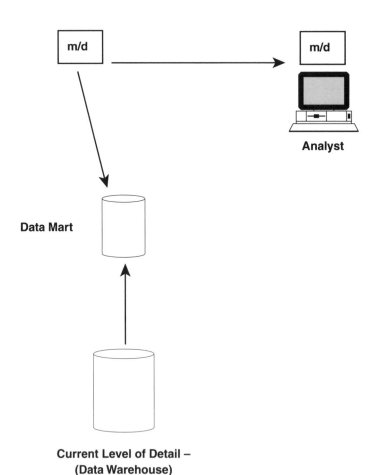

FIGURE 4.6

Metadata is an integral part of the data mart environment, both at the data mart level and at the end-user workstation.

process of discovery and exploration. Data mart metadata contains the following components:

❏ Identification of the source of data

❏ Description of the customization that has occurred as the data passes from the data warehouse to the data mart

❏ Simple descriptive information about the data mart, including tables, attributes, relationships, and definitions

Data mart metadata is created by and updated from the load programs that move data into the data marts. There needs to be linkage between the metadata found in the data mart and the metadata found in the data warehouse. Among other things, the metadata linkage between the two environments needs to describe how the data in the two environments is related. This description is necessary if there is to be drill-down capability between the two environments. With the link, the manager using data mart metadata can easily find the heritage of the data in the data warehouse. In addition, the analyst needs to be able to see how calculations were made and how data was selected for the data mart environment. The metadata found in the data mart must be available to the end user at the end-user workstation in order to be effective.

Data Modeling for the Data Mart

There is one important question that must be asked when building a data mart: Is a data model required in order to build a data mart? Figure 4.7 illustrates this question.

The issue of whether a data model is required depends on the size and formality of the data mart. Some data marts are very small and informal. For this kind of data mart, no data model is required. Other data marts are large and formal. In those data marts it is normal to have some amount of repetitive, predictable processing. For data marts where there is much data and where there will be predictable processing, it makes sense to build a formal data model. One of the challenges of building and using a data model in building the data mart environment is the influence of the data mart database. Some data mart databases, especially the MDDBMS, require the data be placed in such a rigid format that it is questionable whether a data model is of much use. The

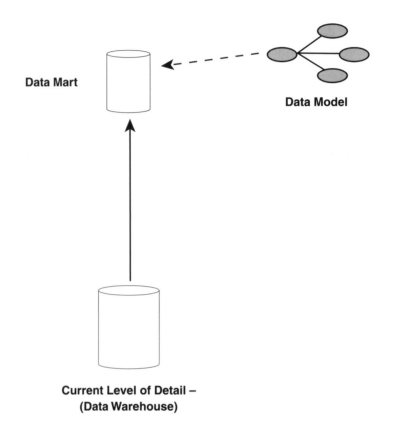

FIGURE 4.7
In some cases, the data model is applicable to the building of the data mart.

MDDBMS dictates so much of the data structure that attempting to apply a model to the database may be an exercise in futility.

The data mart data model follows the same conventions as a data model for any other part of the information processing environment, with the following exceptions. The data mart data model is strongly influenced by the department for which the model is built, and the data mart data model frequently incorporates detailed data and summary data.

Purging the Data Mart

Like the data warehouse, periodically the data mart needs to be purged, as shown in Figure 4.8.

The data mart in Figure 4.8 is being read and some data is selectively removed. The data that is removed may be purged,

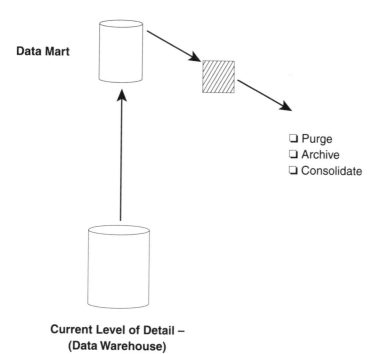

Data Mart

❑ Purge
❑ Archive
❑ Consolidate

Current Level of Detail –
(Data Warehouse)

FIGURE 4.8
An important part of the data mart processing infrastructure is the program that purges, archives, and consolidates data mart data.

archived, or condensed. The criteria for purging can be related to date and time, or it can be based on some other criteria.

Data Mart Contents

The data mart contains whatever data is needed for departmental decision support processing. As such, there is a diversity of data in the data mart, as shown in Figure 4.9.

The data mart contains both summary data and detailed data. In addition, the data mart contains prepared data and ad hoc data. As a rule, the data mart has lots of ad hoc summary data and lots of prepared detailed data. While other data can be found in the data mart, these two categories comprise the bulk of the data that is found there.

Structure within the Data Mart

The data is structured in the data mart along the lines of star-joins and normalized tables. The farmer-oriented tables that are

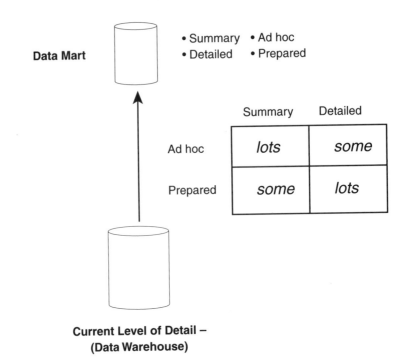

FIGURE 4.9
There are different types of data in the data mart environment.

produced for the data mart center around star-joins. Star-joins are created where there is a predictable pattern of usage and where there is a significant amount of data. Relational tables are used as a basis for design where there is an unpredictable pattern of usage. Figure 4.10 shows the two predominant patterns of design that are found in the data mart. Both forms are able to reside in the data mart without conflict.

REFERENCE TABLES   Reference tables play an important role in the data mart environment. Data marts allow the end user to relate data back to the expanded version of the data. In doing so, the end user can operate in data "shorthand" if desired. Figure 4.11 shows the use of reference data in the data mart environment.

The reference data typically is copied over from the data warehouse. Although it can happen, it is very unusual for the data mart to store and manage its own reference tables. When reference tables are stored and managed in the data mart, there is a need to manage their contents over time. Time management of reference data is a complex task that is best managed in the data warehouse.

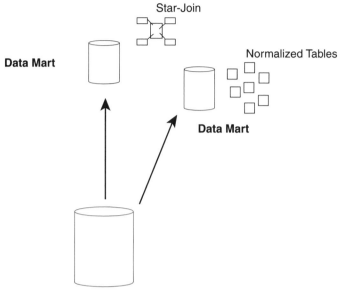

Star-Join

Data Mart

Normalized Tables

Data Mart

Current Level of Detail –
(Data Warehouse)

FIGURE 4.10
The two common types of design for the data mart environment.

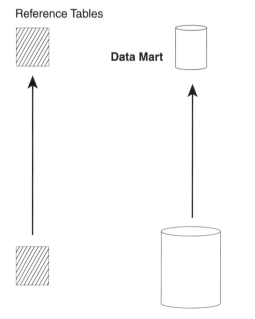

Reference Tables

Data Mart

Current Level of Detail –
(Data Warehouse)

FIGURE 4.11
Reference tables are a normal part of the data mart environment. Reference tables can be copied over from the data warehouse environment.

PERFORMANCE IN THE DATA MART

The issue of performance in the data warehouse environment is an entirely different issue from that in the OLTP environment. In the data warehouse environment, response time requirements are relaxed. One minute up to 24 hours is the expectation for performance in the data warehouse environment. The issue of performance is especially relaxed for the data warehouse, where there is an abundance of data and where there is a lot of exploration occurring. Performance in the data mart is somewhat different from that in the data warehouse for two reasons: the data mart services mostly farmers, and there is much less data in the data mart environment than the data warehouse environment. Where the designer is working with farmers, there can be an anticipation of requirements. And where there is an anticipation of requirements, reasonable performance objectives can be attained. The star-join is one way in which the needs of farmers in the data mart environment can be accommodated. Figure 4.12 illustrates the need for performance in the data mart environment.

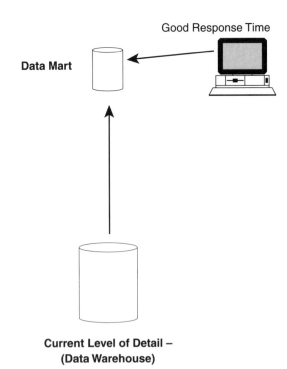

FIGURE 4.12

The expectations for performance are high in the data mart environment. Given the small amounts of data and the level of the user, it is easy to see why the end user expects good performance.

When the data mart is managed by an MDDBMS, there is a different expectation for performance. As long as the analysis is being done within the boundaries that have been defined, and as long as the MDDBMS has not been overburdened with too much data, then there is the expectation of very good performance.

Therefore, it can be simply stated that performance is achieved in several ways in the data mart by:

❏ Using star-joins
❏ Making extensive use of indexes
❏ Limiting the volume of data found in the data mart
❏ Creating arrays of data
❏ Creating profile records (i.e., aggregate records)
❏ Creating prejoined tables
❏ Using MDDBMS technology

MONITORING THE DATA MART ENVIRONMENT

Like the data warehouse, the data mart requires periodic monitoring, as shown in Figure 4.13. The two types of monitoring that are

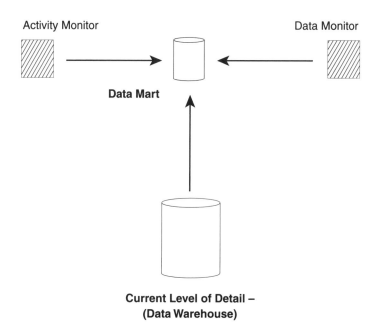

FIGURE 4.13
Monitoring the data mart environment is mandatory when the data mart grows large enough.

required are activity monitoring and data monitoring. The activity monitor looks at the types of requests the analyst is submitting. The activity monitor outlines things such as

❏ What data is being accessed
❏ What users are active against the data mart
❏ What response time is being achieved
❏ How much data is being requested
❏ The busiest times of the day, of the week, of the month

The data monitor looks at other aspects of the data mart and addresses things such as

❏ The actual contents of the data mart
❏ Bad data in the data mart
❏ How much the data mart is growing
❏ The most effective way to access data in the data mart

The monitors for the data mart grow in importance in relation to the volume of data in the data mart and the amount of query activity that passes through the mart. When the data mart is new and small there may be no need for monitoring the environment. But when the data mart grows in volume of data and/or in use of the data, then a monitor facility makes sense.

SUMMARY

The data mart is a powerful and natural extension of the data warehouse. The data mart extends decision support to the departmental environment. The data warehouse provides the granular data and the different data marts interpret and structure that granular data to suit their needs. The appropriate source for the data mart is the data warehouse. Under no circumstances is the operational environment an appropriate source for the data mart. The data mart can contain external data.

There are different types of data marts: MDDBMS data marts and general purpose data marts. Each type of data mart plays a different role. In addition to the database, the software found in the data mart includes

❏ Access and analysis tool(s)

❏ Automatic interface generation

❏ System management

❏ Purge/archival

❏ Metadata management

Metadata is an integral part of the data mart environment. Among other things, metadata allows the different data marts to achieve a degree of cohesiveness. In addition, the metadata allows the end user to efficiently access data in the data mart. The data structures found in the data mart include star-joins and normalized data emanating from the data model.

So far, we have discussed how the platform for the data warehouse environment is shaped by the unique workload demands of the explorer and farmer, and the use and design of architectural components (e.g., data warehouse, exploration warehouse, data mart) to meet their query performance objectives. In the next chapter, we will take a look at a second factor that will also shape the complexion of the data warehouse platform, dormant data.

5

Dormant Data

The first step toward managing volumes of data in a maturing data warehouse environment is to identify and dispose of data that is known as dormant data. Dormant data is data that exists inside a data warehouse that currently is not being used and has little or no prospect of ever being used in the future. Dormant data refers to the data loaded into the active storage area managed by the database. Dormant data does not refer to the system data (such as buffer space, sort merge space, join space, spooling space, etc.) that accompanies any database. By identifying the dormant data in the data warehouse environment, the data warehouse administrator can remove data that will not be used, providing better performance for data that will be used. Figure 5.1 shows that dormant data creeps into the data warehouse over time.

In the first year of operation, the data warehouse is small and all or nearly all of the data is used. There is effectively no dormant data in the data warehouse in the early days. Year two comes and now the data warehouse starts to grow. Dormant data starts to appear but it represents only a fraction of the data in the data warehouse. At this point, dormant data does not pose a real problem. Year three comes and now dormant data is a large part of the data warehouse. Year four comes and the data warehouse is truly large. At this point, the amount of dormant data is ponderous. Dormant data makes up a very large percentage of the data in the data warehouse at this point in time.

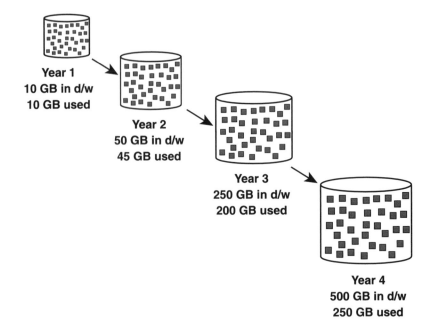

FIGURE 5.1

As data warehouses grow in size, the amount of dormant data grows.

Upon arriving at day four, the amount of data found in the data warehouse poses tremendous (in reality, almost insurmountable) performance problems. Not only does the data warehouse contain huge amounts of data, but a vast majority of that data is not being used.

UNDERSTANDING DORMANT DATA

Dormant data enters the data warehouse in many ways. Some of the more important and obvious ways that dormant data enters the data warehouse are shown in Figure 5.2. As you can see, there are at least four ways that dormant data can creep into the data warehouse:

❏ Through the creation of summary tables

❏ Through the misjudgment of how much history is actually needed

❏ Through the reality of requirements becoming apparent over time

❏ Through the insistence that detail data reside in the data warehouse

Summary Tables

Many summary tables are
created then never used.

| customer id |
| customer name |
| customer address |
| customer phone |
| name of spouse |
| number of children |
| birthday |
| money spent on Xmas last year |
| color of house |
| make of car |
| home owned or rented |
| fireplaces in home |
| number of garages |
| .... |

Reality of Requirements

Extraneous types of data which
are created then never used.

Jan 97   xxxxx xxxxx xxxxx
Feb 97   xxxxx xxxxx xxxxx
Mar 97   xxxxx xxxxx xxxxx
Apr 97   xxxxx xxxxx xxxxx
May 97   xxxxx xxxxx xxxxx
Jun 97   xxxxx xxxxx xxxxx
Jul 97   xxxxx xxxxx xxxxx
Aug 97   xxxxx xxxxx xxxxx
Sep 97   xxxxx xxxxx xxxxx
Oct 97   xxxxx xxxxx xxxxx
Nov 97   xxxxx xxxxx xxxxx
Dec 97   xxxxx xxxxx xxxxx

Misjudgment of History

Using only the last
few months of
data.

Historical data which is
stored then never used.

FIGURE 5.2
*Some of the common ways
that dormant data creeps
into the data warehouse
environment.*

Summary Tables and Dormant Data

The first way that dormant data enters the data warehouse is through the creation of summary tables. The creation of summary tables is a normal and natural part of the data warehouse environment. When a summary table is created there is every intention that it will be used on a regular basis. Unfortunately, over time the summary table either gets lost or becomes irrelevant. The usefulness of the summary table greatly diminishes, but the summary table still takes up space. But because the summarization has been placed in the data warehouse, the data warehouse administrator may be reluctant to remove the data from the system because the administrator has no idea of the importance of the data. In this way summary tables enter the data warehouse and become dormant.

Misjudgment of History and Dormant Data

The second typical way that dormant data creeps into the data warehouse environment is through the misjudgment of the amount of historical data that is necessary and useful. When the end user first hears about the data warehouse and the possibility of historical data, the end user becomes very excited. In most cases the end user has never before had access to any amount of historical data. The database designer asks the end user how much historical data is required and the end user says "as much as we can get." This usually translates into two to three years worth of data. However, after three or four years, the end user discovers that really only the last three or four months of data is useful for most processes. As a result, there is much more historical data in the data warehouse than is being used. At this point, much of the historical data has gone dormant because of the initial overestimation of the requirements for historical data by the end user.

Reality of Requirements and Dormant Data

The third way that data goes dormant is through the reality of requirements becoming apparent over time. In the initial specification of the requirements for the data warehouse, the end user requests that all sorts of data be put into the data warehouse without consideration for how the data will be used. As a result, the data warehouse begins to collect data that may or may not be useful in future processing. Over time some types of data prove to be useful, and other types of data are of little worth. But it is only with hindsight that the exact worth of any type of data can be established. After doing processing for a while, the end user will know what data is and is not needed. But by this time all sorts of data has been placed in the data warehouse, whether it is of use or not. In such a manner, a different class of dormant data creeps into the data warehouse.

Insistence of Detail and Dormant Data

Yet another way that dormant data enters the data warehouse is through the insistence that detailed data reside in the data warehouse. When the end user first encounters the data warehouse, the end user intellectually attaches herself to the lowest level of detailed data. The end user falls in love with the detailed data and becomes attached to it as if it were a security blanket. Only after the end user has become experienced in doing decision support processing does it dawn on her that much processing can be done at a very high or a mid-level of summarization. Once the end user makes this dis covery, the end user transfers her processing allegiance to summary level processing, but the detailed data remains in the data warehouse. It is at that point that detailed data becomes dormant.

There are then many reasons why data becomes dormant in the data warehouse. Each unit of dormant data slows down processing and performance suffers.

CALCULATING DORMANT DATA

There is a simple formula that gives a rough idea of how much data is dormant in the data warehouse or any other component of the data warehouse platform (e.g., data mart). There are three variables used in this calculation:

TXYR. The number of transactions run in a years time against the data warehouse.

TXBYTE. The average amount of data, expressed in bytes, that a given transaction uses.

WHBYTE. The amount of actual storage containing data in the data warehouse.

The simple expression (TXYR × TXBYTE)/WHBYTES estimates (roughly) the amount of dormant data (expressed as a percentage) in a data warehouse.

If, for example, a shop has 10 terabytes of data and runs one million transactions per year, and each transaction operates against 10,000 bytes of data, then the dormancy ratio is approximately 0.1%. In other words, in a configuration like the one described, it is unusual for any given unit of data to ever be accessed, and there is a tremendous amount of dormant data in the data warehouse. The formula used produces only a raw estimation. There are several refinements to the formula that can be, and in some cases should be, made.

The overlap of transaction processing can be accounted for. In a year's time, where one million transactions are done, transactions will overlap and access the same data as other transactions. The overlap can be accounted for by adjusting the amount of data looked at:

$$((TXBYTES \times TXYR) \times OVERLAP)/WHBYTE$$

In this case, the overlap factor would be a percentage represented by a number that is less than one and greater than zero. Given the overlap encountered in most data warehouse environments, it is probably prudent to include this refinement.

The time frame—one year—that has been considered is arbitrary. In order to reflect on the amount of dormant data you have, you may want to extend the time frame to two, three, or even more years. If you do extend beyond one year, you should recognize that the overlap factor will decrease (meaning that there will be more overlap data over a lengthy period of time).

The amount of data for an average query is a very speculative number in an environment where farmers are mixed with explorers. Farmers will typically operate on a very predictable number of bytes while explorers will operate against a truly unpredictable number. When farmers are mixed with explorers, determining the average amount of data used per query is most difficult.

Another important refinement to the calculation is to the variable WHBYTE. WHBYTE represents the space taken by the actual raw and index data. It does not represent idle space, mirror space, backup space, sort/merge space, join space, or any other such system required space. Adding in unused system space inflates the amount of dormant data the system has.

Despite the frailties of the calculation, the simple formula described gives the database designer a good idea of just how much dormant data there is in the data warehouse.

FINDING DORMANT DATA

Understanding that there is dormant data in a data warehouse is one thing. Finding the dormant data is another matter altogether. The best way to find the dormant data is to monitor the end-users' query activity against the data warehouse.

Figure 5.3 shows that the monitor sits between the end-users' query activity and the data warehouse server. The monitor does essentially two things:

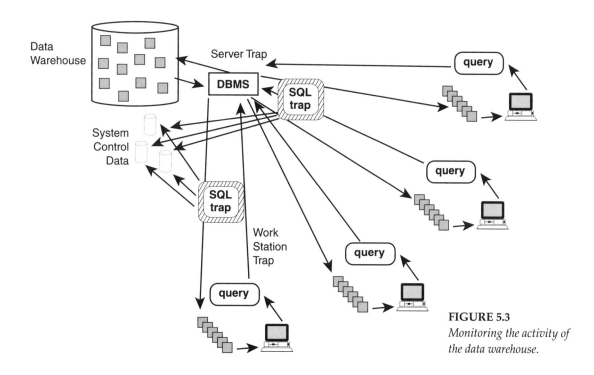

FIGURE 5.3
Monitoring the activity of the data warehouse.

❑ Traps the SQL as the query is passed to the monitor

❑ Traps the query result set as it is passed back to the end user

By looking at the query and the results, the activity monitor is able to determine what data is actually being used in the processing of the queries. Once the database architect knows what data is being used, by extension, the architect knows what data is not being used. In other words, the unused data of the organization equals the total data of the organization minus the data that is being used.

It is of interest to note that there are several ways data can be used in query processing. Some data is selected for qualification of the result set, some data is used in calculations, and some data is used for parameters of selection and qualification. The activity monitor needs to capture and specify them all.

REMOVING DORMANT DATA

So what do you do with dormant data? For dormant data that has the probability of access equal to or closely approximate to zero, there are several choices. Figure 5.4 shows that data can be discarded. While discarding data certainly is an option, and is better than allowing the data to remain idly in the data warehouse, usually this alternative is not chosen. The corporation has gone to a lot of trouble to capture and standardize data from the legacy environment, and it just doesn't make sense to throw it away (especially given the inevitable that it will be needed the moment it is discarded). If data has been captured, standardized, and commit-

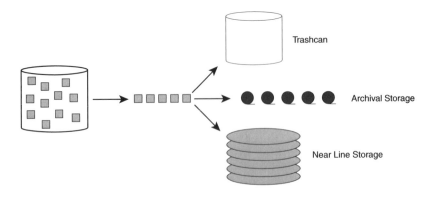

FIGURE 5.4
Where dormant data goes
when it is removed from
the data warehouse.

ted to an electronic medium, then it is easy enough to move the data elsewhere rather than throw it away.

The second alternative shown in Figure 5.4 is to archive the data to a bulk storage medium like tape. Archiving data is a complicated subject and there are many issues to be considered. Some of the issues of archiving are

❑ How physically reliable is the medium on which the data is archived?

❑ How much time is required to re-create the data in an on-line mode?

❑ How will the descriptions of the data that have been archived be stored?

❑ How long is the archived data to be kept?

The third alternative shown in Figure 5.4 is that of moving dormant data to near-line storage. Near-line storage is a happy midpoint between archival storage and on-line storage. Near-line storage costs more than archival storage and less than on-line storage. Near-line storage makes the data reasonably available to on-line storage. The issues of archival storage apply to near-line storage as well.

Selecting Data to be Removed

At first glance it seems that any data that is not being used should be removed from the data warehouse. The intuitive approach is to remove all data that has not been accessed. But that is a most naive way to go about managing large amounts of data. The data warehouse administrator needs to be more sophisticated about deciding what data should be removed from the data warehouse. In order to illustrate what data should (and should not) be removed from the data warehouse, suppose a data warehouse administrator has monitored the data warehouse and has determined the pattern of past usage. Figure 5.5 shows that the data warehouse administrator has removed all data that has not been accessed.

The problem is that the day after the data is removed, an analyst wishes to do a report and finds whole masses of data missing that are needed for analysis. The analyst complains that the necessary data is not in the data warehouse. The problem with removing

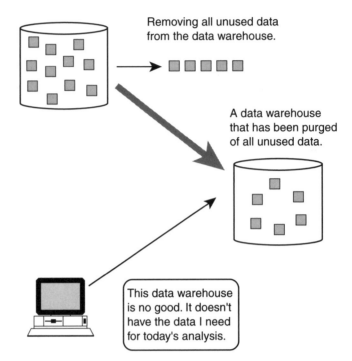

Removing all unused data
from the data warehouse.

A data warehouse
that has been purged
of all unused data.

This data warehouse
is no good. It doesn't
have the data I need
for today's analysis.

FIGURE 5.5

*There is a problem with
removing all unused data
from a data warehouse.*

data that has not been used in the past is that there is much data in
a data warehouse that has not been used in the past but nevertheless
has a high probability of use in the future. By the same token, there
is data in the warehouse that has been recently used but whose
probability of future access is zero or close to it.

Merely looking at what data has or has not been used is only
a crude indicator of the amount of dormant data in a data warehouse. In reality, the data warehouse administrator needs to base
the removal of data on the pattern of access of data, not on what
data has or has not been accessed in the past. For example, it might
make sense to check with the end user to see if there is any future
business initiative that will need access to the unused data. The
determining factor then in removing data from the data warehouse
is the pattern of access, not the specific units of data that have or
have not been accessed. In order to identify the pattern of access of
data in the data warehouse, an activity monitor—a data usage
tracker—is needed. The activity monitor tracks the past activity of
the end users in the data warehouse.

Determining the Probability of Access

There are three steps in determining the probability of access for data in the data warehouse:

❏ Determine what data has or has not been accessed

❏ Create a profile of access based on past activity

❏ Assign a probability of access based on the profile that is created

Once the probability of access has been established, then it is safe to start removing data from the warehouse.

Figure 5.6 shows that the profile of activity is based on three levels of data: a profile for tables, a profile for columns within a table, and a profile based on the occurrences of data within a column within a table. It is sufficient to look at access of data within a table where the table is small and there is little usage of the table and where the table is a summary table.

In looking at data at the summary level, the data warehouse administrator simply looks at how many queries have made access to the table. It is sufficient to look at the profile of usage at the table

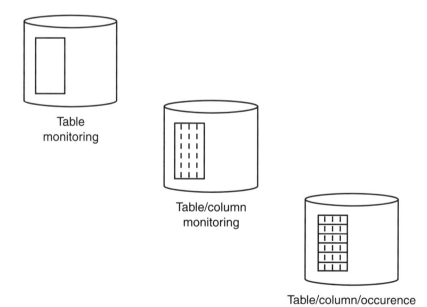

Table
monitoring

Table/column
monitoring

Table/column/occurence
monitoring

FIGURE 5.6
Determining the probability of access.

level where the table receives a moderate amount of activity and where the table is of reasonable size. In the case of table/column activities, the analysis is at the table/column level. The analyst is able to tell what columns are being accessed. It is necessary to look at the table/column/occurrence level where the table is large, used very frequently, and contains deeply historical data.

When analyzing data at this level, the actual occurrences of data are identified that participate in the query and analysis process. From the data usage patterns that have been identified, profiles of usage are created. Once the profile is created, data can be removed because the database designer knows there is a very low probability the data will be accessed.

In Figure 5.7 there is an equal measure of data that has been accessed in the past and data that has not been accessed in the past. However, for the dormant data that is included, the probability of access is relatively high. The activity simply has not gotten around to accessing the dormant data. However, it is likely that future processing will need to access the dormant data. As a rule of thumb, if a data warehouse contains from 25% to 50% dormant data, the warehouse is probably constructed properly. However, when a warehouse starts to contain more than 75% dormant data, then there must be very careful justification for the bulk of the data. When a data warehouse exceeds more than 90% dormant data, serious attention must be placed on managing the volume of data.

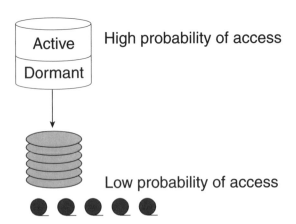

FIGURE 5.7

The results of the removal of data with zero probability of future access.

SUMMARY

The single most profound thing the data warehouse administrator can do to enhance performance is to manage the volumes of data that accumulate in the data warehouse. Volumes of data are managed by removing data whose probability of access is zero or close to zero. This type of data is called dormant data. As data warehouses grow large, the volume of dormant data increases. For a small data warehouse, there may be little or no dormant data. But for a large data warehouse, the percentage of dormant data can grow quickly.

Dormant data enters the data warehouse in a variety of ways. The most common way dormant data enters the warehouse is through the overestimation of the length of time that historical data will be needed. The analyst specifies that 24 months worth of data is needed. But once the 24 months worth of data are loaded into the data warehouse, the analyst discovers that for most processing only three or four months are really necessary. Another way that dormant data enters the data warehouse is through the creation of summary tables that are used once and never looked at again. Yet another way dormant data enters the data warehouse is through the specification of columns of data that are never used in analysis.

The percentage of dormant data can be (roughly) calculated by the following formula:

$$((TXBYTES \times TXYR)/WHBYTE$$

This formula can be greatly refined when the particulars of the data warehouse environment are factored in. One refinement is to factor in the degree of query overlap. This refinement should almost always be considered.

Dormant data can be found by the use of an activity monitor that looks at each activity as it passes into and out of the data warehouse. From this information, assessments can be made as to what data is dormant (i.e., does not have the probability of access).

Now that we have discussed the two factors that need to be carefully considered in building a data warehouse platform to support end-user query response time objectives, let's take a look at another measurement of performance in a high-performing data warehouse environment, data cleanliness.

6

Data Cleansing

Now that we have discussed the planning and implementation of techniques and technology used to optimize query performance, let's talk a bit about another critical dimension of performance, data quality. The data warehouse administrator must ensure that "dirty data" never enters the data warehouse environment. However, for a variety of reasons, it is inevitable that dirty data will enter the environment. Dirty data is a fact of life. Rather than declaring that dirty data should never be allowed to enter, a more realistic stance is to prepare to cope with it. In order to understand how to deal with dirty data, the data warehouse administrator must first understand the causes of dirty data.

HOW DIRTY DATA GETS IN

There are four ways in which dirty data enters the data warehouse environment (see Figure 6.1). The first way that dirty data enters the environment is through entry of the dirty data by the legacy application. For a variety of reasons, the dirty data is not captured or otherwise assigned properly. Perhaps the dirty legacy data element is optional and is never edited properly at the moment of capture. Or perhaps the dirty data element is defined one way and the programmer privately decides to use the element for an entirely different purpose. Or perhaps the programming specifications have been incorrect from the beginning. There are a multitude of reasons

FIGURE 6.1

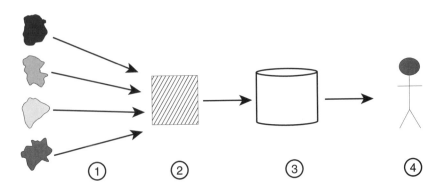

Four ways dirty data can get into your system: Through unclean legacy systems, through improper integration, through the aging of the data warehouse, and through changing user requirements.

why the dirty data may have been accepted incorrectly into the legacy environment and stored that way. And over time, no one has discovered the error in the legacy environment. The first time that anyone has ever cared about the contents of the data is the moment when they attempt to use it in the data warehouse environment.

The second way for dirty data to enter the data warehouse occurs at the moment of integration. At the moment of integration, data enters the system from a variety of sources. These sources of data are usually very different and were never designed for integration. There is incompatibility of key structure, data structure, encoding of data, definitions of data, physical characteristics of data, and so forth. It is the job of the integration and transformation program to bring order and uniformity to this very messy task of integrating the data.

While the analyst tries to get the merging and aggregation of data right, there simply are too many details to get all of the transformation criteria correct. Or perhaps the data warehouse administrator creates the proper transformation for two legacy systems as they feed into the data warehouse. But when another legacy system is added as a source at a later time, the rules of transformation turn out to be incomplete or incorrect.

The third reason why dirty data enters the data warehouse is because data ages once it is entered. Even if an organization has a perfectly clean legacy environment, and even if the organization has perfect integration and transformation programs (which of course, no one has!), there still would be dirty data in the data warehouse because of aging.

In order to explain how dirty data gets into a data warehouse because of aging, consider the following very normal scenario. In

1995, the data warehouse has data entered into it based on the accounting system that has been in place since the company opened for business. Data is entered into the data warehouse for 1995, 1996, and 1997. But in 1998 the company converts to SAP. In converting to SAP, the company changes the chart of accounts and the standard accounting period. In 1998, data is entered based on SAP's interpretation of the chart of accounts and on SAP's accounting period. When the analyst looks over the spectrum of time—1995 to 1998—there is now a massive inconsistency of data. There is a huge disconnect over the years simply because a fundamental business change has occurred. This then is how time can destroy the purity of data in the data warehouse.

The fourth reason dirty data enters the data warehouse is because of changing user requirements or the addition of users who have different expectations of data quality. For example, let's assume that Bob was the primary user of the data warehouse. From day one, we knew that Bob's expectation was that the data would be refreshed on a monthly basis. Then on day two, Anne comes on board as a new user. Almost immediately she begins to complain about the quality of data. As we research the problem, we begin to realize that the data hasn't changed but the end-user expectations have in terms of the timeliness of the data. Anne's expectation (i.e., need) is that the data should not be more than a week old. In this scenario, the end-user expectations have changed causing data quality to come into question.

CLEANSING DIRTY DATA

Given that there are multiple causes for dirty data in the data warehouse, how then is data cleansed?

Cleansing the Legacy Environment

The first way that data is cleansed is by altering the data inside the legacy environment, as shown in Figure 6.2.

It is easy to say that data can be cleansed inside the legacy environment; it is quite another matter to implement such a practice. There are many reasons why managers do not implement this practice:

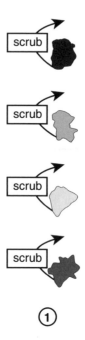

FIGURE 6.2

Correcting data within the legacy system environment.

❏ They do not like to disrupt the legacy code.

❏ The budget for operating on legacy code has long been spent.

❏ The code for the legacy environment is lost or is not up to date and can't be disturbed.

❏ There is no one available who understands the legacy systems.

❏ The legacy systems belong to someone who is at political odds with everyone else and will not cooperate.

❏ The owner of the legacy environment does not see a payback on the cleansing of data, giving the cleansing of data very low priority.

There are then many reasons why making changes to data in the legacy environment is a very difficult thing to do. But there is another interesting perspective. Suppose that all the obstacles to making changes to the legacy environment were overcome. Suppose all data were cleaned perfectly in the legacy environment. Does this mean that dirty data would still get into the data warehouse? Ironically, it does because the cleanliness of the data in the

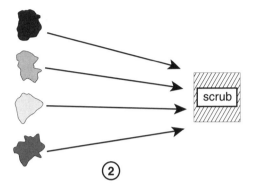

FIGURE 6.3
Cleaning data at the moment of integration.

legacy environment does not speak to integration. You could have perfectly clean legacy data and still have terribly unintegrated data inside the data warehouse. Therefore cleaning the data at the legacy level is only the first step in achieving clean data inside the data warehouse.

Cleansing at the Point of Integration

There is always a need for recleansing data as it passes through the integration and transformation process. The second major opportunity for cleansing data is at the moment of integration and transformation (see Figure 6.3).

Two types of cleansing are done at this point in time. The first is the activity of integrating the data. In order to integrate the data, it is standard practice to use a data model as a guide. The data model describes how the data ought to look as it comes out of the integration and transformation process. The job of the data warehouse administrator is to reshape the data into the desired form. The challenge here is that the data comes from many sources, none of which was ever designed for the data model that is now the flagship.

The second kind of cleansing that occurs is the scrubbing of data if it was not done within the legacy environment. If data comes out of the legacy environment without being scrubbed (as is often the case), then the data needs to be scrubbed as part of the integration and transformation process.

The activities of integrating data are many and complex, and include

❑ The resequencing of data

❑ The encoding of data according to a single predetermined scheme

❑ The conversion of data using a common formula

❑ The standardization of data into a common format

❑ The structuring of data into a common data structure

❑ The interpretation of data according to a common definition

❑ The summarization of data into a common level of granularity

❑ The structuring of keys based on a common definition of the basis of the key

❑ The indexing of data according to a common key

❑ The movement of data from many DBMSs into a common DBMS

❑ The movement of data from many operating systems into a common operating system

❑ The movement of data from one hardware architecture to another hardware architecture

There are then many activities performed in the integration and transformation of data. In addition to these activities, the integration and transformation layer generally assumes the added responsibility of scrubbing the data. This is due in part to the inertia and politics that prevent scrubbing from occurring in the legacy environment.

Cleansing after Loading

The third place that data cleansing needs to be done is after the data has been loaded into the data warehouse. Figure 6.4 shows that data inside the data warehouse needs to be cleansed. There

FIGURE 6.4
Scrubbing data after it has been loaded into the data warehouse.

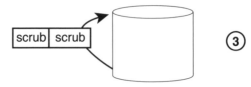

are two distinct steps to this cleansing process. The first step is the monitoring of the data to determine just how much dirty data there is. The second step is to actually go in and clean the data.

The first step, that of monitoring the content of the data, begins with the specification of business rules to which the data in the data warehouse must adhere in terms of completeness and accuracy. These rules are generally documented in a Service Management Contract (SMC). Then a monitor of the content of the data warehouse is made and all rows or records of data that do not conform to the rules are identified. This seemingly simple scenario has many implications and considerations:

❏ How often is the monitoring being done?

❏ What overhead is required to execute the monitor?

❏ If data has been monitored once in the warehouse, is it necessary to monitor it repeatedly?

❏ What is to be done with the results of the monitor?

In some regards, the monitoring of the data inside the data warehouse raises more questions than it answers. For example, when dirty data is discovered, does that mean that the data must be immediately corrected? The answer is, not necessarily:

❏ If there are only a few records that are incorrect, it is possible that the work required for correction will not be worth it.

❏ If entire masses of data are incorrect, the remedy is to fix the program causing the problem before the data can be corrected.

❏ In some cases, it is known that data is incorrect, but there is no way to know what the proper values should be.

In many cases, it is possible to get a reading on how much dirty data there is without actually going in and correcting the data.

There are many other issues that relate to the monitoring of the content of the data inside the data warehouse. One of those issues is the sophistication of the logic of monitoring. There may be a very large payback from simple monitoring of the data. For example, suppose the column representing gender should be encoded with an "M" or an "F." Suppose a simple audit is made and it is found that some rows contain a "1" or a "0" for the contents. Such an audit could very quickly help assess whether the data actually exists under the rules they were thought to exist under. However, a more sophisticated audit might look like, if medical procedure equals "birth" then gender must equal "F." Or an even greater sophistication of audit might look like, for payments made to provider, have payments been made for appointments made at the same time?

DIFFERENT KINDS OF AUDITS

Data audits can be as simple or as sophisticated as desired. However, there is a cost to sophistication. Figure 6.5 shows the mechanics of two different kind of audits. Some audits can be done entirely within the confines of a single row. First one row is audited, then another row, and so forth. The audit goes efficiently. Another kind of audit starts with one row of data then goes to one or more rows of other data in order to verify data found in the original row. Such an audit must be careful in its use because of complexity and resources consumed. The audit that is sophisticated can also be a resource constraint when the amount of data needed to be accessed for the verification of a single row involves the interrogation of data in other rows. This is fairly common when trying to validate the degree of referential integrity in the data warehouse.

One technique that is useful when specifying audits that will consume multiple resources is to "bound" the audit. When an audit is bounded, the audit is not done for all occurrences of data in the data warehouse. Instead the audit is done only for selected rows of data. For example, there may exist 10 years worth of data in a data warehouse. The bounded audit will be for only the last two years.

MANAGING REQUIRED RESOURCES

Unless care is taken at the outset, the resources required to manage the cleansing of data can be considerable. The position the data warehouse administrator does not want to arrive at is having to make a sweeping change to all of the records in a data warehouse. Depending on the operating system and the database, such a

A single row
sequential audit.

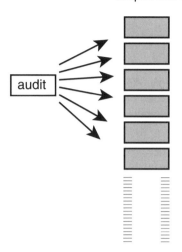

A multi row audit.

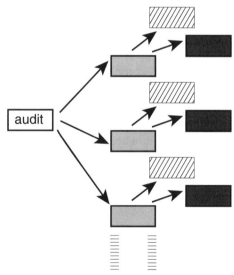

FIGURE 6.5
Single row versus multiple row audits.

change may be very difficult to implement, especially if the data being changed is indexed. An appropriate consideration for the structuring of data is the separation of data into different partitions. The partitions are divided so that the database has no knowledge of their relationship to each other. Only the application programmer has knowledge that the partitions have a relationship.

In Figure 6.6, the data warehouse designer has taken a large table and physically defined several smaller tables that collectively are the equal of the larger table. The database sees the smaller tables—one for a year's worth of data—as merely a bunch of tables. Only the programmer realizes that the yearly tables can be combined to logically form a larger table. By breaking up a larger table into smaller tables, the data warehouse designer has paved the way for efficient cleansing.

Suppose the data warehouse designer finds that there is a problem with data for 1995. The data warehouse administrator can isolate the 1995 data from all other data and make changes to it with no consideration for the performance and analysis that is occurring to other tables. Or suppose that the data warehouse administrator discovers that there is a problem with all occurrences of data in the table. The data warehouse administrator is able to mend the tables one at a time. Or the administrator can even decide to mend some years' worth of data and not mend other years. In other words, the data warehouse administrator has quite a few options at her disposal when the tables are divided into small physical tables. Of course, such a division of data may have an effect on the end user. When data is divided by year, as suggested in the example and as is common in the data warehouse, the end users need to be aware of the fact that in order to get to all of the data, multiple ta-

Tables that are logically related

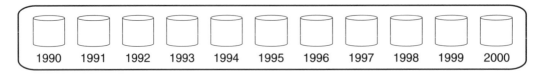

FIGURE 6.6
Improve performance by dividing a single (large) table into several smaller tables based on date.

bles will be needed. But such a burden imposed on the end user is not unreasonable at all. To circumvent this constraint, "views" can be created that are a "union" of the individual tables.

CLEANSING DATA OVER TIME

Along with discussing the cleansing of data over time arises the issue of whether data should be retrofitted once correctly written. For example, suppose in 1995 marketing has territories divided one way and records all sales according to the way that the territories were assigned. Now suppose that in 1997 marketing reassigns territories. Marketing also decides to reassign 1995 sales even though those sales were properly recorded in 1995. Such a scenario is played out in corporations daily. There are several issues that must be addressed before proceeding:

❑ Is the reassignment exercise to be a permanent one? Will marketing never want to return to the reality that existed in 1995?

❑ Is it all right to destroy the basis for all sales reporting that has occurred since the sales data were recorded in 1995? In other words, does management have no concern for the loss of reconcilability that will occur once the 1995 data is destroyed?

❑ Can the values for 1995 be reconstructed in 1997? In some cases they can be easily reconstructed; in other cases they cannot.

Once the organization has decided to rewrite history and has gotten through the issues that surround such a decision, the questions then remains, are there resources to effect such a change? If there is only a modicum of data, then the resources expended will be minimal. But at some point in time the sheer number of resources required to restate history becomes prohibitive.

Figure 6.7 shows that if there is only a small amount of data to be restated, resource consumption is no problem, and if there are a significant number of rows to be restated resource consumption must be considered carefully. But at some point there is so much historical data that it becomes prohibitive to even consider a wholesale restatement of history. When a corporation reaches this

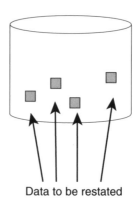

FIGURE 6.7
*Small amount of historical
data to be restated.*

Data to be restated

advanced stage, alternative strategies for the management of the
quality of data over time become mandatory.

BOUNDED REFERENTIAL INTEGRITY

The notion of referential integrity for data stored inside the data
warehouse has been around for a long time. The implementation
of referential integrity in one form or another has been around
since the early days of IMS and DB2, among others. But as the
world enters the arena of data warehousing, the implementation of
referential integrity—as currently implemented in current database technology—simply does not work when applied to the
world of data warehousing.

Why is it that current implementations of referential integrity
do not work for data warehouses? They do not work for three primary reasons:

❏ The volumes of data that are collected inside the data
warehouse are so great that the current implementation of
referential integrity is impractical to implement. When the
data warehouse is loaded, the referential integrity facility is
turned off.

❏ Update is not done in the data warehouse. Current implementations of referential integrity assume that updates will
be done. There is then a very poor fit between the data
warehouse and a facility that is optimized for operational
processing.

❏ Data warehouse data is time variant. This means that on
occasion there will be a relationship between two units of

data at one moment in time and no relationship at another moment in time. Current implementations of referential integrity do not allow for there to be a time variant relationship.

There are then three reasons why the data warehouse administrator finds the current implementation of referential integrity to be inapplicable in the data warehouse. But just because referential integrity as currently implemented is unusable does not mean that referential integrity is not needed. What is needed for the world of data warehousing is a different approach to referential integrity.

The approach to referential integrity that applies to the data warehouse is one that can be called "bounded" referential integrity. Bounded referential integrity is very similar to classical referential integrity except for two features. Bounded referential integrity applies to a subset of a table or tables found within the data warehouse, not to an entire table, and it applies after the data has been loaded into the warehouse, not as the data is being loaded.

With these two exceptions, bounded referential integrity is the same as classical referential integrity. Bounded referential integrity operates on the basis of a foreign key/key relationship between two or more rows. The data warehouse administrator defines the existence criteria by assigning a key and its one or more foreign key correspondents. Existence criteria are established. Furthermore, the data warehouse administrator determines the moments in time when the relationship is valid. The dates for the validity may be open or closed. If the dates are closed, there is a starting date and a stopping date. If the date range is open, there is either a starting date and no stopping date or there is a stopping date and no starting date. In any case, the relationship is bounded—either fully or partially—by dates. But the relationship can be bounded by other parameters as well. For example, the relationship can be bounded by

❏ Part types—only parts with "R", "W", or "J" as the first digit in the key participate in the relationship

❏ Only employees who are management participate in the relationship

❏ Only insurance policies where coverage is greater than $1,000,000

The net result is that only a small number of occurrences participate in the relationship. The relationship is not normally tested at load time. There is too much data for the test to be made, and the testing of the relationship will require too many separate rows of data to be accessed. Consequently, testing of the relationship to see if the relationship conforms to the specifications set up by the data warehouse administrator is done by an independent audit program. The independent audit program operates when there are spare machine cycles. The independent audit verifies that all the foreign key/key relationships are in place. If the independent audit program discovers an anomaly, then the audit program reports this condition back to the data warehouse administrator. Once reported to the data warehouse administrator, the administrator decides how to remedy the situation. This rather passive approach to the enforcement of data warehouse referential integrity applies to the data warehouse environment because there is no active update that occurs in the environment. Should active update occur, then a much more proactive approach is required.

Of course, one assumption made is that efficient access can be made to the data warehouse data. If data monitoring is already being done, it is an easy enough matter to be able to attach the bounded referential integrity processing to the data content tracker. But if there is no efficient way to access the data warehouse, then bounded referential integrity has another level of complexity.

SUMMARY

Dirty data is a fact of life in the data warehouse. Dirty data enters the data warehouse through four sources: invalid or incorrect legacy applications that collect the data in an incorrect state, improper integration and transformation programs, aging of the data inside the data warehouse, and through changing user requirements. Dirty data is not normally cleansed in the legacy environment. Instead the cleansing of the data occurs at the point of data warehouse integration and transformation. In order to find the dirty data inside the data warehouse, a data monitor is executed that does audits of the data. These audits can be simple or complex. In order to run efficiently, the audits need to be run in parallel and need to be executed incrementally. Once a unit of data is audited, it should not be reaudited for the same criteria.

Referential integrity applies to the data warehouse just as it does to other environments. However, because of the massive volumes of data found in the data warehouse, the referential integrity specification needs to be bounded.

Now that we have discussed performance from the perspective of query response time and data cleanliness, let's take a look at the tools used to capture key information to support this tuning process. In the next chapter, we review the monitors needed to capture the information necessary to support tuning of the data warehouse environment in terms of query response time and data cleanliness.

7

Monitors

As we discussed in Chapter 5, the biggest impediment to good long-term performance in the data warehouse environment is the huge volume of data that collects in the data warehouse. The massive volume of data in the data warehouse hide data that is desired by the end-user's queries. As discussed in Chapter 5, the volume of data that comes with a data warehouse appears gradually. First there is a little data. Then there is a lot of data. Then there is a massive amount of data. With the increase in the volume of data found in the data warehouse comes a significant increase in the dormant data. And there is no return on investment on dormant data. All dormant data does is take up space, cost money, and make searches for nondormant data inefficient. The single most effective thing the data warehouse administrator can do to enhance performance and reduce costs is to remove dormant data. But in order to remove dormant data from the data warehouse, the dormant data must first be identified. Dormant data is identified by means of an activity monitor, also known as a data usage tracker.

ACTIVITY MONITORS

There are two basic types of activity monitors: SQL intrusive and SQL nonintrusive. An SQL intrusive monitor is one that intercepts an SQL query and has the potential to reformulate it. An SQL nonintrusive monitor is one that is unable to alter SQL text. Figure 7.1

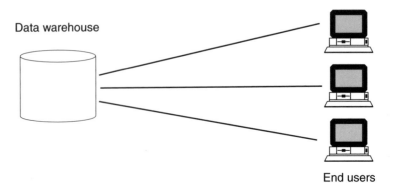

FIGURE 7.1
The tracker looks at text and result sets that are returned as a result of processing.

shows a data usage tracker. The data usage tracker is an SQL nonintrusive monitor that keeps track of all end-user activity.

The activity monitor—the data usage tracker—sits between the end user and the server housing the data warehouse. The monitor can sit on the server or it can sit on the end-users workstation and looks at two important things:

❏ The SQL syntax as the query is passed to the server and the host database management system (DBMS)

❏ The result set that is returned to the end user from the DBMS

There are other parameters that can be accessed and reported by an activity monitor. These parameters include CPU time used by the query, rows accessed, intermediate result sets, and subquery results. An SQL nonintrusive activity monitor is able to use a minimum of resources in its monitoring of data usage. From an efficiency standpoint, the minimization of overhead is a very important feature. However, an SQL nonintrusive query monitor has limited interaction with the DBMS.

An SQL intrusive activity monitor has access to many more system parameters, but there is also the distinct possibility that the intrusive aspect of the monitor will be much more of an impediment to system performance.

Finding Dormant Data

What is it that a monitor finds as a result of activity monitoring? Three types of dormancy can be detected, as shown in Figure 7.2:

❏ Dormancy at the table level
❏ Dormancy at the column level
❏ Dormancy at the occurrence level

TABLE LEVEL DORMANCY   All three types of dormancy have their own considerations. Dormancy at the table level occurs when a table, in its entirety, is not used. Table dormancy typically occurs for small tables and for tables that contain summary data. These

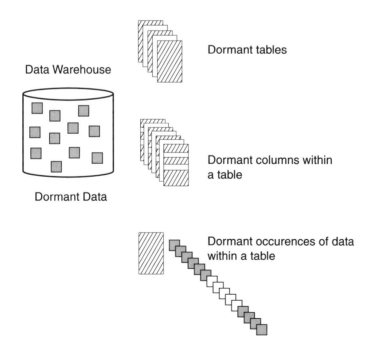

Data Warehouse

Dormant Data

Dormant tables

Dormant columns within a table

Dormant occurences of data within a table

FIGURE 7.2
Types of dormancy.

types of tables are often created when a temporary study of data is being done. At the end of the analysis, the developer forgets to purge the system of the working tables that have been created. Another possibility is that the system created summary tables that were useful at the time when they were specified but are no longer needed. Indeed, there are many reasons why a table is created and then "gets lost in the shuffle." For further information on how data becomes dormant, refer to Chapter 5. Dormant data at the table level is easy to remedy. The table in its entirety is removed from the data warehouse.

COLUMN LEVEL DORMANCY   The second type of dormant data occurs when an entire column or columns are not being accessed. There are a variety of reasons why a column of data goes dormant. The most obvious reason is that the end user specified the column at the design of the data warehouse without really knowing that there was going to be a use for the column. Given that data warehousing entails exploration into the unknown, it is not unreasonable for such a requirement to appear. Another reason for the dormancy of a column is that the end user does not know that the column exists. Or perhaps the end user has found a better source for the column. There may be any number of valid reasons why a column has been specified and then not used.

Unfortunately, eliminating dormant columns is not an easy thing to do. The row of data containing the dormant column must be read into another medium where the column that is dormant is removed. The remainder of the row is then written back into the data warehouse. Such a reorganization of data cannot be taken lightly. Enormous resources may be required for this type of reorganization of data. However, there is a wholesale savings of space that cannot be achieved in any other way.

OCCURRENCE LEVEL DORMANCY   The third type of dormancy occurs when occurrences of data within a table are not being accessed. This is a very common type of data dormancy, and fortunately is very easy to remedy. Occurrence dormancy occurs for a variety of reasons. The most common reason is that an end user has specified at the design of a table that a large amount of historical data is needed. The end user may state that two years' worth of data is required. However, once the data warehouse is built and loaded with two years' worth of history, the end user discovers that only three months of history are actually needed. However, by this time a full complement of two years' worth of data (or more!) has been loaded into the data warehouse. The result is that massive amounts of historical data are just sitting in the data warehouse doing nothing.

Another way that occurrences of data become dormant is when the data reflects business venues that are of no interest. In fact, there are many reasons why occurrences of data within a table go dormant. Removing occurrences of data once the occurrences have been identified is an almost trivial thing to do. The occurrence is identified, read, and deleted or archived from the data warehouse. The space is then reclaimed by the DBA (database administrator) managing the data warehouse.

Understanding Dormant Data

Now that we have discussed it a bit, it seems intuitive that dormant data is data that does not have a probability of being accessed. It appears that any data being returned back to the end user is not dormant data. But this understanding of dormant data still needs a bit of refinement. Data is used in query processing in many ways where the data is never returned back to the end user as part of the result set. Some of these ways include

❑ Data used as selection criteria where the data is not actually returned to the end user

❑ Data used in subquery processing where the data is never returned to the end user

❑ Data used in a calculation or summarization where only the final results are returned to the end user

Because of these uses of data which are "hidden" from the end user, a careful definition of what dormant data is and is not needs to be carefully thought out. See Chapter 5 for a detailed discussion of dormant data.

Removing Dormant Data

Dormant data can be removed by simply deleting the data and discarding it. But there are other strategies for the removal of dormant data from the data warehouse. Figure 7.3 shows the removal of dormant data from the active data warehouse to the near-line storage environment.

When data is archived off to near-line storage, if the data is ever needed again, it can be retrieved in a reasonable amount of time. If the data that is removed from active storage is truly discarded, then it cannot be easily re-created. But if it is placed in near-line storage, the data can be restored to active storage. The time to retrieval for the first occurrence of data that is restored may be as long as a minute or two. But the time to retrieval for all the subsequent records that are retrieved is no more than that of the time required to access active storage. Near-line storage makes sense because it can hold very large amounts of data and it does not cost nearly as much as active online storage.

Capturing Activity Information

In order to capture needed activity information, the activity monitor sets up a software "trap." Figure 7.4 shows where the trap can be set. One place the trap can be set is at the data warehouse server. The other place the trap can be set is at the workstation of the analyst.

There are advantages and disadvantages to placing the trap at either place. The advantage of placing the trap at the data warehouse server is that at the server the trap is simple to install and

Data Warehouse

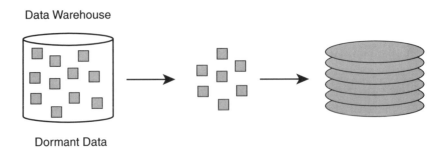

FIGURE 7.3

Passing dormant data to near-line storage.

Dormant Data

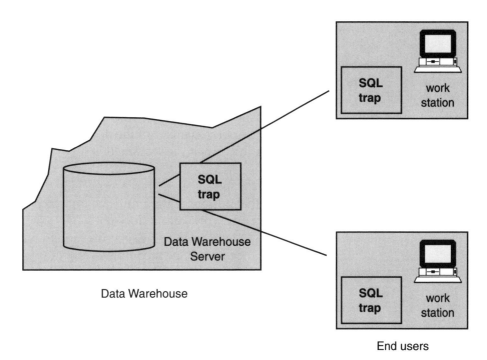

FIGURE 7.4
The SQL trap can be placed in any number of places.

maintain. When set at the server, the trap has to be set and maintained at only one place. Another advantage of setting the trap at the data warehouse server is that there is no possibility of anyone getting a transaction that bypasses the trap into the system. The disadvantage of setting a trap at the data warehouse server is that the trap has the potential of becoming a performance bottleneck. If there are enough transactions passing through the system, the trap itself may become an impairment—a bottleneck—to performance.

The advantage of placing the trap at the workstation is that performance of the system will never be impaired. The end-user's workstation uses its cycles to do the trapping, and the system never knows that software trapping is being done. The disadvantage of placing the trap at the end-user's workstation is that the software trap must be administered across all workstations. In the case of a network that supports the data warehouse platform, there may be many users. Furthermore, the users do not have a uniform profile. Some users are very active; other users are inactive. Some users have hardware ABC; other users have hardware BCD. Some users have a clerical position; other users have a managerial position. In short, there is little uniformity from one user to the next. Because of the extreme heterogeneity of the data warehouse network, administering the trap at the workstation level is very difficult.

Administration of the software trap is especially difficult when you consider that administration must be done across all workstations. If even one workstation does not have a trap installed, then some activity running against the system will be omitted and the monitoring will be incomplete. Not only is installing the software trap an issue, but keeping the versions of the software trap up to date is also an issue. Trying to do a software release change or maintenance across all the workstations in the data warehouse network is a real headache.

A third possibility for the placement of the software trap is a mixed approach of the monitoring being done at both the server and the workstation. In this case, most activity is monitored by the server and only a few selected power users are monitored at the workstation. With this mixed approach there is no performance bottleneck at the server, and there is no administration nightmare.

One of the considerations of monitoring the network for activity is that internal activity is not trapped. Activity traveling across a direct channel attach is not monitored, and internally generated triggers may not be caught. With a server activated network trap, it is necessary to have a way to trap these other activities, if indeed these activities are important. In some cases, these nonnetwork activities will be important. In other cases, there will be no or negligible activity that occurs, and trapping at the network level is all that is required.

TYPES OF MONITORING   There are (at least) three types of monitoring, one for each type of dormancy:

❑ Table monitoring
❑ Table/column monitoring
❑ Table/column/occurrence monitoring

Figure 7.5 shows the different levels of monitoring that can occur.

Each of the types of monitoring has its own considerations. Table monitoring is applicable to summary tables, small tables, old tables, and infrequently used tables. Table monitoring simply states that a table has had some activity run against it, with no detailed explanation as to what that activity might have been. Table monitoring is useful when there is a desire to see whether a table is being used and to what extent.

Table/column monitoring applies to larger tables, frequently used tables, and tables where it is desired to see precisely what data is being accessed. In table/column monitoring the database analyst can see what tables and what columns of those tables are being accessed.

Table/column/occurrence monitoring is used for very large tables and for very active tables. Monitoring at this level is useful for peering into the system and seeing precisely what occurrences of data are and are not being used. This type of monitoring is used to determine what data is dormant and what data is not dormant.

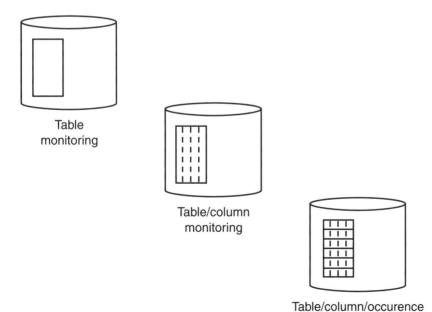

Table
monitoring

Table/column
monitoring

Table/column/occurence
monitoring

FIGURE 7.5
Three different levels of monitoring.

There are several ways that data can be used in query processing that show up at the table/column/occurrence level. Some of these include

❏ Selection processing

❏ Result set formulation

❏ Calculations for result set formulation

OVERHEAD OF MONITORING   One of the important considerations in which type of monitoring needs to be done is the overhead of monitoring. Figure 7.6 shows the differences in the monitoring of the different levels.

Monitoring at the table level requires the least amount of overhead. Almost any type of table level monitoring can be tolerated from an overhead perspective. Table/column level monitor-

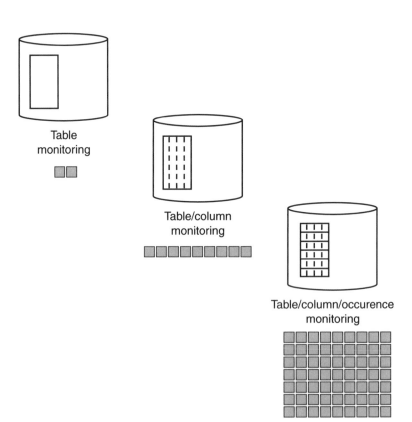

FIGURE 7.6

There is an overhead of monitoring that must be taken into consideration.

ing entails an order of magnitude more overhead than simple table
level monitoring.

Table/column/occurrence monitoring can become a major
issue in terms of overhead unless great care is taken. Table/col-
umn/occurrence monitoring needs to be done on a very selective
basis, for only certain important subsets of data. If care is not
taken, it is easy to see how the overhead of table/column/occur-
rence monitoring can start to consume many resources and produce as much data as is found in the data warehouse.

Minimizing Overhead   The best way to minimize overhead is to
balance the granularity of what is monitored. Using this approach,
architectural elements (i.e., tables, columns, and occurrences) are
selectively measured by the activity monitor. All tables except a
few are monitored at the table level. A few tables are monitored at
the table/column level. And only a few selected tables or columns
are monitored at the table/column/occurrence level. By control-
ling what tables are monitored and at what level, the data warehouse administrator can optimize and manage the resources used
during the monitoring process.

Another good way to minimize the overhead of monitoring is
to allow the monitor to be run selectively at different hours of the
day. As long as the data warehouse administrator does not want to
know what processing has occurred at certain hours of the day,
monitoring only during selected hours can greatly reduce overhead (see Figure 7.7).

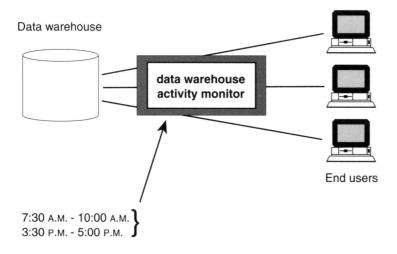

FIGURE 7.7
*The monitor can be run at
selected times throughout
the day.*

Yet another approach to the management of overhead is to move the transactions through multiple ports into the DBMS and attach the monitor at all ports. This has the effect of minimizing the chance of a bottleneck forming in a single port. A final approach for minimizing the chances that a monitor will become a bottleneck is to move the monitoring to the workstations of power users.

Reviewing the Output

The output of the monitoring can be reviewed as often as desired. Figure 7.8 shows that the results can be reviewed daily, weekly, monthly, or at any frequency desired by the database analyst.

AVERAGE DAY PROFILE   While the activity monitor generates many useful pieces of information, putting the information into perspective is another matter altogether. A useful technique is to create an average day (week, month, etc.) profile, as shown in Figure 7.9.

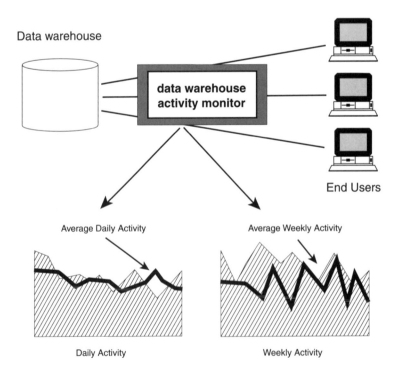

FIGURE 7.8
Reviewing the output of the monitor.

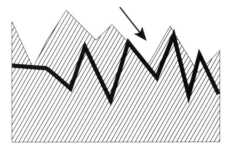

Average Daily Activity

Daily Activity

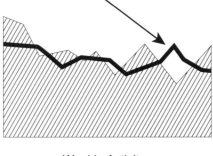

Average Weekly Activity

Weekly Activity

FIGURE 7.9
There is much value in comparing average activity against actual activity over a period of time.

The average day profile is created by gathering together many days activity, then averaging the profile over time. Once the average day profile is created, any given day can be compared to the average to see if the peaks and valleys of the day were normal or extraordinary.

RESOURCE GOVERNORS VERSUS QUERY BLOCKING

Now that we have looked at the activity monitor in a passive sense to support effective management of dormant data, let's look at a more active use of activity monitoring in support of resource governoring. A resource governor is a software monitor that dynamically oversees the activity of each transaction in the data warehouse environment as the transaction is in execution. If the transaction exceeds a predetermined amount of resources, then the offending transaction is removed from active execution by the resource governor software. There are any number of ways to measure the resource consumption—CPU utilization, I/Os executed, etc. The effect, in theory, of a resource governor is to improve response time for all users of the system by removing long-running transactions from the execution queue.

Resource Governors—Nothing New

Resource governors have been in existence for a long time, starting with the world of OLTP. For a short time, resource governors were widely used in the OLTP environment. Then just as quickly as resource governors appeared, they disappeared, and are hardly seen anywhere today in OLTP. Occasionally the idea of a resource governor resurfaces in the data warehouse environment. And when resource governors do resurface, they prove to be no more effective or useful in the data warehouse world than they were in OLTP world.

Why Are Resource Governors Inadequate?

There are a number of reasons why resource governors are not a solution to performance problems (or anything else) in the data warehouse environment. What then are the fundamental flaws with resource governors?

The first is in setting the parameters at which the resource governor will cause the transaction to cease execution. The problem is that the actual parameters can never be set in an optimal manner. If the parameters are set too high, then there is no purpose to the monitor. If the parameters are set too low, then perfectly valid transactions are unnecessarily terminated. Furthermore, it is inevitable that wherever the parameters are set, some users will have a transaction that needs to use just a few more resources than the predetermined parameters. These users are never happy to find out that their transaction has been terminated when only a few more cycles of machine time would have carried the transaction to a successful conclusion.

Second, is what to do when a transaction is terminated. What steps the system should take upon the termination of a transaction are ponderous. There are two basic approaches:

❏ Throw everything away and start the transaction again later

❏ Store the results that have been calculated and processed and resume processing at a later time

Neither of these approaches is practical, but for different reasons.

Throw all results away. When this approach is taken, there is the potential for huge wastage of resources. What if a transaction has been running for 30 minutes and has done 350,000 I/Os. The transaction is terminated by the resource governor. Later in the evening when the machine is quiet, the transaction is rescheduled. Upon rescheduling, the machine must do 30 minutes of processing and 350,000 I/Os in order to reposition itself where it was before it was interrupted. This is a tremendous waste of resources even when there are slack hours of processing.

Store intermediate results. When the intermediate results are stored and processing resumes where it left off, there are some very basic questions that must be asked. For example, what guarantee is there that the data already processed has not changed since the transaction was terminated? What happens is that the query is made where some data is valid as of one moment in time and other data is valid as of some other moment in time. In fact, the body of data on which the query is made is only valid for a single moment in time. The integrity of the analytical query can thus be seriously compromised.

❏ How does the system know what data has and has not been processed? Just because a restart has been done, there is no guarantee the system can remember what data has and has not already been processed.

❏ What resources are required to store the intermediate results? Depending on the transaction, there may be a significant amount of resources consumed saving the intermediate results.

❏ What is to prevent the transaction from being terminated once again?

❏ How will the system know to reschedule and restart the system?

In short, neither throwing away results nor storing intermediate results upon termination of a transaction by the resource governor is satisfactory.

OTHER REASONS WHY THE RESOURCE GOVERNOR IS INADEQUATE   But there are other issues as well. In order to dynamically monitor the progress of a transaction, on-line interactive resources—the most precious of resources—are required. In addition, there is the issue of having to go in and modify and manipulate the internal kernel of the DBMS. The resource governor may not cause any problems with the internal workings of the system. On the other hand the resource governor may indeed foul up the internal workings of the DBMS. From a systems standpoint there are then many serious objections to the use of a resource governor as a means to optimize performance in the data warehouse environment. But there are some other very fundamental objections as well.

DORMANT DATA—THE REAL ISSUE   The first fundamental objection (and probably the most damning) to the resource governor as a systems management tool for the data warehouse environment is that the resource governor says nothing about what data is and is not being used for decision support processing which is the key to management of data in the data warehouse. The real enemy of performance in the data warehouse environment is massive amounts of dormant data, and resource governors say absolutely nothing about what data is dormant and what data is not.

What to Optimize   The second reason why resource governors are only a temporary stop along the way to long-term system management in the data warehouse environment is that resource governors say nothing about where optimization needs to be done. There are many different approaches to optimization in the data warehouse environment:

❏ Repartitioning data
❏ Creating new partitions
❏ Adding indexes

❏ Creating star-joins

❏ Restructuring data

❏ Altering key structures

❏ Changing the hardware platform

❏ Affecting the physical colocation of data

All of these approaches are long-term cures for performance problems, and all of these approaches depend on information about the use of the data inside the data warehouse. Unfortunately, a resource governor does nothing to address the information needed to make these fundamental design decisions.

Resource Governors—Farmers and Explorers   Perhaps the biggest shortcoming of the resource governor as a systems management tool for the data warehouse environment is that it does not recognize that there are two types of legitimate users in the environment—explorers and farmers.

Farmers are those individuals who have a predictable profile of resource utilization. Farmers regularly submit transactions that access a modest amount of data. Farmers know what they want before they set out to look for it. Farmers seldom find huge nuggets of information but frequently find flakes of gold.

Explorers are individuals who do not know what they want and who act in a spontaneous manner. Explorers are people who look at massive amounts of data. Explorers often find nothing, but occasionally they stumble upon huge nuggets of information. Explorers have a very different profile of utilization than farmers. Both types of users need access to the data warehouse.

Resource governors can be used in a very compatible manner with farmers because of the nature of the query submitted by the farmer. But resource governors are anathema to explorers, yet explorers are some of the most important users of the data warehouse.

It is for these reasons that resource governors are no more appropriate to the systems management of the data warehouse environment than they were to OLTP systems. In short, resource governors are a band-aid covering a wound that has been caused by cancer. Resource governors are simply a superficial approach to the achievement of performance in the data warehouse environment.

Query Blocking

A much better idea than a resource governor (which is never a very long-term or satisfactory solution) is a query blocker. A query blocker operates on the same principles as a resource governor but with some important exceptions. A query blocker stops a query from going into execution if it is suspected that the query is going to be a resource problem. Because the query is blocked from going into execution, massive amounts of resources are saved.

The query blocker analyzes the query before execution and estimates how many resources the query will use. Based on the resource usage predicted, the query blocker then decides whether the query should be allowed to execute. One of the reasons why a query blocker is a superior choice to a resource governor is that a query blocker does not allow intermediate results to be calculated. With a query blocker, there is no dilemma as to what to do with a query that has been half executed. For this reason alone, a query blocker wastes far fewer resources than a resource governor.

Another reason why a query blocker is a better solution than a resource governor is that it can account for the difference between farmers and explorers. When an explorer enters a query and the query blocker senses it, the explorer can be allowed to manually override the query blocker. Thus explorers have their opportunity to access data. Used this way, the query blocker will halt only unintentional resource consumptive queries, which is the purpose in any case.

In order for a query blocker to work effectively, the blocker needs to know quite a bit of information about the query and the data on which the query will operate at the outset of processing—before the query is executed. Some of the things the query blocker needs to know about include

- ❏ Will the query use indexes or will a full table scan be required?
- ❏ Will the query do joins? If so, will the query do the joins on large amounts of data or on data that will require intensive machine resources?
- ❏ Will the query do "group by" processing on large amounts of data?

❏ Will the query operate on tables that contain a large amount of data?

❏ Will the query operate on large sets of data?

❏ Will the query operate on tables that are constantly being accessed, or will the query operate on tables that are seldom used?

❏ Will the query operate on tables that are being updated and contain data that is locked?

❏ Will the query operate during a time of day when the system is busy?

There are undoubtedly many other questions that need to be asked prior to the execution of a query to determine whether the query will be a resource problem. These are only the most basic questions. In order for these questions to be answered properly, the data warehouse controller (i.e., the intelligence that examines the query to see if the query should be blocked) needs to know a lot about the data and the system that the query is going to operate on. Some of the information that must be known in order to do query blocking properly includes

❏ How much data is in a table?

❏ What is the demographic content of the data in the table?

❏ What does the system profile of usage look like?

MONITORING DATA CONTENT

As important and as useful as it is to monitor the activity that flows through the data warehouse environment, it is equally important to monitor the content of data within the environment. There are many benefits to monitoring the content of data:

❏ The quality of the data can be audited.

❏ The demographics of the data can be established.

❏ The patterns of growth can be determined so that capacity planning can be done.

One of the concerns with monitoring data is the overhead of the work of monitoring. If care is not taken and monitoring done with finesse, the load monitoring overhead on the system can be very burdensome. While the cost of overhead can be minimized, it of course cannot be eliminated.

The first consideration in minimizing the burden of monitoring the data in the data warehouse is to determine monitoring frequency. A weekly frequency is common. A monthly frequency is not unheard of. Even running the monitor on a quarterly basis may be optimal in some environments. The second consideration in minimizing the overhead of the data monitor is the parallelization of the activities of monitoring.

Figure 7.10 shows that the data monitor has been split into several programs. The programs are divided so that every row of data is accessed only once and that no row of data is not accessed. The monitor programs can be run independently so that a complete snapshot of the data in the warehouse is taken by multiple programs operating in coordination with each other.

Just how the programs split the data into partitions to be monitored is a function of both the data and the DBMS on which the data warehouse resides. The partitioning can be made along application lines, hardware lines, or DBMS lines (or for that matter, any combination of the above). In any case, the result is not a single program that goes from one row of data to the next in a sequential order looking at the contents of the data. The data warehouse administrator can create as many programs as desired.

FIGURE 7.10
Parallelization of the data monitor is the first step in achieving efficient monitoring of the data in the data warehouse.

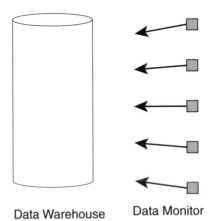

Data Warehouse   Data Monitor

The second technique used to minimize the overhead of monitoring is that of doing only incremental monitoring. A data warehouse usually contains large amounts of data. But the data that is contained is very stable data. For example, from one week to the next only 1% or less of the data in the data warehouse changes. As long as data inside the data warehouse is very stable, there is no point in scanning and monitoring the same data that has been previously scanned and monitored. Therefore a useful technique is to monitor only the data that has changed from one run to the next. There is a wholesale savings of resources by doing only incremental monitoring of the data warehouse as depicted in Figure 7.11.

An incremental monitor operates almost exclusively on the basis of the selection of data for monitoring based solely on time. Another useful technique for minimizing the resources required for the monitoring of data is to combine all monitoring requirements into a single pass of the data warehouse.

Figure 7.12 shows that multiple requirements are gathered together before the monitor run is made. A single pass is made against the data warehouse data. At the end of the pass of the data, the data that has been requested is passed to each of the different requestors. Yet another technique for the minimization of the resources required for the monitoring of data within the data warehouse is that of bounding the monitor.

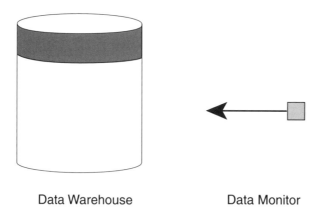

Data Warehouse   Data Monitor

FIGURE 7.11
The monitor only looks at data that has changed since the last monitor run.

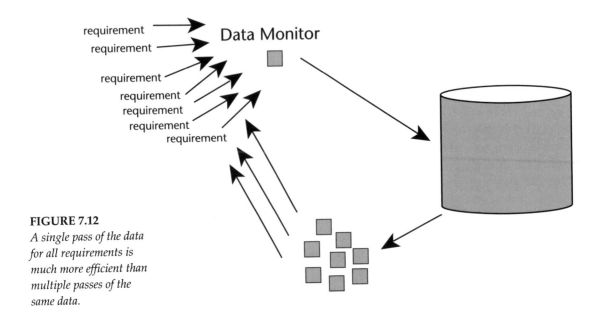

FIGURE 7.12

A single pass of the data for all requirements is much more efficient than multiple passes of the same data.

Figure 7.13 shows that before the request for monitoring is set into motion, the monitoring is limited as to what kind of rows will be accessed. In other words, the monitor run will only look at a subset of data as part of the monitoring exercise. A final consideration of data monitoring is whether the results of the data monitor can be stored historically. Figure 7.14 shows that at the end of each monitor run, the results are stored.

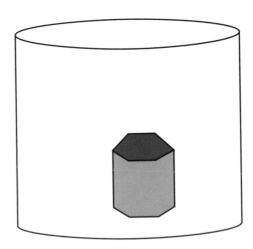

FIGURE 7.13

Bounding the monitor before the execution of the process is a good way to prevent unnecessary resource consumption.

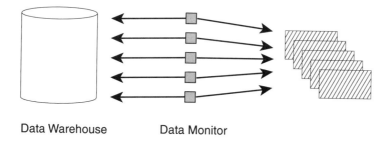

FIGURE 7.14
Storing the results historically is a possibility with the data monitor.

Data Warehouse   Data Monitor

Historical results are quite useful for a number of reasons. Historical results show a progression that can be used as a basis for capacity planning. In addition, changes in the demographics of the data over time can be very useful to the analyst having to look at long-term projections.

DATA WAREHOUSE ALARM CLOCK

Let's take a look at a variation on the data content monitor that capitalizes on this technology in delivering direct and proactive business value. This variation is referred to as the data warehouse alarm clock. Data warehouses are reactive in the sense that data is placed in them and then it becomes the job of the analyst to write reports and perform other calculations to unlock the information. In the case where the analyst retrieves the data in the data warehouse—the normal case—the data warehouse waits for the analyst to cause something to happen. The data warehouse is only as active and as useful as the analyst who is operating on the data warehouse makes it.

But the data warehouse does not have to be passive. There is a way of turning the data warehouse into a proactive facility by means of an "alarm clock" facility. A data warehouse alarm clock facility is one where a data monitor is run against the data warehouse. The data monitor looks at every row of data in the data warehouse and examines the content in each row. As the data monitor is running, predefined variables are being calculated as the monitor passes from one row to the next. A predefined variable is designed to be calculated from looking at many rows of data in the warehouse. A predefined variable can take many forms, such as

❏ A count of all rows in a table.

❏ A count of the subset of rows in a table, such as all customers in the Midwest, all customers who have made more than three purchases this year, all customers who have just entered the system this year, and so forth.

❏ A calculation that is made for all records, such as total sales.

❏ A calculation against selected records, such as total sales in Illinois, total units of products sold in the month of July, total orders for products for Dallas, Texas, in June and July.

The simple count of records or subsets of records is called a profile. The calculations made by looking across the entire data warehouse at multiple records is called a threshhold. Once the data warehouse administrator has defined the profiles and threshholds to be calculated, the data is monitored, looking at each record in the data warehouse. At the end of the monitor execution, the profiles and the threshholds that have been calculated are subjected to conditional checks that have been prespecified by the data warehouse analyst. The checks might be things such as

❏ Is the total number of records in table ABC greater than 100,000?

❏ Is the total number of customers in Illinois greater than 10,000?

❏ Are the total sales in Texas in January, February, and March greater than $1,000?

Predefined variables that are calculated by looking at multiple occurrences of data warehouse records can be used in tandem with each other as part of a comparison, such as

❏ Is the ratio of Texas expenses divided by Texas revenues for August greater than 1.0?

❏ Has the revenue in California exceeded the revenue in Illinois for any month in 1998?

In short, the data warehouse administrator is able to use the predefined data warehouse variables that have been calculated in the monitoring of the data warehouse in any manner imaginable. Once the data monitor has been run and the conditions checked, the data warehouse administrator specifies actions to be taken upon satisfying the condition. The actions typically take the form of messages to be sent, messages to be placed on a general purpose bulletin board, or programs to be set in motion.

As an example of messages that can be sent, the following might be transmitted:

❑ (To the vice president of sales) Total sales this quarter exceed quota. Congratulations.

❑ (To the manager of accounting) The ratio of sales to expenses has exceeded 2.0. You are now in the danger zone.

❑ (To the shop floor foreman) Assembly line 202 is two days behind schedule.

Or messages can be sent to a general purpose bulletin board, such as:

❑ **Congratulations.** Total production goal has been met for the year on November 18.

❑ **Alert.** Quality control has found 13% more rejects than allowed this month.

❑ **Congratulations to all.** The ratio of expenses to sales has just dropped below 0.75.

Another possibility is setting a program in motion upon satisfying a condition. A typical scenario might be: When total sales drop below 75% of quota, set into motion the report that analyzes individual sales representatives by region by district and send the results of the analysis to the vice president of sales.

In short, the data warehouse administrator is able to position the data warehouse as a proactive reporting facility rather than in the classic posture of a reactive facility that depends on the analyst to uncover information and then instigate activity based on the findings. At first glance, the alarm clock facility for a data warehouse appears to be similar to the trigger facility of a traditional DBMS. The trigger facility of a DBMS operates under the same principles, except for the fact that a trigger facility operates against a single row of data in the warehouse. A trigger facility does not look at variables that are created by looking across all the rows that exist in the data warehouse. Instead, a trigger facility operates on the basis of the variables that are present when there is a single occurrence of data.

SUMMARY

The best way to manage volumes of data is to remove dormant data. But in order to remove dormant data it is necessary to find out what data is in fact dormant. The best way to identify dormant data is through an activity monitor. The activity monitor sits between the end user and the data warehouse and looks at each activity flowing through the system. The SQL that flows into the data warehouse and the result set that is generated by the query activity are examined by a nonintrusive SQL monitor. Monitoring can be done at the table level, the table/column level, and the table/column/occurrence level. The overhead of monitoring becomes a large issue when the monitoring is done at a very fine level of detail.

Resource governors and query blockers are variations on the activity monitor. These monitors strive to make use of activity information as it happens to support workload management. Resource governors generally prove to be inadequate for a variety of reasons, while query blockers offer a much more sophisticated and strategic approach to workload management.

As important and as useful as it is to monitor the activity that flows through the data warehouse environment, it is as useful to monitor the content of the data once the data has entered. There are many benefits to the monitoring of the content of data:

❑ The quality of the data can be audited.

❑ The demographics of the data can be established.

❑ The patterns of growth can be determined so that capacity planning can be done.

A variation of the data content monitor is the data warehouse alarm clock, which uses the data content monitor to automate the discovery and notification of key business events.

The chapters presented so far have discussed building a high-performance data warehouse environment from the perspective of usage and data. In the next three chapters, we will discuss building of the platform on which the data will reside, and users and monitors will operate.

Platform and Performance

In the previous Part, we talked about the elements of the high-performance data warehouse environment that shape the landscape, usage, and data. In this section, we talk about a third element in this environment used to house the data and support usage, the platform. Suffice to say that a high-performance platform is at the heart of any high-performance data warehouse environment. In Chapter 8, we will talk about the components of a high-performance data warehouse platform. In Chapter 9, we talk about how to combine and apply these components in arriving at an implemented solution. In Chapter 10, we talk about advanced topics to consider in the planning, implementing and maintaining of your solution.

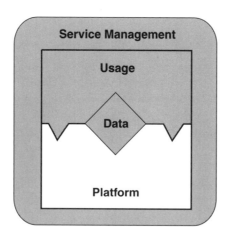

CHAPTER EIGHT

Components of the High-Performance Platform

So far we've discussed high-performance data warehousing from a variety of important usage and data perspectives:

❏ User community (farmers and explorers)
❏ Data mart
❏ Dormant data
❏ Data cleansing
❏ Monitors

These perspectives are important because they fundamentally shape the data warehouse environment. In this section we review a second important element of the data warehouse environment, the platform on which the data resides and the users operate. Beneath the usage and data, and beneath all the performance monitoring tools, lies the platform of the data warehouse environment. A high-performance platform is always at the heart of any high-performance data warehouse environment. It is the platform that determines how much processing power and I/O bandwidth is available, how many users can be supported, how much data can be stored, and how easily the environment will be able to adapt to growing and changing user requirements. In this chapter we describe the fundamental concepts and technologies that form the architecture of a high-performance data warehouse platform and, subsequently, a high-performance data warehouse environment.

PERFORMANCE CHAIN

As a starting point, it is important to realize that a high-performance platform is comprised of a large number of components, all linked together in a chain. It is not sufficient to have some or even most of these components be high performance. If one component is weak, then it becomes the weak link in the chain, and the result will be that some or all of your users will have poor performance. For the overall platform to be high performance, *every* component must be high performance end to end.

Another important issue regarding the performance chain is that data warehouse platforms must be viewed as organic; that is, they change over time in response to changing business requirements. Just as your organization is organic, your data warehouse environment must be able to grow as users' needs grow and it must be able to adapt as your users' needs change. This means that all components in your performance chain must be able to support this organic nature. They each must be able to support rapid growth and rapid change in order to ensure that your data warehouse platform not only performs well initially, but performs well over time.

SCALABILITY REQUIREMENT

Data warehouse environments were originally built for several common reasons. First, one of the original goals was to have a consolidated view of the data in otherwise disjointed and completely independent operational systems. This made integrated data accessible to the organization for improved strategic decision making. Second, they were built as a way to offload the data analysis functions from the performance-sensitive and response-time-sensitive operational systems. It was realized that rather than trying to manage a single system to address the fairly different needs of operational and analysis users, it was far more efficient to create two systems (the operational system and the analytical system), with each one optimized to the specific needs of its users. However, we've gone far beyond these original goals. We are now collecting far more data and analyzing it far more thoroughly to increase our overall effectiveness. In retail, we now want to track and analyze every interaction with a customer (including not just store visits, but also phone calls and mailing responses). In addition, we want to track every product sitting in our line and use the information to make sure the right products are in the right stores and are promoted to the right people at the right time. In telecommunications, we want to track the calling patterns of our clients to determine what types of calling plans would be most relevant to them. After that we might want to analyze whether these calling plans helped retain more customers longer. In finance, we want to build a unified view of each customer, understand which banking products they hold and which additional banking products or services they might be interested in. And we'll want to keep longer histories of our interactions with our banking customers to determine their long-term credit worthiness. These new goals mean we're asking far more from our modern data warehouse environments.

Combine these new goals with the original goals and the result is that modern data warehouses have a set of requirements unlike any other application. Since data warehouses can be viewed as a global collection of data from a number of different operational systems, the volume of data being managed is far larger than that found in traditional operational systems. But it's not simply the fact that they're often unusually large that makes them unique. It's the fact that, regardless of how large they are when first deployed, they will inevitably grow much *larger*. They need to support more users, more data, more complex queries, and more functionality. This is why data warehouses must be viewed as organic, constantly growing applications.

There are at least two intuitive reasons for a data warehouse's natural inclination toward growth: increasing data volumes and an increasing number of end users (see Part 1 on usage and data for a more detailed discussion on the factors that shape the data warehouse platform). As discussed in Chapter 1, a number of factors contribute to the growth in volume of data:

❏ Data warehouses collect historical data.

❏ Data warehouses involve the collection of data to satisfy unknown requirements.

❏ Data warehouses include data at both the very detailed and the summary level.

❏ Data warehouses contain externally generated data (e.g., demographic, psychographic, etc.).

Growth in the number of end users generally results from a phenomenon that we call "usage begets usage." As soon as one group in an organization begins using a data warehouse environment, others begin to see how valuable it is to the first set of users, and they too want access. Soon other organizations catch on and want to get in the game as well.

The performance implications here are significant. Not only must you be able to build a data warehouse platform to meet today's performance needs, but you must also build it so that it can meet tomorrow's too. A data warehouse platform that can achieve this is called "scalable." A good working definition of scalability has two related parts. First, a scalable platform must be able to grow in terms of end users, data, complexity, and functionality, as stated earlier, and second, it must be able to maintain existing performance levels as it grows. If your data warehouse platform grows larger, but suffers from poor performance as a result, users will not be satisfied. A rule of thumb that we've learned from experience is that if your data warehouse platform is not built to be scalable, it will collapse under its own weight within roughly 18 months. The conclusion is that for a data warehouse environment to be high-performance and maintain its high-performance over time, the platform must be scalable.

For all but the smallest data warehouses, traditional hardware and software technologies are not well suited to meet performance and scalability needs. These technologies do not provide sufficient raw horsepower to process the large amounts of data or support the diverse needs of the end-user community. Even if they did, they do not support the ability to incrementally increase their processing capabilities to support the organic, growing nature of a data warehouse environment.

PARALLELISM AND ITS RELATIONSHIP TO PERFORMANCE

If traditional technologies are inappropriate as the basis of a data warehouse platform, then obviously new hardware and software technologies are needed, and new techniques are needed to design and build data warehouse platforms based on these technologies. Fortunately these new technologies already exist, and they have been used successfully to create the underlying platforms of the largest, most complex, most rapidly growing, and fastest data warehouse environments in the world.

The technologies we're referring to are known as parallel technologies. To understand these technologies in terms of how they work and their effect on performance, we must first understand what parallelism is. With that understanding, we can then see how it is used in hardware and software to improve performance and to maintain existing performance levels as the amount of data, the number of users, and the overall application complexity increases.

What Is Parallelism?

Fundamentally, parallelism is a straightforward concept. It is simply the computer industry's name for a "divide and conquer" approach to problem solving. Concretely, parallelism solves a large problem or accomplishes a large task by dividing the problem or task into smaller, more manageable pieces, working on those pieces simultaneously (for example, by different CPUs), and then merging the results (if necessary). In everyday life we often use the parallel approach without even knowing it. For example, every time we ask a group of friends to help us paint our house, we are using parallelism. That is, rather than having one person (usually ourselves) paint the entire house, we divide the house into sections, and have each section painted simultaneously by a different, and obviously loyal, friend.

There are two main benefits of using parallelism. First, the level of performance that can be achieved is far beyond that which could be achieved via traditional technologies. There are two ways to measure this performance increase: speed-up and scale-up.

Speed-up means that your individual task (e.g., the execution of a database query) is completed more quickly. Therefore, it is implicitly tied to the notion of response time, and as such can be measured by dividing the original response time for your task by the sped-up response time.

Scale-up, on the other hand, means that although your individual task isn't necessarily completed any more quickly, more users can be supported without any degradation in the response times of the tasks you submit. Just as speed-up relates to response times, scale-up relates to overall system throughput (usually measured in queries completed per minute or per hour). You can measure scale-up by dividing the new system throughput by the original system throughput.

Parallel hardware supports multiple CPUs in order to achieve speed-up and scale-up. As more performance is required (either in the sense of better response times, higher throughput, or both), more processors are added. It's similar to the notion of adding more people to a project team in order to speed up the completion of a project. In fact, this is actually an extremely appropriate analogy. Unless you're careful, adding an additional person to a team can often create coordination overhead and communication problems that can in fact slow the team down. As you'll see, the same holds true for parallel technologies. Unless you're careful, adding more computing resources can sometimes have the seemingly counterintuitive effect of slowing down the execution of tasks. Why? For exactly the same reasons noted with a project team—sometimes the overhead required to coordinate all the processors (and coordinate all the resources that must be shared by all the processors) can outweigh the potential performance gains.

The use of multiple CPUs is actually a clever way to get around the limits of physics. In a utopian world, we would have infinitely fast processors (and, since we're talking about utopia here, they would also be infinitely inexpensive, i.e., free). In this world, since all machines would be uniprocessors, we wouldn't have to worry about the above-mentioned coordination issues that are an inherent part of parallelism hardware. However, in the real world, signals within a CPU cannot travel faster than the speed of light. Also, circuits can only be made so small or packed so densely before heat and certain quantum mechanic effects cause electrons to begin behaving randomly. Since we can't make a single CPU that meets our needs, we have to gang together multiple CPUs inside a single computer and use their collective power to address our processing needs. It was for this reason that parallel hardware architectures were devised in the first place.

Unprecedented performance levels are the first advantage of parallelism. The discussion of infinitely fast processors brings us to the second major advantage: superior price/performance ratios. Granted, infinitely fast processors don't exist, but there are certainly processors that are very fast. The problem is that the world's fastest processors are also the world's most expensive. This wouldn't be so bad if a processor that cost twice as much as another processor was also twice as fast. Unfortunately, this isn't the case. A leading-edge processor that is twice as fast as another often carries with it a price tag that is 10 times as much. To make a processor twice as fast as the competition requires pushing the limits of fabrication technology, meaning that the fabrication plants are extremely expensive, and the initial yields are very low, because using these exotic fabrication technologies takes a long time to master. All of this means that the price of the processor rises at a more rapid rate than the corresponding performance level.

Parallel platforms, on the other hand, yield far more linear price/performance ratios. If a single processor costs $100, then if I buy two processors, I double my cost but also double my aggregate processing power. If you (and your checkbook) are willing to go even further, you can buy four processors and get four times the total processing power. And so on.

Relating this to everyday life, a 450 horsepower Ferrari costs $160,000, which is eight times more expensive, but only three times more powerful, than the cars from General Motors that have 150 horsepower for $20,000. The Ferrari engine requires exotic design and production techniques, whereas the GM engine is mass-produced using common techniques. Now, imagine building a car that is comprised of three GM cars welded together side by side (making it the world's first "parallel" car). The combined horsepower of our imaginary vehicle would equal that of the Ferrari, but would only cost $60,000, not $160,000. The use of parallelism has improved the price/performance ratio. However, you might wonder how one could drive such a vehicle. How would you coordinate shifting gears? How would you coordinate steering? These questions are reminiscent of the questions that are asked about coordinating all the separate CPUs within a parallel computer. In both our car engine example and our analysis of parallel computers, the advantage of greatly improved price/performance ratios does incur a cost: increased operational complexity.

Types of Parallelism

We discussed the performance and price/performance benefits of using parallel hardware. But the hardware is useless unless the software that loads, manages, and analyzes data within your data warehouse platform takes advantage of the parallelism in the hardware. While it's true that enabling this software to leverage parallelism (i.e., creating "parallel-enabled" software) is predominantly the responsibility of the software vendor rather than the data warehouse administrator, it is still important to understand the different types of parallelism that software developers employ. Why? Well, racecar drivers who study the detailed functioning of their car's engines are better able to squeeze out the last bit of performance from their engine. In the same way, the more you understand about the architecture and the technologies that comprise your data warehouse platform, the better you will be able to design it and manage it for optimal performance.

There are three types of parallelism employed by software developers:

❑ Functional parallelism
❑ Data parallelism
❑ Pipeline parallelism

Let's take a look at each of these technique in more detail.

FUNCTIONAL PARALLELISM The first type of parallelism, and the type that is most common, is functional parallelism. This approach takes advantage of multiple processors by having each CPU work on a different task. Essentially, requests (such as data warehouse queries) come into a request routing service and are handed off to the next available CPU. Each processor is generally able to handle any type of request (see Figure 8.1).

There is a variation of this that can be called partitioned functional parallelism. With this modification, each processor is dedicated to performing a single type of task and the request routing service passes the request to the appropriate processor. In data

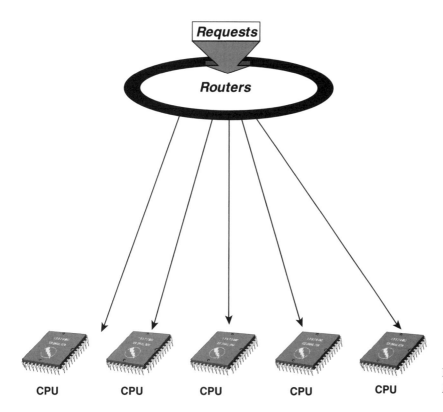

FIGURE 8.1
Functional parallelism.

warehousing, this technique is often used as part of performing parallel queries (described later), where some processors are dedicated to disk scans, others are dedicated to joining tables, and others are dedicated to sorting.

The goal of functional parallelism is to achieve scale-up. Since each request is still processed by only a single processor, each request completes in the same amount of time as before. However, as shown in Figure 8.1, five requests can be processed simultaneously. Therefore five times as many users could be supported without any performance degradation (assuming that I/O and other parts of the system were sufficiently configured so that they do not become bottlenecks when the user load increases).

DATA PARALLELISM   Data parallelism (often loosely referred to as "partitioning") takes a different approach. Rather than assigning a different task to each processor, this technique takes a potentially large amount of data that needs to be processed for a single task and divides it into smaller, more manageable pieces. These pieces (often referred to as "partitions") are then distributed to the various processors. Essentially each processor executes the same routines against smaller portions of the data. For example, a data cleansing routine may be written to identify and correct invalid values in data that is being imported into the data warehouse. If you have a machine with five processors, rather than having one processor execute that data cleansing routine on the entire set of incoming data, data parallelism can be used to divide the data into five partitions, distribute each partition to a different CPU, and have each CPU run the data cleansing routine on its smaller portion of the data (see Figure 8.2).

The main focus of data parallelism is speed-up. In the example mentioned above, since each CPU has to run the data cleansing

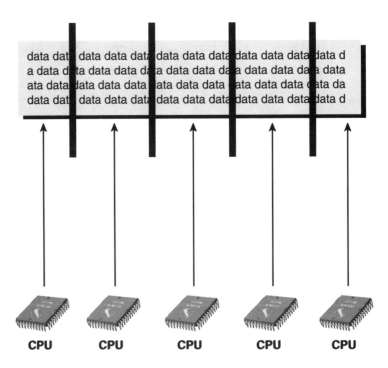

FIGURE 8.2
Data parallelism.

routine on only one-fifth of the amount of data, the data cleansing process will finish in roughly one-fifth of the original time using a single processor.

PIPELINE PARALLELISM With pipeline parallelism, requests and data are processed in various stages, and each stage is handled by a different processor. The first processor in the pipeline applies the first stages of processing to the data, then hands that data off to the second processor which applies the second processing stage, and so on until all the required processing is complete. For example, with a query, the first processor may scan the appropriate table for rows that satisfy the selection criteria of that query. It would then hand off the results to a second processor which would be responsible for joining the scanned rows with the rows from another table. The second processor would in turn take the joined result set and hand it to a third processor which would sort the result set and return it to the user.

But as we've described it, there doesn't really seem to be any advantage to this approach. If, using a single processing machine, the scan, join, and sort stages each require 20 seconds of processing time, then processing the query using pipeline parallelism will still take 60 seconds. A single processor is still executing each stage, so each stage will not run any faster than before.

While it is true that this type of pipeline parallelism will not speed up queries, it can dramatically effect scale-up and improve system throughput. To understand how this happens, we need to look at what occurs after a processor completes its stage and hands off the results to the subsequent processor. Rather than having the first processor wait until the entire query is finished, it immediately begins scanning tables for the next inbound query. As soon as the second processor finishes joining the data from the first query, it begins the join for the second query, and so on (see Figure 8.3). Think of it as a manufacturing assembly line where different people work on a different stage of automobile production.

Returning to our query example, as we follow this process, we see that the third processor returns query results to a user every 20 seconds. Although each query still requires 60 seconds to process, we now get three queries completing every 60 seconds instead of just one.

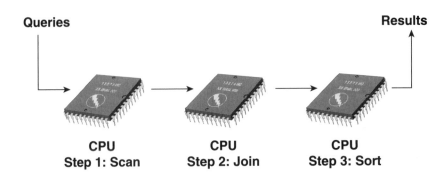

FIGURE 8.3
Pipeline parallelism.

HIGH-PERFORMANCE HARDWARE

There are a number of different hardware architectures that are available today that make extensive use of parallelism and are therefore highly scalable. It is their scalability that makes them particularly well suited for the high-performance data warehouse platform. However, it is not simply the case that you can choose any scalable solution and be assured that it will meet your performance needs. Different architectures exist (and most have been around a long time), and each has its strengths as well as weaknesses. Choosing the appropriate architecture requires understanding these issues.

To begin this discussion, let's look at a uniprocessor architecture. Distilled to its essence, a uniprocessor hardware solution is comprised of a single CPU, a pool of memory, an I/O subsystem, and a system bus that allows all the pieces to communicate. For data warehouse platforms, you will quickly find that the processor becomes the bottleneck (see Figure 8.4). The amount of data that needs to be processed and the number of users grows, but the amount of processing power available can't grow. The hardware doesn't permit it. Hence performance degrades as a linear function of increasing workload.

To solve the problems created by the fact that the uniprocessor solution doesn't scale well, scalable hardware was developed.

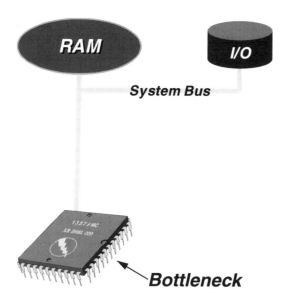

FIGURE 8.4
Uniprocessor architectures (the CPU can become the bottleneck).

In the rest of this section on hardware, we discuss four different scalable hardware architectures:

❏ Symmetric multiprocessors (SMPs)

❏ Clusters

❏ Massively parallel processors (MPPs)

❏ Nonuniform memory access (NUMA)

Each approach addresses the scalability limitations of the previous architecture, but does so at the price of increasing the complexity.

Symmetric Multiprocessors (SMPs)

Naturally, if the problem with a uniprocessor is that you cannot add more processing power, then the solution is to create a computer architecture that does allow you to add more processors when needed. These architectures are called symmetric multiprocessors (SMPs). In these architectures, instead of connecting a single CPU to the system bus, you can connect multiple CPUs and have all of them share the same bus and the same memory pool. Because all hardware components are shared, SMPs are often referred to as "shared-everything hardware architectures." Currently most major vendors provide SMP hardware, and the maximum number of processors with which they can be configured varies by vendor. Some vendors provide systems that can only be configured with a few processors, while others can be configured with as many as 64 processors. Most SMP systems built as data warehouse servers can contain at least a dozen processors.

To get all of these processors to efficiently share the system bus requires that the system bus be intelligent, and it must arbitrate when two processors want to use the bus at the same time. In addition, with multiple processors sharing the bus, the bus bandwidth needs to be much larger than in a uniprocessor. Since building very fast buses is quite expensive, hardware vendors use a series of caching techniques, whereby a copy of recently used data is cached locally to the CPU that requested it. This helps decrease the bus bandwidth requirements, but it does add the need for even more intelligence in the bus itself, since the bus has to synchronize the locally cached copies with the original copy in main memory.

The advantages of such an architecture are obvious. You can start with a small number of processors, or even a single processor, and add new processors as your workload increases. In addition, since the operating system transparently handles assigning processes to the various CPUs, and since all the CPUs share the same memory, application developers do not need to learn a new programming paradigm. SMPs can therefore be programmed in much the same fashion as uniprocessors. To be sure, in order to exact optimal performance out of these systems, you need to have an understanding of how the multiple processors work together. However, your programming model is still the uniprocessor model of multiple processes all running on a single copy of the operating system within a single shared memory space.

A final advantage is that the single shared pool of memory means interprocess communication is easy. That is, all processes can easily, quickly, and efficiently communicate by writing to and reading from shared memory. Ultimately this means that development is fairly straightforward on SMPs, and the efficient shared memory communication mechanism means communication overhead is minimal.

But SMPs still have a bottleneck. We removed the uniprocessor's CPU bottleneck by connecting multiple CPUs together on a single bus, but in doing so we created a new bottleneck, the bus itself. Since an SMP bus has a fixed bandwidth, at some point the workload generated by the CPUs will saturate that bandwidth, and adding additional processors beyond that point will not increase performance. In fact, it will often decrease performance. To understand why, think of the system bus as a freeway. As CPUs begin to do work, they generate bus traffic, which can be visualized as cars on the freeway. If the freeway is relatively empty, adding a few more cars increases the "throughput" of the freeway—more people get to their destinations per unit of time. If we add even more cars, we begin to form a traffic jam, and the cars all slow down. At this point, the freeway's throughput probably does not change much. More people are on the freeway, but they are all traveling more slowly. Finally, if we add still more cars, the freeway becomes a veritable parking lot. The freeway is now saturated, people barely move at all, and throughput plummets. In the same sense, if we put too many CPUs on the system bus, the bus saturates, and performance plummets as the CPUs spend all their time contending for the bus rather than performing useful work (see Figure 8.5).

In most high-end SMP systems, this saturation point tends to occur at around a few dozen processors. Increasing the speed and

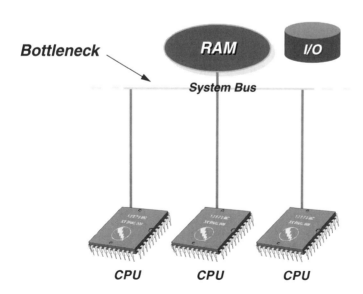

FIGURE 8.5
SMP architectures (the system bus can become a bottleneck).

bandwidth of the bus will push the saturation point farther out, but it won't eliminate it. Higher bandwidth will allow you to support more CPUs, but it can quickly become an expensive solution.

Clusters

Following the same line of reasoning we used before, if the problem in an SMP is that the bus becomes the bottleneck, then the natural solution is to provide multiple buses. The processors are then divided between these buses, and so is the memory. This combination of a set of processors, a pool of memory, and a bus is referred to as a *node,* and a set of nodes is called a *cluster.* To allow the nodes to communicate and coordinate with each other, the nodes are all connected to a special high-speed network called an *interconnect.* In a cluster with three nodes, each bus will only have to support one-third of the total number of processors in the system and will also only have to handle memory requests that pertain to its particular third of memory. Therefore the need for an ultra-high-performance (and therefore expensive) bus is removed.

If you look at the definition of a node, you will realize that it is identical to an SMP. The cluster approach says that if one SMP begins to run out of steam, then just bring in another SMP. That's really all a cluster is, several SMP systems connected via a fast interconnect.

Clusters can take two different approaches to handling disks. In most clusters, each node not only has its own pool of memory, but also its own set of disks that are physically connected to that node. Disks that are connected to a particular node are referred to as "local" to that node, and all other disks are considered "remote." Processors on one node cannot directly access the data that resides on remote disks. That's not to say that they can't get to the data at all—it just means that they can't get to it directly. Specifically, if a processor needs data that resides on a local disk, then the processor can simply directly issue an I/O request to that disk. But if the data resides on a remote disk, then the processor must send a message to that remote node requesting that one of the processors on that node issue the I/O request. Once the I/O is completed, the remote node will then send the data back to the requesting processor in the form of another message. Thus a request for data on a local disk requires issuing just a single I/O, but a request for data on a remote disk can require an outbound message, then an I/O, and then an inbound message containing the resulting data. Since nodes do not share buses, memory, CPUs, or disks, this architecture is referred to as a "shared-nothing hardware architecture."

The other approach to handling disks in a clustered environment is called a "shared-disk hardware architecture." In this environment, each node has its own physically separate pool of memory, but all disks are attached to a single, centralized disk control subsystem (rather than directly attached to a node), and all nodes are directly connected to this subsystem. Any node can directly access any piece of data residing on any disk by simply issuing an I/O request directly to that disk. In these systems the concept of local and remote disks doesn't apply. However, if you were to insist on using those terms, then all disks would have to be considered remote.

ADVANTAGES AND DISADVANTAGES OF CLUSTERS   Regarding data warehousing, the most significant advantage of clusters is that they give you increased scalability. If you build your warehouse on an SMP, given the average growth rates of a data warehouse platform, you will likely hit the throughput limit of the SMP in 18 to 24 months. At that point, performance degrades, and no more growth is possible from that single SMP. But with clustering, you can bring in another SMP, cluster the two together via an interconnect (assuming the hardware vendor designed the SMP to support clustering), and roughly double your available throughput. For a growing data warehouse environment, this capability is essential.

Clusters also provide the advantage of improved fault tolerance. Because each node in a cluster is essentially its own complete computer, there is an element of redundancy built into the architecture. If one node fails, the other nodes can still operate. In a shared-nothing hardware architecture, to avoid losing access to the disks that are local to the failed node, most disks are "multi-initiated" or "twin tailed," meaning that they are each connected to both a primary and a secondary node. In normal operation, a disk is exclusively controlled by its primary node, but if that node fails, the designated secondary node will take over control of the affected disks. Although fault tolerance is generally considered to be more important in the OLTP arena than in the decision support arena, it is, at a minimum, a beneficial side effect of clusters.

Not everything about clusters is advantageous. By linking together multiple SMPs, you've now created one fundamental difference between a clustered hardware architecture and the uniprocessor or SMP architecture. For the first time, we've introduced physically separate pools of memory. Each node has its own local pool of memory that it can directly see, but all other memory pools are remote, and a programmer cannot write code that can directly read or write to memory locations that are remote. To intuitively understand this, think of a cluster as multiple computers hooked up to a local area network (LAN)—each computer can directly read and write to its own local memory, but not to the memories of any other computer on the LAN.

These separate memory pools add complexity to the system. Before, on an SMP, if eight processors wanted to coordinate their actions while executing some task in parallel (say, using data parallelism and/or pipeline parallelism), they could communicate to each other by writing to and reading from a shared section of memory. If one processor wanted to let the others know its status, it could write a status message to memory. Then all the other processors could simply look at that message by reading a memory address. Or if one processor wanted to send data to another processor, it would again just have to write that data into some shared section of memory for the other processor to read. This communication between processors is easy, efficient, and fast because it happens at memory read/write speeds.

In a cluster, the separate pools of memory mean that this straightforward form of communication and coordination is no longer possible. Assume we have a three-node cluster, and each node holds eight processors. If we want to involve more than eight processors in processing a parallel task, we then have to coordinate processors that reside on at least two different nodes. But these processors can't let all the others know their status just by writing to a piece of memory, because not all of the processors involved will have access to that memory. For the same reason, they can no longer pass data to each other by using shared memory.

How then do they coordinate their actions? The answer is that two processors that want to communicate but which reside on different nodes must now explicitly pass messages to each other over the interconnect (which is just like sending messages over any other network). This form of communication is far slower than communicating at memory speeds (often 100 times to 1000 times slower), so obtaining good performance on a clustered hardware platform means constructing the application so that only the absolute minimum amount of communication occurs over the interconnect. Lots of internode communication increases the amount of communication overhead required, and this in turn causes performance to degrade. Performance on clusters is therefore very sensitive to how much data must be passed between nodes.

Conceptually the SMP communication and coordination model can be thought of as having a few people (say, eight) in a room that has a chalkboard at the front of the room. If each of these people wanted to keep the others posted regarding their status, they would write messages on the chalkboard. Whenever anyone wanted to see the status of the other seven, they would glance at the chalkboard and quickly see what everyone was doing.

But in a cluster, this isn't possible. Instead of having eight people in a single room with a chalkboard, you would have eight people in each of three rooms, each with its own chalkboard. So within a room, a person could still easily see what the other seven were up to. But to truly coordinate their actions systemwide, they need to know what is happening in the other rooms as well. Since they can't see the other chalkboards directly, we have to introduce telephones (the "interconnect") into the picture to allow them to communicate information back and forth. But this means that communicating sometimes requires more than simply looking at a chalkboard. It requires explicitly picking up a phone, dialing it, and then waiting for someone at the other end to pick up the phone. This process of communication involves significantly more overhead.

Also, clustered systems are not bottleneck free. As before, we removed one bottleneck only to replace it with another. The system bus is no longer the bottleneck, but the new bottleneck is now the interconnect. It has a fixed bandwidth, which means it can only support a fixed amount of communication. As mentioned earlier, for performance reasons, it is important to keep the amount of communication flowing over the interconnect to a minimum. But at some point, as you keep adding nodes to the system, you will hit the interconnect bandwidth limit. Figure 8.6 shows a shared-nothing cluster architecture, highlighting where the interconnect bottleneck can form. (A shared-disk cluster would look very simi-

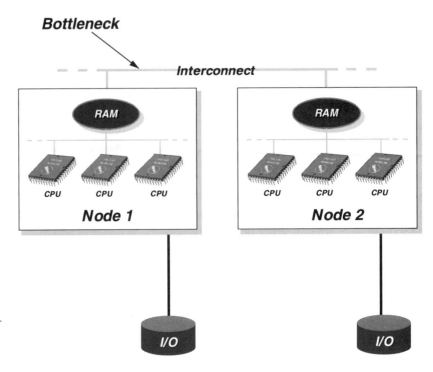

FIGURE 8.6
Shared-nothing cluster architecture (the interconnect can become a bottleneck).

lar, and the interconnect bottleneck would be identical. The only difference in the picture would be that instead of having disks directly attached to nodes 1 and 2, all disks would be directly attached to a central disk control subsystem, which would in turn be connected to nodes 1 and 2.)

In most clustered systems, the sweet spot for performance is around four nodes, but this is certainly application dependent, and we've seen systems with eight nodes that have performed well. However, once you go beyond the sweet spot, the performance advantage of adding another node quickly declines. If you continue to go farther by adding even more nodes, overall performance will in fact decline because of the excessive amount of communication over an already saturated interconnect. The freeway analogy used previously applies here as well.

Massively Parallel Processors (MPPs)

Often, for many of the largest data warehouse platforms, processing the data within the required time frames requires more processing power and more I/O bandwidth than you can get from even the largest SMP or clustered hardware architectures. For these data warehouse platforms, the requirements call for a massively parallel computer which is really nothing more than a very large cluster. Massively parallel machines often support many dozens of processors, and the largest commercial configurations contain well over 100 processors. Originally massively parallel machines supported only uniprocessor nodes, but more modern MPP machines have SMP nodes (just like a cluster). The introduction of SMP nodes into MPP machines means you can still have the same aggregate processing power as before, but now with few physically separate nodes, and, therefore, fewer physically separate memory pools.

Because MPP machines essentially look like very large clusters, they also have the same two approaches to handling disks— some vendors employ a shared-disk hardware architecture, others employ a shared-nothing hardware architecture (although the former is far more common for MPPs). Also, because they look like very large clusters, MPP machines also act like clusters, except the advantages and the disadvantages are magnified. Looking at the advantages, the single biggest benefit of using an MPP machine is the ability to achieve scalability levels that exceed even the largest traditional SMP and/or cluster solutions. As mentioned above, it is possible to build MPP machines with over 100 processors, and there are a number of real-world sites that prove this. Because they have the ability to be configured with such a large number of processors, and because they can handle such large amounts of I/O, MPP machines are frequently the architecture of choice for the largest of data warehouse platforms. Several of the world's largest financial institutions, retailers, airlines, and telecommunications companies have used MPP machines to obtain the performance they need for their large data warehouse environments, which often contain several years of information and which have tables with hundreds of millions (or in some cases billions) of rows.

However, as with all architectures, there are disadvantages to MPP architectures as well. You still have message passing latencies that are 100 to 1000 times slower than SMP messaging latencies, and in general it can be quite a challenge to manage a machine with dozens or even possibly hundreds of separate nodes. In addition, given the large number of nodes, the performance of an MPP machine is notoriously sensitive to the amount of data movement and communication across the interconnect.

OVERCOMING BOTTLENECKS WITH MPPS   But we've glossed over one important point regarding MPP architectures. We still have an interconnect between the nodes of an MPP, and we've explicitly stated that MPPs are really just large clusters. Yet we've somehow managed to add many more nodes than was possible in a traditional clustered environment. How then did we overcome the interconnect bottleneck problem that was identified in the previous section on clusters?

Essentially there are two ways to do this. The first way is a bit more elegant, because it rethinks the whole interconnect approach. Rather than having an interconnect that has a fixed bandwidth, some MPP machines have a clever connection scheme whose total bandwidth increases as more nodes are added to the MPP (see Figure 8.7).

This particular MPP machine connects all the nodes in a two-dimensional grid, often referred to as a "mesh." The spheres represent standard SMP nodes (each with their own set of processors, memory, system bus, and disks), and the lines between the spheres represent a point-to-point connection between the nodes. Starting with configuration A, we have a nine-node machine with 12 point-to-point connections. Assuming each connection has a bandwidth of 40 megabytes per second, if all connections are simultaneously active, the aggregate bandwidth is 480 megabytes per second.

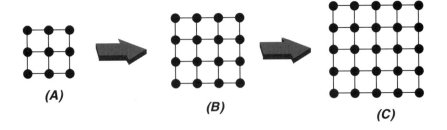

(A)   **(B)**   **(C)**

FIGURE 8.7
Massively parallel architecture (the interconnect bandwidth scales).

● = *Node*

In configuration B we've scaled up the number of processors. Not only have we added more processing power, but we've also added more point-to-point connections for a new total of 16 processors and 24 connections. Not only has the processing power been increased, but the aggregate bandwidth has also increased from the previous 480 megabytes per second to the new aggregate of 960 megabytes per second. In fact, the aggregate bandwidth has been increased by a larger percentage than the aggregate processing power. The number of CPUs increased from 9 to 16 (a 78% increase in processing power), whereas the interconnect bandwidth increased by 100%.

This scaling up process is again repeated in configuration C. Here, we've again increased the number of processors, this time to a total of 25. And accordingly we've added more point-to-point connections, bringing the total up to 40 (for an aggregate bandwidth of about 1.6 gigabytes per second). Again, the interconnect bandwidth has increased at a faster rate than the processing power.

It should be clear that this type of MPP machine is able to overcome the traditional cluster's interconnect bottleneck by making the interconnect itself scalable. As you add more processing power, you add more interconnect bandwidth. Think of it as adding more lanes to the freeway every time you add more cars. The real beauty of MPP machines with scalable interconnects is that they theoretically don't have any inherent components that become bottlenecks as we scale-up the system. Also, because each connection is only point to point between two nodes, each connection can be built fairly inexpensively, so this is a cost-effective way of connecting very large numbers of processors.

MPP TRADE-OFFS By now you should realize that with hardware, as with all things, there's no such thing as a free lunch. There is a price to pay for having a scalable interconnect. In the particular architecture described above, the price is that the average length of the communication path between any two nodes increases as the mesh gets larger. In configuration A, a message sent from the node in the lower left corner to the node in the upper right corner must hop across four connections. In configuration C, the number of hops to get from the lower left corner to the upper right corner increases to eight. This means that the time it takes a piece of data to get from corner to corner increases by a factor of two. This increased latency is yet another challenge that must be managed in this type of MPP environment. There are a few optimizations that hardware vendors make to improve this situation a bit, but regardless, the average number of hops will always increase as the mesh gets larger.

Other MPP architectures overcome the cluster interconnect bottleneck problem using a completely different approach, brute force. Rather than making the interconnect scalable, this solution focuses on taking a standard cluster interconnect scheme, which has all the nodes directly connected to a single interconnect (as shown in Figure 8.6), and making the interconnect very, very fast. Using this approach, vendors implement an interconnect that has the lowest latency and the highest bandwidth possible. The notion is that if you make the interconnect able to support very large amounts of bandwidth, then the single interconnect can support a very large number of nodes, and even the largest data warehouse applications won't hit the bandwidth limit. The advantage of this architecture is that the latencies between nodes doesn't increase as the number of nodes grows, because every node is directly connected to the single interconnect. The drawback is that this interconnect can be expensive to build. Also, it is true that the interconnect can still become a bottleneck in this architecture, but in reality they are usually built with enough bandwidth that most applications don't even come close to hitting the saturation point.

Nonuniform Memory Access (NUMA)

The final major scalable hardware architecture is called the nonuniform memory access architecture (NUMA). For many people, 1997 was the first time they heard of NUMA. In reality, NUMA is not new. The first computers based on this architecture were built in the early 1980s. These first machines had various technical and performance problems, and therefore didn't gain much market share. But it appears that most of these problems have finally been solved, and vendors are starting to promote NUMA-based hardware solutions for commercial use.

As we saw earlier with SMP platforms, end-users are able to harness the power of multiple processors, yet they still are able to treat the computer as a single, unified system because all physical memory is shared. Any coordination that must occur to ensure that two processors don't try to modify the same data element at the exact same time is handled by the hardware itself. Ultimately this keeps things simple for the application developer.

But as we also saw earlier, SMPs have their limitations because the system bus can become a bottleneck. That's why non-shared memory architectures (that is, clusters and MPPs) were created. However, we saw that there is a price for these nonshared memory solutions, and it is the application developers who pay. Rather than living in the single, continuous memory model of an SMP (or a uniprocessor, for that matter), programmers must manage multiple discrete pools of memory. It is the programmer's responsibility to track which pool of memory contains which pieces of data and to coordinate the changing of any particular piece of data. This is done via explicit message passing between nodes, and it is ultimately up to the programmer to manage the entire message passing process.

At first blush, it seems like we have a classic trade-off. That is, you can choose either a simpler programming model with less scalability or a more complex programming model with more scalability. But what if we could build an architecture that had multiple separate memories and buses to avoid bottlenecks, which also had mechanisms built into the hardware that transparently managed all the memory pools as if they we all part of one logical, contiguous pool of memory (thereby removing the burden from the programmers)? Well, that is exactly what NUMA is.

At the hardware level, NUMA looks a little like a traditional clustered system. However, there are significant differences from traditional clusters. First, at the hardware level, NUMA introduces the concept of *local memory* (memory that physically resides on that node) and *remote memory* (memory that physically resides on other nodes). It is important to note, however, that the concept of local/remote memory exists only at the hardware level. From the application developer's perspective, it is all treated as local memory. That is, if a NUMA system has three nodes, and each node contains 1 gigabyte of physical memory, then the application developer sees a single, contiguous 3 gigabyte address space.

Some NUMA architectures also include the concept of a "remote memory cache." In these machines, each node not only has its own local memory, but also a local cache for storing pieces of remote memory. This cache stores local copies of recently accessed data that natively resides on other nodes. Figure 8.8 depicts a NUMA architecture with a local cache.

However, the most significant difference between NUMA architectures and other architectures is that NUMA machines contain additional hardware that is responsible for creating the illusion of a single address space. For example, when a program on node 1 references a piece of memory, the hardware looks at the address that was referenced. If the address falls within the address range for node 1, then the data is directly retrieved from node 1's local memory. However, if it's not within node 1's address range, and if the architecture contains a cache for remote memory, then node 1's remote memory cache is checked. (Remember, this cache is still on the same node, so accessing it is quick.) If the data isn't found there, or if there is no remote memory cache in the first place, then the hardware automatically sends a request to the node that natively contains that memory address and the node to which the request was sent will return a copy of the data to node 1. It is

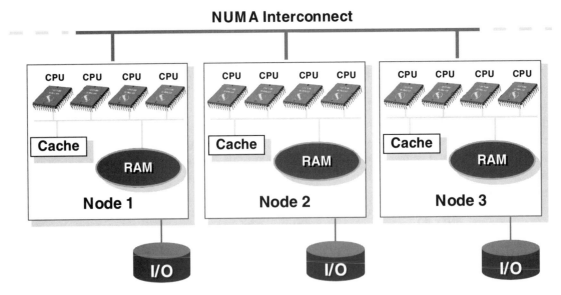

FIGURE 8.8
NUMA architecture (with local cache).

up to the hardware to ensure that all copies of a piece of data are synchronized on a systemwide basis.

From the preceding description, you can see why this architecture is called nonuniform memory access. Any piece of memory can be accessed, but accessing local memory is much faster than accessing remote memory. Hence the nonuniformity refers to the fact that memory access latencies differ depending on what pieces of memory are referenced.

NUMA PROS AND CONS As mentioned before, the main advantage of NUMA systems is that you obtain increased scalability over traditional SMP systems, yet you still retain the single memory programming model of SMPs. How about the disadvantages of NUMA systems? On paper there really aren't any. If the hardware can successfully pull off the illusion of a single memory space, then there aren't any disadvantages. However, that's a big if. There are major issues that must be addressed if NUMA systems are to succeed. The main issue is that the ratio of remote memory access latency to local memory access latency must be as close to 1:1 as possible. In other words, if the single memory space illusion is to be believable, then remote memory accesses can't be inordinately painful. In 1990, the best a NUMA system could offer was a ratio of 10:1, which was wholly unacceptable. Today's systems are close to 2:1.

Also, caching can help reduce the need for remote memory accesses, but it is only effective if a program has good "locality of reference," which means that it tends to work on a particular set of data for a little while before moving on to the next set of data. If a program accesses data completely randomly, or has the characteristic that once it accesses a particular piece of data it tends not to access that data again for a long time, then caching will be ineffective.

Ultimately the main advantage of using any of these scalable platforms (SMPs, clusters, MPPs, or NUMA) is that they enable you to build a data warehouse platform whose performance levels continually meet end-user requirements. When your data warehouse environment doubles in size, as it inevitably will, if you do not have a scalable hardware solution, your performance levels will rapidly degrade. But with scalable hardware platforms, as the data warehouse grows, and as the demands against it grow, you can add additional computing resources to maintain the required performance levels.

HIGH-PERFORMANCE DATABASES

High-performance scalable hardware solutions are only useful for data warehousing if the databases themselves are able to take advantage of the hardware's scalable capabilities. In other words, the database management system must be able to put the multiple processors to good use when processing data warehouse workloads. For traditional relational DBMSs, this means they must be able to process queries in parallel in order for the data warehouse platform to achieve scalability.

Parallel Queries

Although the optimization details can become extremely complex, the general concept of performing a query in parallel is fairly straightforward if you already understand the basic types of parallelism. Earlier we discussed three fundamental types of parallelism:

- ❑ Functional parallelism
- ❑ Data parallelism (also known as "partitioning")
- ❑ Pipeline parallelism

All three can be used in conjunction to make sure your scalable hardware solution is being fully utilized and to obtain very fast query response times for even the largest of queries.

With large numbers of concurrent users, functional parallelism can be used to assign different users' queries to different sets of processors. This means that different sets of processors can be working on different queries concurrently. Theoretically the number of processors to which the query is assigned can be determined at run time. For example, if the system workload is very high, a query could be assigned to only use a few processors. If the workload is low, it could be assigned a larger number of processors. Or the number of processors could be assigned based on the priority level of the query, with higher priority queries being assigned a larger number of processors. In truth, however, current database systems are very limited in their ability to automatically and dynamically assign varying numbers of processors to a query based on system load or query priority. For most systems, the number of processors that will be used is determined by the way the tables are laid out on disk or by defaults that are set up by the data warehouse administrator.

Once a query is assigned to a set of processors, heavy use is made of the concepts of partitioning and pipelining to both speed-up the query response time, and to increase the overall throughput of queries systemwide. Let's reuse the example we introduced earlier in the section on pipeline parallelism, where our query first scans the tables, then performs a join of the results of the scan, then sorts the results, and finally returns the sorted set to the user. Let's assume that the join involves two tables, each containing 20 million rows, and that running this query sequentially on a uniprocessor shows us that each of the three stages (scan, join, and sort) takes four minutes to execute. (We're using completely fictional results here for simplicity. The actual times for executing each stage would likely be very different from each other.) Again, to keep the following explanation simple, let's assume that all queries submitted against this data warehouse platform have this same profile.

In this example, the nonparallel execution of this query will take 12 minutes. By using partitioning and pipelining, we can improve this result dramatically. Now let's run this query on 12 processors instead of 1. The stages in our pipeline are clear—scan, join, sort. Let's assign four processors to each of the stages and evenly partition the workload of each stage among the four processors assigned to that stage. For the scan stage, we can assign two processors to evenly split up the workload of scanning the first table and assign the remaining two processors to evenly split up the workload of scanning the other table. Now instead of having a single processor scan both tables (for a total of 40 million rows), each processor only has to scan half of a table (or 10 million rows). So the scan stage should complete in one-quarter of the time, or one minute.

Next, we see the identical effect in the join phase. Instead of one processor joining all the rows returned by the scan stage, the workload is evenly partitioned across four processors. Since each processor has only one-quarter as much work to do, the join stage should also take only one minute instead of the original four minutes. Finally, the same effect also occurs in the sort stage, where each of the four processors has to sort one-quarter of the overall dataset that will be returned to the user, which should complete in one minute.

There is certainly some overhead involved in all this to partition the workload for each stage and to merge the four sorted subsets of data into a single sorted set before returning it to the user; but if the query is large enough, this overhead is negligible. Given that, our query should now complete in 3 minutes instead of 12.

That's quite an impressive improvement. Or is it? Yes, our query now runs four times faster, but remember that we went from a uniprocessor machine to a 12-processor machine. We used 12 times the computing power, but only achieved a 4× improvement. Why is this the case? Because we have not fully looked at how pipelining is really used. As soon as the four processors that are assigned to the scan stage finish the scan for a query, they hand off their results to the processors executing the join stage, and then they immediately begin scanning the tables for the next query. They don't just sit there idle until the entire query finishes. The same holds true for the join stage processors. As soon as they finish joining the rows for the first query, they hand off their results to the sort stage processors and immediately begin joining the next set of rows that are being sent to them by the scan processors. As described earlier, think of it as a common automobile manufacturing assembly line. All workers on the line are always busy, working on different stages of the various cars that are progressing through the line.

Each minute the sort stage receives a new set of rows to sort, and at the end of each minute it completes the sort and hands the query results back to the user. After a period of 12 minutes, it has completed 12 queries (see Figure 8.9). Given that the sequential processing originally took 12 minutes, using parallel queries we now have 12 times the throughput. Each query runs four times faster, and overall system throughput is increased by a factor of 12.

The above description of the use of parallel queries applies directly to SMP hardware architectures. As described earlier, that architecture is known as a shared-everything hardware architecture because all hardware components (such as memory and disks) are physically shared by all the processors. This sharing makes it easier to divide the workload of a parallel query among multiple

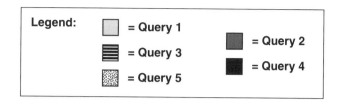

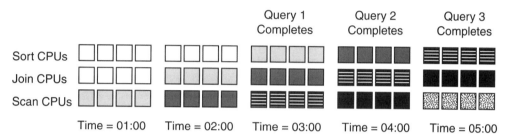

FIGURE 8.9

Parallel query execution.

processors because each processor can directly query the data residing on any disk drive.

We also previously discussed that some non-SMP architectures (including some vendors' cluster, MPP, and NUMA platforms) fall into a second category known as shared-disk hardware architectures. On these solutions, even though there are physically separate pools of memory, all the disks are shared equally among all the nodes. Since any node can still directly access any piece of data residing on any disk by simply directly issuing an I/O request to that disk, the above description of parallel queries also directly applies to these shared-disk hardware architectures.

However, most clusters and MPP implementations fall into the category we previously called shared-nothing hardware architectures. Since processors on one node cannot directly access data that resides on disks connected to another node, the above description of parallel queries doesn't apply directly. Although the main concepts of parallel queries don't change in a shared-nothing hardware architecture (i.e., functional parallelism, partitioning, and pipelining are still alive and well), there are new performance considerations to take into account, because accessing data on a remote node involves more overhead in the form of message passing across the interconnect.

Shared-Disk and Shared-Nothing Database Architectures

At the database level, database vendors have created two different architectures targeted toward addressing the issues that appear in shared-nothing hardware designs. The first approach is referred to as a "shared-disk database architecture," the other is a "shared-nothing database architecture." (Note that we're referring to these as shared-disk or shared-nothing *database* architectures, as opposed to the shared-disk or shared-nothing *hardware* architectures we discussed earlier.) Both database architectures have their relative strengths and weaknesses, in both theory and reality. It is important to understand which issues are important and which are not. Also, it's important to keep in mind that we're now talking about the architecture of the database servers, not the hardware. As we'll see, both the shared-disk and shared-nothing database architectures can (and do) run on shared-nothing hardware architectures.

SHARED-DISK DATABASE ARCHITECTURES   Briefly a shared-disk database architecture means that at a conceptual level, any processor is allowed to query data residing anywhere in the entire database. If a set of rows needed by a processor happens to be on remote disks, then the appropriate message passing will automatically occur behind the scenes to send all the rows back to the original processor for local querying. This process of sending all the rows back to the requesting processor is called "data shipping." With this architecture, the DBMS has no notion of a certain node "owning" a certain set of disks—it views all the disks as logically shared, even though they are not physically shared. The "behind the scenes" message passing is responsible for allowing the database to treat all the disks as accessible to all processors.

The theoretical advantage of this database architecture is increased flexibility regarding how your system's resources are used. This is because the database management system can dynamically choose not only how many processors and how many nodes will be involved in executing a query, but it can also choose which processors and which nodes will be used. This improves your ability to perform load balancing. The theoretical drawback, however, is that this flexibility incurs additional communication overhead between nodes due to data shipping (that is, because many rows may need to be sent across the interconnect as messages).

If you are already familiar with shared-disk database architectures, you may have heard about (or have had direct experience with) the phenomenon known as *pinging,* which is unique to shared-disk architectures. Pinging refers to the process that occurs when a node needs to access a data block that is currently being modified by another node. In this scenario, the node that currently holds the data block must give up the block to allow the other node to read it (or modify it). The first node is required to give up the block to ensure that only one version of the block exists within the DBMS. If one node were allowed to read (or modify) a block while another node was making changes to a different copy of that block, significant data integrity issues could arise. (Different queries may end up looking at different versions of the same piece of data, which would obviously create problems.) By ensuring that only one version of the block exists if that block is being modified, the data integrity problem is solved.

Unfortunately, pinging can create performance problems when users on different nodes want to update the same data block. There will be high levels of contention between the nodes for that block, and performance usually suffers. However, note that we stated that pinging only occurs when data is being modified. In a typical data warehouse environment, the data is generally read-only. Since nodes will be accessing the data blocks in a read-only manner, each node is allowed to cache its own local copy of the block. Since the database management system recognizes that the block is not being modified by anyone, it will allow multiple copies to exist in the DBMS, and it will be assured that all the copies will be identical to each other. What does this mean to you? If you have a typical data warehouse environment where the amount of data modification is low, then you don't have to be concerned with pinging. In fact, we only mention it here to remove the misconception that pinging can create performance issues within your data warehouse platform.

SHARED-NOTHING DATABASE ARCHITECTURES   In contrast, a shared-nothing database architecture focuses on minimizing the message passing overhead by dividing each table into "partitions" based on some partition key that you choose, assigning each partition to a different node. For example, if you have four nodes, a trivial partitioning scheme for your customer table could use the customer's last name as the partitioning key, assigning names in the range A–F to node 1, G–L to node 2, M–S to node 3, and T–Z to node 4. In essence, each node exclusively "owns" a partition of each table. If a processor needs to query rows that reside on a remote node, the database does not send the rows back to the original processor for local processing. Rather, via a process known as "function shipping," it sends the query to the remote node, processes it there, and then returns the query results back to the original processor.

The theoretical advantage is reduced internode communications overhead (and therefore more efficient use of interconnect bandwidth), because rather than sending all the rows across the interconnect network, you just send the query itself, and you only get back the results of the query (rather than each row that was queried). However, there are a few theoretical drawbacks as well. The first drawback is simply reduced flexibility, because a query that involves a particular database partition can only be processed by the CPUs of the node that owns that partition.

The second drawback involves two by-products of the strategy of partitioning the database tables and highlights the critical importance of choosing a good partition key. The first by-product is that queries that do not query against a table's partition key must be sent to every node that manages a partition of that table. In contrast, if a query does involve the partition key, then it is possible for the database management system to send the query to only those nodes that manage the data being requested. For example, if you partition your customer table based on the customer's last name, to find John Smith you only need to involve the node that has "S" within its partition. But if you want to look up a customer based on his or her social security number, then the database management system has no way of quickly determining which node has that social security number, and the query must be broadcast to each node that might have the data. The downside of this is that you incur additional overhead broadcasting the query to multiple nodes.

The second by-product is that response times for queries are very sensitive to data skew. Data skew occurs when a poor partition key is chosen, leading to one partition having a disproportionate amount of data. An example of this would be to partition a sales table by month if you sell products that have most of their sales during the Christmas season. The result would be that nearly all of the data would end up in the December partition and very little data would be in any other partition. This is problematic if you need to perform a table scan because a table scan requires each node to search its own partition—the query will not complete until all nodes are done scanning their partition of the table. If one node has a disproportionate amount of data due to a poor choice of a partition key, that node will slow down the query because it is not possible for the other nodes to help off-load some of the scanning work.

WHAT'S REALLY IMPORTANT   Previously we very carefully used the term "theoretical" when referring to the advantages and drawbacks of the shared-disk and shared-nothing database architectures. How much should you believe the theories about these architectures and how well they should run data warehousing applications? Can you make your product choices based solely on these theories? No—it would be a mistake to do so. Although understanding the theoretical pros and cons of these two architectures is critical to understanding whatever architecture you choose, in reality the actual quality of a database vendor's implementation is much more important than its architecture. This will likely be true for many more years until the products become fully mature.

For example, the quality of a vendor's query optimizer often has a far greater affect on performance than any of the pros and cons mentioned previously. In another example, one database vendor's code path to perform a certain operation might be 50% of the length of one of its competitors. For this operation, the first vendor has an enormous advantage over the competitor, regardless of the architecture. In these and many other cases, the differences in how well the vendor's developers wrote various parts of their products are the true determining factors of performance. This is the issue on which you should focus. Although this might sound like heresy, architecture is currently only a secondary consideration.

So how can you determine which database products are built better in the areas where it matters most to you? Industry standard benchmarks are of only limited use, since they are highly specified and highly controlled. The only way to really know is to test your own data warehouse application. The larger the test, the more you will learn, because larger tests will put more stress on the system, highlighting its strengths and exposing its weaknesses.

OTHER PARTS OF THE PERFORMANCE CHAIN

Earlier in this chapter we noted that a system must be viewed as a set of components that are linked together in a chain. Also, we noted that to have a system that delivers high performance overall, each component in this chain must deliver high performance and must be scalable to handle rapid increases in user populations, amounts of data, application complexity, and application functionality. We've already discussed two major components in the chain, the hardware and the database. These are the components that manage and maintain the data. However, there are clearly more components to the data warehouse platform than just the hardware and the database. In this section we'll look at two additional components: the extract, transform, load component and the end-user access tools component. We'll then finish this section with a discussion of a new class of tools, known as scalable application frameworks, which essentially allow you to take any otherwise nonscalable software component in your data warehouse platform and make it scalable.

The Extract/Transform/Load Component

We know that data warehouses must be able to handle rapidly growing amounts of data. But where does that data come from? Predominantly the data sources consist of your internal operational systems as well as some external sources (such as demographic data that has been purchased). If data warehouse environments grew solely due to the continual stream of data coming in from a fixed set of data sources, then the tools and routines that were responsible for extracting the data, transforming it and consolidating it, and then loading it into the database would not need to be scalable. But these tools and routines absolutely must be scalable, because the data sources for a data warehouse are never fixed. As data warehouse environments mature, they begin to bring in data from an ever-expanding set of sources. Initially the data warehouse might only include data coming from the sales and marketing operational systems, enabling users to understand which types of customers buy certain products. Then a few months later, users might want to include externally purchased demographic data to add to their customer profiles, thereby enhancing their understanding of their customers' purchasing patterns. Later still, users might want to begin including information from their accounts receivable operational system to enable users to determine not just who buys which products, but who pays for them on time if the products were purchased with credit.

For an extract, transform, load tool to be scalable, it must be able to take advantage of one or more of the various types of parallelism. The earliest tools did not meet this criteria. For example, assume the data source was a data file residing on a mainframe. The first (nonscalable) tools would create a single routine to read the raw data in that file, transform the data following the user-defined transformation rules, and then hand off the transformed data to be loaded into the data warehouse. Clearly this routine can quickly become a bottleneck, and if it does you will be unable to feed your data warehouse platform the data it requires within the time frames required. Ultimately this means your data warehouse environment will no longer be able to scale to meet your needs.

In contrast, scalable extract, transform, load tools make effective use of the various parallel techniques of functional parallelism, data parallelism/partitioning, and pipelining to ensure that this component of your data warehouse platform will not become a bottleneck. Instead of using a single routine to extract the raw data from the source data file, the extract routine is usually replicated, and each replicated copy works on a different partition of the source data file. In addition, the transformation routine is also replicated, to allow the multiple data streams coming from the extraction routines to be processed simultaneously. Finally, database vendors now supply parallel loading tools, to allow multiple data files to be loaded into the database in parallel. So each file that is output by the transformation routines can be loaded into the database simultaneously (see Figure 8.10).

Another characteristic of a scalable extract, transform, load tool is its ability to distribute the workload across different computers. This gives you the ability to better balance the workload across your entire data warehouse platform and allows you to take advantage of whatever processing power is available. For example,

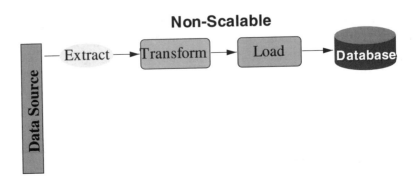

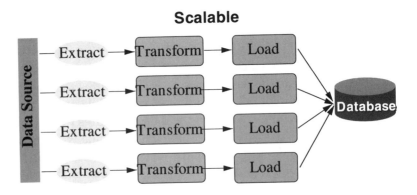

FIGURE 8.10

Scalable versus nonscalable extract, load, transform processes.

if the extraction and transformation routines were required to run on the machine that contains the source data, then you might hit the performance limitations of that machine, particularly if it's not scalable. (For example, if the source machine is uniprocessor, then executing multiple copies of the extraction and transformation routines will not improve scalability. Rather than having each routine truly run simultaneously on different CPUs, each routine will instead have to share the horsepower of a single CPU. Your performance will therefore be no better than having a single copy of the routine, and will likely be worse because of the additional overhead involved in coordinating the multiple routines.) But if a scalable platform exists elsewhere in your environment, then the ability to distribute the workload to a different machine (or even to multiple machines) means that your extract/transform/load routines can take advantage of the additional processing power, resulting in a much more scalable platform.

End-User Access Tools

End-user access tools must also be savvy of scalability issues to ensure that your data warehouse environment will truly scale. The first issue involves the queries that these tools submit to the data warehouse platform. If database query optimizers were perfect, then there really wouldn't be much to say about this topic. The tools would just submit a properly formed query and the optimizer would choose the optimal way to parallelize and process the query. However, we all know that query optimizers aren't perfect, which is why there is a lucrative market for talented application developers who know how to tune data warehouse queries for performance. To complicate matters further, different databases have different parallel query capabilities and require different tuning techniques. While it is true that adequate performance can be achieved by simply sending "generic" SQL queries to any of the databases, better performance can be achieved if the tool is aware of the specific capabilities of the database underlying the data warehouse platform, and if it can use this awareness to tailor the query accordingly.

The second scalability issue concerns those end-user access tools that are multitiered, meaning that not only is there the client portion of the tool that runs on the end-user's desktop machine, but there is also some additional component (usually some type of application server) that runs on a separate machine. The functionality supported by these server components completely depends on the end-user tool, but some common types of functionality include caching precalculated query results or supporting complex manipulations of the data (such as multidimensional analysis). The notion is that it is inefficient to support this advanced functionality on each of the client machines because it would require each end user to purchase a large, powerful computer (often called a fat client). Instead, it is often more sensible to support only the minimal functionality necessary on the client machine so the end users can purchase smaller and cheaper desktop computers (often called thin clients), and to put the advanced functionality on a server that is shared by multiple users. However, this means we have just added another shared component to our performance chain, and, therefore, it too must be scalable. Therefore, just like the database server, the application server must use the basic concepts of parallelism to allow it to take advantage of scalable hardware.

Scalable Application Frameworks

Up to this point, we've been talking about making sure that the various components used at any point in the entire data warehouse performance chain are all scalable. However, what happens when you have some legacy components that you still want to use in your new data warehouse environment, but which were built a long time ago and weren't originally designed to be scalable? For example, you may have very large and very complex batch processing programs written in COBOL that contain critical data manipulation routines. In many cases, due to their complexity, rewriting these programs (in order to make them more scalable) may be a very expensive proposition. In other cases, any individual legacy program may not be very complex, but there may be hundreds of these programs that were developed over time, and each one would have to be rewritten. Again, the time and the resources needed to rewrite all these programs might be prohibitive.

A similar issue can arise even if we don't have legacy applications, but we want to use off-the-shelf applications that simply weren't written to take advantage of scalable hardware solutions, and therefore cannot scale in their generic form. Or, there may be cases where your data warehouse environment will need some custom code, forcing you to write scalable/parallel applications (which may require that your developers become trained in how to write scalable/parallel programs).

Until recently, organizations that found themselves in this situation had very few alternatives, if any. But, fortunately, a clever new class of tools is now available that can help solve the problem. Rather than forcing you to rewrite legacy programs, or live with nonscalable off-the-shelf programs, or write parallel programs from scratch, these frameworks can take nonscalable programs and by leveraging the concepts of replication and data parallelism, allow these routines to be run in parallel.

First, these frameworks create multiple copies (known as replicated copies) of the routine and assign them to run on separate processors. Then, they make heavy use of data parallelism/partitioning techniques and divide up the data so that each of the replicated copies only has to work on a portion of the data. In essence, what these frameworks do for you is automatically create the scenario depicted in Figure 8.10. In the example shown, rather than having to rewrite the extract, transform, and load routines to be able to run in parallel, these frameworks automatically will create multiple copies of each routine (four replicated copies are created in this case), run the copies on different processors, and then divide up the input data into four streams so that each replicated copy only gets one-quarter of the overall data.

These frameworks aren't quite that simple, however. In fact, quite a bit of magic needs to occur behind the scenes to ensure that everything works as intended. In particular, automatically dividing up the data is not trivial. If your nonscalable routine expects to open a file, read the data from beginning to end (processing it as it goes), and then write out the results into a single file, what happens when you now have four copies doing this? These frameworks work their magic by "fooling" the routines. When the routine issues an I/O request to open a file and start reading from the beginning of the file, the framework catches that request and determines what to do with it. In the example in Figure 8.10, if the request is coming from the third replicated copy of the extract routine, then the runtime components of these frameworks will automatically and transparently start returning data from the third partition of the original data file, rather than from the beginning of the file. The original routine simply thinks it is reading from the beginning of the file. And, when it reads the last piece of data from the third partition, the framework will automatically return an end-of-file message to the routine, making the routine think it has finished reading the entire file. Even more complexities exist with the creation of output files (that is, we might be expecting one sorted output file, not four smaller files), but these scalable application frameworks are sophisticated enough to ensure that the right things occur.

In essence, these frameworks make it far easier to ensure that all your application components will be scalable. They can be used to make legacy or off-the-shelf applications highly scalable with little or no modification required, and they can remove the burden on the application developers to have to write parallel code. They can help save time and money when building a high-performance scalable data warehouse.

SUMMARY

When we consider the entire process of data warehousing, we realize that not only must the hardware and database server be scalable, but, in fact, each component in the process must be scalable. If any component or any part of the process is not scalable, your data warehouse platform will eventually hit bottlenecks whenever the bandwidth limit of the least scalable component or process is reached. Therefore it is imperative that each component be analyzed, not just to ensure that it meets your functionality and performance requirements today, but to ensure that it is scalable enough to meet your needs in the future. It is this scalability that enables you to maintain the required performance levels even in the face of rapid and unpredictable growth of your data warehouse environment. In the next chapter we discuss how to combine and apply these components in arriving at a high-performance data warehouse platform.

9

Building a High-Performance Platform

In the last chapter, we introduced the notion of the performance chain for the data warehouse platform and discussed the various components that can be used to make the performance chain scalable. In addition, we discussed how each part of the chain has to be scalable in order to maintain the required performance levels as the data warehouse environment inevitably grows over time. If any single link in the chain isn't scalable, or if any single step in the entire data warehousing process isn't scalable, then the environment as a whole is not scalable. This means that although you may not notice it at first, a nonscalable component means there is a bottleneck lurking in your platform, and it is only a matter of time before it becomes the cause of significant performance problems.

But having the right scalable components is only one of the issues that must be addressed when building a high-performance data warehouse platform. The technologies do not by themselves represent a solution—they are merely underlying infrastructure. And like any set of technologies, they can be used well or used inefficiently. Therefore, another issue is the techniques with which these technologies are integrated. These techniques must focus on leveraging the components to give you a data warehouse platform that is capable of meeting performance and functionality needs, even for the largest, most complex, and most rapidly growing data warehouse environments. It is only when scalable technologies (i.e., components) are used with the appropriate implementation techniques that you can achieve a scalable data warehouse platform. Using one without the other will not give you the high-performance, scalable data warehouse solution you need.

In reality, the technologies are the easy part of the solution. Why? Because these components are readily available, and you can buy them by simply writing a check to your chosen vendor. But, you can't buy a data warehouse platform. It would be wonderful if you could go to your favorite vendor and buy the data warehouse platform of your dreams, but that notion is nonsense. A data warehouse platform is something that you have to build yourself. And that is why the techniques with which you architect your data warehouse platform and integrate the scalable components into that architecture are so critically important. This chapter will therefore focus on the various techniques for building a high-performance data warehouse platform.

The key to success in building a high-performance, scalable data warehouse platform is to begin with a scalable architecture. If a poor architecture is in place, then your solution will hit limitations early in its life cycle. Thus in this chapter we first focus on a system architecture that allows the largest degree of performance and scalability for large and rapidly growing data warehouse platform. Once we define the issues from an architectural level, we then discuss how to assemble a high-performance and highly scalable hardware, database, and disk I/O environment within that architecture.

SYSTEM ARCHITECTURE

The system architecture is the overall blueprint that you will follow when building your data warehouse platform. It is the underlying foundation that governs many of the decisions you will need to make when building and managing your data warehouse platform. Given this, it is no surprise that there are probably as many different data warehouse architectures as there are data warehouses. However, they can usually be grouped into one of two main categories: a three-tiered architecture or a two-tiered architecture.

Three-Tiered Architectures

In a three-tiered design, the first tier is comprised of your operational systems that are already in place. These are the transaction processing systems that collect the data about all the events that occur within your company. The data collected by these systems is fed into your data warehouse. The second and third tiers of this architecture are the data warehouse and the data marts, respectively (see Figure 9.1.)

Why do we recommend separating the data warehouse and the data marts into different tiers instead of combining them both into the second tier? Because there are two different types of functions that must be addressed when building a large-scale data warehouse environment: data consolidation (i.e., getting data in) and data analysis (i.e., getting information out).

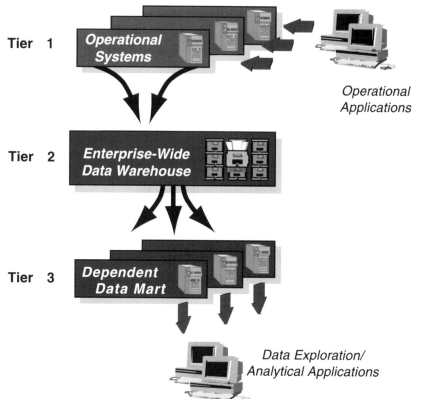

FIGURE 9.1
Three-tiered data warehouse architecture.

Data consolidation refers to the process of extracting, cleaning, and transforming the data from disparate, unconsolidated operational systems into one consolidated repository. Data analysis refers to the process of having end-users access, manipulate, and generally analyze the data looking for useful insights. With two different needs, it is much more scalable to split those functions into two different tiers. In essence, we're using a form of functional parallelism here to improve scalability. We're assigning different tasks to different computers. Also, it is simply easier to address these different needs if we have one tier focused on optimally solving data consolidation issues and another tier focused on optimally solving data exploration issues.

With a three-tier architecture, the data warehouse tier is responsible for the consolidation activities. Its goal is to take data from the operational systems, consolidate it, and then feed portions of the consolidated data to the various data marts that are responsible for the exploration activities. Since these data marts get their data from the data warehouse, we refer to them as "dependent data marts"—they are dependent on the existence of an enterprise data warehouse.

Highlighting the differences between data warehouses and data marts, the data warehouse is fed by multiple operational systems (with additional externally purchased data occasionally included as well), so it must therefore perform the required extractions and transformations. The data marts, on the other hand, only need to extract data from a single source that is already consolidated, the data warehouse. The marts will also occasionally include additional external data, but the amount of consolidation that must be performed is still far less than for the data warehouse.

Also, the data warehouse needs to store its information in a form that is "application generic," since it will be feeding multiple data marts, each of which is focused on a different set of business problems. As a data warehouse designer, you therefore want to keep the data stored in the data warehouse tier in its most flexible form, which is the unsummarized, detail level form. This means you should design a database schema for the second tier that has much of the flavor of a traditional third-normal form schema. In contrast, data marts need to store their information in a form that is "application specific," tailored to the needs of the explorer or farmer. This means that you will want summarizations, subsets, and/or samples in your data mart that are specific to the particular business unit that is using the data mart.

You also want the data in your data marts to be easily accessible by the end-user community. Traditional third-normal form schemas, though they excel in minimizing data redundancy, are fairly poor models for end users to try to understand and analyze, and are, therefore, usually a poor choice for data marts. Instead, data marts should use dimensional models and star schema designs, which make heavy use of redundancy to make it far easier for end users to navigate their way through large volumes of data without getting lost.

Even the choice of optimal hardware and DBMS is different for the data warehouse and the data marts. The data warehouse tier has to act as a repository for enormous amounts of data that span many different organizations and subject areas. In addition, more data from both existing and new subject areas is constantly being added to the data warehouse. And the data warehouse tier must be able to feed an ever-growing number of application-specific data marts. This means that the data warehouse tier must be an industrial-strength, highly scalable, enterprise-class hardware and DBMS.

The data marts, however, need only focus on a single business problem. To be sure, they will see growth in their particular subject area, because new transactions relating to that subject area are continually being collected from the operational systems, but the magnitude of this growth is far less. Therefore the data mart tier is usually a smaller (though still scalable), department level hardware and DBMS solution. The differences between the requirements of the data warehouse and the data mart tiers are summarized in Table 9.1.

BENEFITS OF A THREE-TIERED ARCHITECTURE The main benefits of a three-tiered data warehouse architecture are high performance and scalability. The high performance comes from the fact that the inclusion of data marts allows us to partition different query workloads across different data marts. This means that users of one data mart will not be affected by the workload levels of users of other data marts. For example, if users of the sales data mart are executing complex, long-running queries that are highly resource intensive, this will have no effect on the performance seen by users of

TABLE 9.1   *Data Warehouse and Data Mart Differences*

	Data Warehouse (Tier 2)	Data Mart (Tier 3)
Data source	Extract from many sources (the operational systems)	Extract from a single source (the warehouse)
Applications focus	Application generic	Application specific
Type of data	Detailed, unsummarized data	Highly summarized data
Schema design	Looks very much like a traditional (i.e., normalized) relational schema	Uses dimensional modeling/star schemas
Platforms	Very large, highly scalable, enterprise-class machines	Smaller (though still scalable) departmental platforms
End users	Data marts are the "end users" of the data warehouse	Departmental workers are the end users

the completely separate finance data mart. The resulting increase in end-user satisfaction levels is enormous. In our experience, end users get frustrated by their own queries slowing down their machine, but nothing infuriates end users more than having someone else in some other department bring a machine that everyone must share to its knees. By separating the workloads into physically separate marts, you can prevent different sets of users from adversely affecting each other.

This architecture is also very scalable. As we stated above, we're assigning extraction and consolidation functions to one tier and end-user query and data analysis functions to another tier. This is nothing more than a straightforward use of the concept of functional parallelism, which we described in the previous chapter as one effective method for improving scalability. Both the second and third tiers can be individually scaled up as well. Since the data warehouse tier is a large and highly scalable, it can be scaled up by adding more resources to it (such as processors, disks, I/O controllers, and so on). Scaling up the data-mart tier is done by simply adding more data marts to service new user populations, address new subject areas, or focus on providing a new type of functionality such as data mining. Since data marts are usually far cheaper to build than data warehouses, it is fairly easy to add another data mart when you need to explore a new business area.

COSTS OF A THREE-TIERED ARCHITECTURE   However, the cost issue raises a much larger issue concerning three-tiered architecture. The main issue is the multisubject, enterprise-wide data warehouse that is at the center of this architecture. To design this data warehouse is a complex process. You must spend time consolidating various subject areas, and this can involve many long meetings (and many long debates) with representatives from various organizations. In addition, there is quite a large time investment involved with building an enterprise-wide data warehouse. Defining what business problems you want to solve, finding where all the data required to solve those problems is located, writing all the required extraction, cleansing, and transformation routines, loading all the data into the database, and then tuning the resulting system is no trivial task. In fact, the average enterprise-wide data warehouse takes about 18 months to build. Finally, the cost of such a system is not trivial, often reaching into the many millions of dollars.

For many organizations, the complexity of the project and the required time and cost investments are prohibitive. And even if they weren't, having the first step in a data warehouse development project be the development of a centralized, enterprise-wide data warehouse is a risky proposition. The dynamic, organic nature of a data warehouse environment means that it doesn't really make sense to build something that large as your very first step. Your organization's needs will likely change by the time you finally deliver your data warehouse. You will have spent a large amount of effort building a wonderful system that helps give answers to questions that are no longer the most important questions that need answering.

Because of these issues, many organizations have dropped the notion of a three-tiered architecture and moved to a simpler two-tiered architecture. We'll first describe the advantages of this approach, but then we'll highlight the serious flaws with this approach. To avoid leaving you with the feeling that there's no approach that doesn't have significant problems, we'll present a simple solution that gives you the performance and scalability advantages of three-tiered architecture, but doesn't incur the initial up-front cost and time investments.

Two-Tiered Architectures

There are two ways to build a two-tiered solution. The first involves just building the enterprise-wide data warehouse without the data marts, and having all the end-users directly access it. With this architecture, you may save some money because you don't have to buy separate data mart hardware to store copies of the data that already exists in the central data warehouse, and you may save some time by not having to build data marts. But data marts are generally not as complicated to build, so the time savings won't be dramatic. Ultimately there are two main problems with this approach. First, you are starting by building the central data warehouse, so the majority of the complexity, time, cost, and risk are still factors. Second, since all departments and all users will be sharing a single database, you lose the ability to separate workloads among different user groups. Since there really aren't many advantages to this version of the two-tiered approach, we won't discuss it further.

The other far more common approach is to build the data marts without building the centralized data warehouse. Since these data marts do not depend on the existence of a consolidated data warehouse, we refer to them as "independent data marts" (see Figure 9.2).

The advantages of building a two-tiered environment using the independent data mart approach are fairly enticing:

❏ The data mart traditionally will only have data pertaining to one or two subject areas, so there is much less complexity involved in the design and implementation of this architecture.

❏ Since you are dealing with fewer data sources and less data, the time required to build a data mart can be on the order of 3 or 4 months, not 18 months.

❏ As we discussed earlier, the hardware required for the data mart, though still scalable, are generally much smaller departmental machines, not enterprise-class machines.

The costs will be far lower as well. Essentially, since few organizations have the multiple millions of dollars and 18 months it takes (on average) to build an enterprise data warehouse all at once, the only option is to be less ambitious and start with a data mart.

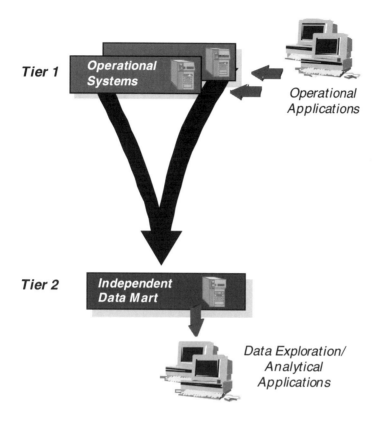

Tier 1

Tier 2

FIGURE 9.2
Two-tiered architecture with independent data marts.

GROWING PAINS WITH TWO-TIERED ARCHITECTURES As compelling as these advantages may seem, there are also some serious potential dangers associated with the independent data mart approach. If you're not careful, independent data marts will inevitably set you up for a fall. Because data marts are indeed useful, everyone in the enterprise ends up wanting access to one. Typically there are two ways to handle this growth in demand. The first solution is to simply add to the existing data mart. If the new users want new subject areas included, just add the new subject areas to the data mart. But this solution never works for long. Almost by definition, independent data marts weren't designed with the enterprise in mind, and they weren't designed for scalability. They can grow a little, but the hardware, DBMS, etc. on which they are built will eventually collapse under their own weight.

The second and more popular solution is to create additional data marts for people in different organizations. If people want access to a different subject area, they can build their own data mart to address their specific needs. From a local viewpoint, this solution works. Each group gets what they need. But from a global enterprise viewpoint, this solution is a disaster. Each data mart performs its own extractions from the operational system, and as the number of data marts proliferates, the combined effect of all the extraction processes puts enormous strain on the operational system's resources, creating bottlenecks and limiting scalability. In addition, each mart takes its own approach to performing data transformations, which means that the data in each mart is not integrated with the data in any other data mart. Each independent data mart becomes its own island of unintegrated information. But this is exactly the problem we were trying to solve in the first place. That is, one of the main reasons for building a data warehouse is to consolidate previously unintegrated data, not to create more of it.

The Solution: Scalable Data Marts

At this point it seems that neither three-tiered nor two-tiered approaches are optimal. Three-tiered architectures give you the required performance and scalability, but they're too complex and costly to be used as a starting point. Two-tiered approaches with independent marts are simpler and less costly and are, therefore, a better starting point, but they ultimately become a mess as your needs grow over time.

Thankfully there is a solution that gives you the best of both worlds. The trick is to take advantage of the benefits of starting with the simpler and less expensive two-tiered environment, but to define an architectural road map that will allow this two-tiered approach to incrementally transform into the more robust three-tiered architecture that will be required when your needs become too much to be efficiently handled with two tiers. We refer to this solution as the scalable data mart approach.

BUILDING SCALABLE DATA MARTS Essentially the key to building scalable data marts is to logically design a three-tiered architecture, but to initially implement it using two tiers. As the data mart grows to encompass more subject areas, you will eventually need to move to a three-tiered architecture where the operational systems feed a large, multisubject, highly integrated data warehouse, which in turn feeds individual subject area data marts (see Figure 9.3).

But how do you define a system that starts off with one architecture and moves to another? This is not a trivial problem, especially because we have seen that data warehouses and data marts have different needs. In the initial two-tiered architecture, should the second tier have a database that's designed to address the needs of the current data mart or should it have a database that's designed to address the needs of the future data warehouse? The answer is yes! In other words, you initially need to have both types of databases on your second tier (the scalable data-mart tier). The first database is a "mini data warehouse" and the second is a dependent data mart.

The mini data warehouse should be thought of as a not-yet-fully-populated enterprise data warehouse. It starts with a single subject area and stores detailed (unsummarized) data in a normalized schema. However, even though it starts with a single subject area, since we know it will grow, it must be architected to scale. This means that you must define a logical data model for this mini

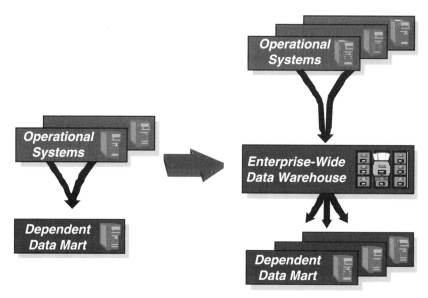

FIGURE 9.3
Starting with two-tiers and moving up to three tiers.

data warehouse that includes not the initial subject area, but any other subject areas that you reasonably think might eventually be added. Only a high-level logical model is needed, which should take no more than three or four weeks of effort to build (any more than that and you're getting into too many of the details, which are likely to change anyway). The goal is to determine what the common threads are throughout the subject areas and make sure that the integration is based on those threads. For example, in the finance industry, a common thread is often the individual account holder. In retail, common threads are individual stores and individual customers. As you add more subject areas to your system, you already have a design that allows these areas to be included without requiring a redesign of previous work.

The second database (the dependent data mart) then performs the equivalent of an extract against the data stored in the mini data warehouse. It summarizes and aggregates the data as necessary and then stores it in the data mart tables. This is all done on a single physical machine (see Figure 9.4). In fact, even though we've been referring to two separate databases on the second tier, in reality, it is often implemented as a single physical database

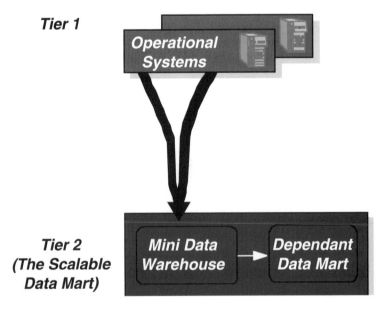

FIGURE 9.4

Scalable data mart architecture.

where certain tables are logically designated as data warehouse tables and others are data mart tables created by "extracting" data from the data warehouse tables.

In effect, the mini data warehouse is really a sort of staging area from which the dependent data mart extracts its data. This is how you achieve a three-tier architecture logically, even though you are physically implementing it on two tiers.

As the number of subject areas grows, the data warehouse component grows, and more data marts can be extracted from it. Since the operational systems all feed one data warehouse, there is no proliferation of multiple extraction processes, so we've solved that scalability problem. Also, all the data in the data warehouse is integrated, so the data marts are all reading from one consistent version of the data.

This design also solves the other scalability problem, that of data marts eventually collapsing under their own weight. It is true that eventually you will exceed the capacity of your hardware, especially since data marts are usually implemented on smaller machines. But this is where logical partitioning of the data warehouse from the data marts pays off. When you reach your machine's limits, you can leave the data mart where it is but move the data warehouse to a larger, more scalable machine. The system now has the standard three-tiered architecture shown in Figure 9.1. By doing so, your solution now becomes much more scalable. And since you've always logically treated the data warehouse as a separate entity, physically moving it to another machine is not a difficult exercise.

For those organizations where the cost and complexity of starting with a three-tiered architecture is prohibitive (which is usually the case with most organizations), scalable data marts are the right starting place. They allow you to start small and deliver initial functionality quickly, but they also give you a clear path to get to the three-tiered architecture that will ultimately be required for a large, high-performance, scalable data warehouse environment.

With an architecture in place, you can now start building your data warehouse platform. This means you need to assemble the hardware components, design the database, and lay out the data on your disks. The rest of this chapter discusses these phases in order, focusing predominantly on highlighting the relevant performance and scalability issues.

BUILDING A BALANCED HARDWARE SYSTEM

Regardless of whether you start with a three-tiered architecture or a two-tiered architecture that will evolve into three tiers, you will need to deploy your data warehouse and your data marts on scalable hardware. This raises the issue of how to correctly configure your hardware. Also, it's important to realize that hardware configuration for a data warehouse environment is not a one-time exercise; as your enterprise data warehouse and your data marts grow, you will need to scale up the configurations of your hardware to meet the new processing requirements.

Whether your hardware is a large, enterprise-class server being used to store your enterprise data warehouse or a smaller departmental machine being used for data marts, the goal of any scalable system configuration exercise is to build a *balanced system*. A balanced system refers to a system where the throughput and/or processing capabilities of each major hardware component are matched to the capabilities and needs of all the other components. In very simple terms, a balanced system is one where there's enough CPU power to process the data coming from the disk controllers, and where the disk controllers have enough bandwidth capacity to handle the data coming from the disks (see Figure 9.5). If any of these components is underconfigured, then your system is unbalanced and you have a bottleneck in your machine. Referring back to the notion of a performance chain, if there's a bottleneck in your machine, your data warehouse environment will not be able to scale. (Note: You may have noticed that memory is not shown in Figure 9.5. We discuss how memory affects building a balanced system later in this section.)

Aside from the technical reasons for avoiding bottlenecks, an additional goal of a balanced system is the wise spending of your hardware dollars. If you have a system where one of your components is a bottleneck, then some of the money you spent on the other components is wasted. For example, if your disk controllers are a bottleneck, then it's a signal that you spent too much money

FIGURE 9.5

Components' capabilities are matched in a balanced system.

on disks or CPUs and not enough on disk controllers. Even worse, if you then buy additional CPUs, you would be wasting even more money because you would not see any performance gains. The current set of CPUs is already being limited by the bandwidth of the disk controllers.

There are three steps critical to building a balanced high-performance system:

1. Estimate the business requirements.
2. Determine the technology.
3. Iterate.

Let's look at each of these steps in detail.

Estimating the Business Requirements

A basic tenet of system sizing is that the selected configuration provides a technical solution that meets the needs of the business, both now and in the future. Therefore the first step in building a balanced system is determining what the business requirements are for the system. There are four main business requirements (or "business drivers") that will ultimately be used to determine the technical configuration of your system:

❏ Raw data size
❏ Average query complexity
❏ Desired query response time
❏ Number of concurrent queries

RAW DATA SIZE This is the size of the raw data being housed in the RDBMS. It is not the size of the total database, which would include internal RDBMS space (discussed later). Raw data size can usually be estimated by evaluating the data feeds that are expected to create the data warehouse, usually by using the formula "X records × Y bytes per record." The record count and sizes are usually estimates, based on the representation of the data in the legacy system. It is important to take account of the differences in representations between legacy systems and relational databases. It is usually necessary to create a mapping of legacy data types to RDBMS data types and sizes using the documentation of each

RDBMS to find byte counts for each data type. Small errors introduced in this section tend to be multiplicative and can have a large effect on system sizing.

AVERAGE QUERY COMPLEXITY This is a breakdown of the queries into high, medium, and low complexity categories. Typically these are divided by the number of joins performed, nested selects, and any aggregations, such as sort or group by. For example, queries that join four tables, have an embedded subquery, and then perform a group by on the results would typically be considered high complexity. The categorization is somewhat arbitrary, though any experienced DBA will be able to formulate categories that he is comfortable with.

This query categorization factors into other areas of the configuration analysis as well. For example, once you define the categories, you can then estimate desired query response times for high (e.g., extracting and classifying), medium (e.g., profiling), and low (e.g., modeling and multidimensional analysis) complexity queries. A simpler model might just choose to utilize queries of "average" complexity, but these will necessarily ignore worst-case scenarios.

DESIRED QUERY RESPONSE TIME This is an estimate of how long an average query should execute. If a breakdown of queries by category has been done, then each category will have its own desired response time (e.g., high complexity queries in 4–6 hours, medium in 1–2 hours, and low in 20–40 minutes). These are difficult to estimate and are usually arrived at by considering the workload of the business units using the data warehouse, estimating how much they will use the data warehouse in a given day or week, and then working backward to calculate what time frame the queries must complete in. When estimating this, it is important to know when the actual users will be logged in. For example, a data warehouse with users in only one time zone will usually have an 8 to 10 hour peak demand cycle. If the same number of users were located across the United States in four time zones, the same amount of work would have 11 to 14 hours to complete.

NUMBER OF CONCURRENT QUERIES This is the average number of queries that will be executing concurrently. This number is usually estimated by typing the user community and their data access tools, and determining how much work they need to complete in a given day. As an example, if a data warehouse is being used for marketing mailings, and five marketing analysts usually each produce one mailing every week, and each mailing usually requires analysis by querying for 50 different customer segments (each one a separate SQL query), then we can expect about 250 queries per week, or roughly 6 queries per hour. If we estimate our desired query response time at 30 minutes per query, then we can estimate that at any one time there will be an average of three concurrent queries. If we also assume that four marketing managers will be performing ad hoc reporting on the same data warehouse (usually a highly complex, long-running query), it could be estimated that it is necessary to increase this number by one concurrent query. Thus an estimation of the mixed workload would be four concurrent queries.

Determining the Technical Configuration

The estimated business requirements do not directly give you the system configuration. Rather they define requirements that need to be met by any potential configuration. These requirements generally provide the basis for the service management contract (more on this in Chapters 11 and 12). Once these requirements are understood, the next step is to translate these requirements into a physical, balanced system configuration. This involves balancing five major system components:

- ❏ Total disk capacity
- ❏ Disk subsystem throughput
- ❏ Disk controller throughput
- ❏ CPU processing power
- ❏ Memory capacity

TOTAL DISK CAPACITY Total disk capacity is usually defined as the ratio between the raw data size and the total database size. The total database size is always larger than the size of the raw data it contains because it includes the raw data plus things like indexes, system overhead, and the database's internal temporary working areas. These work-in-progress areas are used to execute such SQL statements as joins (especially sort/merge joins), sorts, group bys, and selects using nested subqueries. For large decision support queries, where a subquery may return 50% or more of the total database, the working space needed can be quite large.

However, the database size is not just a function of raw data size. It is also driven by the number of expected concurrent queries, because as mentioned earlier, each query requires its own working space. For example, if three concurrently executing queries have subqueries that each return half of the raw data in the database, then the total database size must be at least 2.5 times the raw size. As a baseline rule of thumb, for most data warehouse applications with only a small amount of denormalization (as might be expected in the enterprise data warehouse tier), the average ratio of database size to raw data size tends toward 3.0 to 3.5. However, if there is a substantial amount of denormalization (as might be found in the potentially highly aggregated data of the data-mart tier), then this ratio could be much higher, with the database easily being 10 or more times the raw data size.

DISK SUBSYSTEM THROUGHPUT   The previous exercise tells you the rough amount of total storage space you need, but it doesn't tell you how many disks you need. For example, if you need 400 gigabytes of disk storage, should you buy 400 one-gigabyte disks, 200 two-gigabyte disks, or 100 four-gigabyte disks? The more disks you have, the higher the I/O throughput you will be able to generate. However, a larger number of smaller disks will also cost you more than a smaller number of larger disks, because smaller disks are less cost effective than larger disks in terms of dollars per gigabyte of storage.

To determine the required amount of throughput involves looking at the business requirements defined earlier. By looking at the amount of data that each query must scan and dividing that by the desired response time for that query, you can determine the I/O throughput required for that query. Next, factor in the number of queries that are executing concurrently and you can estimate the total I/O throughput needed. Finally, divide the total I/O throughput by the average scan rate capabilities of the particular disk drives you are considering to get the actual number of disk drives you will need.

A word about RAID devices is important here. Most RAID systems appear to the hardware platform as one large disk with very high throughput. Clearly this will affect the calculations above, because the definition of a disk becomes a little fuzzy. However, don't let this confuse you. The main point to focus on is disk subsystem throughput, not the number of disks. Since you still know the overall disk throughput you need, you can divide that throughput by the average throughput capabilities of the particular RAID array you are considering to determine the number of arrays you will need.

DISK CONTROLLER THROUGHPUT   To keep the system balanced, the next step is to ensure that you have enough disk controllers to handle the aggregate amount of data coming from the disk I/O subsystem. As a first cut, divide the aggregate I/O bandwidth (calculated above) by the average throughput capabilities of the particular disk controllers you are considering. As a rule of thumb, it is usually wise to increase this number by about 20% to give you headroom to handle any momentary peaks in I/O throughput demands.

CPU PROCESSING POWER   The next step in building your balanced system is determining the number of CPUs that you will need. As a first step, you need to determine how much data an individual processor can process in a given amount of time. Then, because you already know the throughput capabilities of the disk controllers, you can determine how many processors will be needed to handle that throughput.

However, published CPU performance measurements have only limited value. First, many of the published metrics are not really relevant to a data warehousing workload. While most vendors will quote millions of instructions per second (MIPS) for their processors, this is not considered an important measurement for data warehouse operations. The MIPS rating contains many floating point metrics that are not typical of a data warehouse's database instruction mix (although this will change as multimedia and other complex object databases become more commonplace). Instead, most data warehouse operations depend heavily on the ability to compare strings and binary values, which is used in index searching and table scanning. These are integer operations, and the most accepted metric for processor integer operations is SPECint95. Although the SPECint95 rating is more relevant than the MIPS rating for data warehouses, it still is only partially useful. Unfortunately there are still a lot of hidden factors that affect system performance, so comparing SPECint95 ratings between vendors and between different hardware architectures is not very accurate.

However, within a particular platform, the SPECint95 rating can, in fact, be useful. Assuming there are no other bottlenecks on your hardware, the ability of the CPU subsystem to process data will be nearly linearly related to the total SPECint95 rating. So the best approach to determining how many CPUs are needed for your configuration is to run a small test of your system (with one or two processors) to determine the relationship between SPECint95 ratings and data processing throughput for your specific query mix. For example, you might determine that 1 SPECint95 implies an ability to process 2MB per second. Then, configure enough CPUs to give you the total SPECint95 rating that you need for the desired aggregate throughput.

MEMORY CAPACITY   Finally, we turn to memory. This component is a little different from the others, however, because memory doesn't really become a bottleneck. As long as the minimum amount of memory is available to run your database, then any amount of memory beyond that amount has the effect of reducing the workload on the I/O subsystem. The more memory there is to cache data, the less the application will have to generate disk I/Os and the lower the actual throughput requirements will be for the disks and the disk controllers. As a baseline, for most relational databases, count on having at least 500MB of memory to be able to make effective use of caching in an SMP. In MPP environments, you should have at least 250MB per node if the nodes are uniprocessor, and 500MB per node if they're multiprocessor (i.e., SMP) nodes.

Iterate

Following these guidelines, step 2 almost seems too easy, doesn't it? Well, as always, beware of things that seem too easy. In truth, these are generic guidelines, and they lead only to configurations that are balanced for "generic" data warehouse environments. They may not be very suited to your actual workload.

Therefore the previous guidelines should only be used as a starting point for your configuration. After that you will need to iterate on your configuration for a number of reasons. First, you must tailor and tune your system to the demands of your particular data warehouse. For example, does your data warehouse have a large number of indexes? If so, what effect does that have on reducing the disk subsystem bandwidth requirements? How about the increase in total disk capacity that will be needed to store the additional indexes? Do your data warehouse users access the same data frequently? If so, then a database's ability to cache parts of the database in memory will be very effective and will reduce the overall disk subsystem throughput requirements, but only if your memory cache is sufficiently large. If your users have random access patterns to the data, even a large memory cache won't have much effect on the system. Or, how much aggregated data do you have? The more you have, the more disk space it requires, but it will reduce the CPU processing power requirements. Also, depending on the actual access patterns to certain tables, you may want to purchase additional disks and store only a single, frequently accessed table on this set of disks to ensure that the bandwidth available from those disks is entirely dedicated to that one table.

A second reason why you will need to iterate your configuration is that there are complex interactions between all of the system components. That is, changing the capabilities of one component can have an effect on the demands placed on other components. In some cases it may just move the bottleneck to another component, while in others it may decrease the throughput requirements of another component. Earlier we discussed the obvious interaction between memory capacity and disk and disk controller requirements. As you increase memory, the requirements for the other two decrease. Other interactions are not so obvious. For example, the database/raw data ratio also has an effect on the average query response time. If insufficient working space is available, SQL statements will either fail to execute or be blocked from beginning, which will have a detrimental effect on total database throughput. For similar reasons, the amount of available disk space will also effect the number of concurrent queries that can run. Figure 9.6 shows just some of the potential interactions between business requirements and the various components in the technical configuration.

The fact that your data warehouse environment is constantly changing and growing is yet another reason why you will need to iterate your system configuration. As we mentioned earlier, config-

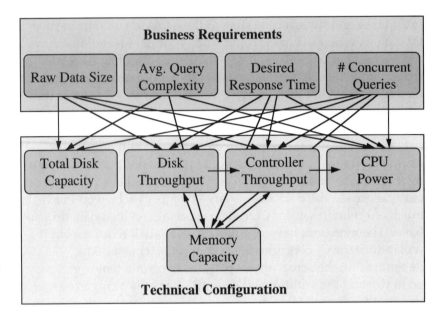

FIGURE 9.6

Business requirements and technical components have complex interactions.

uration is not a one-time exercise but is rather a continuous process that ensures that your system is not only balanced, but that it is capable of meeting the changing needs of your organization. And because we are using scalable technologies, we have a platform where the capabilities of all the major system components can be scaled up dramatically, as dictated by business requirements.

DESIGNING THE PHYSICAL DATABASE FOR PERFORMANCE

With a balanced hardware platform in place, the next step is to focus on the design of the database. In general, as described earlier, in a three-tiered architecture, the data-warehouse tier generally follows a standard (i.e., fairly normalized) database design, while the data mart often uses a star schema database design. But the purpose of this section is not to guide you through either conventional schema design or star schema design. Instead, the focus of this section is on techniques you can use to enhance the performance of either design.

To be effective at this, you need to have an understanding of the type of workload you will be handling. In OLTP systems, the workload is characterized by queries that are highly selective and which usually don't involve complex joins or scanning lots of data. In contrast, data warehouse and data mart queries frequently involve complex joins and large scans through mountains of data, and often these queries have repetitive components. For example, one user might want to look at revenue by sales region. Another user might want to look at product A's sales as a percentage of regional revenue across all regions. Another might want to see a salesperson's performance as a percentage of regional revenue. In each case you are recalculating regional revenue. Each query involves scanning the sales table to group the data by region and summing up the totals for the regions.

Certainly you can use parallelism when scanning and joining tables to improve the response time for these types of queries, and later we discuss how to lay out your data on disk to make optimal use of parallelism when scanning large tables. But it would be far better to avoid having to recalculate the results each time. By understanding the specific queries that users execute, we can determine which parts of their queries are being repeated. Then, rather than recalculating the required values each time a query executes, you can precalculate the values once and store the results, and then use these results over and over. This technique is one form of what is called denormalization.

Denormalizing the Database

From a performance perspective, denormalization delivers two main advantages. First, query response times can be improved by multiple orders of magnitude because large, long-running table scans or complex joins can be replaced with a simple lookup of a precalculated result. Second, as a corollary to the first benefit, use of your system's resources is much more efficient because you can dramatically reduce the amount of work that needs to be done to get the results for a particular query. There are three main denormalization techniques that we will cover: preaggregation, column replication, and prejoin.

PREAGGREGATION Earlier we discussed the problem of having to calculate regional sales revenues multiple times and proposed that it would be better to calculate the regional sales revenues once and then store the results for later use. The general approach of storing the results of an aggregation function (such as summations and averages) for later use is called preaggregation. In the earlier example, as a final step in our data warehouse load procedure, we would execute a query against the newly refreshed sales detail table that would summarize sales by region, and then we would store those results back in the database. Subsequently, if a user wanted those results, a simple lookup is all that's needed rather than having to actually execute the query against the entire sales detail table.

Where are these aggregations stored? Almost always, they are stored in separate tables in the database. This leaves the original table alone, so you won't affect any queries that need to look at the detail table, such as would be the case when a particular query doesn't have a preaggregated result and must therefore scan the detail table. There are some specific cases where the aggregates might be placed back into the original detail table as new rows in that table, but that generally requires adding new columns to the table to identify which rows are detail rows and which rows are aggregate rows. Since there can be multiple types of aggregations (sales by product, sales by store, average sales by quarter, etc.) and multiple levels of roll-up (sales by store, which then rolls up into sales by state, which in turn rolls up into sales by region), there will often be a large number of aggregation tables in your database.

Most relational OLAP (i.e., ROLAP) tools make heavy use of this type of preaggregation. This technique gives users the ability to quickly look at summarizations at multiple different levels and to drill down to the next level of detail easily. And since most of the commonly used results are preaggregated, performance can be excellent with response times for queries that are nearly real time. The question arises, however, regarding how you actually use these aggregate tables. Certainly you can query them directly, but that requires knowledge of which aggregate tables exist. A more elegant solution is to use a decision support tool that is "aggregate aware." With these tools, the user always formulates queries against the detail table and submits the query to the tool. The tool is responsible for knowing which aggregate tables exist and will use some intelligence to automatically rewrite the query to take advantage of aggregate tables where appropriate. This means that an administrator can add or remove aggregate tables as needed without affecting how the users interact with the system.

As described so far, preaggregation is a fairly simple process of taking a simple aggregation of a column. However, there is no reason why our aggregations can't be much more complex than this; that is, we can perform an arbitrarily complex calculation against any number of rows (and can include multiple columns from each row in the calculation) and store that result. In fact, we can even perform such a calculation on individual rows. For example, a bank will typically look at multiple attributes of an individual customer to calculate their credit rating, and it might want to use this calculated credit rating in a number of analyses. Information on each bank customer can be extracted from the database via a query, a credit scoring routine can then be run to calculate the credit rating of that customer, and the result can be stored for later use. In this case, for convenience it is probably best to add a "Credit_Rating" column to the customer table rather than storing these calculated results in a separate table, because this separate table would have just as many rows as the original table (each table would have one row for each customer).

Some purists might claim that this credit scoring example is not truly preaggregation because you're not actually aggregating multiple rows into a single value. Honestly, it doesn't matter what you call it, but it is clearly an example of calculating a result and then storing it for later use, and it certainly is a form of denormalization (because it is a value that is derived from other values in the database).

COLUMN REPLICATION   We mentioned earlier that denormalization is useful when users execute the same query (or the same portion of a query) repeatedly. If the query action that is being repeated is an aggregation function, then preaggregation can greatly improve performance. But what about the cases where users are repeatedly executing the same join? In these cases, column replication can often give you the same order of magnitude performance improvements that we saw with preaggregation.

Assume you have a table called Sales and a table called Customer, as shown in Figure 9.7. Also, assume that the data warehouse users frequently run queries and reports that are focused on the actions of individual customers (such as how much a customer spends per order, how much a customer spends per year, how

Sales Table

Store_ID	Prod_ID	Cust_ID	Date	Qty	Unit_Price
279	405723	4983	11/26/97	3	$45.77
404	649825	2933	11/26/97	4	$22.29
863	964267	4983	11/26/97	2	$ 7.68
279	583794	9341	11/27/97	9	$99.62
863	723450	2933	11/27/97	3	$26.61
863	556968	5372	11/27/97	9	$72.88

Customer Table

Cust_ID	Cust_Name	Cust_Addr
2993	Runner's Paradise	122 Main St.
4357	Athlete's Universe	129 Chestnut Rd.
4983	ProSport	147 22nd St.
5372	Sports 'n More	7 Davis St.
6323	The Winner's Edge	1233 Saw Mill Rd.
9341	The Finish Line	1688 Seaview Ln.

FIGURE 9.7

Sales and customer tables before column replication.

often a customer places an order, etc.). To make these reports more readable, users always want to see customer names instead of customer IDs. To do this requires a join between the Sales and Customer tables, using the Cust_ID column as the join key.

Since these reports are run frequently, the join on the Cust_ID column to retrieve the customer name is executed over and over. If the Sales and Customer tables are large, this join can consume a very large amount of computing resources. However, there is a more efficient way to approach this problem. Rather than forcing a join to be executed each time, simply replicate the Cust_name column of the Customer table directly into the Sales table, as shown in Figure 9.8. This solution means that the expensive join is no longer necessary. Not only is query performance dramatically improved, but your system's resources are being used more efficiently, which means the system will be able to handle a larger workload, thereby increasing the overall scalability of your data warehouse.

PREJOIN The third common form of denormalization is a prejoin. In reality a prejoin is nearly identical to the column replication technique, except rather than copying a single column from the second table (that is, the table where the join key is the primary key), all the columns of the second table are replicated. In other words, the two tables are joined using the specified join key and the results of the join are stored as a permanent table. Then, whenever a user wants to execute a query that would normally have required a join on these two tables, they can instead run the query against the prejoined, denormalized table. Scanning this single table will be many times faster than performing a join on the two original tables.

COSTS OF DENORMALIZING DATA Clearly the advantage of denormalization stems from the fact that it reduces the amount of work that needs to be done to get the information that the users request. And because the amount of work is reduced, response times are greatly improved and system resources are used more efficiently. But as might be expected, there are issues regarding denormalization. Denormalization isn't free. There are multiple costs associated with any denormalization technique.

Sales Table

Store_ID	Prod_ID	Cust_ID	Cust_Name	Date	Qty	Unit_Price
279	405723	4983	ProSport	11/26/97	3	$45.77
404	649825	2933	Runner's Paradise	11/26/97	4	$22.29
863	964267	4983	ProSport	11/26/97	2	$7.68
279	583794	9341	The Finish Line	11/27/97	9	$99.62
863	723450	2933	Runner's Paradise	11/27/97	3	$26.61
863	556968	5372	Sports 'n More	11/27/97	9	$72.88

FIGURE 9.8

Using column replication in the Sales table.

Increased Disk Storage Denormalization also increases the amount of disk storage your data warehouse requires. In the case of preaggregation, there are significant disk costs associated with storing large numbers of aggregations. Depending on how much preaggregation you want to perform, the space required for storing the aggregations can be many times larger than the space required to store the original detail information. Column replication (and therefore prejoins) also increases disk storage requirements because each of the values from the replicated column usually appears multiple times in the table to which the replicated column is added. In Figure 9.8, notice that "ProSport" and "Runner's Paradise" each appear more than once. Even worse, as you can see from this example, the replicated data is often textual rather than numeric, and storing a text string takes more disk space than storing a number. Storing aggregates and using column replication and prejoin techniques improves query performance, but means you'll have to spend more on disks to achieve that performance improvement.

CPU Cycles The denormalization techniques we discussed all require CPU resources. You pay a certain price (in CPU cycles) up front with the hopes that you will save far more CPU cycles when users execute their queries. If the amount of denormalization is large, this up-front cost can be quite large. Also, it is possible to denormalize your data so much that the CPU cycles it takes to perform all the preaggregations, column replications, and prejoins is greater than the amount of CPU cycles that are saved when processing users' queries. How can this happen? If you spend resources denormalizing data that is either never or hardly ever used, you will not be efficiently using your system's resources. For example, it is very common for people to want to create large numbers of preaggregated tables in an effort to try to speed up any query that a user might want to execute. However, in reality, only a small percentage of these queries are actually ever executed, so the resources spent denormalizing the data are wasted.

Increased Refresh Cycle Time Requirements Denormalization also increases the time required to complete your data warehouse refresh cycle. Not only must you load the detail data, but you must now also denormalize the data as part of the refresh cycle. Data warehouse usage is held up while users wait for the refresh cycle to complete, and there is certainly a cost associated with this delay.

Decreased Performance for Some Queries Column replication and prejoins have an unfortunate side effect, which is that while they might speed up some queries, they can actually slow down others. In the column replication example shown previously, we increased the performance of any query that would otherwise have had to perform a join between the Sales and Customer table to retrieve the customer's name. However, what about all the queries that just want to scan the Sales table? The Sales table has now become wider and therefore larger (and in the case of a full prejoin, it can become significantly larger), which means that it will take longer to perform a table scan on the Sales table. So it speeds up some queries and slows down others. We always have the option of keeping the original table around as well as the new version of the table that includes the replicated column(s), but this further increases the disk storage requirements.

Determining What to Denormalize Given that denormalization has various costs associated with it, how do you determine what to denormalize? We've seen that denormalizing everything you can think of is extremely costly and wasteful. To make intelligent decisions about what should be denormalized and what should not, you need to have a good understanding of how your data warehouse is being used. You need to know what aggregates are frequently requested in order to know what preaggregations to perform. Also, you need to know what joins are frequently executed in order to determine where you might want to use column replication of prejoins. And you'll also need to know what table scans are frequently executed to understand which queries might be adversely affected by column replication or prejoins.

There are tools on the market to help you collect this information. Some of the end-user client OLAP tools will watch what queries users are executing and will automatically make suggestions to the database administrator about what data should be denormalized. Other tools take the approach of being on the server side and monitor all the queries that are sent to the database. These tools can then generate sophisticated statistics regarding how often each query is executed, average execution times, average amount of data returned, which users are executing which queries, and so on. These tools make it much easier to gain a solid understanding of what should be denormalized and what should not (see Chapter 7 for a more detailed discussion of monitors and performance).

Wise use of denormalization will increase the performance of your data warehouse (and data mart) on a per query basis. In addition, denormalization will also make your data warehouse more scalable because intelligent denormalization reduces the overall workload on the system, so more users or more data can be supported with the same amount of computing resources.

Indexing Your Data

Techniques for reducing the amount of work that needs to be performed to execute a query are not limited to denormalization. The standard technique of indexing is also another way to achieve the same result. By intelligently indexing data in your data warehouse, you can increase both the performance and scalability of your data warehouse solution.

B-TREE INDEXES   The most common type of indexing technique is the B-tree index. The principle is straightforward. Rather than scanning an entire table to find rows where a certain column satisfies a WHERE clause predicate, you instead create a separate index structure on that column. This index structure contains a sorted list of all the actual discrete column values, and each value in the index is associated with a list of pointers to the rows in the original table that contain that value. To allow the database engine to quickly find any element in the sorted index list, the index is stored internally using a binary tree (or B-Tree) representation.

When a query is executed on that table, the database engine's query optimizer first determines whether or not to use the index (more on that later). If the database chooses to use the index, the database engine

❑ Traverses the B-tree to find the appropriate key(s) in the index list

❑ Collects the associated list of pointers to the row(s) in the table

❑ Uses those pointers to immediately hone in on those disk blocks that contain the rows we want

Using indexes, a full table scan can be replaced by a quick read of the index followed by a read of only those disk blocks that contain the rows needed. In an optimal situation, the cost savings can be quite large, greatly improving the performance and scalability of your data warehouse.

Costs of Using B-Tree Indexes However, indexes are not a panacea and must be used intelligently. In an OLTP environment, administrators realize that indexes can be costly because modifying the value of the column that is indexed (either via an update, or by inserting or deleting a row) requires not only modifying the row, but also modifying the index to keep the index synchronized with the table. So adding many indexes usually has the effect of slowing down the OLTP performance of your application. However, in a data warehouse, aside from the refresh cycle, the database is generally not modified. So the (incorrect) conclusion is that you might as well index everything. However, as with denormalization, indexing isn't free. In fact, the costs are almost identical. Indexing requires increased disk storage, requires valuable CPU cycles, increases the refresh cycle time requirements, and as we'll see, can even decrease performance for some queries.

Regarding the space issues, it is obviously a poor choice to create an index that won't be used. Generally indexes with low selectivity will rarely or never get used, because the query optimizer will determine that it will always be faster to perform a full table scan than to access the index.

To understand this, let's look at an example. Assume you are a retail company, and your Customer table holds various types of information about individual customers, including a column labeled Gender. Also assume that a customer record is about 200 bytes, and that the disk block size is 32K (meaning that the smallest amount of data we can read from a disk drive is 32K). Finally, assume that 50% of our customers are male, and that we have 10 million customers total. This means that our table takes up roughly 61,035 disk blocks (200 bytes per row × 10 million records/32K per disk block). If we create an index for the Gender column, and if we assume each pointer into the original table requires 10 bytes, then we will have 1525 disk blocks worth of pointers to rows containing "male" (10 bytes per pointer × 5 million male customers/32K per disk block), and 1525 disk blocks worth of pointers to rows containing "female." If we want to determine the average income of our female customers, there are two ways to execute the query.

First, the database engine could ignore the Gender index and perform a full table scan, requiring that all 61,035 disk blocks be read. Second, the database engine could choose to use the index, in which case it will first read in all the pointers to the "female" rows (1525 disk blocks), and then it will read in all the blocks that contain rows pointed to by the index.

But an interesting phenomenon occurs. Since each disk block contains about 164 rows (32K per disk block/200 bytes per row), it is extremely likely that every disk block will contain at least one "female" row. (On average, it will in fact contain 82 such rows.) That means that the list of pointers provided by the index will essentially point to every disk block. So not only must you read in the initial 1525 disk blocks of the index, you must then read all 61,035 disk blocks of the Customer table. Clearly, using the Gender index will hinder performance and would hopefully never get used by the query optimizer. Therefore creating the Gender index is a waste of disk space and CPU cycles.

Actually the relative performance of using the Gender index as described above is worse than has been described so far. Up to this point, we've only discussed the number of disk blocks that need to be read. But the time it takes to read a disk block will differ depending on whether or not the disk head has to seek to the desired disk block. When performing a full table scan, the disk head performs a sequential read, meaning that the head will move smoothly across the disk. By minimizing disk head movement, we get optimal I/O throughput from that disk. In these situations, modern disks can read about 5MB per second. Our full table scan will therefore complete in under 7 minutes (200 bytes per row × 10 million customers/5MB per second).

However, when using the Gender index, not only do you have to read more disk blocks, but the disk head that is reading the Customer table will not be doing a sequential read. Instead the head will read blocks in the order they are identified in the index, and this order is determined solely by the sorted order of the rows of the table, not by their physical placement on the disk. Even if we assume that once a disk block is read, the database's memory cache is large enough to keep the block in memory, we will still generally be seeking 61,035 times (once for each block). Modern disks can perform about 50 seeks per second, so our query will require a little over 20 minutes (61,035 blocks/50 blocks per second). Because the index has such low selectivity (meaning each index entry points to a large number of rows), in this case it is far faster to perform a full table scan than to use the index.

The next logical question is, for our Customer table, how selective must an index be before it is useful to use it? (As clarification, when discussing indexes, higher selectivity means that fewer rows are actually selected. The term "selectivity" is used in the same way that it is used when we talk about a club being "highly selective" about its membership.) We can calculate a quick-and-dirty answer to this fairly easily with the information we already have. First, we just saw that if every block has to be read, using an index is slower. So, at a minimum, we can safely assume that the index has to be selective enough that not every block has to be read. And if not every block needs to be read, we can also assume that if a block does need to be read, then we will usually want only one row from that block. Why is this so? If our index were to select 100 rows, given a random distribution of these 100 rows across all 61,035 blocks, it is unlikely that any two selected rows will be in the same block. So if you want to read X rows, you will likely have to read about X blocks.

We know that a sequential scan of the entire table will require just under 7 minutes. In that same 7 minutes, how many rows could be read if we used an index? Given that a disk can perform 50 random I/Os per second, which means 50 blocks per second, we can locate 50 rows identified by the index per second. In 7 minutes, we could therefore locate 21,000 rows (50 rows per second $\times$ 60 seconds per minute $\times$ 7 minutes); 21,000 rows out of a total of 10 million rows represents a selectivity of 0.2%. If we need more than 0.2% of the rows, a table scan will be faster than using an index.

So we can see that some queries would be hindered by the use of an index. But a query optimizer should be able to determine this, meaning that although creating some indexes may be a waste of disk space and computing resources, they should never have a detrimental effect on query performance. Earlier we stated that indexes can in fact slow down some queries. How can this be? Really the answer is simple, query optimizers often make mistakes. Therefore, unless the index selectivity is very high, it is generally best not to add a B-tree index. If you add an index and performance decreases, don't be perplexed. Just remove the index.

BIT-MAPPED INDEXES   For a B-tree index to be selective, the column that is indexed needs to have a large number of discrete values. B-tree indexes are optimal when the indexed column has values that are all unique or nearly unique, such as Order_ID or Social_Security_No. This means that B-tree indexes are not good for columns that only have a small number of discrete values. If you sell your product in five different colors, putting a B-tree index on the Color column of the Product_Sales table is probably not useful, because each index entry will point to a very large number of rows. For example, if all colors were equally popular, each index entry would point to 20% of the rows, which is two orders of magnitude larger than the 0.2% shown in the example above. Nor would it be useful to place a B-tree index on the Income_Level column of your Customer table if you classify your customers into only a few different income levels (e.g., <$25,000, $25,001–$40,000, $40,001–$60,000, etc.).

However, just because B-tree indexes aren't effective at enhancing performance in situations where the number of discrete values is small, this doesn't mean that other indexing techniques aren't useful. In fact, bit-mapped indexes are optimal for enhancing performance in these low-selectivity situations. Bit-mapped indexing techniques have been around for many years, but have only recently found their way into mainstream database products. Like B-tree indexes, a bit-mapped index is also a structure that is separate from the original table. However, its structure is very different. The first step in the process of building a bit-mapped index is to determine the exact number of discrete values contained in the column to be indexed. Then, for each discrete value, a bit map is created such that if the row contains that particular value, then the bit map contains a 1 bit in that position. Otherwise, it contains a 0 bit. Figure 9.9 shows the bit-mapped index for the Color column.

There are many advantages to bit-mapped indexes. First, they are usually much smaller than B-tree indexes when the number of discrete values in the column is small. For example, assume the Product_Sales table in Figure 9.9 had 10 million rows. Assuming 10 bytes per index entry for a B-tree index, a B-tree index would require about 100MB (10 million index entries × 10 bytes per entry). However, a bit-mapped index would only require about 6.25MB ((10 million rows × 1 bit per row × 5 bit maps)/8 bits per byte). Not only are there storage savings, but it is far faster to read

Color Index

Red	Green	Yellow	Black	Blue
1	0	0	0	0
0	1	0	0	0
0	0	1	0	0
0	0	1	0	0
0	1	0	0	0
0	0	0	1	0
0	0	0	0	1
1	0	0	0	0
0	0	0	0	1
1	0	0	0	0

Product Sales Table

Store_ID	Cust_ID	Date	Color
09	15342	11/29/97	Red
14	82234	11/29/97	Green
11	12239	11/29/97	Yellow
19	42276	11/29/97	Yellow
03	34221	11/29/97	Green
11	86746	11/30/97	Black
06	43629	11/30/97	Blue
14	98531	11/30/97	Red
08	95679	11/30/97	Blue
12	16277	11/30/97	Red

FIGURE 9.9

Indexing a column with a bit-mapped index.

a 6.25MB index than it is to read a 100MB index (about 16 times faster).

Also, for certain types of queries, bit-mapped indexes are extremely fast. For example, to find out how many products were sold in red, the database engine just needs to count the number of

1 bits in the Red bit map. Bit-mapped indexes can also be easily combined with other bit-mapped indexes on the same table by using logical AND and OR operations. For example, if you had 20 different store locations, you might also want to create a bit-mapped index on Store_ID which would require 20 different bit maps—one for each store. The database engine could then easily find out how many products were sold in red in Store #11 by ANDing the Red bit map with the Store #11 bit map, and then counting the number of 1 bits in the result. Because each bit map is small, and because computers excel at these logical AND and OR operations, you can understand why bit-mapped indexes can deliver tremendous performance improvements.

Costs of Using Bit-Mapped Indexes Like the other techniques we've been discussing that improve performance by reducing the amount of work that needs to be done, bit-mapped indexes also have the same up-front costs. The index increases disk storage requirements, creating the index uses valuable CPU cycles, and the data warehouse refresh time is increased. The earlier discussion of these issues applies directly to bit-mapped indexes as well, so there is no need to repeat that discussion here.

In general, the denormalizing and indexing techniques we have discussed are all critical to designing a high-performance and highly scalable data warehouse platform. Rather than using the brute force approach of throwing more and/or faster hardware at your platform, they can make far more efficient use of the computing resources already allocated. If used appropriately, the performance and scalability benefits can be dramatic.

Designing Your Disk Layout

With the rest of your database design in place, the next step is to focus on the aspect of physical database design that deals with determining exactly how your data will be laid out on the disks. This step is critical because the actual location of the data will have a tremendous impact on the performance and scalability of the data warehouse platform. No matter which hardware architecture is chosen for the data warehouse (SMP, clusters, MPP, or NUMA) or which database architecture is used (either a shared-disk database architecture or a shared-nothing database architecture), scala-

> ### A WORD OF CAUTION
>
> Whereas B-tree indexes are always the same size regardless of the number of discrete values in the indexed column, bit-mapped indexes grow in linear proportion to the number of discrete values. In Figure 9.9, since we have five discrete values, we have five bits of index associated with each row. But if we had 10 discrete values, our bit-mapped index would be 10-bits wide. And so on. Therefore, at some point, the number of discrete values will be so large that the bit-mapped index will be larger than the B-tree index. If you were to use our assumption that each indexed row requires 10 bytes (that is, 80 bits), then you may think that once you exceed 80 discrete values, your bit-mapped index would be more than 80-bits wide and would therefore be larger than a B-tree index. However, this isn't true. Database engines use advanced compression techniques on bit-mapped indexes, sometimes yielding a 25:1 compression ratio. So the actual number of discrete values can in fact be quite large before the size of a bit-mapped index will exceed the size of a B-tree index. That's not to say that it would be ineffective to use a bit-mapped index just because it's larger than a B-tree index on the same column. If your queries can be solved by counting bits in a bit map, or by ANDing or ORing bit maps together, you may still get better performance using bit-mapped indexes rather than B-tree indexes.

bility will not be obtainable unless the data in the data warehouse can be accessed in parallel.

As we saw earlier, many queries can make effective use of denormalization or advanced indexing techniques to bypass the need for executing long-running queries. However, it is not feasible to precalculate the results of every possible query or to index every possible data element. In fact, it's not even desirable to do so. As we saw, the computing resources that would be required to precalculate every possible query would greatly overwhelm the savings that we normally get from denormalization. In addition, the disk storage required to store all the precalculated results and all the indexes would be prohibitive.

Obviously, then, we will still need to frequently execute large and complex queries. To get good response times, we will make heavy use of data parallelism to get the performance and scalability we need out of our I/O subsystem. The goal is to use parallel techniques to push the system components (disks, controllers, CPUs, and memory) to the limits of their capacity, thereby fully utilizing the hardware's capabilities. This section concentrates on techniques that can be used to ensure optimal performance in your current environment, as well as ensuring scalability as the data warehouse environment grows in terms of both data and users.

TAKING ADVANTAGE OF I/O PARALLELISM

At a high level, you can think of your CPUs as engines, and data on your disks is the fuel that keeps them running. A disk reader process, commonly referred to as a "scan thread" or "scan process" is responsible for getting data off of a disk and sending it to a CPU to keep the CPU supplied with fuel. It is important to realize that at any given point in time, a scan thread can only read from a single disk, and can only ship that data to a single CPU. In addition, each disk can only serve the requests of one scan thread at a time. Therefore if we have four CPUs in our system, unless we have four scan threads and at least four disk drives, all four CPUs will not be able to run simultaneously. This means that at any given point in time, at least one of the CPUs will be idle, and the benefit of having that additional CPU will be nil (as depicted by CPU 4 in Figure 9.10).

Our goal is simple: Keep data flowing to all CPUs at all times. If we were to put all the data on one disk, then only one scan thread could be active at a time, and we would not be able to take advantage of any I/O parallelism. Therefore we need to spread the data out across multiple disks. There are two main techniques for doing this: striping and database partitioning.

Striping Techniques

To make our data warehouse platform more responsive, we must use a combination of multiple CPUs, multiple disks, and multiple scan threads. For each CPU we add to our system, we must also create another scan thread to ensure that the CPU will not be idle. Assuming that all current disk drives are being fully utilized,

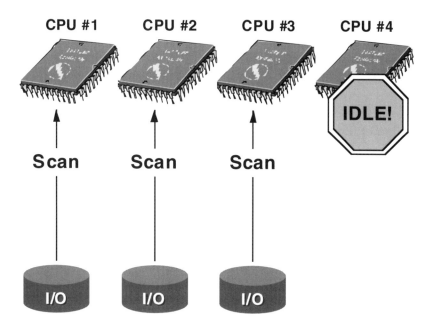

FIGURE 9.10
CPUs are idle when not being fed by a scan thread.

whenever we create another scan thread, we need to also add another disk drive to ensure that the scan threads will not have to contend with each other for access to an available disk drive. If all disks are being fully utilized and you add more CPUs without adding any more disk drives, you won't see any improvement in system response time or scalability whatsoever. The money you spend on the additional CPUs will be wasted.

But, obviously, simply having more disks drives isn't useful unless you spread your data out across these new disk drives. The process of taking a pool of data and evenly dividing it up across a set of drives is called *striping*. The main purpose of striping is simply to increase the level of data parallelism at the I/O subsystem level.

To illustrate, let's look at a data warehouse that stores information pertaining to foreign automobile sales for the United States. Assume that your platform has four CPUs. Also, for simplicity's sake, assume your data warehouse only has information on Mercedes, Porsche, BMW, and Volvo, and that it has roughly an equivalent amount of information on each type of car, all of which is stored in a single table called "Car_Sales." If you put all the information on a single disk drive (assuming for a minute that it would fit), then only one scan process would be able to read the table at a time. Choosing this as a physical database design would mean that your data warehouse would not be able to scale. The optimal solution is to spread the data (i.e., stripe the data) across at least four disks, as shown in Figure 9.11. We say "at least" four disks, because it could very possibly be the case that the data might not fit on just four disks.

Now, when you query the Car_Sales, you can use four scan processes, and each process will read one-fourth of the total table, completing a query in approximately one-fourth of the time it would have taken to scan the table without parallelism. You can see that by combining the throughput of multiple disk devices you can greatly enhance the performance of large queries against the data warehouse. You can continue extending this principle even further by adding more CPUs, striping the data over more disk drives, and using more scan processes.

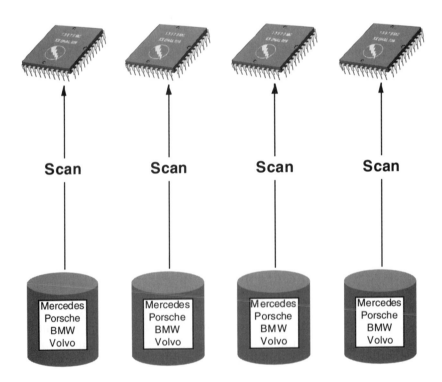

FIGURE 9.11
Striping increases the level of parallelism.

Previously we said the optimal solution was to stripe the data across "at least" four disks, because it could very possibly be the case that the data might not fit on just four disks. In fact, in almost all cases, the number of disk drives greatly exceeds the number of processors. What happens when you stripe a table across more disks than there are CPUs? Figure 9.12 illustrates this. Here, we have eight disks, but we still only have four CPUs, and our level of parallelism will still be limited to four scan processes. Each scan process will first scan one drive, and when finished it will scan the second drive. So although table size often requires you to stripe data across more disks than there are CPUs, doing so will gener-

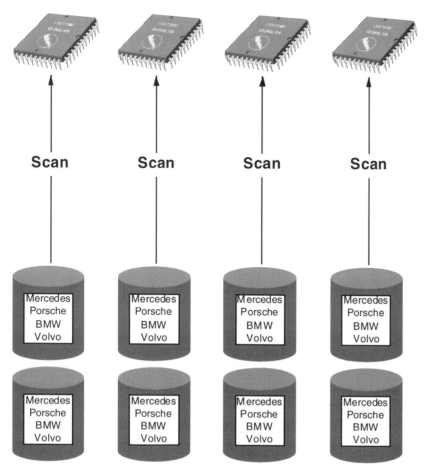

FIGURE 9.12
Striping across more disks than CPUs won't improve performance.

ally not improve performance. (Note: Having eight scan processes, one for each drive, would mean that each CPU would be fed by two scan processes. This will only help performance if a single scan process were unable to keep one CPU busy, but this is usually not the case.)

Up to this point we've been talking about striping in the generic sense of distributing a pool of data across a set of drives. However, in reality, disk striping can be performed by different components of your system: the hardware, the operating system, and the database. Before we proceed any further, let's look at each of these.

HARDWARE STRIPING   This method of disk striping involves purchasing specialized intelligent disk array technology which includes additional hardware that automatically handles striping the data across the multiple disks in the disk array. To the rest of the system, this disk array looks like a single (albeit very fast) disk drive that has the ability to simultaneously handle multiple I/O requests. The striping is usually done in a round-robin fashion, meaning that the first chunk of data is written to the first disk in the array, then the next chunk is written to the second disk, and so on. When you hit the last disk in the array, you go back to the first disk and repeat the process until all of the data has been written out. The process is similar to a card dealer dealing out a deck of cards to a set of players. These chunks of data are referred to as "stripes" and are usually 32K to 64K. The benefit of using this technique is that data is transparently and evenly spread over many physical devices, balancing the I/O load across all the disks. This therefore minimizes the risk of having disk "hot spots," which occur when data is requested from some drives much more frequently than others.

Another advantage is that these intelligent disk arrays also automatically handle various RAID levels. This provides a greatly increased level of fault tolerance to the disk subsystem, which due to its mechanical nature is the most likely component to fail in your computer system. Finally, because all of the striping is done by separate hardware contained in the disk array itself, there is no system CPU overhead required for maintaining the disk array.

However, there are some disadvantages as well. First, the hardware striping solution is usually the most expensive method of achieving disk striping. Second, while the disk array's capability to handle multiple I/O requests means you can use multiple scan threads to simultaneously read from the array, the resulting parallelism is not what you would hope for. In general, to maximize I/O throughput you always want to have the disk head move smoothly across the disk in one continuous motion, streaming the data back to the system as it goes. That means you want to have a single scan thread start at the beginning of a disk and then read all the data from that disk. Unfortunately, because the database is unaware of how the data is actually striped (remember, with hardware striping the striping is intended to be transparent to the system), the I/O requests issued by a single scan thread will almost always reference data that is on multiple different drives. This problem affects each scan thread, so all the disks in the array are constantly satisfying requests from multiple threads. The disk heads will therefore have to constantly seek back and forth, significantly lowering I/O performance for queries.

OPERATING SYSTEM STRIPING   Operating system striping introduces the concept of a "logical volume group," which (similar to hardware striping) appears as a single disk device to the database. However, it actually consists of pieces from multiple physical disk drives logically grouped together to give the appearance of one physical device. The data is distributed across the pieces of the various disks in a round-robin fashion using a stripe width of 32K to 64K. As with hardware striping, this approach removes hot spots and gives us a balanced I/O load across all the disks in the logical volume group. And because there is no special hardware required, this solution is cheaper.

However, more system resources are needed to manage the logical volume group. This overhead is seen as system CPU time if you were to monitor the CPU utilization of the system. Also, it suffers from the same head-seeking problem we noted in our discussion on hardware striping, since a scan thread can only issue a request to the logical volume group, not to a specific disk within that group (see Figure 9.13). Because of this, the use of logical volume groups is better suited for OLTP applications or other environments where user concurrency is very high and I/O requests are small, because the logical volume group allows an even distribution of disk access for the online users. In a decision support environment where there is low user concurrency and large sequential

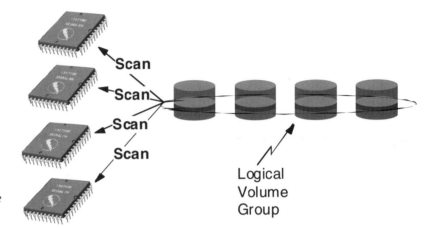

FIGURE 9.13
Scanning a logical volume group.

scans, database striping (described next) yields superior performance because head seek movement is minimized by having each
disk drive service just one scan process.

DATABASE STRIPING   Of the three striping techniques available, database striping is the easiest to employ and offers the best performance when there is a smaller number of concurrent users (than in
typical OLTP applications) running parallel queries. This
technique does not require any special hardware or extra overhead
from the operating system, relying solely on the database's ability
to allow tables to span multiple physical devices. A database table
is divided up into a number of sections (called fragments or extents), and each section is assigned to a specific drive. The database
then has the ability to assign a single scan process to a single fragment or extent and be assured that head seek movement will be
minimized. This is largely due to the fact that the scans are sequential and the disk head does not have to be repositioned elsewhere
on the disk platter to service another request. Figure 9.14 illustrates
database striping.

In Figure 9.14 we show eight different extents, even though
there are only four CPUs. As we stated earlier, this will not give us
any better throughput than if we had only used four extents. We
already discussed one reason why you might do this: If the table is
too big to fit on four disks, then you will be required to use additional disks. However, there is another reason: planning for

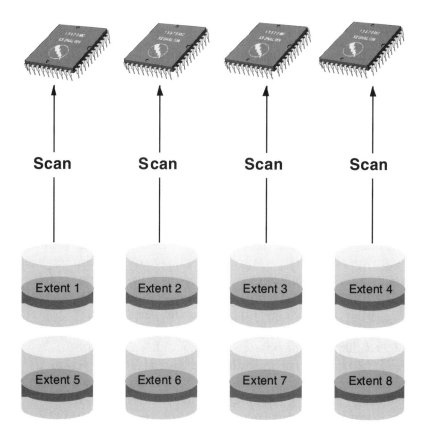

FIGURE 9.14
Database striping.

growth. With the current physical design, if we add four more CPUs to our system, we could have four additional scan threads go directly against extents 5–8. No changes need to be made to our layout, and the table will be scanned twice as fast as with four processors. If we used only four extents, adding additional CPUs would not improve performance without changing the physical layout of the table.

The downside of database striping lies in the fact that each fragment or extent is a separate operating system file. Therefore there will be many more data files to manage compared with operating system striping or hardware striping, where the eight separate sections would be treated and managed as a single file. But since performance and not ease of maintenance is paramount in our warehouse, we usually prefer to use database striping.

Table Partitioning Techniques

Earlier in this section we mentioned that there are two techniques for spreading the data out across multiple disks. The first technique, striping, makes use of data parallelism to allow us to benefit from the aggregate bandwidth of multiple disk drives. While it gives us a mechanism for distributing data, by itself it doesn't let us place various pieces of data at certain physical locations based on the value of the data itself. Why would we want to do that? Well, what if only some parts of the table need to be scanned (such as would be the case if you only cared about BMW sales)? We need a technique that allows us to group data together based on the data values, so we can then hone in on only those parts of the table that are relevant (such as BMW sales), thereby speeding up our query because we don't have to scan through lots of irrelevant data. The technique we need is called table partitioning. There are three common partitioning strategies: range partitioning, hash partitioning, and round-robin partitioning.

RANGE PARTITIONING   The physical design we chose in Figure 9.11 is the easiest to implement and administer. But each time we want to search the Car_Sales table for a specific type of car, we will need to read through the entire table and consume (assuming parallel query/scan) all of the available system resources (CPU, disk, and memory). Let's now look at another example where we partition the data into physical groupings based on the value of the data. The first thing we must do is to choose a partition key. A partition key is the value of a field in which data can be physically separated. Choosing an effective partition key requires an understanding of the types of queries users will be executing. Generally you want to use as your partition key a column that is frequently used in the WHERE clause of your SELECT statement. In the example, assume that you frequently look for a specific type of car in your database; therefore, using the car type column would be a logical choice for a partition key. This type of partitioning is known as range partitioning (sometimes also referred to as expression-based partitioning). Figure 9.15 shows our data warehouse partitioned by car type.

Now assume you want to execute the following query:

```
SELECT type, model, price, dealer, sale_date
  FROM Car_Sales
  WHERE type = "BMW" AND
  price BETWEEN (30000 and 45000);
```

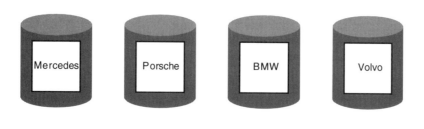

FIGURE 9.15
Range partitioning by car type.

The database engine can use far fewer system resources to find the answer to this query than if you had not partitioned your table. In fact, you will be using only 25% of the available system resources. The database engine knows that the data that has been requested (BMW vehicles) resides only on the third disk drive. As a result, the database engine does not use any other system resources to retrieve the data other than the one disk and one CPU which services the one scan process (as shown in Figure 9.16). What has occurred is known as partition elimination. Instead of using all four CPUs and all four disk drives, you use partition elimination and are able to use just one CPU and one disk drive and scan 75% less data to get your answer.

But how did the database engine know exactly where to find the data? The answer lies in how the table was originally created. To create a partitioned table, you would use a syntax similar to:

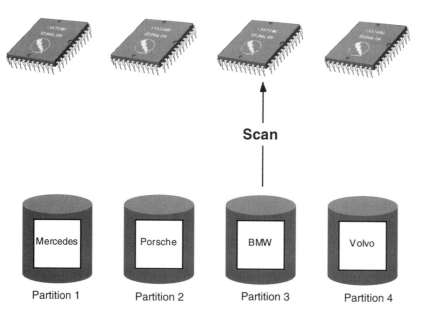

FIGURE 9.16
Partition elimination reduces the amount of data that must be scanned.

```
CREATE TABLE Car_Sales
(
type            CHAR
model           CHAR
price           NUM
dealer          CHAR
sale_date   DATE
)
PARTITION BY VALUE
type = 'Mercedes'      IN partition_1,
type = 'Porsche'       IN partition_2,
type = 'BMW'           IN partition_3,
type = 'Volvo'         IN partition_4;
```

This partitioned syntax tells the database to put all BMW data in the partition named partition_3 when the table is created (and when any subsequent changes are made to the table's data), so the database engine knows that partitions 1, 2, and 4 can be eliminated for the above query.

But even though we eliminate the need to scan the other 75% of the data, did this partitioning really reduce the response time of the query? In the above example, assume that scanning all of the data in all four partitions with a single scan thread (that is, no parallelism) would result in a response time of T_1. Scanning all of the data with four parallel scan threads would therefore result in a response time of $T_1/4$. If we eliminate three of the partitions and just scan one, the time would still be $T_1/4$, the same as it would be if we performed a parallel scan of all the data. Using partition elimination freed up 75% of the resources on the machine for other queries that could be processed at the same time, and this is a huge savings in processing power. But it didn't improve our response time. What if we wanted to reduce the response time of our query and still use only 25% of the system resources? To accomplish this we need to be able to access our partitions in parallel. That is, we need to combine partitioning with striping and stripe each partition over each of the disks. This is shown in Figure 9.17.

If we use this physical layout and execute our query for BMWs again, the database will once again eliminate partitions 1, 2, and 4, but it will now be able to use four scan threads to scan partition 3. Thus, because we only have to scan one-fourth of the data (due to partitioning), and because we can scan the remaining partition using a parallelism level of four (due to striping), our overall

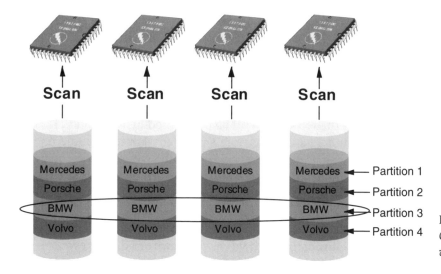

FIGURE 9.17
Combining partitioning with striping.

response time is 16 times faster than if we had no partitioning and only a single scan thread.

Issues with Range Partitioning: Data Skew In the previous, highly simplified example, we made the assumption that there was roughly the same amount of data for each type of car, so each partition would therefore hold roughly the same amount of data. However, very often this is not the case. When some partitions contain much more data than others, the undesirable result is called data skew. To illustrate the effect of data skew on a data warehouse, let's create a new data warehouse which stores information on turkey sales at a supermarket. As our platform we will use a 12 CPU system with 12 disks. Since we frequently want to look at turkey sales by month, we choose to use the month in which the turkey was sold as the partition key.

In general, partitioning based on the most frequently used key is the correct strategy. However, in this case it will be disastrous because we didn't take into account the nature of the data itself. While it's true that this strategy will allow you to perform partition elimination for any of the months that you're not interested in for a particular query, a short time after the system is put into production you would notice that node 11 (containing the November data) is constantly busier than the other nodes. In fact, all the other nodes hardly get used.

Why would this happen? Because the partitioning strategy we have chosen has caused data skew. Since more turkeys are sold during November than any other month of the year, we have a lot more data, and hence a lot more processing, on node 11 (see Figure 9.18). If your data warehouse has data skew, it will not be scalable. Adding more nodes or disk drives will not improve performance because all of the work will still be performed just by node 11.

There are two solutions to this problem. First, we could combine partitioning and striping, and stripe the November partition across all 12 nodes. In fact, we could stripe all 12 partitions across all 12 nodes, although because the other 11 partitions contain very little data, this would likely be overkill. The other option is to simply choose a different partitioning key, one that will still be useful for partition elimination but will not suffer from data skew.

HASH PARTITIONING   Another method for partitioning your data is hash partitioning. Previously we discussed that one of the benefits of range partitioning is that there is deterministic logic behind where a particular row is placed, and that could be used to make some queries more efficient via partition elimination. However, we had to be careful to avoid data skew. Simple striping, on the other hand, avoided data skew, but since the rows were essentially randomly distributed, this technique can't be used to make some queries more efficient. The goal of hash partitioning is to try to get the best of both worlds—deterministic placing of rows while minimizing the chances of having data skew.

To achieve this goal, hash partitioning uses a hashing function coupled with a hash key. Whereas range partitioning fills each

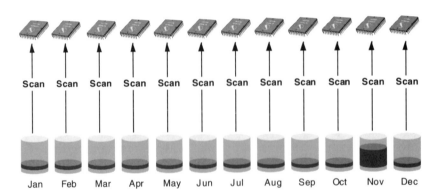

FIGURE 9.18
Partitioning can lead to data skew.

partition with rows whose partition key falls within a specified range, hash partitioning applies the hashing function to one of the data elements in your table (the "hash key") and uses the resulting output value to determine into which partition the row should be placed. The hashing function is chosen so that its output values are evenly distributed given the range of possible input values. The hash key itself must also be carefully chosen so that its values are as unique as possible, because the wide variety of input values will lead to an even distribution of output values (assuming we have a good hashing function). For example, a serial number or a social security number is a good choice for a hash key. Often a product ID is also a good hash key. However, if we were to use the month in which an item was sold as our key, we would have all the same data skew issues that we saw above. Having only 12 possible input values is not sufficient for effective hash partitioning.

Unfortunately, hash partitioning won't really enable us to perform partition elimination when performing table scans because the data in any particular partition is not associated with a single range of data. However, if we're looking for an individual row, hash partitioning can be used to instantly hone in on the correct partition if the hash key is used as part of the query. More importantly, in clustered and MPP architectures, hash partitioning can be used to greatly improve the performance of joins if the join key is used as the hash key. In clustered and MPP architectures, partitions are assigned to physically separate nodes, and these nodes are connected by a high-speed interconnect. Even though the interconnect is a high-speed transfer medium, we must minimize data transfer across this interconnect in order to obtain maximum scalability. The more data sharing that occurs, the more coordination there must be between the nodes, and this increased coordination overhead reduces scalability. We can use hash partitioning to help minimize data movement.

When processing a join on one of these hardware architectures, if two rows that need to be joined are located in different partitions, and hence on separate nodes, then one of the rows must be moved (via the interconnect) to the node where the other row resides before the actual join of those two rows can occur. In a situation where the rows to be joined are not already colocated, a join will require a dynamic redistribution of the data of one or more of the tables so that any two (or more) rows that will be joined will be on the same node. Depending on the particular database implementation, this dynamic reorganization can be an expensive operation, decreasing query performance. But by using hash partitioning on the join keys for all tables that will be joined for a query, we can guarantee that any rows that need to be joined will always be found in the same partition and, therefore, on the same node. Data transfer between nodes will be minimized (because all the joins will be local), dynamic reorganization will be unnecessary, and performance will increase. Because hash partitioning not only gives you an easy way to evenly distribute your data, but also gives you an effective way to improve query performance in certain hardware architectures, it is a commonly used partitioning technique in data warehouses.

ROUND-ROBIN PARTITIONING   The third common partitioning method is basic round-robin partitioning. However, we have already covered this topic, because it is really just another name for database striping. This method of partitioning provides the easiest way to evenly distribute data across multiple disk drives because you don't need to worry about selecting a partitioning key. However, it gives the database no way of performing partition elimination because the rows are randomly distributed.

OPTIMIZING THE QUERIES

Often, the most significant gains in query performance can be realized by reformulating the SQL query itself. The tuning of database queries is a topic for a book in its own right. This discussion will use an example query to illustrate the form and interpretation of query plans, the method by which these plans can be related to the execution characteristics of a query, and some of the basic principles of query optimization.

SQL is a language that allows a user to specify a number of different queries that return the same result set—though the specific way they are formulated might imply quite different execution strategies. In a perfect world, query optimizers would automatically choose the most appropriate strategy regardless of the way the user formulates the query. However, as we write this in 1998, even the best SQL optimizer in existence can be handily trounced by a human who understands the issues that determine SQL performance.

Unfortunately, front-end tools that machine generate their SQL are becoming more and more prevalent in the decision-support world, resulting in fewer and fewer opportunities for direct hand tuning of user queries. Front-end tools are becoming progressively smarter about the SQL they generate, but it is still quite common to see highly inefficient SQL being executed on behalf of OLAP, data-browser, or other query-generating applications.

Still, it is usually possible to hand tune SQL that's used in data center processes such as updates, extracts, or aggregations as well as canned reports. In addition, a significant number of environments include a number of users who often do compose their own queries, such as SAS programmers; many of these environments have successfully implemented a process to identify particularly pathological resource consumers (i.e., explorers) and work with the users to reformulate those queries.

The mechanics of reformulating various SQL constructs in order to execute the query a particular way are specific to each database engine; instead of attempting to present these details this section will stick to a discussion of general principles and methods.

Execution of an SQL Query

The best way to envision the execution of an SQL query (and, indeed, the way database engines represent them internally) is as an inverted tree, with the source tables represented as leaf nodes at the bottom of the picture, and the rows from these tables being processed upwards through filters, joins, and other SQL operators until they become a single result set at the top. An example is shown in Figure 9.19.

Figure 9.19 represents a possible execution plan for the query shown at the top of the figure (the "root" of the tree), which retrieves a list of bank accounts in California branches that wrote checks to other accounts in the same branch. We'll use this query as an example throughout the discussion.

The execution of this query plan occurs *depth-first, left-to-right*. The query is said to be driven by the scan of the ZIP table—that is, the ZIP table is scanned, and each scanned row then proceeds through the rest of the tree, driving the rest of the query processing.

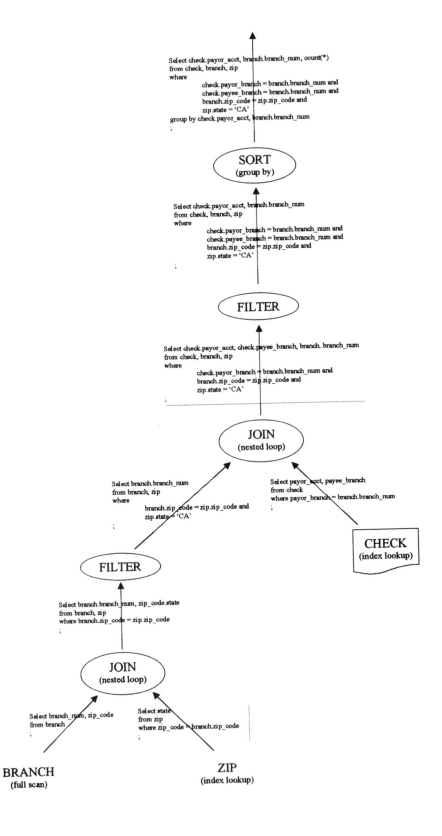

Select check.payor_acct, branch.branch_num, count(*)
from check, branch, zip
where
        check.payor_branch = branch.branch_num and
        check.payee_branch = branch.branch_num and
        branch.zip_code = zip.zip_code and
        zip.state = 'CA'
group by check.payor_acct, branch.branch_num
;

SORT
(group by)

Select check.payor_acct, branch.branch_num
from check, branch, zip
where
        check.payor_branch = branch.branch_num and
        check.payee_branch = branch.branch_num and
        branch.zip_code = zip.zip_code and
        zip.state = 'CA'
;

FILTER

Select check.payor_acct, check.payee_branch, branch.branch_num
from check, branch, zip
where
        check.payor_branch = branch.branch_num and
        branch.zip_code = zip.zip_code and
        zip.state = 'CA'
;

JOIN
(nested loop)

Select branch.branch_num
from branch, zip
where
        branch.zip_code = zip.zip_code and
        zip.state = 'CA'
;

Select payor_acct, payee_branch
from check
where payor_branch = branch.branch_num
;

CHECK
(index lookup)

FILTER

Select branch.branch_num, zip_code.state
from branch, zip
where branch.zip_code = zip.zip_code
;

JOIN
(nested loop)

Select branch_num, zip_code
from branch
;

Select state
from zip
where zip_code = branch.zip_code
;

FIGURE 9.19
Example query tree.

BRANCH
(full scan)

ZIP
(index lookup)

1. The row is passed through "state = CA" filter and discarded if it does not pass.

2. All branch records for that row's zip code are retrieved.

3. For each branch row just retrieved:

   4. Every check written on every account in that branch is retrieved.

   5. Each check row just retrieved is:

      6. Passed through the "payee branch = payor branch" filter (discarded if it does not pass).

      7. Included in the group-by sort to generate the result tally.

It's important to notice that, with the exception of the sort, none of the operations in the above diagram have inter-record dependencies—at any point in the process, the processing of any one record is not affected by anything about any other record. This means that, although the above description implies that the query is executed as a conventional looping serial operation, it is just as valid to execute the workload independently for each row or any group of rows.

In fact, modern database engines take advantage of just this property of relational operators in order to execute queries in parallel. They start multiple processes and assign a portion of the query workload—either statically according to a database partitioning scheme or more dynamically—to each process in order to parallelize the query. Sorting, of course, does have inter-record dependencies, but there are any number of well-known parallel sorting algorithms.

Effects of Parallelism

The effects of parallelism on the execution of a query are complex, are specific to a database engine architecture and implementation —and, most importantly, are logical extensions of the execution characteristics of single-threaded queries. Fundamentally, a parallel query is nothing more than a collection of single-threaded queries executing simultaneously, with the result sets occasionally sorted together, or combined into a single result set for presentation to the user. While parallelization considerations can have a significant effect on query execution performance, particularly in a statically partitioned database architecture, the largest determining factor of query performance is most often evident in the sequential version of the query plan—and even on the simpler single-threaded problem, current query optimizer technology is often hard-pressed to manage "good enough."

The query plan of Figure 9.19 is optimized in a very conventional fashion—the smallest table is scanned and nested-loop joins are used throughout, with the joins into the larger, inner tables making the most possible use of a reasonably complete (though not comprehensive) set of indices.

Let's imagine that this query is being executed on a data warehouse built for a very large, nationwide bank. 10% of this hypothetical bank's 2000 branches, and 10% of the 100 million checks in the CHECK table, are in California. Let's also assume that 10% of the nation's zip codes are in California (and let's assume that all of the 100,000 possible zip codes actually do exist).

The easiest aspect of query execution to quantify is the anticipated I/O workload. Assuming the row size on the branch table is about a kilobyte, the branch table is about 2MB. At that size, there's a good chance it's fully cached in the database server (depending on how frequently it's accessed), but even if not, most databases use large reads to do table scans—256K is a reasonable figure. Thus, we anticipate about eight I/Os to scan the branch table.

The row size of the zip code table is probably considerably smaller—say 100 bytes—but at 100,000 rows the table ends up being 10MB. A B-tree index on the zip_code column is probably about 1MB. This 11MB of data is probably going to end up being cached during the nested-loop join, but it's going to be read in single-block random I/Os; a block size of 8K yields 1408 I/Os.

The check table, on the other hand, is too large to be cached. The way the query is structured, every check that's associated with a California branch is going to be read in individually as an index lookup. This translates into ten million random I/Os to read in blocks of the check table (assuming check records are physically stored in random order). A B-tree index on payor-branch will contain leaf nodes that have multiple entries for the same branch; assuming a fan-out factor of 100 on the index, we anticipate 100,000 I/Os to read index leaf blocks.

We expect that a very small fraction of the checks retrieved by this process will actually satisfy the final filter—that is, will be written to accounts in the same branch as the payor's account. If we estimate that one in every thousand checks has this characteristic, we end up having to do a group-by sort of approximately 10,000 small rows. This sort will probably be done in memory, generating no I/O.

In total, we anticipate that slightly over ten million random I/Os will be required to satisfy this query, with the vast majority of the I/O being to perform the nested-loop join with the check table. Assuming disk devices capable of 50 I/Os per second, we see that this query requires 200,000 device-seconds of I/O time—a 100-device disk farm would be able to perform this many I/Os in just about half an hour. This is not necessarily the anticipated completion time of the query, but a system with a disk farm smaller than this will certainly not be able to complete the query in less time.

CPU Utilization

A query's CPU utilization is more difficult to quantitatively predict, particularly in a manner generic to any particular database or hardware implementation. The CPU usage of a query is very much dependent on the specific implementation of the database engine and underlying operating system, as well as the specific configuration in question. However, it is possible to meaningfully quantify the amount of work involved in the query by examining the number of rows that each step must process. While the way this correlates to the CPU utilization of the system is implementation-dependent, the correlation is direct enough to be meaningful.

So . . . we scan 2000 rows out of the branch table; we do 2000 index lookups and 2000 row retrievals to execute the nested-loop join to the zip code table; we apply the California zip code filter 2000 times; we do 200 index lookups and ten million row retrieves on the check table; we apply the same-branch filter ten million times, and then we sort 10,000 rows. The bulk of the CPU utilization, like the bulk of the I/O, is associated with the processing of the individual check records.

We have enough information at this point to predict some of the operational characteristics of this query. The processing of each check record involves a random read, occupying 10 milliseconds or so during which the query process is blocked, and the processing of the block to retrieve the row and the application of the same-branch filter, which combined will take substantially less than 10 milliseconds of CPU time. Thus, for most database engines, executing this query single-threaded will occupy considerably less than 50% of a CPU; in order to saturate a number of CPUs with the execution of the query, we would expect to have to run the query in parallel with multiple processes *per CPU*.

Query-Optimization Questions

The query-optimization question, then, is "How can we reduce the resource utilization of this query?" Consider an alternate execution strategy: Scan the branch table, pulling out all the rows that have the same payor and payee branch; then join through the branch table to the zip code table to select only branches that are in California.

From an I/O perspective, the table scan of the check table now uses large I/Os. Assuming 250-byte rows, still large for what we'd expect to be a highly normalized detail fact table, we end up executing approximately 100,000 256KB reads to scan the fact table. If we again assume that one check in a thousand has the same payor and payee branch, we end up with 100,000 rows passing our filter.

As with the previous query plan, the branch and zip code tables will probably be cached during the query, and it will take under 2000 I/Os to read those tables into memory. Thus, the bulk of the I/Os executed in this query plan are still associated with the check table (which stands to reason), but we are executing 100,000 large I/Os instead of ten million smaller ones.

In practice, in a multi-user environment, one rarely actually achieves the seek optimization on sequential I/Os that is theoretically possible with a table scan—other users executing other queries are also attempting to access the device. Even so, the fact that with this new strategy the disk heads are only doing 100,000 seeks instead of ten million results in significant reduction in resource consumption in the disk farm. The time it takes to do 256KB I/O is dominated by transfer time rather than seek time, and is approximately 50–100 milliseconds (depending on the disk devices); the total I/O resource requirement then becomes 5000–10,000 device-seconds (as opposed to 200,000 as in the previous example).

CPU, again, is more difficult to predict in a generally applicable fashion, but using the same method as above we scan 100 million rows out of the check table, apply the same-branch filter 100 million times, perform 100,000 index lookups and 100,000 row retrieves on the branch table, and the same 100,000 index lookups and row retrieves on the zip code table, apply the California zip code filter 100,000 times, and sort 10,000 rows.

As with the previous example, the vast majority of the processing is associated with the processing of the check table. The CPU utilizations are actually somewhat comparable: Ten million random, index-driven row retrieves out of the check table for the first plan compared with 100 million scan-based retrieves (which are probably somewhat cheaper) for the second, and ten million applications of the same-branch filter in the first plan compared with 100 million applications of the same filter for the second.

In sum, then, the second query plan has a very different resource utilization profile from the first: The second plan uses somewhat less than ten times more CPUs, while doing 20–40 times less I/O. The execution profile is also very different: A large block of check records is read in a single I/O, and the processing of each record is then completely in memory (either the application of filters or nested-loop joins with completely cached tables). Because a query execution process blocks far less often for I/O (by a factor of around 100), a single process will saturate a CPU, and the ratio of query execution processes to CPUs should be very close to 1-to-1.

The bottom-line question, then: Is the second query plan better than the first? Unfortunately, the above analysis clearly illustrates the first principle of query optimization: There is no simple answer.

In theory, the answer depends on the system configuration: If the limiting resource on the system is CPU (such as on an SMP that is pushed to its limit against a large warehouse), the first query plan is theoretically more suitable; if the scarce resource is the I/O rate that can be sustained by the disk farm, the second is superior. As an aside, this illustrates the limited utility of a "rule-of-thumb" ratio between the capacities of the various system components— the theoretical optimum ratio of CPU capacity to disk device capacity for the former query plan is 200–400 times different from the ratio for the latter.

An important respect in which the above theory falls short comes from the observation that in order to execute the first query plan for best response time, at least two execution threads should be used *per disk device*. This is impractical on a warehouse of any size, particularly in a multi-user environment—in practice, for a variety of reasons, a multi-user warehouse can rarely be configured to support more than a few dozen threads of execution per query. However, because of its greatly reduced CPU usage, the first query would have far less impact on other users—in other words, while compromising response time, the first query plan is much more nice, and quite possibly allows for more throughput on the system as a whole. Thus, depending on the environment, the second plan might be more suitable for data center batch operations such as offline warehouse updates, while the first plan might be preferable for exactly the same query against the warehouse in multiuser operation.

The most germane closing observation, then, is that there is no single "optimal" query plan for a particular query. Among other factors, the appropriateness of a plan depends on:

❏ What the limiting system resource is

❏ Whether the query will be executed purely for response time, or whether impact on other users is a consideration

With due consideration to these factors, application development and database administration staff can be well on their way to cost-effectively utilizing the resources at their disposal for their particular application—in the cases where they actually have control over the SQL being used by the application and the manner of its execution.

SUMMARY

The real key to building and maintaining a successful, high-performance, scalable data warehouse platform lies not in the hardware, software, or individual techniques that you use. While each of these components is a critical piece of a solution, they are really just tools. Real success comes from knowing how and when to use each of these tools and understanding how to integrate these vari-

ous tools into a unified solution. By using these tools and techniques to maximize the performance of any task that needs to be
executed, while at the same time using them to minimize the overall workload on the system, you will create a data warehousing
platform that is flexible, scalable, and fast. In the next chapter, we
will take a look at some advanced topics to consider in building a
high-performance data warehouse platform.

10

Advanced Platform Topics

At this point we've discussed performance from two different high-level perspectives—performance relative to usage and data and performance relative to the platform. This understanding gives us a solid foundation on which to build a data warehouse environment that meets current end-user performance needs while providing scalability to support these levels of service as the environment grows in terms of functionality, users, and data. With that as a basis, this chapter discusses some more advanced topics that are important for an enterprise building and maintaining a high-performance data warehouse platform. We will cover the issue of how you proactively test the performance, as well as a discussion of why managing the performance of a large data warehouse platform is very different from managing the performance of a smaller data warehouse platform. Finally, we cover the effects that three important trends have on data warehousing efforts: the Web, data mining, and the use of object-relational multidimensional databases.

BUILDING A PERFORMANCE ASSURANCE ENVIRONMENT

It's obvious that a data warehouse environment that doesn't meet the performance requirements of the end users will not be successful. But there is often more to meeting performance requirements than many people realize because your data warehouse environment will scale up over time, continually placing increasing requirements and demands on the platform. Therefore, not only must the data warehouse platform perform well when it is first built, but these performance levels must be maintained as the environment grows. In reality, it is not very difficult to double the amount of data in your data warehouse environment—you can simply add more disk drives and fill them up with data. What is difficult is to ensure that response times stay roughly constant even though you're doubling the amount of data and/or the number of users. Successfully maintaining performance levels in the face of rapid growth is the essence of scalability, and to be able to do this we need to build what we call the performance assurance test environment (PATE). This is essentially a series of benchmarks that are continually used to both test and predict the performance of your data warehouse platform.

Defining the Performance Assurance Metrics

The first step in creating the PATE is defining the performance metrics that are most important to the success of your data warehouse environment. These metrics are generally documented in a Service Management Contract (more on this in Chapter 11) and will vary for each environment, but some common metrics are shown in Table 10.1.

By defining these metrics, you can then build tests to determine whether or not your data warehouse platform meets end-user needs and expectations. Clearly, if you haven't defined your requirements, it's impossible to determine whether or not you've satisfied them. You can run these tests before delivering the next incremental phase of the data warehouse platform to your users to ensure that performance requirements will be met and that there will be no surprises when the next incremental phase goes into production usage. Note that the last three items in this table are very important, as they take into account the scalability aspect of your data warehouse platform. Remember, it's important to not only understand the workload your platform must support initially, but to also think about how the demands will be growing over time. As we'll see, these growth rate estimates enable you to proactively test your platform against future demands to determine if there is a scalability bottleneck in your environment before your users find it.

TABLE 10.1 *Common Performance Assurance Metrics*

Common Performance Metrics	Typical Required Information
Extract times	How many sources are we extracting from? How much data comes from each? How much time do we have to complete the extract?
Data scrubbing and transforming times	What kinds of data cleansing must be performed on the data coming from the various sources, and how complex is this cleansing? How much time do we have to complete this cleansing?
Load times	How much data must be loaded and at what intervals? How fast can data be loaded into our warehouse? How much time do we have for our load batch window?
Query response times	What different categories of queries do we have (such as high, medium, and low priority)? What are the required response times for each (such as seconds, minutes, or hours)?
Backup times	How much data will we back up, and how often will we back up our data warehouse? How fast can our database perform backups? How much time do we have to complete the backup?
Recovery times	What amount of downtime is allowable? How fast must we be able to recover from a software failure or a disk drive failure?
Growth rates: Data	How much data do we expect to have initially? In 6 months? In 12 months? In 18 months?
Growth rates: Users	How many users will we have initially and in 6, 12, 18 months (etc.)? What types of users will we have, and what types of workloads will they generate?
Growth rates: Number of queries	How many queries of each type do we have initially and in 6, 12, 18 months (etc.)? How many will be running simultaneously? How will workload patterns be changing over time?

Before we move on to actually building the tests to determine your platform's performance, we must address one other issue. We know what metrics we have to define, but how do we determine the actual values for those metrics? What makes this question even more difficult is that a data warehouse solution is usually a new application (rather than a rewrite of an existing application). There is very little data that you'll be able to collect to help you determine user loads, query workloads, types of queries, or simply just general usage patterns. And users are notorious for incorrectly predicting what data they'll need and what types of queries they'll execute. Even though the predictability of farmer usage will improve over time, we can expect that explorers will always present a challenge when it comes to the predictability of their workload (see Chapters 2 and 3 for more information on farmers, explorers, and performance).

How then do we assign values to these metrics? Our less-than-wonderful answer is to make an educated guess. Since your data warehouse environment is an organic system, workload patterns will change, and people will discover new ways of using it that they never initially envisioned. This is especially true of explorers. This implies two things. First, you must build and refine your data warehouse platform incrementally. Since usage patterns will grow and change, you need to constantly "build" your data warehouse environment and the platform which supports it. Just as a growing plant needs continual care and feeding, so too does this environment. Do not think of this in a negative light, such as "you mean to tell me that I'll never be finished building my data warehouse?" Think of this as a positive aspect—by continually iterating through incremental development cycles for your data warehouse environment, you ensure that your environment remains capable of meeting the changing needs of your organization. The other alternative is to let your data warehouse environment become static, which guarantees that it will become your next system scheduled for replacement.

More importantly, the second implication is that end-user feedback after the first development iteration is critical. You will have made some educated guesses about what levels of performance will be needed, and you now need to validate that with your end users. You do this by both talking to the end users and by monitoring usage patterns. These two forms of feedback are important throughout the entire life of your data warehouse environment, as they are used to continually refine the Performance assurance test (PAT) metrics.

Building Performance Assurance Tests

With the metrics defined, the next step is to measure the actual performance of your data warehouse platform. There are actually a few different performance areas that must be tested. Since we were just discussing performance assurance metrics, we'll begin with those.

BENCHMARKING PERFORMANCE ASSURANCE METRICS   To determine whether or not your system satisfies your performance metrics, you need to build some benchmarks. These benchmarks must be written to either replicate or simulate the specific aspects that you're trying to test. For example, to test load performance you can use your real data and replicate the real load process to test how fast data can be loaded into your platform. Or to test the ability to support the required number of users, you can write a benchmark that simulates users executing various queries at a specified rate. These benchmarks are generally not complicated to build, and many can be built using simple scripting languages or by writing short programs in traditional programming languages. In fact, many organizations already have some benchmarking programs that they've used in the past, and these can be modified to suit the needs of the data warehouse's PATE.

To be able to proactively test the scalability of your data warehouse platform, these benchmarks must also be able to test different scales. That is, you must be able to test load times not only for x amount of data, but also $1.5x$, $2x$, and so on. And you must be able to simulate not just 25 users, but also 50, 75, and 100 users. Each time you run a larger scale test, you also want to add the appropriate amount of computing resources to keep performance stable. That is, if the workload doubles, then you will probably want to double the number of processors, double the disk I/O bandwidth, etc. The goal is to determine not just how your platform performs today, but also how it is likely to perform in the future based on your growth estimates. What you want to look for is unchanging response times as your workload increases. If you increase your workload and increase your computing resources accordingly, then response times should maintain their current level if your system has good scalability. However, if performance begins to suffer, then you have a scalability problem lurking in your platform. Figure 10.1 illustrates this. In the scenario displayed at the top of the the Figure, we show an example where we have good scalability. We increase the amount of data to be processed, and we also increase the number of CPUs (and any other necessary resources) accordingly, so the response times are unchanged. However, in the scenario displayed at the bottom, we also increase the amount of data and the system resources, but we see response times increase, alerting us to a scalability problem.

If you see a nonlinearity, it means that a bottleneck exists somewhere in the platform. Even though it may not be a problem

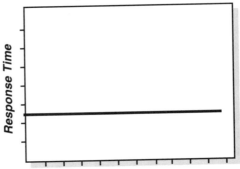

Increasing amount of data and number of CPUs

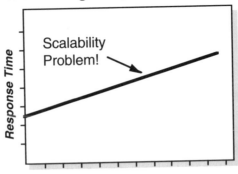

Increasing amount of data and number of CPUs

FIGURE 10.1
Increasing response times gives an early performance warning.

today, it will eventually become a problem. The good news is that as long as you're meeting your performance requirements for today, you've got an early warning mechanism that alerts you to problems before your users discover them. Thus you have time to find the bottleneck and rearchitect the component (or components) that is causing the problem, thereby removing the bottleneck.

A real-world issue arises when we try to test different scales for a data warehouse platform: access to the required amounts of hardware. If our machine has only four processors, how can you test scalability up to six processors? Or if you have only 100GB of disk space available, then how can you test performance with 200GB of data? If possible, borrow resources from another system in your enterprise or see if the hardware vendors will loan you or lease you additional hardware for a brief period. However, it's a fact of life that this isn't always possible. The goal is to test as much scalability as your computing resources will allow. Draw as much of the curve shown in Figure 10.1 as possible. If you simply don't have the available resources, then you must skip this step. However, even drawing a little of the scalability curve is better than nothing at all.

USING SYSTEM MEASUREMENTS   The benchmarks we have been discussing are critical in ensuring that your data warehouse platform meets its performance goals, but by themselves they are insufficient. To ensure scalable performance you must also look at a few critical system measurements that cover how the CPUs and the disks are being used. To do this you need not write any additional benchmarks—you need only use the system measurement tools that are supplied as standard utilities with all major operating systems.

Focusing first on the CPUs, you need to know CPU utilization across the system. If you're at 50% utilization, you might at first think that this is good, because it means you have spare CPU power available to handle unforeseen peaks in system workload and that you have room to grow your platform a bit before you'll have to purchase additional CPU power. You could claim that as long as you're meeting performance requirements, it really doesn't matter how much of the aggregate CPU power you're using. In many cases, this is an appropriate way to think about the situation. That is, if your users are happy, you've done your job well, regardless of utilization levels. However, others would disagree with this notion. Their thinking is that since they've paid for these resources, they should obtain the highest performance levels possible from what they've purchased.

If you fall into this second category, the goal should be to get your CPU utilization to about 90 to 95%. At this utilization level, you're using nearly all CPU resources available, with a little headroom left to handle some workload spikes. In contrast, OLTP systems generally target about 80% CPU utilization, because in an OLTP environment, fast response times are much more critical, so you want to leave much more headroom to ensure that even large spikes in the workload will not adversely affect response times. For those who want to use all the resources available to them, how can CPU utilization be increased? The answer is that you can usually increase CPU utilization by increasing the level of parallelism. If you have spare CPU cycles, then you can more finely divide up a task and apply the spare cycles to the processing of the additional tasks. For example, you can run more queries concurrently to increase throughput, or you can keep the same number of concurrent queries but create more processes (such as scan threads) to process each query, thereby decreasing response times. As long as you're not bottlenecking on some other subsystem, either of these will cause more data to flow to the CPUs and improve performance.

Another important system measurement regarding CPUs is the load balance between the CPUs. In a well-performing system, the workload should be evenly distributed across the processors, and, therefore, all the CPU utilizations for the individual CPUs would be roughly equivalent. If one of the CPUs has a utilization that is markedly higher than the others (that is, one of the CPUs is "hot"), you will have a scalability problem regardless of whether or not you are currently meeting performance requirements. If one processor is hot, that means that the way the workload is being divided is ineffective. Sometimes in a shared-nothing database architecture, this can be caused by incorrectly striping and partitioning the data such that frequently accessed data is being managed by a single CPU. Or sometimes the culprit is a piece of code that was incorrectly written and is only able to run on a single processor. Regardless, if you have a hot processor, you do not have a scalable platform. Adding more processors will not improve performance (at least not very much), because the workload is not being evenly distributed across all available CPU resources. Essentially the one hot CPU becomes a bottleneck. You need to find the culprit and eliminate it.

There are also identical system measurements that you must look at regarding the disk drives. First, you need to look at overall disk subsystem utilization. By utilization, we are referring to how much of the I/O bandwidth is being used, not how much of the storage capacity is being used. As with the CPUs, if your utilization is too low, then you want to either determine if there is a bottleneck elsewhere in the platform or increase the level of parallelism to either increase throughput (i.e., scale-up) or decrease response times (i.e., speed-up). Also, again similar to CPUs, you need to look at the load balance on the I/O subsystem. If one of the disks is hot, then you will have a scalability problem, because adding more disk drives by themselves will not improve performance for the same reasons we saw in our discussion on CPU load balance. To solve this problem, you need to choose a new disk striping and partitioning scheme that better balances the distribution of the data for your current workload.

SMP BUS BANDWIDTH TESTS   If you have an SMP machine, there is a third type of PAT that you need to employ. In an SMP, the system bus can sometimes be its Achilles' heel in terms of performance and scalability, because in a conventional SMP machine, the system bus has a fixed bandwidth. And anything with a fixed bandwidth that is part of a scalable platform can potentially become a bottleneck. Unfortunately, if the bus becomes a bottleneck, you cannot simply incrementally increase its bandwidth. Rather the entire bus must be upgraded, and since the bus usually cannot be upgraded by itself, this generally implies moving to the next larger hardware solution (that is, buying a bigger SMP machine). Since the whole premise of performance assurance is proactively finding performance problems before your users discover them, you need a way to determine how much bandwidth is still available on your SMP bus.

Before we go further, let's look at the two main components that contribute to bus bandwidth utilization: CPUs and disk I/O. The CPUs use the system bus to read instructions and data from memory (if they're not already in a local instruction or data cache, respectively), and to write data back to memory. The bus is also the conduit for all data being read from the disks into memory. Since they share the bus, total bus bandwidth utilization is the sum of these two components.

It would be very nice if there were system utilities that would tell you how close you are to bus saturation, but such utilities don't exist. It would also be nice if you could just calculate the bus bandwidth utilization, but the number of estimations that must be made make this type of calculation fairly inaccurate. For example, just to calculate the CPU component of bus utilization, you would have to estimate how many instructions are being executed per second, what percentage of those are already in the on-chip instruction cache, what percentage are data reads, what percentage of those data reads can be fulfilled by the on-chip data cache, and what percentage are data writes. To point out the difficulty in obtaining a reasonably accurate answer from your calculation, look at the difference between assuming that 94% of all instructions are already in the instruction cache versus assuming 96% are in cache. It makes quite a big difference, because in the first case 6% of all instruction reads must go out to main memory, while in the second case only 4% must do so. That's a 33% decrease in instruction reads that go over the system bus.

The best way is to devise a test that tests your bus utilization directly. Like all performance assurance tests, such a test requires access to your machine and some time during which system tests can be performed, which we understand is always difficult (and sometimes extremely difficult). Regardless, the idea is to write a very simple program whose only reason for existence is to consume a known amount of bus bandwidth. For example, you can write a program that allocates a portion of memory, writes zeroes to every allocated memory location, and then repeats the process. Also, you need to put a simple delay loop in between the memory writes (where you can change the length of the delay as desired) to control the speed at which data is sent over the bus. Since all data writes go out over the system bus and directly into memory (so the writes will be visible to the other CPUs immediately), we don't have to make estimations about the effects of a data cache—100% of all the writes will use the system bus. Also, since writing zeroes to memory locations requires a very small number of instructions, we can safely assume that the instructions that are part of the loop that zeroes memory locations are fully cached. By keeping track of how much memory this "cache buster" program was able to zero, and over what time period, we can get an accurate assessment of how much bandwidth this program is using.

The purpose of this test program is to have a mechanism that will use up all available bandwidth, thereby saturating the bus. So you need to run this test while your machine is processing its regular workload (or has simulated users running a simulated workload), and then see how much more data can be put on the bus before it saturates. Typically, starting with the cache buster program running slowly (that is, with a large delay loop), you will (hopefully!) not see any noticeable performance change in the other running applications. However, as you increase the rate at which the test program writes data to the bus, you will begin to see the performance of your other applications degrade as the bus nears saturation. In some cases, if you have plenty of bus headroom available, you may even need to run multiple copies of the test program to create enough traffic to saturate the bus.

Regardless, at the point where performance starts to degrade, calculate how much additional data is being placed on the bus per second. Next, divide that number by the total bus bandwidth to get the percentage of the total bandwidth that is still available on your platform. You can use multiple copies of this test program running on an otherwise bare system to calculate the total bandwidth directly, but usually the vendor's stated bus bandwidth numbers are accurate enough. In the example shown in Figure 10.2, during normal workloads the machine is using some as yet undetermined amount of available bus bandwidth. However, when we use the cache buster program, we measure that it is able to use 25% of the available bus bandwidth before performance begins to collapse. We can therefore calculate that under normal workload conditions, we are using 75% of the available bus bandwidth.

In summary, creating a PATE (which includes writing benchmarks to test performance metrics, tracking CPU and disk I/O utilization numbers, and testing available bus bandwidth if you're using an SMP) is a critical part of building a successful data warehouse platform and maintaining it successfully. As your data warehouse environment grows over time, the PATE is the primary mechanism you will use to proactively ensure that your platform performance does not drop below your end users' performance

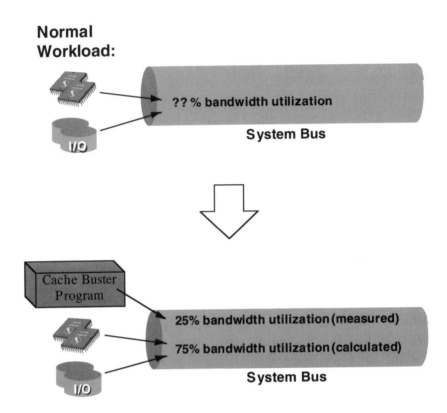

FIGURE 10.2
Directly measuring bus utilization.

requirements. Realize, however, that the performance assurance process is not magical. It will not prevent you from incrementally scaling up your data warehouse environment (either by adding more data, users, functionality, or complexity) in such a way that performance degrades below required levels. It will, however, give you a tool to allow you to proactively test the incremental additions and will alert you to the performance problems before you release the latest incremental additions to your end users. It therefore gives you a way to find problems early and fix them before your users ever see them.

VERY LARGE DATABASE (VLDB) ISSUES WITH DATA WAREHOUSING

Another important topic regarding high-performance data warehouse platforms is the issue of database size. If your data warehouse database is large enough, it will earn the right to be called a very large database (VLDB). The definition of a VLDB is hard to pin down, however, because the term is both relative and constantly changing. That is, what was considered a VLDB a few years ago is considered commonplace today. In this regard, the term VLDB is similar to the term supercomputer, because today's desktop computers are more powerful than the fastest supercomputers that existed only 10 or 15 years ago. A reasonable (although admittedly vague) working definition is that if we were to rank all databases by size, and if your data warehouse database were in the top 5 to 10% based on its size, then your data warehouse database could reasonably be called a VLDB.

Even though it is exciting to work on such large databases, VLDBs have their own set of performance issues that differ from the issues found in more conventionally sized data warehouse databases. It's a flaw to think of VLDBs as simply larger versions of smaller databases. You don't just have to do more of the same old thing as your database becomes larger, rather you often have to take different approaches. As an analogy, consider the differences between building a two-story house versus building a skyscraper. You can imagine what would happen if a skyscraper were built with the mentality that it's just like a two-story house, except that it has 50 stories. The large size introduces a whole different set of design problems that don't exist when building a two-story house. The same holds true for VLDBs.

The goal of this section is to point out why these differences exist. Managing a VLDB is different from managing a smaller database, and we need to understand why this is so. Where applicable, we also present some general approaches to addressing the issues that arise; but be forewarned that generic solutions work best only for generic issues. In many cases, your solution will have to be uniquely created to suit the needs of your specific VLDB. This is often a nontrivial process, but by understanding the causes of the issue, you will have an easier time identifying possible solutions.

Custom Code Requirements

As a DBA or developer of a VLDB data warehouse, one of the first differences you'll encounter is that there's a high probability that one or more of the steps in your data warehousing process will require custom code. As alluded to before, the cause is that issues faced in the VLDB realm are often unique to that specific data warehouse environment. There are probably not many other sites that have run into the same problems you're encountering, because there are not that many sites that are at the same scale as you are. And because of the fact that not many have faced this specific problem, there will probably not be an off-the-shelf solution to address the issue. You will have to develop it yourself, and unfortunately there is not much previous work on which you can base your solution.

One-In-A-Million Odds Occur Frequently

Another difference between VLDBs and non-VLDBs is the frequency with which "rarities" occur in a VLDB. For example, take the process of extracting data from your operational systems and cleaning/consolidating it in preparation for loading it into the data warehouse. Typically you need to define the formats and the range for the input data coming from the operational systems, and define transformation mappings for the data that define how the data needs to be modified before being loaded into the data warehouse database. In a non-VLDB platform, you can usually get away with not having to worry about those one-in-a-million flukes in your operational data that do not fall into the input formats or ranges you've defined. If one of those is encountered, since they are so rare in most databases, you can manually fix the problem.

VLDBs are different because this approach no longer works. Why not? Well let's assume that we have a table in our data warehouse database that contains 500 million rows (tables even larger than this exist). If the chances of a fluke piece of data being encountered are one in a million, then we will hit a fluke 500 times! Clearly we're taking the expression one in a million a bit too literally, but you can still see the point—if your sample size is large enough, it will contain a large number of things that only "rarely" happen. The result is that we must spend considerably more effort in defining our extraction and transformation routines to ensure that we don't leave any holes that will require manual fixing. Fixing 500 occurrences of a problem manually is not a feasible solution.

Statistical Effects

Other differences faced when building and managing a VLDB are caused by the laws of statistics. However, before we delve into the statistics, we first need to describe the situation. As we all know, databases of any size can encounter situations where response times begin to increase as the workload grows, but for a non-VLDB database, this increase is usually fairly linear. That is, you double the workload and find that your response times double. Usually this problem is caused by hitting a bottleneck in a specific component of your platform. Scaling up the bandwidth of that component (possibly along with performing some application tuning) will usually fix the problem. However, in a VLDB, the behavior can be quite different. Often, incrementally increasing your workload can (seemingly inexplicably) lead to response times that grow exponentially.

Statistics can help explain this effect. There is an entire area of statistics that involves modeling the flow of "service requests" through some process (such as modeling the flow of cars through a gas station or modeling the flow of customers through a restaurant). The process itself may have multiple stages, and each stage has a certain throughput capability. For example, the restaurant's kitchen can produce 25 meals an hour. We also assume that the service requests arrive in a random fashion, and that the distribution of the time between request arrivals follows a standard bell-shaped curve.

If the process being modeled is not very close to being saturated (meaning that it is not very close to 100% utilization of its throughput capability), then the average completion time for each type of request (for example, filling up on gas or getting an oil change) also follows a nice bell-shaped curve. In other terms, the standard deviation of response times is stable. However, this all falls apart if the process nears saturation. In this case, incoming requests rapidly become queued up, and the standard deviation for response times grows quickly. The queue length and the response times begin to grow exponentially as you get closer to saturation. In fact, if you were to work out the mathematics, you would discover that if a process is at exactly 100% utilization, and requests arrive in a standard bell-shaped distribution, the average response time becomes infinitely large. You might think that if you're not entirely 100% saturated, then the queue length should just grow linearly, not exponentially. We won't go into the mathematics, but suffice it to say that if queries arrived at exactly regular intervals, and if each query required the same amount of resources to process, then you would be right. However, the random nature of the query arrival times and the varying execution times of the different queries does in fact cause the queue length to grow exponentially.

Applying this to the data warehouse environment, the service requests are end-user queries, and the process being modeled is the execution of the query. In a smaller environment, you might hit the capacity limits of a single platform component, but the other components will usually be safely far away from the saturation point. That is, the database is usually of some manageable size, and we're not pushing multiple limits simultaneously. Since we're not very close to totally saturating the entire platform, we don't see the exponential performance degradation discussed above. However, in a VLDB-sized data warehouse, the sheer size of the database and the overall workload often leads to a scenario where you're pushing all system components (such as I/O, system bus, and CPU) to their limit. You are therefore many times more likely to saturate the entire platform, leading to exponential increases in response times.

What can be done in this situation? There are two options. The first option is to scale up all parts of the platform to alleviate the saturation problem. However, sometimes this may not be physically possible (e.g., traditional SMPs have no means of scaling up their bus bandwidth) or it may be economically infeasible.

The second option is to decrease the workload by restricting usage. You may have to purchase tools or create your own tools which (for example) only allow certain users to execute certain types of queries, or which limit how much time you can remain on the system, or which limit how long a specific query can run before being automatically aborted. The use of these tools and trade-offs is discussed in Chapter 7.

Algorithm Changes

Other differences can be attributed to what are known as algorithm changes. As the size of a database grows very large, you often see a discontinuity in performance levels that you don't see with smaller data warehouse platforms. That is, response times may initially be flat as you add data (and also add the associated amount of computing resources), as shown earlier at the top of Figure 10.1, but you will hit a certain data size where the response times will make a discontinuous jump and may then again remain flat after that (as shown in Figure 10.3).

Performance discontinuities are usually caused by a change in the algorithm that is used to carry out the requested function, and this change is usually necessitated because the amount of data to be processed has reached a size that can no longer be handled by the initial algorithm. For example, let's look at the algorithms for sort-merge joins and hash joins. For the purposes of this discussion, we don't need to analyze the entire algorithm. However, the part regarding the use of memory is critical. If the amount of data to be joined is such that it can all fit into memory, then the sort-merge join will bring all the data that needs to be joined into memory and perform the sort-merge join on it. Similarly the hash join will create all the hash join "buckets" in memory and place all the

Discontinuous Response Times

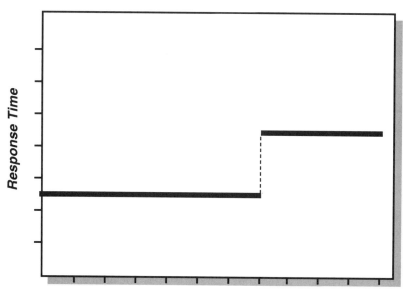

FIGURE 10.3
VLDBs often display discontinuous response times.

data into these in-memory buckets. In both cases, all of the data will be memory resident for the entire join process, so performance will be good.

However, we must look at what happens when there is more data to be joined than can fit into memory at one time. In this scenario (which is common in VLDBs), the first portions of the data are brought into memory, the join is performed on those portions, and the results are written out to disk as an intermediate result. Then the next portions are brought into memory, joined, and written to disk. The process repeats until all the portions are processed. Finally, the intermediate results stored on disk are merged into a final result set.

Clearly the scenario where all the data to be joined no longer fits in memory requires more steps (and therefore more CPU instructions) to be processed. That is, the algorithm itself changes depending on the size of the data. Whereas the initial code path followed is one that is highly efficient and totally memory based, the subsequent code path is more complex and requires more overhead. To minimize the impact, the only real solution is to add more memory. You may not be able to add enough to keep the entire process in memory, but adding memory will have two beneficial effects. First, it will push the discontinuity point farther out (i.e., it will happen at a point farther to the right in Figure 10.3). Second, increasing memory means that the size of each portion read into memory will be larger, so the total number of portions (and, therefore, the total number of times you must read in data and write out intermediate results) will be reduced.

MULTINODE ALGORITHM CHANGES   Another performance discontinuity caused by an algorithm change occurs when the data warehouse platform grows to a size larger than a single SMP can handle, and the organization decides to purchase a second SMP and cluster the two together to obtain the computing resources they need. However, even if the second SMP is identical to the first, you will never obtain twice the throughput you had with a single SMP. You may get close, but you won't be able to get exactly double, even under most optimal circumstances.

An algorithm change (going from a simpler to a more complex algorithm) is again the cause of this performance issue. When you run your database engine on a single SMP, you run it in "single node" mode. However, when you move to a clustered platform, you have to run in "multinode" mode. This means that additional functionality is invoked that is required to coordinate the actions of these multiple nodes. This additional functionality increases the length of the code path that must be executed for most database operations, and therefore has a negative impact on performance. In fact, there will be a noticeable performance difference even on a single-node machine if you do nothing else other than change the RDBMS setting from single node to multinode. So, when adding a second node, it is unreasonable to expect twice the performance that you were used to when you were just using a single node.

When you hit the physical limits of one component, you can always harness together multiple components into a scalable pool of resources. As we have said before, this is the basis of scalability. But the unavoidable downside is that you add coordination overhead (necessitating an algorithm change) when you create this shared pool of resources. The goal therefore is to keep workloads as partitioned as possible between these multiple nodes to minimize the communication overhead between nodes.

Exceeding Batch Windows

A final difference between VLDB data warehouse environments and smaller data warehouse environments is the complexity of the issues involving batch windows. These batch windows are used for many different operations, but the dominant uses are for performing the extract/cleanse/transform process and for backing up your data warehouse platform. It is an unfortunate truism that when it comes to data warehousing, you can expect everything in your system to scale up, with one major exception—the size of your batch windows. Typically your extract/cleanse/transform and backup batch windows will remain the same size over time, or if they do change, they tend to be scaled down, not up. As the rest of the requirements continually increase, you will be forced to perform more and more work in the same size (or smaller) batch window.

Of course, even smaller data warehouses run into this issue. But in these smaller scenarios, the standard utilities that are being used for the batch processes usually have performance levels that are high enough to handle the initial growing workloads without any major changes to how the process is performed. As your environment grows to the point where it is getting closer to the VLDB realm, you will hit the performance limits of your batch utilities. Since these batch utilities are a critical part of your whole data warehousing process, if they can no longer scale, then your platform will also no longer be able to scale.

The solution is to leverage the basic parallel techniques of splitting up the workload (using the concept of data partitioning) and then replicating the batch process to have one replicated copy per data partition. For example, instead of having a single backup process backing up the entire database, you need a parallel backup utility that allows you to run multiple backup processes, each of which simultaneously performs a backup of a different portion of the database and writes the backed up data to a different set of disks (so I/O throughput doesn't become a bottleneck). The good news is that all of the major database vendors supply parallel versions of their load, backup, and restore utilities, because in a VLDB environment, using parallel versions of these tools is always a requirement. Unfortunately the bad news is that only a few of the data extraction and transformation tools that are currently available are designed to run in parallel. This is not to say that they can't be run in parallel, but it usually requires a fair bit of manual effort to run these tools in parallel. For example, you'll need to manually start up multiple copies of the tool and also manually create the data partitions, and then point each copy of the tool at a different partition. But this situation is changing as these tool vendors modify or redesign their tools to run in parallel, thus more directly addressing the needs of VLDB warehouse environments.

As we said earlier, data warehouse databases that can be categorized as VLDB have their own sets of issues that designers and administrators need to be aware of. Because they are so large, they stress many components of your platform simultaneously. Finding solutions to these issues often requires creative thinking, but the better you understand the causes of the issues, the more likely you are to devise an effective strategy for handling them.

DATA WAREHOUSES AND THE WEB

Now let's turn our attention to some important trends that are affecting data warehousing. The first of these trends is the World Wide Web (WWW), which in recent years has forever changed the face of computing. The Web (for simplicity, we use the term Web to refer to both the World Wide Web and to intranets that use Web-based technologies) has rapidly become an effective medium for people and businesses to communicate and collaborate. Nearly every area of information technology has been affected by the pervasiveness of the Web.

Data warehousing is no different. It too has been affected, in that a large (and rapidly growing) percentage of data warehouses are being connected to the Web. Why is there such a rush to connect data warehouses to these networks? From a bottom-line perspective, the more you give people access to your data warehouse environment, the more advantageous it is, and the more leverage you can get out of it. If you've already taken the time and resources to build this environment, then you can increase your return on investment by having as many users as possible use it to understand and explore your business. By increasing access, you can increase the average knowledge level of your organization. Of course, even before the Web, it was true that you could increase the leverage of your data warehouse environment by giving more people access to it, but it was never very easy to do so. You had to struggle with proprietary networks, proprietary client/server protocols, and special client-side applications. But the Web (and Web-based technologies) make it far easier than before. You don't have to worry about installing additional client software (everyone just uses a Web browser) or distributing application updates to all users (the application logic is stored centrally on the server, not the browser).

In addition, end-user training is greatly simplified. No longer do you have to train people on both how the application works and how to use the client tool (which provides the interface to the application). Since nearly everyone already knows how to use a browser, you can focus training on the application, not the tool's interface to the application. Finally, since the Web is ubiquitous, you don't have to worry about connectivity issues. By leveraging the Web, the infrastructure is already in place to enable you to access your data warehouse environment from any place in the world. Essentially the Web simplifies the issues to the point where it is possible to make the dream of universal access to your data warehouse environment a reality.

But universal access via the Web creates a whole set of issues that must be handled. Distilled to its essence, Web access means your data warehouse environment will be exposed to more access by more users to more data. These increases will in turn put more strain on your data warehouse platform. Whatever level of scalability requirements you had will become magnified once you connect your data warehouse environment to the Web.

Web Access Means More Users

Let's look at the "more users" issue. As we discussed earlier, one of the most powerful reasons for connecting your data warehouse environment to the Web is to make it more accessible. Logically, then, it follows that if you increase accessibility, you will have more users than you would otherwise have. And not only will you have more users, but each user will typically access the data warehouse environment more frequently. Because Web browsers are ubiquitous, and because most people keep them running on their computers all the time, it becomes easier for users to use the data warehouse environment more frequently. That is, there is an increased inclination to access the environment simply because it is so easy to do so.

But it's not just the initial increased size of your user population that stresses the platform. It's also the rate at which your user population grows to this increased size. This problem is most noticeable if you have a portion of your data warehouse environment that is public—for example, it's available to all employees via a corporate intranet, or it's available over the Internet to your suppliers or customers. (Note: We are not using the term public to mean making your data truly public to anyone on the Web. Due to the sensitive nature of the data, few corporations would have reason to do this. Rather we're using the term to mean making the data accessible to any large user population that has a real need to access the information.) Once you decide to make the data public, anyone can access it, and you can no longer easily control the ramp-up in the number of users. This can very quickly lead to rapid growth in the number of users. At first, a few users in the population will experiment with the data warehouse environment, and then others will see the benefit and want to use it as well, and so on. Very quickly you will find yourself with a large user population that is growing exponentially.

HYPERGROWTH AND THE WEB   Hypergrowth refers to the fact that your user base will grow faster than your ability to scale up your data warehouse platform to meet these growing requirements/demands. You won't be able to scale up your platform fast enough to keep up with this hypergrowth. You simply can't add new CPUs, disk drives, and memory (and test them all to make sure you have no bottlenecks) fast enough to keep up with demand.

There are two approaches to dealing with hypergrowth. The first approach is to avoid the problem in the first place. Most data warehouse administrators become overzealous about making the data warehouse environment instantly available to the public. But in most cases we would suggest proceeding with caution. If you're not sure of the usage patterns, we would recommend against making it public initially. Instead, use the traditional approach of rolling your environment out to a few users, then a few more, etc. This can be done by password protecting the access and only giving the password to select groups. (Of course, people can share the password with people outside their group, but you can monitor usage to see if unintended users are accessing your data warehouse environment.)

However, sometimes there is a valid reason to make your data warehouse environment accessible to your entire organization. Since you aren't going to avoid hypergrowth, you need a different approach that allows you to handle it. The key to handling hypergrowth is to note that it only occurs during the initial stages of evolution. Continuous rapid exponential growth in the user base isn't possible—at the extreme, the maximum size of the number of concurrent users is ultimately limited by the total number of people in the user population. The trick is to build the first iteration of your data warehouse platform so that it has enough resources to handle where you will be when the hypergrowth subsides. To do this, you have to determine where you think that point will be. This is accomplished by looking at the growth plan for the data warehouse environment. That is,

❑ How many users do you expect?
❑ What workload will they be generating, and in what time frame?

After looking at the growth plans (or at least making your best guesses), you can define a graph that looks something like Figure 10.4. According to this graph, you can see that we expect the hypergrowth phase to level off sometime in May, supporting

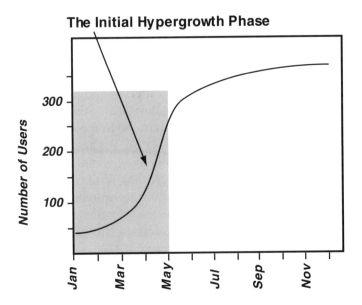

The Initial Hypergrowth Phase

FIGURE 10.4
Hypergrowth only occurs during the initial stages.

roughly 350 users. So even though we plan to start with only about 50 users, since we expect to grow extremely rapidly to 350 users, we build our first iteration to support 350 users rather than 50.

Web Access Means More Data

Next, let's look at why Web-enabled data warehouses imply more data. The answer is intuitive: the graphical nature of the Web makes it natural and simple to make requests for multimedia data. For example, an insurance company may choose to not only store traditional numeric and text data about car accident insurance claims, but might also store a digitized photograph of the car itself. End users could use the numeric and text data types to perform their analytical processing, and then perform drill-downs on specific data items to get not only the traditional data on a particular record, but also the related image as well. With the potential need for storing large numbers of images, this means that the trend to larger and more rapidly growing data warehouse environments will only accelerate. In addition, not only will your environment be responsible for storing more data, but the requests for multimedia data also require much more bandwidth than is required for traditional data types.

Ultimately, what does more access by more users to more data really mean? It means that the requirement for a scalable warehouse platform is increased. Addressing these issues doesn't require any new techniques—the standard scalable design principles discussed in this book will work well. It's just the case that the requirement to use these scalable techniques will be even more critical if your data warehouse environment is connected to the Web.

DATA WAREHOUSES AND DATA MINING

A second trend that is important to data warehousing is the increasingly common use of advanced data mining techniques to extract previously unknown information. There's a good reason for this sudden surge of interest in performing data mining. Traditionally the model for performing decision support within a data warehouse environment was fairly simple. An analyst, armed with his or her favorite query or reporting tool, would derive a set of questions, and then use the tool to run queries against the database. This works fine when the questions are of a quantitative nature: What are my average sales for the quarter? Which products are selling better this year than last year? Who are my 10 biggest customers?

But it doesn't work well for answering more complex qualitative questions: Why do some of my customers take advantage of a particular sale, but others don't? What type of person is likely to be a good candidate for a mortgage loan? What factors most influence the sale of a certain product? Using the traditional approach, the analyst would have to form a hypothesis about the answer to these questions and then use their query tool to collect the information necessary to prove or disprove their hypothesis. This is called a "verification-based" approach. The reason this approach doesn't work well for qualitative questions is that it relies on the analyst to have the correct intuition about what the answer really is. If the analyst doesn't think of the correct answer, then it won't be found. But data mining is a solid step toward solving this problem. It is a process by which a set of algorithms systematically look through your data to automatically find patterns, trends, and correlations that you otherwise might not have found. The burden is therefore no longer on the analyst to have the correct intuition.

Data Mining Requires Scalability

When data mining tools are employed they must be thought of as an integral part of the data warehouse platform rather than as a separate application. Why is it important to think of data mining tools this way? Because it will force you to realize that these tools are really just one step in the overall data warehousing process. And as we mentioned in previous chapters, every step of the process must be thought of as a link in a "performance chain," and therefore every step must be scalable to avoid bottlenecks. This means that if you want to build a data warehouse environment that can give you significant insight into the way your enterprise is functioning (the type of insight that data mining tools excel at delivering), then the data mining component must be able to scale along with the platform. There are a number of reasons why this is true. First, data mining needs to look at individual records to be able to find patterns, and this often means sifting through vast amounts of detailed data. Analyzing smaller amounts of summarized and aggregated data is not very useful, because the process of summarization and aggregation "smoothes" out the data, thereby removing the ability to find subtle correlations between individual data items. Therefore you need enough raw CPU power and I/O bandwidth to process this large amount of data, in the same way that a parallel query needs large amounts of aggregate CPU and I/O power. The scalable hardware discussed in previous chapters is well suited to meeting these requirements.

Also, data mining is usually extremely computationally intensive. If you're using data mining to develop predictive models (such as those that might predict a customer's tendency to respond to a certain targeted marketing campaign), the algorithms will generate dozens, hundreds, or sometimes even thousands of models, and then you'll need to test the accuracy of these models against a significant portion of the database (at least 10%). You need the raw horsepower that multiprocessor scalable hardware can supply to be able to process all these tests in any reasonable amount of time.

But scalability is really about being able to solve problems that get bigger over time, regardless of the size at which they start. As with any data warehouse application, there are a number of different factors that inherently drive data mining applications to grow rapidly in at least three different dimensions: data size, complexity, and functionality. As a component of your data warehouse performance chain, your data mining application must be scalable to handle this growth.

DATA MINING TOOLS MUST HANDLE INCREASING AMOUNTS OF DATA   We've discussed how a data warehouse environment is one that will continually and organically grow over time. Therefore it should be obvious that for this reason alone, any tool that accesses data in this environment must necessarily be able to handle growing volumes of data. However, there are other reasons that are more uniquely tied to data mining that act as additional motivations for growth in data volume. First, an organization will typically begin a data mining project with data captured during the last 12 months of operation. However, it's not uncommon that the analysts will soon start clamoring for a much longer history (say, 36 months) in order to have more history on which they can perform a more complete trend analysis. Also, it's often very valuable to have more than a single year's worth of data in order to detect patterns that repeat on an annual basis. (If you only have one year of data, then you have no way of determining if a particular cycle repeats every year.) These reasons will accelerate the growth rate of your data warehouse environment.

But additional data does not just come from internal sources. Often the data you need is not available internally, and is instead purchased from external sources and added to your data warehouse environment. For example, in order to understand, model, and predict certain customer behaviors, you might need to add demographic data about your customers. Or if you're a clothing retailer trying to understand the sales patterns for your heavy wool sweaters, you might need historical weather data. Integrating this external data with your existing environment can result in a tremendous increase in the amount of data managed by the data warehouse platform.

INCREASING COMPLEXITY   One of the goals of data mining is to be able to model and understand very specific behaviors. As the behavior you're trying to model becomes more narrowly defined, the complexity of the data mining task increases. For example, if you're trying to understand the purchasing patterns of a specific age group, you have a certain amount of complexity involved. If you then become more specific and want to target that age group in a certain geographic region, your complexity increases. If you further want to refine your model to target that age group in that region for a certain time of year, your complexity increases again. Once again, scalability in your entire data warehousing process is required to handle this increasing complexity.

INCREASING FUNCTIONALITY   Not only do analysts find themselves trying to continually refine their models, as described previously, but once they see their efforts begin to bear fruit, they'll want to expand their scope and add more data mining functionality to address other issues. For example, a telephone company's first foray into data mining may be to use "clustering" algorithms to help identify groups of customers (i.e., clusters) that have similar cellular phone usage patterns. They can use the results to better understand their different customer segments, which in turn means they can better tailor particular services to these different segments. Once these efforts begin to pay off, they might next want to add "neural net" algorithms to help them perform fraud detection. And so on. Each additional piece of functionality means increased demands against your data warehouse platform.

The Basics of Scalable Data Mining

Given that data mining systems need scalability, how do you go about putting together a scalable data mining solution? First, you need the right technology components, which means scalable hardware components and scalable database software to manage the data warehouse environment that will be mined. The mining tools themselves also need to be able to take advantage of scalable hardware. (Although the data mining application usually is not run on the same hardware as the database, whatever platform it does run on must be scalable.) If a platform lacks the ability to add more CPUs as the amount of data to be processed increases, the computationally intensive nature of data mining will bring any nonscalable platform to its knees very quickly. Optimally these tools would also be able to retrieve data directly from a database rather than forcing the user to first write the data to a flat file (which is still the case for many data mining applications).

Finally, you need to have a good understanding of how to integrate data mining technologies into your data warehouse platform performance chain without introducing any bottlenecks in your application design. This means that you must be familiar with the techniques defined in this book. When the right technologies are combined with the appropriate techniques, the result is a data mining application that meets not only your current needs, but which can also adapt to meet your future needs.

DATA WAREHOUSES AND OBJECT-RELATIONAL DATABASES

A third trend that will have a significant impact on data warehousing is the recent introduction of object-relational databases. The premise behind being able to put objects into a data warehouse environment is very compelling. Even though standard relational databases are powerful, only a tiny fraction of the world's information actually lends itself to being stored in the row and column format of a relational database. Therefore giving users the ability to store more complex objects of any format and any data type means that users can now put all the rest of their nonrelational data online. Basically, with object-relational databases, if the information can be digitized, it can be put in a data warehouse environment.

Since this technology gives us the ability to manage far more types of data, object-relational databases will inevitably be much larger and will grow much faster than standard relational databases ever did. Multimedia data, complex data types, unstructured data types, and countless other types of data will begin to work their way into corporate data warehouse environments as organizations find creative ways to derive tangible value from these new types of data. Also, since we can put more types of data and more types of functionality directly into the database, we can address the needs of a wider group of users. All of this leads to more data, more users, and more rapid growth. Therefore, similar to the effect the Web has on data warehousing, adding object capabilities to a relational database technology clearly increases the requirement for a truly scalable data warehouse platform.

But unlike the Web, object technology does not simply magnify the scalability requirements/demands. It can also be used to enhance the scalability of the system by increasing the system's efficiency. By using object technology in a relational database, you can define routines (called methods) for handling these new data types that are far more efficient than using the standard relational operators. So, on the one hand, the introduction of object technology means more data, more users, and more scalability stresses on the platform, but on the other hand, object technology can be used to enhance the efficiency of the database to alleviate many scalability stresses.

Scalable Performance for Complex Data Types

While there are certainly numerous operations that can be performed efficiently by relational databases, there are countless others that do not easily fit into the relational model and therefore are woefully inefficient to process using standard relational approaches. For these operations, achieving scalable performance in a traditional relational database is either extremely difficult or outright impossible. However, object-relational databases can help us solve this problem. By allowing users to define their own data storage, data access, and data processing methods, users can define operations that are optimized for a particular data type.

For example, relational databases are notoriously inefficient at processing "time-series" data. Time-series data is used to track the value of a particular entity over time. The classic example is tracking the value of stock market equities on a daily, hourly, or even minute-by-minute basis. Time-series data is actually just about everywhere in a data warehouse environment. Tracking the daily store revenues of each outlet in a retail store chain reflects time-series data; so does tracking on a per-product basis the number of customer service calls you receive each hour pertaining to that product. Essentially anything where you might want to generate a graph that plots a certain value over time fits into the definition of time-series data.

Continuing with our classic equity example, in a relational database, this time-series data typically would be stored in a table that has at least the following three columns: Equity Name, Time Stamp, and Equity Price. While this approach gives you a way to store the information you need, it is not an optimal solution. First, data for a single stock will usually end up being scattered across a possibly very large number of discontiguous disk blocks, completely intermingled with information about other stocks. Because the data is spread across a large number of disk blocks, the time it takes to access all the data associated with an individual stock is increased (see Figure 10.5).

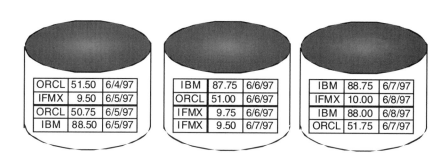

ORCL	51.50	6/4/97
IFMX	9.50	6/5/97
ORCL	50.75	6/5/97
IBM	88.50	6/5/97

IBM	87.75	6/6/97
ORCL	51.00	6/6/97
IFMX	9.75	6/6/97
IFMX	9.50	6/7/97

IBM	88.75	6/7/97
IFMX	10.00	6/8/97
IBM	88.00	6/8/97
ORCL	51.75	6/7/97

FIGURE 10.5
Relational models scatter time-series data.

Also, relational technology doesn't give you an efficient way to achieve the types of functionality that are needed for time-series data. For example, a common request is to plot the "moving average" of a time series for a stock price, which for any given day returns the average of the n most recent closing prices. Or analysts might want to look at the spread between the maximum and minimum stock price for each week to see how the price volatility is changing on a week-by-week basis. Trying to generate these answers using standard SQL is extremely inefficient, often requiring a separate query for each data point desired. In these cases, performance is usually poor, and as data sizes scale up, generating your results using relational technology becomes infeasible.

The solution in the object-relational world is very different. If your application required storing and analyzing time-series data (or any other nonrelational data type that you can imagine), you would simply purchase a database extension (often referred to by object-relational database vendors as a datablade or a cartridge) that supports the storage, manipulation, and analysis of that data type. Or if the extension you need isn't available on the market, you can create your own. Either way, once the extension is plugged into your database engine, all the functionality you need would be available. For example, a time series extension would treat all the time-series data for a specific equity as a single object. Storage mechanisms would be included which know about these time-series objects and which try to keep all the information for an individual time-series object spread across as few disk blocks as possible. That is, it would collocate data from the same equity in the same disk blocks. This greatly reduces the number of disk blocks that need to be read, thereby speeding up data access times and making performance acceptable even for large data sizes (see Figure 10.6).

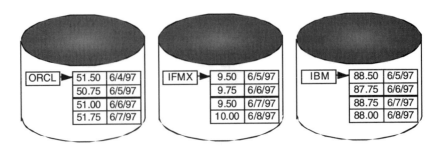

FIGURE 10.6
Object-relational models can store time-series data more efficiently.

This extension would also contain intelligent functions that read a time-series object and generate all the data points for a moving average graph (or a volatility graph, etc.) with only a single pass through the data rather than requiring the execution of a separate query for each data point. Because of the dramatically increased efficiency of these functions, analyzing very large data sizes is no longer infeasible, and the ability for your data warehouse platform to scale is increased.

Scalable Functionality

By definition, scalable data warehouse platforms must be able to handle not only increases in the amount of data managed and the number of users supported, but must also handle increases in functionality. As alluded to earlier, object-relational systems let you add to the database any functionality you want. Third parties will be creating extensions for many common nonrelational objects, and you'll be able to buy these extensions (or write your own) and plug them into your own system. You'll be able to do such things as search through digitized pictures and return only those that contain a particular image, or perform complex statistical analysis on large data sets, or search through unstructured text to find documents discussing a specified topic. The flexibility this enables is enormous, helping ensure that as your needs grow, you can scale-up your data warehouse platform's capabilities with client-specific functionality.

Scalability Issues Regarding Object-Relational Technology

As we write this, object-relational technology is still fairly new. Many organizations have begun to experiment with different uses of the technology to unlock the real business value that object-relational data warehouses promise to deliver. But currently there are still some questions that need answering before this promise becomes a reality. As we discussed, object-relational extensions can potentially increase the scalability of the data warehouse platform, but there are a few technical hurdles that need to be overcome. For example, the use of parallelism is critical to scalability. Can these extensions make efficient use of parallelism? Also, performance assurance and performance tuning are ongoing processes in a scalable data warehouse platform. But do we know how to tune the performance of an object-relational database? Note that we're not implying that the answers to these questions can't be found. We fully believe they can. Rather we're implying that it's going to be up to the early users to discover the answers.

TAKING ADVANTAGE OF PARALLELISM One of the most effective ways to improve scalability is to use parallelism. But to be able to deploy parallelism requires that the problem be broken up into smaller portions and the results from processing each of the portions be meaningfully merged into a final result. For relational databases, running parallel queries against standard tables is fairly well understood, and efficient algorithms exist. But we don't yet have the same level of understanding about how to run parallel queries against other types of objects.

For example, take the problem of running queries against digitized pictures in a data warehouse environment and asking the database to return only those pictures that contain specific visual items. Certainly the problem of enabling a computer to identify visual items within a picture is enormously complex, and current technologies are only mediocre at best. But for the sake of this discussion, let's assume that this problem is already solved and that we therefore have algorithms that can accurately scan digitized pictures to locate specific items contained within. The scalability question is then raised: How would you take advantage of multiple processors to perform this query? Well, you could assign different sets of images to different processes, and each processor would scan its subset of images by itself. However, many images are extremely large (single images can sometimes be even larger than a "large" relational table), and we would therefore benefit even further by enabling multiple processors to work on an image simultaneously.

How do we do this? If we are scanning a relational table, the solution is to hand each processor a portion of the table to process. So, your initial guess might be to follow the same tactics—divide up the image into pieces and have each piece scanned by a different processor. That is, if you have four processors, you can partition the image into quadrants and have each processor look for the existence of the desired visual item in their quadrant. Unfortunately that won't work. If the feature you're looking for spans the boundary between two or more quadrants, you won't find it using this approach because the entire image doesn't exist in any single quadrant. For example, assume you have a simple query that is intended to return all pictures that contain three or more circles. The image shown in Figure 10.7 satisfies this query. However, one of the circles lies on the border between quadrants I and III (outlined in bold in the figure) and would not be found with this simple partitioning scheme. Therefore the query would mistakenly conclude that this image does not satisfy the query.

Let's take another case: using object-relational technology to place data mining functionality directly into the database engine so

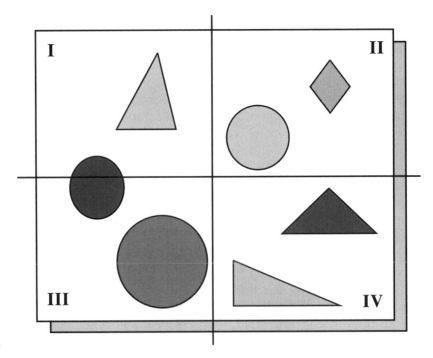

FIGURE 10.7
Simple partitioning doesn't work with images.

you can perform data mining against your data within the database engine itself, rather than having to move the data to another platform on which you would run your data mining processes. To ensure scalability, you'd like to be able to harness the power of multiple processors to work on different subsets of the data. However, you again run into technical hurdles. For example, assume you want to run a neural net algorithm against a very large data set. Rather than having a single processor process each row and develop the neural net by itself, you'd prefer to be able to divide up the data and have each processor build a neural net from its subset of the data. This is shown in Figure 10.8.

Although we've been able to successfully divide up the problem (which is the first step of running an algorithm in parallel), the second step (merging the results from the different partitions) is difficult. A neural net is loosely modeled after the functioning of a brain. When you create a neural net, the result is a complex web of interconnected inputs and weighted values that act as outputs. It is generally considered a "black box" solution, meaning that for a given set of inputs at one end of the neural net, it yields fairly accurate outputs at the other end, but the internal process by which it does so cannot easily be understood by looking inside. In other words, there is no real "semantic meaning" associated with a specific weighted value. And no two neural nets will look exactly alike. So how do you merge each of these "subnets" into one larger neural net? How do you know which values to combine with other values? As shown in Figure 10.8, the neural nets all look different. How would you combine them?

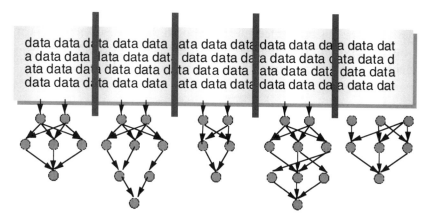

FIGURE 10.8

Creating a neural net from each partition of the data.

In both examples (parallel image processing and parallel creation of a neural net), computer science researchers have discovered some solutions, and some of this research is making its way into commercially available object-relational database extensions. But more work is needed. For an application to be truly scalable, we will have to learn how to make all database extensions work in a parallel environment.

OBJECT-RELATIONAL PERFORMANCE TUNING   Most obvious to any early user of object-relational databases is the fact that as an industry, we're not fully versed on how to tune object-relational database extensions to improve their scalability. A bevy of books exists on how to tune relational databases, but no such resources are yet available for object-relational database users. The techniques have yet to be defined, and the tricks of the trade have yet to be discovered. And it's likely that different extensions will require different tuning techniques. For example, some objects might be hierarchical in nature (meaning that a single object is comprised of several subobjects, each of which can in turn be comprised of several subsubobjects, etc.). Other objects might simply be very large, as is the case with digitized video. We wouldn't consider it going out on a limb to assume that designing and tuning these very different objects for performance will require a different skill set for each.

Ultimately the emergence of object-relational technologies will have a significant impact on what you'll be able to do with your data warehouse platforms. Your platforms will contain more data of more types and will have more functionality that will make them appeal to a wider user audience. This in turn means that a premium is placed on scalability. We have discussed that there are still outstanding issues that need to be resolved, but we are confident that, as has happened with relational databases, we will learn how to build highly scalable data warehouse platforms that efficiently leverage the capabilities of object-relational databases.

SUMMARY

The state of the data warehousing industry is in a period of rapid growth and change. Data warehouse platforms themselves are beginning to have "organic" qualities about them, allowing them to not only grow and adapt as the environment around them changes, but also giving them the ability to affect their environment and change the way organizations work. Throughout all this it is important to understand how building and managing these data warehouse platforms differs from what we've been used to in the past. To be able to build a very large data warehouse environment, and to be able to take advantage of the important new trends as they occur (such as the Web, data mining, and object-relational technologies), we must build high-performance, highly scalable, and highly flexible data warehouse platforms. If we have given you some insight into how to do this, then we have achieved the goals we defined when we first set out to write this Part.

We have discussed a variety of topics critical to the successful delivery of a high-performance data warehouse environment. We have talked about the usage and data that fundamentally shape the complexion of the data warehouse environment. In addition, we have talked about building an "organic" platform to house the data and support the various usage characteristics of explorers and farmers. In the next Part we talk about the critical, ongoing role of servicing the high-performance data warehouse environment.

Service Management and Performance

Chapter 11, "Service Management and the Service
Management Contract"
Chapter 12, "Putting the Service Management Contract in
Motion"

In the previous Part, our focus was on the elements of a high-performance data warehouse environment that pertain to the delivery of data warehouse services (i.e., usage, data, and platform). In this Part, we shift our focus to the "pearl" of the data warehouse environment, service management.

This layer strives to ensure that the services delivered meet user expectation initially and over the life of the environment. This discussion is divided into two chapters. Chapter 11 details the history of service management, its importance, and the role of the Service Management Contract in providing form. In Chapter 12 we focus our attention on putting the Service Management Contract in motion.

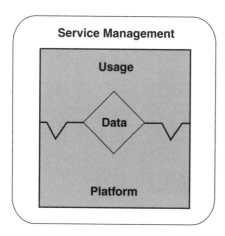

11

Service Management and the Service Management Contract

In the first Part of this book we emphasized that one of the biggest challenges facing the data warehouse environment is the ever-increasing accumulation of dormant data. Although the heart of this environment is to provide a consistent, historical store of data, needlessly collecting data without knowing who is going to use it and/or how it is going to be used is simply not a good (or career enhancing) idea. Dormant data can place a great burden on the data warehouse platform and require expensive cycles and disk storage space from the source systems to capture data that will never be used. As we will see, service management is an effective tool for dealing with this dormant data. In addition, service management provides the basis for managing the high-performance data warehouse environment (usage, data, and platform) such that customer expectations are understood and met. It places IT in the position of providing a valuable service to its customers and not just a "technology."

First, let us begin with a definition of service management. Later we will cover the history, future, and the business imperatives of service management. Finally, we will go through the steps for creating a winning service management contract or SMC. In the next chapter we will talk in detail about putting the SMC in motion.

299

SERVICE MANAGEMENT DEFINED

Service management is the strategic discipline responsible for defining, building, and maintaining IT services at a level that supports the organization's business goals and objectives at a cost that is justified and appropriate. According to the *IT Infrastructure Library*, the definition of service management is "the process of managing the quality and quantity of delivered IT service according to a written agreement or 'contract' between the customers and IT services. This contract defines the responsibilities placed on these parties and in particular binds the IT services group to offer an agreed quality of service so long as the customer constrains the demands they place upon the service within agreed limits." For the remainder of this discussion, we will use the abbreviated phrase "service management" to refer to the all activities related to IT service level and objective management. [There are many good sources of information about ITSM that can provide the interested reader with more detail than the available space and intended scope of this book allows. In particular we reference the *IT Infrastructure Library* (IT-IL). This comprises a set of books ("modules") that offer accumulated best practices and recommendations for the establishment of ITSM and its supporting functions. IT-IL was originally developed under the auspices of the CCTA (UK government body for IT standards) by the Exin Foundation. Exin's web site is www.exin.nl.]

While many have heard of service management, most think of it in the context of outsourcing, where one company provisions and manages computer-related services from another company. While service management plays a large role in outsourcing, it is also used quite effectively in house to ensure computer-related services meet customer expectations.

It is worth noting that service management is a *strategic* management discipline. It is important to differentiate between tactical fire-fighting behavior that tends to be the norm when tackling day-to-day performance and availability issues and the proactive and heavily business aligned practice of service management that operates at a business level. Let's look more closely at the origins of service management to better understand how it is used today and how you can apply it within your organization.

If you can't measure it, you can't manage it. [Anon.]

Service management is not a new discipline. Service management has been practiced by many organizations for more than a decade. In the beginning, service management was created in response to the sheer cost of the IT infrastructure, largely due to the price of mainframe hardware and software. For investing a certain amount of money, users or consumers of the IT service wanted commitments on measurable events like response time and system availability. With investment decisions for hardware upgrades requiring board-level approval, the ability to demonstrate return on investment (ROI) and value to the business was imperative. Service management provided the measures and controls to demonstrate that they were delivering and managing a high quality service at optimal cost. This activity was key to the budgetary process, ensuring the necessary funding for key initiatives was secured.

Service Management Today

Until recently, industry adoption of service management has been slowed for a number of reasons. Most prominent of these reasons is the move to open systems, fueled by the availability of low cost, but powerful, computers running the Unix operating system. This trend was driven by the very reason IT implemented service management—cost optimization. Unix hardware is considered inexpensive and the associated software license costs are an order of magnitude less when compared to mainframe alternatives. Another reason for the service management slowdown is the challenge presented by the new, distributed computing paradigm. Many progressive organizations implemented systems based upon this technology, but few knew how to implement and manage them effectively. Tactical day-to-day issues of implementation made strategic initiatives such as service management a low prior-

continued

ity. IT managers were less concerned about the quality of service they offered and more concerned about being able to offer any service at all! Now that most well-run organizations know how to effectively use open systems, organizations are rediscovering the benefits of service management and are weaving its discipline and structure into new and existing distributed computing application projects.

BUSINESS NEED FOR SERVICE MANAGEMENT

As Figure 11.1 shows, there must be a direct link between the goals and objectives of the business and the supporting IT infrastructure. Service management is built upon the foundation of many IT management activities. To provide a common understanding, following are brief definitions of each activity:

> **Availability management.** Best thought of in terms of the service or applications that are expected to be available during business. Simply put, it is the service or application available to all customers during business hours (which may be different than 9 to 5).
>
> **Capacity management.** Defines, tracks, and controls IT service capacities to ensure that the platform is able to meet growing demands of its customers.

FIGURE 11.1

Service management relationship to IT functions.

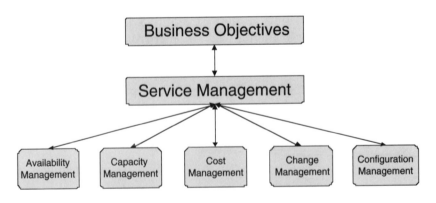

Cost management. Defines, tracks, and controls service costs associated with IT applications. It enables IT to recover or, at a minimum, track costs of providing these services.

Change management. The process of planning, coordinating, monitoring, and measuring changes that affect the data warehouse environment.

Configuration management. A disciplined process to specify, track, and report on each IT component under configuration control, which is often referred to as a configuration item. Data is stored in a logical entity known as the configuration management database, typically consisting of multiple distinct databases. Configuration items vary widely in complexity, size, and type. Typically they are defined down to the lowest possible level at which a component can be independently installed, replaced, or modified.

Today this is well documented and understood. As organizations align resources to focus on those initiatives that are business critical, those resources that are not in alignment are either reengineered or removed. For this reason, there seems to be a significant level of renewed interest in service management to facilitate business alignment between IT and customers in all types of computing environments, from departmental systems to mainframes and everything in between. With the advent of client/server systems and more complicated computing architectures (as discussed in the previous section on platform and performance), service management has become a principal way of managing customer expectations. The software solutions (i.e., enterprise management solutions) for monitoring and managing complex distributed system infrastructures have evolved to the point where they make service management a practical proposition for the new breed of IT services now in production. Even with these improvements in management of IT infrastructures, many companies are questioning whether their IT is a necessary and important function.

For many organizations, the prospect of outsourcing has not gone away. Organizations are looking to "do more with less" by concentrating on their core business and selectively outsourcing those things that are not considered strategic (e.g., management of a wide area network). For these organizations, service management plays a vital role in ensuring the level of service meets the needs of the business. Without service management, and all of the associated metrics and reporting capabilities, companies that outsource would not have a predictable service provided from their outsourcer. For example, if data is not loaded into the data warehouse environment as needed, critical decisions may not be able to be made or, worse, the wrong decision is made. Let's look more closely at service management and its relationship with other IT functions. Following is an illustration of how a company's business objectives and imperatives must be translated into business value, cost, and measurement for IT and other company functions. Once this is documented, service management is the vehicle to monitor and report on the company's progress toward its business objectives.

THE SERVICE MANAGEMENT CONTRACT

Service management creates an environment that encourages teamwork between the IT service supplier (typically an internal entity within the organization) and the service consumers (customers). It provides a forum where they can discuss the service offering on a professional and businesslike basis. These meetings typically occur on a regular basis, such as weekly or monthly. Topics of discussion range from service performance for the current period to any trending or recurring problems that seem to be present.

Central to the service management process is a document known as the service management contract (SMC). The SMC is jointly developed by the data warehouse administrators and the customers, as the customers will not typically have sufficient knowledge to understand that some of their perceived requirements are unreasonable or just not possible. For example, the customers might see no reason why all profiling or multidimensional analysis queries can't complete within two seconds. The key question is, do the customers really need a two-second response time in order to meet their business objectives or is this simply a "nice to have" requirement? It may be technically possible to deliver two-second query response times if it is a business imperative; however, the cost of doing so may be disproportionate to the value received. Is the business prepared to pay the money necessary to achieve a guaranteed two-second response time? Chances are probably not.

The SMC is an articulation of what customer needs are to be met with the data warehouse environment. Most contracts identify activities that must be completed to meet the objectives set by the business and, consequently, what IT needs to know in order to plan and monitor the data warehouse environment. Some SMCs contain sections that relate to a specific application and, in some cases, a particular population of customers (e.g., farmers or explorers) of the application. Remember that customers will place different demands on the system based on their job function. For example, explorers will tolerate longer response times because of the type and complexity of information they request. It is common for explorers to have queries that run in hours or even days (e.g., extracting). In addition, explorers are less likely to expect consistent response times given the unpredictability of their requests (e.g., profiling).

Farmers, on the other hand, are more sensitive to response times, since their queries take from minutes up to an hour (e.g., multidimensional analysis). Farmers know what information they are looking for and approximately how long the query should take. Wild variations in farmer response time will not be tolerated. Knowing that each group of customers will likely require their own response time goal will save the data warehouse administrator a lot of time and frustration. For more information on the different types of customers and their expectations, see Chapter 2.

In addition, the SMC may define additional generic customer services defined by the data warehouse administrator (such as a Help Desk service), which do not relate to a single customer application but must be in place to serve the global customer community (e.g., data quality, availability).

CREATING THE SERVICE MANAGEMENT CONTRACT

Can all applications benefit from the service management process? The answer is yes and no. Defining and supporting an SMC can be a time-consuming activity. Not every application needs one. Most often, only mission critical applications should have detailed SMC definitions. Thus service management focuses on understanding and aligning the delivery of data warehouse environment services with the organization's strategic goals and objectives. It should be readily evident which applications require a service management contract and which do not (e.g., the HR vacation data warehouse is unlikely to be mission critical). This is not to say that IT should not measure service for those noncritical applications. Indeed, the more IT appropriately measures and adjusts, the better the service offered. The distinction that is being made is that the level of service management detail that is required for mission critical applications is far greater and will have a greater positive impact on the company than spending time on the less critical applications. Having said that, once all mission critical applications are covered by an SMC, it would be appropriate to create a simple SMC for other applications that are used by non-IT staff.

In broad terms, most applications that are customer facing should be considered mission critical. In addition, applications that play a "near-time" role in determining how the business operates and interfaces with its customers and competitors is also likely to be, at the very least, "mission sensitive" and warrant an SMC. An additional factor that may also dictate that an SMC is warranted is how politically visible the application is. New applications that may not yet directly contribute to the business's goals, but are seen as holding great promise, fall into this camp, as do those requiring high levels of capital investment. The nature of data warehouse environments dictates that they will often play a mission critical or at the very least a mission sensitive role in the organization, and therefore SMCs are highly appropriate.

From this discussion, one thing is clear. SMCs come in all shapes and sizes, depending on the environment and application. Some contracts are less than one page, and others can exceed ten. With the wide range of complexity and alternatives, how does one go about implementing an SMC? The following section gives the reader a systematic process for creating and maintaining successful SMCs.

One last thing to note is to start small. Find a well-defined application that would benefit from a service management contract and start there. Too often a Herculean effort that covers all services quickly collapses under its own weight because it is too complicated (sounds similar to a data warehousing effort). One approach would be to start by creating a contract for data warehouse availability, data quality, or recoverability (i.e., backup and restore). This will contain the scope and maintain the focus of the service management contract team until they have iterated through the process enough times to be comfortable at handling the more complicated aspects, such as query performance.

The seven steps to creating and managing a winning SMC include

1. Establish relevant data warehouse resources inventory or services catalog.
2. Characterize usage of data warehouse resources.
3. Determine current or project service levels.
4. Understand the customer's requirements.
5. Determine cost and feasibility of customer's requirements.
6. Create the service management contract.
7. Track compliance to the service management contract.

Now let's take a look at each of these steps in detail.

STEP 1: Establish Relevant Data Warehouse Resources Inventory or Services Catalog

The essential building block in understanding what levels of service can be delivered is in knowing and cataloging the data warehouse platform that supports the service. This includes all components of the performance chain as referenced in the section "Platform and Performance" (hardware, operating system, database, etc.). This information is vital to knowing if the shared or common infrastructure components can support the needs of the data warehouse user. For example, the corporate networking backbone, which all applications and customers share, may not be able to handle the incremental amount of activity that the new data warehouse application will generate. Since the network is usually outside the purview of the data warehouse team, the assumption that network planning will just increase the bandwidth may be erroneous. Typically this information can be found in the IT capacity plan or services catalog. (The *IT Services Catalog* is a reference guide that details, by application, all IT resources required and any pertinent details, such as current release of the application software, etc., for all IT supported applications.) If no such service resource exists, this may be the appropriate time to create one.

STEP 2: Characterize Usage of Data Warehouse Resources

For existing data warehouses, understanding how both the data warehouse environment and other applications use the current platform is important (e.g., profiling, extracting, modeling, multidimensional analysis, etc.). When components of the platform are being shared (e.g., the aforementioned corporate networking backbone), it's necessary to take a global view when planning service levels for the data warehouse environment. It is important to acknowledge that changes in the usage of these other applications will have an impact upon the level of service that can be delivered in the data warehouse environment.

For an application that is in the process of being developed or implemented, a heavy reliance must be placed on the IT capacity planning function. They can use predictive techniques (typically analytic techniques which may make use of automated modeling tools) to arrive at a best estimate of resource requirements. This activity should, of course, be conducted during the implementation of any new application regardless of whether or not an SMC is being defined to ensure that the project does not fail as a result of poor performance when implemented. That is, that the proper performance boundaries should be set as new applications are released to customers, so expectations regarding performance can be managed. For example, if customers think that a data warehouse query that has four multimillion row table joins and a group by and order by can return a 10,000 row result set in five minutes (which is probably not realistic), they will be disappointed unless expectations are set before they begin running queries.

STEP 3: Determine Current or Projected Service Levels

If the data warehouse environment is currently in production, then it is a relatively straightforward matter to determine the current levels of service being delivered ("baselining"). This can be derived from measurement data (where available) and supplemented with information from interviews with the customers. Measurements of query performance, availability, and other areas are used to help determine the level of service currently provided. This is used to measure improvements that are made to performance over time.

For a new data warehouse, the performance prediction activities conducted in step 2 should provide data to characterize the level of service that will be delivered once the data warehouse application is moved from the pilot phase into production.

STEP 4: Understand the Customer's Requirements

Steps 1–3 are important precursors that must be completed before engaging in discussions with customers regarding what levels of service they feel they need and want. For existing data warehouse environments, it is important to understand how well the warehouse is serving the customer and whether there are additional needs that are not being met. For new data warehouse environments, it is important to understand the expectations the customers have so that these needs can be accommodated during the design phase of the data warehouse environment. These discussions should be conducted in the customer's own terms, referencing the business objectives and how the data warehouse environment will contribute to helping the customer meet the organization's strategic goals.

Armed with the information gathered thus far, it is now evident whether the current levels of service are meeting expectations and if not, how large the gap is. The potential business impact of not meeting service levels can also be determined during these discussions. This allows the data warehouse administrator and the customer to arrive at a minimum level of service to support the business objective and the associated cost to the business if it is not met. This process is important because it helps to separate the needs from the wants, a critical task if the data warehouse administrator is to provide services that support the business' objectives at optimal cost.

For a new data warehouse environment, customer needs should have been determined by the application architects and developers and incorporated into their design goals and customer acceptance-testing plan. It is still important to revisit these require-ments and perform this separation of needs from wants as rigor-ously as possible.

STEP 5: Determine Cost and Feasibility of Customer's Requirements

For an existing data warehouse environment, there are two poten-tial scenarios at this point. The first (and typically least likely) is that the service being provided is totally acceptable and no further work is required at this stage (skip to step 6). In most cases, how-ever, the service being delivered does not meet all of the customer's needs. Therefore the purpose of this step is to analyze what must be done to address this gap (what the customer has versus what they need) and what the associated cost will be. Hav-ing assessed the cost and time to implement, return to step 4 to determine if this cost is acceptable to the customer (typically the Line of Business manager) or senior IT management. Finding a need that cannot be financially or technically accommodated is a serious matter, as needs are directly driven by the organization's business objectives. While this is clearly not good news, it is better to know that a problem exists and proactively resolve it than to wait and allow it to get worse. Finally, customers and IT must agree on how to fund the service. Typically IT receives full com-pensation if it meets the service levels and a portion thereof if it does not meet all of the prescribed objectives.

For a new data warehouse environment, the best advice is to use the requirements that went into building the data warehouse to jump-start the SMC process. The following items should be con-sidered:

- ❏ Hours and days of data warehouse availability
- ❏ Maximum number of total and concurrent users
- ❏ Incremental load process frequency
- ❏ How and when to escalate problems
- ❏ How and when enhancements will be made
- ❏ How long the data is going to be kept
- ❏ How security is going to be maintained
- ❏ Expectations with regards to data quality (in terms of accu-racy and completeness) and data currency

STEP 6: Create the Service Management Contract

Once having arrived at agreed-upon requirements for the service, formally document these in the SMC as service level objectives. In order to assess the impact of each requirement, supporting activities such as capacity management and change management must be in place and engaged. The reason for this is that some of the requirements may be contrary to current processes and cannot therefore be accommodated or the cost of supporting the requirement is not consistent with the value received.

For an existing system, as was stated earlier, it is often simpler to define the SMC based upon the current measured level of service being delivered.

The service delivered is reviewed and refined, and the SMC updated over time, prioritizing improvements to the quality of service based on business drivers. One of the keys to creating a successful SMC is to build it in an incremental fashion. Given the unknowns of a new data warehouse environment, it is best to focus on a few areas of the SMC that are of most value to the customer. As you become successful in managing compliance in these few areas, other areas can be added as needed to ensure the data warehouse environment is addressing the needs of the customer. In some ways, we can look at the development of the SMC in a similar fashion to that of the data warehouse environment itself. That is, the SMC should be created in an iterative fashion.

Looking more closely, most SMCs include the following:

- ❏ Definition of the business environment
- ❏ Definition of the service to be provided
- ❏ Definition of the parties involved
- ❏ Date when the SMC is active
- ❏ Response time targets
- ❏ Data storage limits
- ❏ User concurrency
- ❏ System availability
- ❏ Data quality
- ❏ Data currency
- ❏ Monetary remunerations
- ❏ Performance objective
- ❏ etc.

Let's take a look at each of these in a bit more detail.

DEFINITION OF THE BUSINESS ENVIRONMENT   This section should include a brief discussion of the business environment and associated events that have led to the establishment of the service. Any characterization of past services that were provided before this service are helpful in setting the context for the agreement. For illustration, let's look at the XYZ Company. XYZ's inventory department has managed the data warehouse environment for the last year. XYZ's environment started small and has grown in size and complexity. Now the inventory department would like the IT staff to manage the data warehouse environment. The SMC would have an entry that would look something like this:

```
XYZ has been in the widget business for over 10 years.
Recently XYZ found that in order to increase profits,
their inventory must be more efficiently managed. The
current inventory system has worked well, but due to
limited staff, users have had difficulty receiving re-
sponses to their requests for changes and the response
time has nearly quadrupled in the last three months.
The current staff is unable to meet the demands of the
users. By transitioning support to XYZ IT, they are
better equipped to deliver credible, timely, and cost-
effective services to their users and will offer a
service that meets the needs of the XYZ inventory sys-
tem as defined in the SMC.
```

DEFINITION OF THE SERVICE TO BE PROVIDED   The definition of the service to be offered should describe, at a high level, all the people, processes, and resources that comprise this service. Quite often, customers do not understand the amount of effort expended on behalf of an application. Therefore items worthy of mention in this section are common support areas, like Help Desk, that constitute part of the service value offered. It may be useful, depending on the service, to categorize the service into standard and nonstandard types. The standard services are those covered by the Service Management Contract and are explained in the customers' terms, such as XYZ IT will support the corporate user interface for the inventory data warehouse environment. The nonstandard are those services outside the scope of the SMC. Typically, items mentioned in the nonstandard SMC are services that require large incremental investment by IT to support. For example, supporting five different user interfaces into the data warehouse environment. Other examples of standard and nonstandard services are

> **Standard.** IT will provide an immediate response to problem calls from XYZ inventory when corporate standard tools are used.
>
> **Nonstandard.** XYZ IT will provide best-effort responses to questions from inventory when noncorporate standard tools are being used.

DEFINITION OF THE PARTIES INVOLVED   This section outlines the parties to the agreement and their responsibilities. Most often there are only two parties to the SMC. In some cases, such as with the network departments, customer communities subscribe to an SMC. Each department within the community has an opportunity to include any specific requests, but for efficiency, only one master SMC should be created to ensure consistency of approach and service. Additional sub-SMCs can be created that are unique for customer groups or locations.

One important point to remember is that customers of a service also have responsibilities. A well-written SMC acknowledges responsibilities on both sides. One common responsibility to include is securing corporate information assets by complying with password and authentication policies. Another example could include the "good corporate citizen clause," which covers training of customers, ensuring those using the systems have appropriate competency to safely and effectively use the service.

Signing authority for the SMC should be completed by the IT CIO or director in charge of providing the service (operations). For the customer side, the business unit manager or equivalent should sign.

DATE WHEN THE SMC IS ACTIVE   Here is where the commencement and conclusion dates are stated. It is customary to have a one-year term for most SMCs. For the first year, it may be appropriate to have a three-month period to acclimate everyone to the process. Once that SMC is complete, and everyone is more comfortable, create the one-year SMC. Establish quarterly meetings where all aspects of the Service Management Contract are reviewed to ensure that customer expectations are being met.

RESPONSE TIME TARGETS   Tools that track and report on queries have not caught up with the need to provide granular tracking of queries. The need exists for allocation of platform resources based on the customer and the behavior of queries. As stated in earlier chapters, having the capability to stratify usage based on the customer and the complexity of the query is important. Since the very nature of usage is nondeterministic (especially in the case of explorers), it is nearly impossible to manage performance in the data warehouse environment without being able to schedule queries based on business need. For example, performing a four-table join with a group by in the predicate is usually much more resource intensive than a qualified single table inquiry. Given today's data warehouse environments, both queries would receive the same priority. In the future, SMCs will be created for various types of customers and queries. For example, explorer queries that are often complex (meaning four or more table joins) will complete 80% of the time within six hours. Farmer queries are less complex and will usually have three or less joins and will complete 80% of the time within 2 hours.

Some tools exist that allow SMCs to be created for data warehousing. While these tools are immature, they hold great promise to manage both customer expectations and data warehouse performance.

DATA STORAGE LIMITS   With every data warehouse environment, there is a finite amount of disk storage available. Take the time to identify not only the amount of data that will be initially loaded but also include the size and growth if incremental data will help in correctly sizing the amount of storage needed. In addition, addressing the number and relative size of summary (aggregate) tables that will be supported is a vital task. The latter activity is difficult unless the data warehouse is already in use and summary tables are being used. Another caution is needed at this point: The raw size of the data to be loaded in the data warehouse is a multiple smaller than the data that has already been loaded. For example, without including overhead like mirroring and RAID, it is common for raw data loaded into a relational database to increase fivefold in size. This is due to a variety of factors, such as internal database structure overhead and table indexes. This does not include summary tables. For more detail on sizing the platform, see the previous section on "Platform and Performance." Summary tables, if the compression ratio is low and density percentage is high, will at times be larger than the underlying fact and dimension tables. (Along with the size of the fact and dimension tables, two additional factors work together to determine the size of summary tables. Compression ratio represents the average cardinality of the dimensional hierarchy levels that are summed by the aggregate. Put another way, if a retailer wanted to create a summary for brands that are sold quarterly, and the average number of products that are represented by a brand name is 15, the compression ratio is 15:1. This says that 15 individual products (SKUs) are summed in the brand entry. Lower compression leads to larger summary tables. Density represents the expected occurrences of the compressed hierarchy in the fact table(s). For example, in the earlier example, only 10% of all products are sold on a daily basis, while 60% of all brands are sold. The higher the density, the larger the summary table.) So one must carefully consider adding summary tables.

Once the rough size of the data warehouse is determined, monitoring the usage of data in the data warehouse environment will not only identify dormant data, it will also show the different users of the data warehouse environment and their usage by workload type (e.g., profiling, modeling, etc.). Tracking both rows touched and returned are valuable metrics to understand when determining the sustainable amount of activity that the data warehouse environment can support. It may be the case that the data warehouse platform will support only 10 or fewer (often the case) explorers. Conversely, if the users are not creating complex queries, or if the majority of queries use aggregates, the number of farmers that can be supported will be much greater. Additional factors to consider are time-of-day and month-end activities, which often follow a pattern of increased usage.

The amount of data that users require changes over time. Data warehouses will usually have a rolling window of first in, first out (FIFO) data. Data that is too old to be in the data warehouse environment will be archived off and available to another period of time and associated cost.

USER CONCURRENCY　It is very difficult to determine the number of users that can be supported by a data warehouse environment. Since the queries are nondeterministic, and the users themselves will have different needs from day to day, it's often a best guess effort to identify the number of users. Good advice is to be conservative: Lean on the capacity planner in conjunction with the vendor published numbers to decide on a supportable number.

The best case is that the data warehouse environment has been in service and its behavior can therefore be categorized. The capacity planner should be able to characterize the number and types of users the data warehouse platform is able to sustain. Using this information, the next step is to segregate users based on the demand they place on the data warehouse environment. A rule of thumb is to limit the number of explorers to 10% of the overall user base. This will ensure that the relative ratio of intense requests from explorers will be moderated by the farming community. Also, limit the number of concurrent users to approximately 25% of the overall users supported. The idea here is not to limit the number of available users. Instead, the notion is to be prepared and properly equipped to support a given number of users. Then if additional users need access, the SMC can be reviewed to see if the new users can be accommodated with existing capacity.

SYSTEM AVAILABILITY   It is critical that you understand all of the dependencies of making the data warehouse environment available to its customers before setting the hours the system is available. Many related processes must be completed before the data warehouse environment is considered available, such as current data is validated and loaded, backups have been performed, and other routine system maintenance is complete. Normally availability is something approaching normal business hours; that is, unless the data warehouse environment is used by groups across the country or globe. Remember that explorers will often request complex combinations of data. Explorer queries can sometimes span hours or even days. Be sure to plan for this when committing to availability. You will often need blocks of time to load incremental data and create new aggregates. Having a few "killer" queries running with no way to cancel them is not a good situation.

Once the hours of operation are agreed to, the actual versus planned availability of the data warehouse environment can be measured with the ratio *service availability = actual service hours delivered/planned service hours*. The actual number of service hours delivered may, for a variety of reasons, be less than planned, such as hardware or software failure, network outage, data unavailability, etc. There are automated methods of gathering this ratio from the customer perspective. It involves using remote terminal emulation (RTE) to test if the service is available. The metrics captured at the RTE terminal can be fed to the SMC reporting system for proper tracking.

Two additional and related dimensions of availability that are worth noting are the number and duration of failures. Many availability agreements specify the maximum acceptable number of failures during a period of time (typically one month). For example, it may be acceptable to have three failures during nonpeak hours and only one failure during peak hours. Perhaps even more important than the number of failures is the duration of the failures. Typically there are two categories of failures. Critical failures are those lasting more than 4 hours and general failures last less than 4 hours. The distinction between critical and general failures depends on the business impact resulting from the lack of availability. For those situations where the availability requirements of the data warehouse platform approach 100%, the data warehouse administrator and customers should consider whether this is the appropriate place to support the business application (given the strategic nature of the environment). Perhaps what is needed is an operational data store; however, this is a subject for another book.

DATA QUALITY Measuring and scoring the quality of data is vital to properly managing a data warehouse environment. Performing these activities allows SMCs to be created and used to identify when a data quality problem exists and when a noteworthy trend has potentially been discovered. Data quality problems usually occur in one of two places: when data is moved and transformed before being loaded into the data warehouse or when the source systems themselves contain incomplete or inaccurate data. Experience shows that the most common cause is the latter, and it is the most difficult to change.

The cleanliness of data is preeminent in data warehousing. Even still, this area is ignored by many who are involved with building the data warehouse environment. Perhaps this is because there is little in the way of tools and techniques to improve the quality of data, or maybe because many (wrongly) assume that the data in source systems is clean, or maybe because in the rush to deliver capabilities that demonstrate business value the importance of data quality became a lower priority. Whatever the reason, very few tools exist to assist in the arduous process for creating and maintaining accurate warehouse data. Few tools can comprehensively address the data quality issues customers have. For more on data cleansing, see Chapter 6.

The best advice to remember when talking to customers is that the data warehouse itself does not create any data. All of the data in the data warehouse is gathered from other IT source systems and outside agencies. Therefore the customers must realize that while many of the errors in the data have been corrected, the source system that created the error has not been changed. And as new features are added to the source system, new errors will invariably follow. Improving the data quality of the source system is not often supported as a data warehouse activity. It is largely for this reason that a new business role is gaining popularity—the data steward. The data steward is responsible for ensuring data quality standards (among other things) within the operational systems as well as the data warehouse environment.

The recommended approach is to work closely with the customer and see what amount of inaccurate or incomplete data they are willing to accept. Clearly the goal is to have 100% accurate and complete data. Unfortunately for most organizations, that is unrealistic. Instead, create a step-function improvement goal for data quality. For example, in the first three months, customers will accept a data defect rate of not more than 20%. After three months, the defect rate will drop to 15%, and so on. In this way, data quality is addressed, and while bad data is unacceptable, it's impossible to commit to 100% clean data in the data warehouse environment right from the start.

DATA CURRENCY   Data acquisition is the complicated process of extracting the source data needed by the business, transforming it to a usable, time-correlated format, and loading it into the data warehouse. It is understood that the quality of the data loaded must be very high. Bad data can lead to bad decisions. How often this process is performed leads us to data currency. Customers may require a portion of the data from yesterday to be loaded into the data warehouse by a certain time every day. Therefore the currency of that data is daily. Other parts of the data warehouse may need data refreshed on a weekly basis. The important point here is that all of the data coming in and out must be synchronized. That is, the data in the data warehouse and queries asked of it must maintain integrity.

The recommendation for handling data currency is that the more frequent the loading of data the more expensive it is to support. The next chapter will go into more detail about this; however, having a data currency of less than one day is difficult to support from a business point of view. The best starting place is to work with the customers and see if weekly currency is acceptable. Once the processes are automated and everyone is comfortable with weekly currency, transitioning to a greater frequency can be investigated. Remember, if summary tables are part of the data warehouse environment, incremental loading of new information may require some summaries to be rebuilt. For most environments, this is a time-consuming and complicated activity.

MONETARY REMUNERATION BASED ON SERVICE PROVIDED The best way to ensure customers and IT agree on the provided service is to institute a pricing schedule for the services. The money may never change hands, but it is still important that customers and the data warehouse administrator understand that there is a cost to providing the service. The pricing may be based on the number of rows returned, the amount of storage kept online, the complexity of the query, or more simply by the cost of the system divided by the number of customers. Whether one or all of these are computed in the monthly cost of the service, it is important that customers see and understand the costs associated with the service. Once both parties (data warehouse administrator and customer) are happy with the SMC wording and metrics, it is signed and becomes a working document.

STEP 7: Track Compliance to the Service Management Contract

Thus far the SMC has defined a number of objectives, which must be met if the business is to operate smoothly and meet its goals. As with any objective-driven endeavor, it is important to review performance against the objectives. However, identifying and capturing metrics is difficult. Very few tools exist to help with monitoring and reviewing service levels. It is for this reason that SMCs are fluid and should be refined over time. Initially some tools that are needed to capture metrics may not be available or commitments for service may have been too optimistic. As the service becomes better understood, a more complete contract can be created. As was stated earlier, the initial SMC should cover a period of three months. This will give both sides (the IT and the customer) the ability to make any changes to the contract as more is learned. The next period should be for at least six months, but one year is better.

The activity monitors that were mentioned in Chapter 7 will assist with capturing data warehouse usage, although this is only part of the equation. More metrics need to be captured and monitored to enable service management for the enterprise. We talk more about activity monitors and their role in providing key information to support tracking compliance to the SMC in the next chapter.

A report should be completed that highlights identified gaps and commensurate corrective actions along with those measurements that were met or exceeded. Once an SMC is in place, a monitoring process must be established to collect the relevant compliance information. This report can be used both reactively, to detect and resolve violations on a day-to-day basis, and proactively during service review meetings with the customer. Service delivery metrics can be trended to predict potential issues to ensure steps are taken to mitigate any potential risks. Service review meetings will typically be conducted at least once per month; but for new customers or customers who have a critical need, these meetings may be performed weekly or even daily.

SUMMARY

The benefits of service management are clear: It is a valuable tool for managing customer expectations and ensures that the data warehouse is addressing the needs of the business. With an SMC, IT and customers agree on a rich set of activities which, if performed, provide the customers with satisfactory service. It provides a service centric rather than system (hardware and software) centric view. This is an important distinction. As IT begins to use business terms for describing its value and service, it removes some of the barriers that have kept IT from working closer with customer departments. Customers are not interested in whether another CPU has been added to the data warehouse platform. Instead, they are interested in having their queries complete in roughly the same amount of time it took the last time they ran it. It's that simple. IT should be a solution provider, not a technology pusher.

We now know that the key to a successful SMC is the measurable metrics themselves. Without the ability to measure how well or poor the service is performing, it's impossible to clearly understand if the business objectives are being supported.

Note that the term "customer" is often used to refer to the users of the application. This is an important, if seemingly trivial, point since it highlights the mind-set change that is required in moving to a service provider mentality. It is also important to differentiate between the customer's "needs" and "wants." A *need* is a requirement that is vital if the customers are to be successful in meeting the business's objectives. Needs should be considered nonnegotiable unless they are financially or technically infeasible. On the other hand, *wants* are things that the customer would like to have or approaches to take, but they are not critical in meeting the business's objectives. For example, a customer might want continuous availability of the service, but is unable to articulate a clear business reason for this.

Defining an SMC is an activity that requires much communication and research within the organization. The data warehouse administrator will require input and assistance from several of his colleagues within IT who are responsible for key tasks.

In this chapter we introduced the concept of service management and its growing popularity in bringing much needed discipline and order to mission critical applications. Service management contracts were also covered as an important tool in the service management process. The challenge for data warehouse environments will be to use this tool to better understand, meet, and manage customer expectations by providing a consistent service. In fact, it's important to note that customers must participate in the design, creation, and maintenance of the data warehouse environment. Using service management to facilitate and focus this discussion makes sense and will work well for setting and meeting their expectations with regards to high performance. The next chapter dives further into service management, discussing how to put the service management contract in motion.

12

Putting the Service Management Contract in Motion

In the last chapter we covered the history and importance of service management and its role in the data warehouse environment. In particular, we stressed the importance of service management as a strategic management discipline used to ensure that data warehouse services are delivered predictably and reliably, and that these services meet evolving customer expectations. In addition to discussing the critical nature of service management, we discussed the role of the Service Management Contract (SMC) in defining the objectives by which the success of service management (and the data warehouse environment) is measured. But how do we measure and report on the success of these objectives? What about the organization which tracks and strives to ensure compliance with these objectives? This chapter answers these questions and, in doing so, provides the basis for putting the SMC (and subsequently service management) in motion. Before jumping into the details, a brief overview of this chapter's topics will be provided to introduce you to the components, in addition to the SMC, that together comprise service management.

PUTTING THE SMC IN CONTEXT

Applying service management in your data warehouse environment involves many components that must work together to be successful as depicted in Figure 12.1. The process for evolving these components is similar to that of how a pearl develops in an oyster. The pearl begins as a grain of sand, or in this case as an expressed need to proactively understand and fulfill customer expectations. Much like the grain of sand that irritates the oyster, customer dissatisfaction with the data warehouse environment often is the impetus behind beginning the service management process. If managing customer expectations is the core of service management and the SMC defines these expectations, the next ring or layer out from that is the IT infrastructure, or data warehouse administration

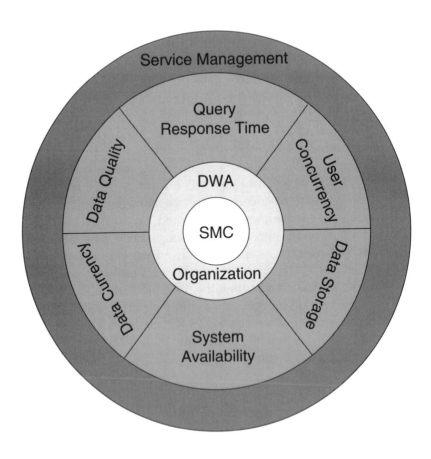

FIGURE 12.1

The service management pearl.

(DWA) organization. The DWA organization generally focuses on such things as data acquisition, data management, and DSS/reporting (application stuff). In addition, referring back to the ITSM hierarchy (Chapter 11), there are other groups or functions supporting service management. Groups such as network operations, system administration, DBA, etc. all play key roles in supporting service management. It is therefore critical to have the proper organization that can understand, influence, and execute the SMC.

Organization Layer

Having the right DWA organization means that not only will this group assist in identifying the right metrics to capture and measure, they will also solicit assistance from other groups to meet their SMC objectives. Therefore, for most organizations, several groups support the service management process. Typically this results in the DWA being both a provider and a customer of an SMC. That is, the DWA supplies services that are predicated or built on top of services that are provided by other groups. In this sense, the DWA is a customer of these other groups. For example, while response times are of key interest to data warehouse customers, the response time itself is influenced by a number of components in the performance chain such as network efficiency (see Chapter 8 for more on the performance chain). And for most organizations, the network is usually outside the purview of DWA. How then can the DWA create an SMC that has a response-time component? The answer is by entering into an SMC with the network group that stipulates the network performance expectations needed by the DWA to support customer response time. Because of this interdependency between IT and other groups, the core service management function for most organizations should be in a functionally impartial group.

Service Dimensions Layer

Turning to the components that are within the DWA's influence, the DWA group should engage their customers in discussions of the data warehouse service dimensions. These dimensions comprise the next layers of the pearl and consist of activities performed by the DWA organization to ensure that the data warehouse environment is meeting customer expectations (which are embodied in the SMC at the center of the pearl).

The first service dimension, query response time, is perhaps the most important to data warehouse end users. Having predictable, well-performing queries is high on the list of end users' wants. How to measure and improve query response time is covered later in this chapter.

Looking next at user concurrency, we will explore the implications of increasing the number of users allowed to access the data warehouse. As you'll see, there are a variety of considerations that must be weighed before adding more users to a system. For most customers, the number of end users is perhaps the biggest factor influencing data warehouse performance.

As you learned in earlier chapters, most data warehouse environments have data that is never accessed. This type of data, known as dormant data, is expensive to support. It not only takes up space that needed data could be occupying and gets in the way of needed data, it is expensive to support operationally—from extraction to backups. Creating a data warehouse environment that effectively uses its storage, from the user's point of view, can be achieved through an SMC.

Data warehouse availability, from the end-user point of view, is the ability to send queries and receive the results. With the advent of more complicated computing architectures and end user environments, maintaining availability is a difficult task, and accommodating the unique needs of each user community taxes service capability. For example, explorers will have extract, profiling, or modeling queries that span hours and sometimes days. These protracted run times may spill into the time that the system was scheduled to be unavailable for backups and other operational activities. This section will identify ways to create successful SMCs given the many complicated issues associated with availability.

The next dimension is data currency, that is, the length of time it takes for a transaction in the source systems to be propagated into the data warehouse environment. Users will often insist on data currency that approaches near real time, but that level of data currency is difficult to support from a business value perspective.

Closely related to data currency is the quality of data that is presented to end users. For a variety of reasons, data quality is a troublesome area for many customers. The goal is to have 100% accurate data in the data warehouse. Unfortunately this goal is nearly impossible to attain. In this section we will cover the more common data quality issues and provide ways to improve data quality.

Service Reporting Layer

The final layer in the service management pearl is reporting. Having the ability to accurately report on the agreed-upon SMC metrics is key to the service management process. By reporting periodically on the attained versus committed levels of service, the SMC allows the DWA team and their customers to capitalize on two opportunities. First, it allows the DWA team to publish the success of the service. By reporting in this way, it reinforces the notion that the service delivered is meeting its commitments. Two, it also enables the costs and benefits of the service to be periodically measured and adjusted over time. As expectations of the data warehouse environment change, the report and SMC can provide a near-complete picture of the current environment that can be used to determine the potential impact of the proposed changes.

Now let's take a look at each of these layers of the Service Management pearl in more detail.

DATA WAREHOUSE ADMINISTRATION (DWA) ORGANIZATION LAYER

A great deal of discussion thus far has been focused on the process for creating the SMC (i.e., the sand of the service management pearl) itself. Now let's talk about the next layer in our pearl, the DWA organization (Figure 12.2). Clearly this is an important consideration of successfully implementing an SMC. Looking back at the pearl, if there is a grain of truth that users are not satisfied with their data warehouse service, use this opportunity to verify why this is so. Look critically at the organization and its capability to implement service management. Are the departments working together and do they have common organizational goals? In one case, a telecommunications company that was ready

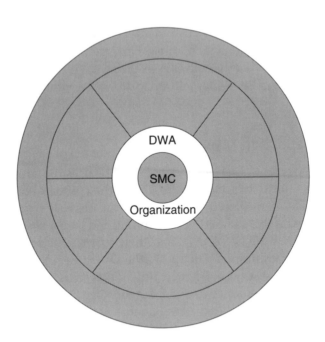

FIGURE 12.2

The data warehouse organization layer.

for service management planned its implementation over six months.

Unfortunately, many companies do not have this much time to implement service management. In another case, a manufacturing company that was not ready for service management allowed IT to manufacture the metrics with no objective way to verify the results. This can be a tough situation because the service customers must have confidence in the metrics. If customers agree with IT creating the metrics, this will work. Most often, this is the approach. Usually the issue is not with the metric identification or creation, rather it is with monitoring compliance to the metrics. Ideally the service management group should take the initiative and work with the customer to arrive at agreed-upon metrics and subsequent measurement of compliance. However, it must be noted that some customers are suspicious of IT and will not agree with this approach. While this may seem trivial, it is a driving factor for those processes that use the SMC. Therefore, before service management is implemented it will likely become necessary to have a role dedicated to the oversight and administration of service management.

Service Administrator

A person should be identified to oversee the compliance to the data warehouse SMC. This role can be thought of as the service administrator. Ideally this person will be responsible for not just the data warehouse, but all SMCs and should be someone who is impartial to all parties of these agreements. Often this person is found in or added to the change management group. Folks in the change management group typically have a good handle on processes that impact production, like changes, and they are well equipped to handle service management. Change management also knows about the pressure points in the operational systems and will be a good resource for data warehouse service management metrics. Quite often the customers of the service will be able to define, from a business perspective, the salient service metrics. The role of the service administrator is to translate these business metrics into quantifiable and objective metrics that can be captured and reported.

For smaller organizations, the functional service representative can perform the role of service administrator. For example, the data warehouse administrator could also wear the hat of service administrator. The concern is that the person performing in the latter role must be an advocate of the customer or end user, and will sometimes be expected to make difficult choices with respect to service remuneration, among other things. For large IT environments, a new functional group can be established whose charter is to manage all aspects of service management. All service administrators would report to this group. This group of people would not only be responsible for defining and ensuring compliance to metrics, but they would also facilitate the role as the single point of contact for all requests (enhancement, ad hoc, or otherwise) to the data warehouse environment.

Measuring the Right Metrics

Before committing to performance metrics, it is critical to look for good indicators of health. Often this is the most difficult part of service management because these indicators are often unique to a company and application. Once identified, these indicators will be measured and monitored over time. Many otherwise viable indicators of system health, such as end-user query response time, are not used because no automated or simple means exists to capture and report on these metrics. If an indicator is not measurable, performance is subjective, and therefore these indicators should be used sparingly. Also, keep in mind that just because a metric already exists, for example, the I/O rate, does not mean that it is appropriate for service management. Unfortunately, too often metrics are used because they are available and yet are really poor indicators of service health. Surveying the already available measurements that are captured is the first step. If appropriate metrics do not exist, consider creating the necessary metrics. Remember, however, that measurement for measurement's sake is of no value. In fact, taking system measurements has a cost associated with it that can be burdensome. Therefore, make sure that the measurements performed are useful. As one would expect with a database-centric service, many of the measurements will be defined with the assistance of the data warehouse administrator and end users. It's important to be mindful of the goal of service management: to proactively manage customer expectations.

DWA May Not Be In IT

Depending on the company structure, the data warehouse administrator may be found in different parts of the organization. She may reside in the IT department or in the end-user business unit. Since the evolution of data warehousing has been outside the confines of traditional data centers and is instead found in the line of business that sponsored the data warehouse effort, management of the data warehouse environment has been more difficult than with other applications. This is one of many challenges posed when implementing service management for a data warehouse environment. Not all data warehouse administration personnel report to the corporate IT management structure. As Figure 12.3 notes, the DWA function is sometimes outside the traditional IT structure.

Challenges Existing DW Support Structure

Quite often, service management support activities such as the help desk and problem management are, like the application being supported, performed in an ad-hoc manner, mostly by telephone.

Data Warehouse Organization

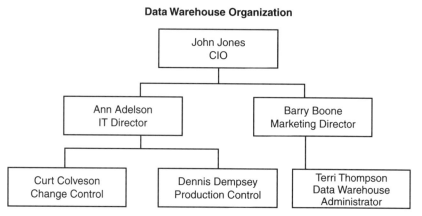

FIGURE 12.3
Functionally isolated data warehouse administrator.

The SMC must address and articulate the manner and process by which all problem management will be performed. This will greatly improve the effectiveness of administrators and users that interact with the data warehouse environment. Unfortunately, scenarios such as Figure 12.4 are somewhat common in data warehouse environments.

As Figure 12.4 illustrates, it starts with a telephone call to the data warehouse administrator. The customer states that the data warehouse response time is too slow and that their query is taking forever. Hearing this, the data warehouse administrator reviews the system and finds no problems, so a telephone call is placed to other support groups, such as network, DBA, and the system administrator. Each representative explains that his or her part of the service is performing well. So what is the problem? Is it the data-

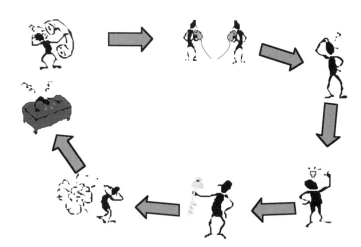

FIGURE 12.4
Example of DWA without the benefit of an SMC.

base? Network? Who knows? That, too often, is the fool's errand that data warehouse administrators find themselves in. There is little assistance available to the data warehouse administrator to track down exactly what is causing the problem.

Adding to the confusion is that with no other information to go on, the administrator begins the next level of investigation by examining the query syntax and the underlying database structure. Without having a firm understanding of what is going on in the environment, he will sometimes make the problem worse! For example, if he is lucky he will perform some analysis and find indications that the problem is the lack of an index or aggregate. Then he creates a new aggregate that fixes the problem. Unfortunately, problem resolution performed in this manner may create a problem somewhere else, sometimes with another query.

As this example demonstrates, not having processes that facilitate the management of the data warehouse service engenders a reactive, fire-fighting mentality. Trying to predict performance in such a chaotic environment is nearly impossible. Compounding this problem is that if problems are not logged and reported, it's difficult to know what problems are recurring and which are new or unique. This leads us to our next topic, service management reporting.

FIGURE 12.5

The service management reporting layer.

SERVICE REPORTING LAYER

Rather than working our way out from the center of the pearl from the data warehouse administration organization layer, we will start with service management reporting (Figure 12.5). The reason for this is that service management reporting is one of the most important elements of a successful service management environment. It will help the reader to think of how to report on the service as we review the dimension of the service later. For IT, service management reporting validates both investment in the service infrastructure and also allows improvements to the service to be measured and tracked. For customers, service management reporting is a valuable tool for understanding how the data warehouse environment is performing relative to their expectations and needs. These reports can communicate important service-related information to customers. For example, customers may want to see their performance information (average query response time, average number of users, data currency and quality, etc.) for both current and historical time periods. More progressive IT departments create Web sites for this information. These sites include a rich set of service-related information, from both a current and historical perspective. As with any user-centric activity, asking the customers what they want reported is vital; with complex computing environments, one must be careful to keep reports simple and relevant.

When considering service management reporting, it is important to differentiate between the service itself and the myriad of complex components that comprise the service. The service is really the value the data warehouse application provides, and for most data warehouse environments, the components include application software, middleware, operating systems, and hardware components such as servers, network infrastructure, and client workstations (PCs or otherwise). Most users are not interested in the performance and subsequent reporting of any one component; instead, they are interested in the end-to-end performance of the service. For this reason, the user does not care, nor does he need to know, all of the components that comprise the service. He simply knows that the data warehouse service is either available and valuable or it is more trouble than it's worth. Service management reporting will greatly assist with keeping data warehousing in good standing by measuring compliance to the SMC. How does one measure the value of the data warehouse service?

As previously stated, a service is in many ways a representation of the value delivered by an application, such as decision support systems that are delivered with a data warehouse environment to the users (e.g., profitability analysis, sales analysis, inventory analysis, etc.). How is the service valued? Increasingly, the effective return on investment (ROI) is used to gauge the success of the data warehouse environment. The effective ROI assesses if the business is receiving the forecasted business value. This is difficult to measure. Typically the business value translates into soft financial returns; for example, better customer intimacy, better ability to respond to competitive pressures, and similar business imperatives that are fueling the interest in data warehouses. Unfortunately, measuring and reporting on the benefits and ROI in these and other areas can be illusive. One must know the magnitude and extent of the problem for comparison purposes.

Consequently the successful data warehouse environment is created in response to a known business problem and the associated requirements must be documented. The data warehouse benefits can then be measured by the progress made against the requirements. These requirements are often in business terms and the same requirements that were mentioned earlier must translate into appropriate, measurable metrics. Consequently, reporting on these metrics will directly link the success of the data warehouse back to the business requirements and ROI. In addition, user performance will have more relevance and context when linked with user requirements. An example could be a customer inventory problem. The company is having a hard time aligning demand with inventory. Having this business problem in mind will help quantify the value of time lost by analysts if the data warehouse environment is not working properly for its users. Conversely, when it is performing as expected, the customers must be able to identify business improvement attributable to the data warehouse environment. Let's look at a case in point.

A good example is a telephone customer. They do not need to understand the technology between themselves and the person being called. They just know that when a fast busy signal or no dial tone is received, something is wrong with the telephone system and it needs to be fixed. Whether the user is a phone customer or data warehouse customer, all they care about is whether the service is accessible, usable, responsive, and delivers the correct information when it is needed.

Furthermore, the fact that other users can access the service is not particularly relevant to a user who, for some reason, is not able to. The reported availability of individual hardware and application software components does not mean that the service is available for all users. If, for example, a user's PC or workstation has failed, the data warehouse environment is unavailable to the user. When reporting on service availability and delivery, the perspective of the user must be maintained. Too often there's a tendency to limit the view to only include the components, sometimes not even in their entirety, of the service. For example, the DBA may say that the database is working properly and therefore the data warehouse platform is available. Clearly, this is not the case. To the customer, the platform is available only if all necessary components are working properly such that service is being delivered.

As these illustrations point out, there other essential dimensions which are important to consumers of the data warehouse service that must be considered to successfully manage and report on the service. Let's look at these now by looking at the different service dimensions that provide input to reporting.

SERVICE DIMENSIONS LAYER

Deciding "what" service objectives to track and measure over time is fundamental to service management. In addition, it is equally important to understand the implications of tracking and measuring these service objectives. As the saying from the previous chapter pointed out, "if you can't measure it, you can't manage it." In the sections that follow, we will talk about considerations and implications of service management for your organization. Armed with a solid understanding of service management and all of its complexities, you will be able to quickly begin to manage your customers' data warehouse service expectations. As was stated in the previous chapter, it is not necessary to implement all of these dimensions. In fact, depending on the customer, they may not be interested in all possible service dimensions. Therefore the best advice is to start with the service dimension that is easily deployed and will inspire confidence with those who provide the data warehouse service (Figure 12.6).

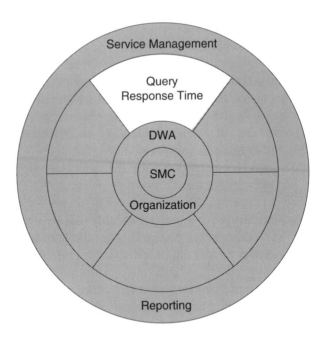

FIGURE 12.6

The query response time dimension.

Query Response Time Dimension

Tracking and measuring response time, from the customer's perspective, is likely to be ranked as the most important aspect of the service. Unlike traditional online transaction processing (OLTP) applications where reasonably consistent performance can and is expected (for example, 95% of the time a new customer account will take less than 3 seconds to complete), the performance of data warehouse transactions will have much greater variation. This is due to the nondeterministic nature of the requests. Therein lies the most obvious difference between OLTP and DSS. In the former, all questions have already been asked and the only choice is to select one; with the latter, the population of questions has been set, just not all of the questions have been asked. It really is a system that strives to let users ask any question they're interested in. Extending this comparison to the user community, for OLTP transactions it matters little who is submitting the transaction, the data required, result returned, and elapsed time to complete will be largely the same. By and large, OLTP users are really only interested in a handful of rows being returned or inserted into the database. Contrasted with DSS, the user submitting the query will have a large influence on the aforementioned dimensions and is not

---

ACID

ACID is an acronym describing a transaction: Atomic—the transaction completes or everything is returned to the way it was; Consistent—the transaction leaves the DB in the proper state; Isolated—each transaction is independent; and Durable—applied transactions will survive failures.

---

only interested in the first few rows being returned, they are interested in all of the rows that answer their query. Imagine for a moment comparing explorer and farmer queries. There is a significant difference in the returned result set as well as the complexity of their queries. This comparison between OLTP and DSS is important because it helps in defining where data warehousing is today.

OLTP AND DSS   OLTP, unlike DSS, has been around for quite a long time, and in many ways it is the essence of computing. Many of the earliest business computers were based on the concept of transactions. Aside from the ACID properties of transaction processing, let's consider what a transaction processing monitor like CICS or Tuxedo has done for OLTP processing. If we agree that one of the major functions of a TP monitor is to schedule transactions to ensure the host system is not overburdened, this is a key piece of the puzzle that is missing from the OLTP environment. Looking at Figure 12.7, expected system utilization would be reduced and the

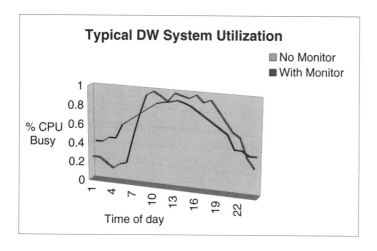

FIGURE 12.7

Affect of a TP monitor on a data warehouse.

response time would be more predictable if query scheduling through a DSS monitor were employed.

Since the OLTP processing environment has been around for a relatively long time, the computing infrastructure and management is well known. Most IT staffs that support OLTP processing have at least one person responsible for the TP monitor. Add the production control, change control, help desk, capacity planning, and documentation that exists for OLTP and you have a substantial support infrastructure. In addition, consider the path a new or modified module takes in the OLTP environment before it is released into production. Most of us who have experience in operations can recount at least one horror story of an OLTP module gone bad. The amount of testing and rigor in the performance, reliability, and manageability of OLTP modules is well known and documented. In contrast, little formal testing goes into today's data warehouse environment. It's no wonder that providing a predictable high-performance service is so hard to do. This is magnified by the earlier point of how many and what type of end users are supported in the data warehouse environment. These users have arguably the most influence over performance—certainly more influence than system tuning or even system size can dictate.

USER AND PERFORMANCE   There is a great temptation, therefore, to adopt a view that says, "the users are responsible for how long their transactions will take. They have much greater flexibility in the questions/requests that can be made of the data warehouse." This viewpoint neglects to understand that one user's query can have a profound impact on another's. So while user's do have a wide latitude of questions they can ask, they also have a responsibility to others to use the service wisely. With the wide latitude given to customers of data warehousing service, how do you keep them content with query response time?

One way is to properly set user expectations with regards to the levels of responsiveness that they can expect. In the future, users will be able to receive an estimate of elapsed run time before a query is submitted (see Chapter 7 for a more thorough discussion on resource governors versus query blockers). Unfortunately, no tool is available today that can do this very well. However, a few tools are nearing this capability, but they will need to be proven over time since they are new and comprise another layer of middleware that is in the queries' critical path. Just because it is difficult to predict the behavior of queries (some may be impossible with any real confidence) does not mean that we should shy away from trying. In fact, it is the authors' belief that in the next three years a process for throttling and queuing queries (i.e., query blocking) based on their expected execution profile will be available and widely used. This will be the first significant step toward having OLTP-like performance predictability, though not performing all of the functions that a TP monitor would be expected to perform.

Clearly, when the thought of a TP monitor for OLTP was first conceived, it was probably derided at first as not being practical. Now it is mandatory for most OLTP applications. Without knowing the amount of resources that will be consumed by a data warehousing request, it will be a self-fulfilling prophecy that the query response time will be unpredictable. To improve this, users must be made aware of the resources they are allowed to consume if the data warehouse environment is to become more manageable. But this only solves part of the performance problem. Knowing the amount of resources is good, but knowing how to more efficiently use these resources is even better. As evident in the last example, perhaps even more important than predicting query run times is to have a user education program.

Education of the users, in this case with proper query formulation, is a meaningful aspect of service management environments. Training in the proper syntax of queries, along with the structure of the underlying data, will benefit all its users. Knowing what is required to execute a query serves to set user expectations correctly and optimizes the way in which users consume the service. However, even when users are properly trained, performance of the system will likely still be an issue.

PRIORITIZING QUERIES Should IT always strive to deliver the fastest possible response to queries in a data warehouse environment? The answer to this question is both yes and no! Queries should be prioritized to ensure that the most critical ones receive maximum throughput, while the less important ones are given background status, allowing them to complete in a time scale that is satisfactory but does not impede other, more important, business imperative transactions. At a high level, query precedence should be based on three factors:

❏ Importance of query to fulfilling business objectives

❏ Amount of resources required for the query

❏ User submitting the query and whether she has other queries currently executing

If this precedence is used, it will encourage some positive behaviors. For example, if a query receives a committed 24-hour turnaround it is more likely to be correctly structured, or formulated, to ask the right question and in return get the right answer. If, on the other hand, all queries receive a committed 30-minute turnaround time, there is a greater temptation to simply launch a query and see if it was correctly phrased by observing the result set—thereby wasting valuable resources and possibly impeding other users. The latter behavior is actually somewhat common. For a variety of reasons, users submit queries without knowing exactly what they are looking for. For example, users will submit a test query to validate a hunch. Another reason might be that they submitted a similar query before and they are getting a different response now. Perhaps the schema has changed, or worse, the data has been archived or removed. Both of these points demonstrate the need for tighter management of modifications. This brings up an interesting question: How many IT shops have both a test data warehouse environment and production environment?

TEST AND PRODUCTION ENVIRONMENTS   This type of segregation is vital to testing patches, new operating systems, and database versions among most other change control activities. It is also an ideal end-user training environment. The best use of this arrangement is as a controlled test environment. In this way, IT can formulate a suite of queries that can be run repeatedly as the data warehouse environment changes over time. Perhaps, it is best suited to run the baseline suite of queries that test the performance over time on a system that is exclusively dedicated to running the baseline test. The notion is to have the ability to replay this known and understood data warehouse load at appropriate times, as the configuration and assumptions change over time. The baseline environment is typically comprised of the following items (ideally one per subject area/mart):

Base data warehouse. A clean subset of data from the data warehouse that has been validated with the full test suite of queries. The only time the base data warehouse changes is when the production data warehouse requires schema changes. The purpose of the baseline is not for stress testing but instead is to test new versions of SW and HW, from the clients to servers and everything in between. All proposed schema changes are first made to the baseline data warehouse before making any changes to the production data warehouse. If the changes are not successful or the HW/SW is not performing properly, the baseline data warehouse should be restored to it original state—typically from a tape backup/archive. Once testing is complete the modifications can either be applied to the production system or removed from the baseline data warehouse. In a similar fashion, you may also create test data mart environments to be used to assess changes prior to production migration.

Load files. Load files represent the current set of data being sourced from the operational systems. As the structure of the production load files changes, so too should these files. The purpose of these files is to have a validated, proven set of files to test the data warehouse population and its associated load time.

Load query suite. This set of queries tests the amount of time it takes to execute the set of baseline load files.

Simple DSS query mix. A representative set of actual queries that are of short execution duration and minimal disk utilization. This is typical of a multidimensional analysis. Ideally these queries should have a client and server component. These queries should be executed against the baseline DW and production DW. The latter information will then feed capacity planning efforts.

Complex DSS query mix. A representative set of actual queries that consume significant resources. This is typical of a profiling query. Ideally these queries should have a client and server component. These queries should be executed against the baseline DW and production DW. The latter information will then feed capacity planning efforts.

The importance of having this baseline environment is that once established the data warehouse administrator can begin to analyze and characterize the behavior of the data warehouse and/or data marts. Use performance monitoring and reporting tools to compare and validate performance improvements in cache increases, query plans, and the full range of other modifications that can be made to the data warehouse environment once reference points such as these have been established. For example, if the administrator upgrades the database to a new version, running the full complement of queries against the database will validate the performance and other important qualities of the change. Another example is that as the environment changes over time, running the suite of benchmarks will help in understanding any differences found in performance (e.g., the impact of growing data volumes). This is an important facet of service management: to have the ability to measure and assess whether the platform (data warehouse or data marts) is not performing well; to have the ability to diagnose and repair the reason for not meeting the expected performance objectives.

On a related note, if there is any application development work on behalf of the data warehouse, another mini development system should be created for this work. It will ensure development does not affect testing and production. In conclusion, using this segregated approach to managing change and performance in the data warehouse environment will be beneficial to both customers and the DWA support staff. Another area that will improve the data warehouse service is capacity planning.

CAPACITY PLANNING   Perhaps one of the biggest differences between OLTP and DSS is in the area of capacity planning. It is not only practiced, it is a science in the OLTP world. Unfortunately, since most data warehouse activity is so chaotic, most otherwise process-oriented people shy away from even attempting to bring structure and discipline to it. Using the baseline query information discussed earlier, as the data warehouse grows in size and the number of users, the impact of increasing either can be forecasted, albeit in a rudimentary way, to facilitate capacity planning. The objective of capacity planning is to smooth out the peaks and valleys found in the data warehouse query performance. One way to smooth is through the creation of summaries or aggregates (for a detailed discussion on this topic, refer to Chapter 9).

SUMMARIES AND AGGREGATES   Aggregates are simply precalculated queries. Most often, they are created for the most often executed queries. As these aggregates are created, what is really happening is that on the continuum of data warehouse processing, the system is becoming more transaction oriented. More of the questions that can be asked are anticipated, planned for, executed, and stored for users to use later. The data warehouse administrator executes these queries once the warehouse has been refreshed, and thus enables the known queries to perform better. The benefits of aggregates, if the environment is equipped with an aggregate-aware client tool, are improved response time and that users will not have to reformulate their queries. The client tool will automatically translate the query and redirect it to take advantage of an aggregate without end-user intervention. This enables the DWA to create and retire aggregates based on changing user demands.

USAGE TRACKING   Beyond transparently using aggregates on behalf of user queries, another interesting feature that is causing interest in these client tools is the ability to capture and compare response times for identical queries. The challenge of these tools is that while they are great rulers for comparing previous query run times, they are misleading in that they do not account for other activities on the system. There are many examples of administrators chasing perceived problems by users because the last time the query ran it took less time than it's taking now. The issue here is not availability. The issue here is that it only took 1 hour before, now it has taken 1 hour and 10 minutes.

IMPORTANCE OF PEOPLE   The harsh reality is that we must invest a similar amount of resources, people, and processes that are currently invested in OLTP in order to secure the success of data warehouses. Trying to solve data warehouse management with only individual tools, such as a response time indicator, will not be as successful as when a more holistic approach is employed that incorporates the processes to exploit the tools.

User Concurrency Dimension

There are two types of consumers of a data warehouse environment—explorers and farmers. These two categories can be further analyzed by separating those consumers that are logged on but not active and those that are currently using the service (Figure 12.8). These distinctions are important as service management is used to

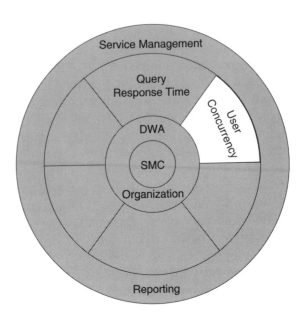

FIGURE 12.8

The user concurrency dimension.

manage performance. Certainly one of the biggest factors affecting data warehouse query performance is the number of connected and active users. Ideally, SMCs should describe both the maximum number of explorers and farmers and how many can be active at one time. This is half the story. With the advent of asynchronous query processing, one user can have more than one query executing concurrently. This has the potential to be a major performance consideration.

Unlike relatively fast turnaround times found in OLTP environments, where users will typically only have one transaction pending at any one time, the extended turnaround time of data warehouse queries may tempt users to submit additional queries in parallel. This can lead to excessive system loading and cause degradation of service for all users. This practice can be managed through software measures; however, the SMC should also specifically stipulate what is and is not acceptable in terms of parallel query submission. Taking this approach may be too heavy handed. Often the only time concurrent user queries pose a threat is during the busiest processing times.

During the "online day" or period of time when the system is its busiest, it is important to limit the amount of non-business-critical activity that occurs on the system—everything from extract and transform to superfluous concurrent queries should be restricted from consuming precious system resources. If the data warehouse administrator cannot fully control the resources being consumed on the system, she will have a very difficult time in managing performance. Until such time that there is a TP monitor for DSS environments, it will be necessary to exert control over what can be run during the system's busiest times. One approach to assist with smoothing out the peaks and valleys of the on-line day is to implement a charge-back program. Charging higher rates for queries that run during the busiest times encourages users to submit speculative or non-business-critical queries during off-peak, less costly times.

Along with concurrent queries, there are other concurrency considerations worth mentioning.

Figure 12.9 shows the balance of controlled versus uncontrolled queries. If this balance is not properly struck, the data warehouse environment will have moderate acceptance and limited success. The other side of the balance is that as you bound the questions and capabilities of the environment, you lose flexibility, and important business questions may remain unanswered.

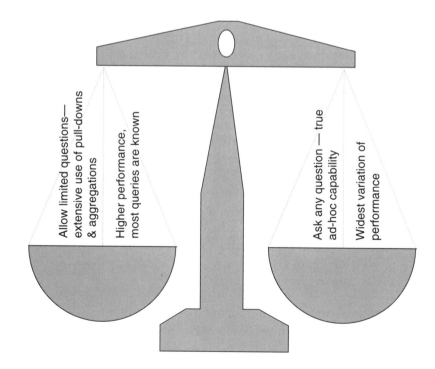

FIGURE 12.9
Controlled versus uncon-trolled queries.

TURNING POINTS   There are really three major tuning points to the data warehouse: the number of users submitting queries, the complexity of their queries, and the supporting platform (for more on platforms refer to the previous section on platforms and performance). When faced with performance problems that are jeopardizing your SMCs, areas to focus on include the following:

> **Number of users.** Has the number of explorers or farmers gone up recently? The SMC should clearly denote the number and types of users and the uses that are supported. For more information on the types of users and their use of the data warehouse environment, refer to Chapter 2, "User Community and Performance."
>
> **Complexity of queries.** As explorers and farmers gain proficiency with the data warehouse services, they will inevitable ask more complicated questions. This type of evolution should be anticipated and planned for.
>
> **Clients.** Typically the problems are not here, unless there are poorly behaved applications that reside here. Some Java-based applications do not perform well. If more than one client is having trouble, it may point to a network or an intermediate server problem. As was mentioned earlier, end-to-end performance is another area of increasing interest in the data warehouse platform. Today, as more complicated computing architectures are being deployed for data warehouses, users are increasingly becoming more disillusioned with all of the possible choke points in their query paths. For the vast majority, the client is the least problematic component of the environment. Fortunately there are tools available to assist with capturing performance data. One example is the application response measurement (ARM) application programming interface (API). This measurement tool allows IT to capture metrics at discrete points in the platform. Application response measurement was jointly created by Hewlett-Packard and Tivoli. For further information, please visit the following web sites: www.hp.com/openview/rpm/arm/docindex/.htm or www.cmg.org/regions/cmgarmw/sdk.

As more companies implement the ARM API into their part of the overall solution, it will enable the DWA to properly assess how much time is being spent in each of the components (network, server, etc.). Another important consideration, which was mentioned earlier, is that there must be a balance to what is measured. While it may be interesting to measure time spent in each application on the desktop, all of that measurement has an overhead associated with it. Therefore it's important to carefully weigh what is going to be measured and how critical that measurement is in validating performance per the SMC. Some of the components and their relative impact on overall performance are discussed as follows. Figure 12.10 gives is an analysis of typical data warehouse problems and their relative frequency.

Network. Most LAN-based networks between clients and the data warehouse are sufficient. If users are remote, this could be an area that needs attention.

Servers. This should be an area of focus for performance problems, especially if more than one server participates in the warehouse environment.

Applications. This should be an area of focus if the application is multitiered, meaning that parts of the applications reside on the client, server, or other participating systems.

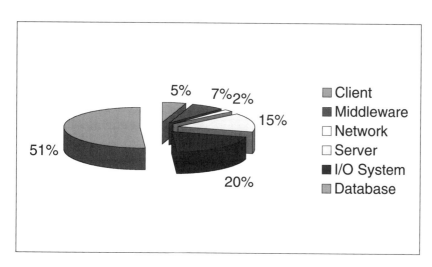

FIGURE 12.10
Percentage of response time issues in a data warehouse.

Middleware. May be an area of focus if other areas have been reviewed and no problems were found.

Database. Most of the wait time associated with data warehouse queries will be in this component. The average time spent in queries is predominately with the database and associated required components—DB server and I/O subsystem. As Figure 12.10 demonstrates, most of the time is spent in the database; this in turn places demands on the server and I/O subsystem.

Given all of the areas that may pose performance problems, it is important to remember that data warehousing is really in its infancy. OLTP has 30 years of focus and refinement. Even though few tools exist to help data warehouse administrators tame the performance problems that exist in data warehouses, service management offers the discipline and structure to improve the performance and management of end-user expectations through service-level agreements. During the next five years, data warehouse administration infrastructure will continue to improve and more closely resemble traditional OLTP processing.

Data Storage Dimension

In Chapter 5, dormant data was covered in detail. And while it's not important to review all of the details, it is important to understand that by tracking and reporting on dormant data, users will be able to make more informed decisions on how their storage is managed. Without the ability to report on data usage and nonusage within a data warehouse environment, everyone associated with the environment will wrongly assume that all of the data is being used. That is why tracking and reporting dormant data and other appropriate storage information is so vital (Figure 12.11).

How much storage is needed for a data warehouse? It's difficult for the DWA to articulate exactly how much data warehouse detail is necessary. On the one hand, users hear that availability of transaction-level data is critical to a data warehouse. Users tend to believe that detail from a sales transaction will be needed several years from when it was created. This scenario highlights the need for users to ultimately be responsible for the amount and type of data kept in the data warehouse environment. The corporation

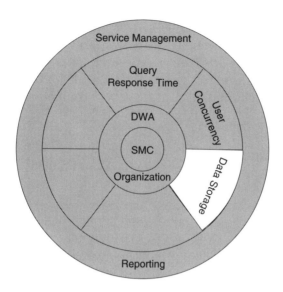

FIGURE 12.11
The data storage dimension.

must also bear some of the responsibility of ensuring it has adequate information to make decisions, irrespective of user communities. However, the decision of how long to keep data is one that is best addressed by service management. Having a contract that stipulates how much data will be kept for how long will go a long way toward more effectively using the storage available.

Aggregates are a powerful tool that can dramatically improve query response time. There are two cautions associated with aggregates that must be mentioned. The first is that customer access patterns for any data warehouse environment are dynamic and will change over time. Therefore the DWA must be committed to constantly reviewing the usage to determine if users are using the aggregates already created and must be ready to retire and build new aggregates as customer needs dictate. The management of aggregates is a difficult process. Few tools exist that enable the DWA to automate this arduous task.

The second caution is that aggregates tend to be large entities in their own right. It is not uncommon to have a robust aggregate environment that actually takes up more space than the underlying transaction or reference. Consequently, the notion of creating aggregates must be carefully considered and the performance implications must outweigh the issues around their management and size. Clearly, aggregates are beneficial if used judiciously.

THE BIGGER THE DATA WAREHOUSE THE BETTER?   Just three years ago, a large data warehouse was 500GB. Now a large data warehouse is in the 5TB range. Why is this? Have corporations generated that much more data in the last three years? The rationale for this explosion in size can often be traced to be an element of competition between corporations to have the largest data warehouse. The notion that large databases have large business value is common, but that is not always the case. Consider the adage "one in a million." This saying usually refers to either being lucky or unlucky. Let's look at applying it to the data warehouse environment. It could mean that because of its size and ability to sift through lots of information, a corporation may be able to find a new competitive trend. The users would say, "finding that was one in a million!" Now think about a DWA that is responsible for a large data warehouse. Having multi-million row tables is commonplace. When errors occur in this environment, the one in a million can be expected with relative frequency. As data warehouses push the size envelope, robust data structures and processes become fragile. Therefore keeping the data warehouse down to a manageable and in some ways minimal size is critical to the success of the delivery of service.

When it comes to OLTP (and DSS for that matter) environments, bigger is not better. Systems seem to break down or fail under the weight of their own size. This happens for a variety of reasons. First, the mission-critical nature of these systems typically demands little or no downtime, at least during the on-line period. Moreover, these are the source systems for the data warehouse and have narrow windows in which to extract the data destined for the data warehouse. As the amount of sourced data grows and the concurrency of the data (covered later) is accelerated, these fragile source systems are not able to keep pace. These computing environments have backup requirements, maintenance, and the like that have little or no time or tolerance for error.

Deciding what and how much data is needed is the rub. For OLTP systems, it's easy to identify what is needed to support the application. Creating a data warehouse that is correctly sized to provide business value is the crux of creating the SMC with the user community. The idea is that a properly constructed data warehouse will contain data required for the business—customer demographics, payment history, shipping information, etc. OLTP systems have discreteness to their storage needs. For example, customer invoices are maintained until paid and are then stored for another six months. Therefore, for the OLTP environment to grow in size, it means that new customers or sales are being added, because changing the information in the OLTP environment for a given customer does not really increase the amount of storage needed. This is clearly not the case for the data warehouse.

Unfortunately, for data warehouses, the same notion of discreteness doesn't apply. The allure of being able to compare current sales with the slump of 1987 is too great for many organizations. The idea, "that is what data warehouses are for," is prevalent. Consequently, data is stored and quite often never read again. Another interesting item is that data warehouses rarely, if ever, create new data (though some derived data is created). That is left up to the source systems. The trick, therefore, is to capture data, at the right interval, to enable trending and analysis on the data while not retaining data that is no longer of value. Assuming that the right data is captured and retained, there are additional considerations for storage requirements.

Along with data mirroring (RAID and full-duplicate copy), which was covered in earlier chapters, there's another type of data redundancy that should be reviewed. Many customers employ a two-copy approach to data warehousing. This approach uses a live and a backup copy of the data warehouse. For example, users are active against copy 1 while copy 2 is receiving updates. Once validated and complete, users are then pointed to copy 2 for processing. Thus only one copy is available to users at any time.

System Availability Dimension

Simply defined, data warehouse availability is the ability of users to submit queries and receive timely and appropriate responses from the data warehouse platform (Figure 12.12). Therefore all components of the data warehouse environment must work together and operate properly. Planning the availability of the data warehouse is more complex than for most OLTP services. And as with planning any IT service, the customer's requirements must be known and well understood.

For example, when planning for availability, the biggest difference is that query response time is much slower than in an OLTP environment. Users want to use the service between the hours of 8:00 A.M. and 8:00 P.M., Monday through Friday. However, what they really mean is that they wish to submit queries during

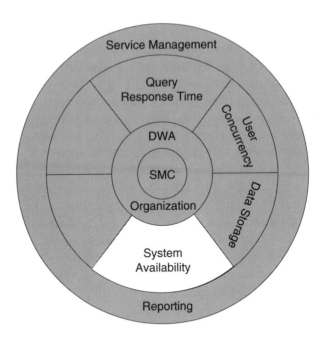

FIGURE 12.12

The system availability dimension.

these times. Since a long-running query from an explorer could take many hours or even days to complete, the DWA needs to understand the types of queries and their elapsed times before any commitment to service availability can be made (see Chapter 2 for further discussion on the type of queries).

Continuing with the previous example, it may be necessary to specify that no long-running queries be submitted after 8:00 P.M. on Thursday if the IT knows that one or more components of the system need to shut down on Saturday to perform routine maintenance. Of course, if this restriction is unacceptable to the business, then it should be highlighted during the SMC negotiation process, and suitable technology measures (such as on-line backup, highly available configurations) should be investigated and priced to address the need. Therefore, as has been stated many times thus far, service management is an iterative process. Consequently, when committing availability to service levels, proceed conservatively (only commit to what you are sure you can provide) and revise as experience gives you better insight into your limitations. As the saying goes, "You have to know your limitations."

The availability of the data warehouse service at specific times cannot always be guaranteed since unforeseen events such as hardware failures are unavoidable. Typical availability clauses in the SMC for OLTP services will quote percentage availability such as "99% available during the specified time intervals." The SMC will define how availability is calculated and provide a definition of what constitutes the service being unavailable. This is an important point, because a hardware failure in a user's desktop workstation may be considered as rendering the service unavailable. If, however, the user has the ability to move to a different workstation and continue working, then this can be defined within the SMC as not constituting a service failure. In addition to defining the maximum amount of unplanned downtime per occurrence, the SMC also defines the number of service failures that are allowable within a specific period, which is typically the service review period. Understanding availability from the user's perspective requires the DWA (focused on the data warehouse) and IT (supporting infrastructure) to have a richer, more complete view of the environment. This is a fundamental dilemma.

Availability is an important challenge facing data warehouse administrators. This challenge exists due to the lack of any mechanism to readily capture application availability with nonintrusive measurement tools. While one or more of the data warehouse components may be available, all components must be available and performing within agreed specifications (please see previous section on performance management) to consider the data warehouse service available. Since there are no automated tools to assist with capturing and reporting availability, other means must be employed.

One tool that assists with this problem is the use of the aforementioned application response measurement application programming interface (ARM API). It provides a mechanism, along with other customer definable components, for addressing this key service management issue. Using this tool, along with proven IT approaches, will enhance data warehouse availability capabilities. Let's look at how this can be accomplished.

RTE WILL MEASURE DATA WAREHOUSE AVAILABILITY   The recommended approach for measuring data warehouse availability is to use a process called remote terminal emulation (RTE). This technique has traditionally been employed in benchmarking and performance stress testing facilities to simulate large populations of users accessing and interacting with one or many applications. This approach works equally well in measuring the availability of the data warehouse. In fact, this approach can be used to assist in capturing end-user performance data as well. An example of this architecture is illustrated in Figure 12.13.

In this environment, it is useful to monitor end-user availability (and performance) at a number of points in the data warehouse platform. This will enable the DWA, in conjunction with IT, to identify service degradation resulting from failures in a variety of components—remote LANs, the LAN/WAN bridges, servers, clients, etc. Each service management availability monitor installed in the environment will provide valuable information about the service levels being delivered to specific subsets of the user population. For example, a data warehouse RTE could include a simple query of a table, retrieving a specific row, by date, to ensure not only availability but also currency of data. The resulting availability report should describe the objective for the measured transactions and performance against those specified in the SMC. Determining where and how many monitors to use is a step-by-step process.

The actual number of service management monitors deployed is driven by a number of factors including:

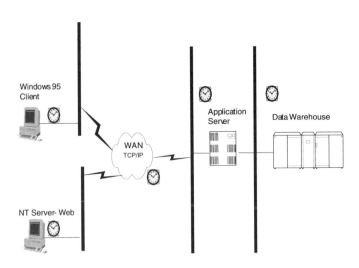

FIGURE 12.13
Measurement points in a
simple data warehouse
platform.

❑ The physical infrastructure

❑ The definitions of data warehouse service management objectives

❑ The criticality of the service to specific segments of the user population

Using the time-tested RTE approach will allow you to provide a comprehensive, reasonable, low-cost approach to measure, monitor, and report on data warehouse platform availability across the enterprise. Reporting on the availability is important; however, even more important is being able to positively influence the availability over time. This means being able to proactively detect and correct availability problems with the data warehouse platform.

In the event of a failure, users will want the service to recover and be available as quickly as possible. Therefore it is normal practice to define a number of different levels of failure severity, with corresponding time targets to resolve each type of failure. For example, IT might define a complete failure of the service for all users as a severity 1 (highest priority) failure with a target time to respond of 2 hours. A failure of the service for a subset of users, perhaps less than 10, might be defined as severity 3 with a time to respond of 4 hours. A failure of the service to a single user might be defined as severity 9 with a time to respond of 1 day. Determining the levels of service is a function of the value it provides to the company.

RESPONDING TO AVAILABILITY FAILURES   Clearly the value to the business of the service, and indeed the importance of particular sections of the user community, will dictate how the severity and time-to-resolve targets are defined. It is also important during the negotiation of the SMC to articulate the cost impact of having every failure defined as severity 1 with a time to respond of 30 minutes. Responding to the failure is the first step in correcting it. It should be noted that responding to the failure is not the same as resolving it. Depending on the severity, it may require IT to invoke disaster recovery procedures. Typically if the failure is of this magnitude, it will take many days to recover, and the data will not be as up to date as usual. When the service suffers an outage, what happens to all of the work in progress? Perhaps explorers are running critical day-long queries. Is all of that work lost? Today it is.

The ability to restart long-running queries without losing the intermediate result set is another function that is becoming important in data warehouse environments. Again, this functionality is not currently available in off-the-shelf tools. If this capability is important, you will have to code it into your application yourself. Other service failures may not affect the ability of a previously submitted query to complete, for example, a failure in the users desktop workstation or the network infrastructure that connects the user to the data warehouse. In these situations, the ability to "reconnect" the user with the output of his query when it completes and the failure has been rectified becomes an important factor in service delivery.

Data Currency Dimension

The short definition of data currency is the delay in time from when the data is generated in the source system to when it is available to the customers of the data warehouse environment (Figure 12.14). Data currency is the complicated process of extracting the source data needed by the warehouse, transforming it to a usable, time-correlated format, and then loading it into the warehouse.

For example, in a simple data warehouse environment, there are three stores that provide sales information. Users expect to be able to interrogate sales from all three stores and would be dissatisfied if all three stores were not consistently loaded. This is not to say that there won't be times that one or two stores may not have sales data—this can and will likely happen. In fact, planning for this and being able to alert users that they are using a subset of data is valuable. The issue here is that this data, whether it's daily, weekly, or monthly, may not be available to the users in the time required. How can service management assist in data currency?

USER REQUIREMENTS ARE ESSENTIAL   At the risk of sounding like a broken record, the DWA must first have the user requirements. The user requirements should spell out how often the data needs to be refreshed. It depends on the users' needs. One example of a service management agreement for data currency would be that sales data from the previous day will be loaded by 8:00 A.M. the following

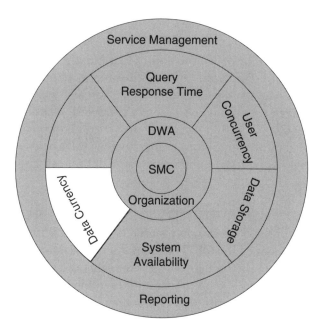

FIGURE 12.14
*The data currency
dimension.*

day. Another example would be to have a rolling window of 3 months' detailed and 9 months' aggregated sales information available at all times. This way, if the amount and/or timeliness of information required by users changes, the SMC will serve as the mechanism to change the storage and processing requirements. If, for example, the users want to increase the amount of data stored, the SMC for data currency could be reviewed and modified, reflecting the increase in data storage costs. Similarly, if IT planned for and agreed to the growth of stored data at a 10% level, and it is growing at 15%, a change to the SMC is in order.

DETERMINING CURRENCY OF DATA   While the next section will more fully cover data quality, it must be mentioned that the quality of the data loaded must be very high. Bad data can lead to bad decisions. Users may require a subset or a portion of the data from yesterday to be loaded into the data warehouse by a certain time every day. Reconciling that data with data already loaded can be tricky; nevertheless, the currency of that data is daily. Other parts of the data warehouse environment may need new data on a weekly basis. The important point here is that all of the data coming in and out must be synchronized. That is, the data in the data warehouse environment and queries asked of it must maintain integrity. Having a set schedule will improve the ability to maintain integrity.

Today most data warehouse environments operate on a weekly or daily currency schedule. That is, on a weekly or daily basis, changes in the source system are extracted, massaged into data warehouse formatted data, and then loaded and made available to users. However, before going in to the intricacies of currency, let's spend a few moments on some of the history behind currency.

HISTORICAL AND CURRENT VIEW OF DATA NEEDED   Referring back to OLTP systems, the value of its data is that it's up to the minute. It may be the case that areas of the OLTP system are not updated frequently, but the essence of the system is that it reflects the current state of known information. The point is that data in the system is constantly being overwritten to reflect the current state of values. Data warehouses are designed and created to capture and report on these changes.

For data warehouses, the data that is of interest is that which has changed (and why) over time. Whether the difference is in sales or in inventory levels, or whatever the subject area of interest, capturing the changes is the essence of data warehousing. How often should the data be captured? The answer is, it depends. In highly volatile OLTP environments, such as airline reservation systems and retail systems, if data is not being captured at precisely the right moment, it degrades the value of the data warehouse environment because time-correlated information regarding transactions is not available. Often, though, the window of time to capture the changed data is not conducive to business needs. For example, having weekly or monthly extracts of the source system may not be frequent enough. How often should source data be readied and loaded into the data warehouse?

The answer is as often as necessary and practical to maximize the business value of the data warehouse environment. Depending on the needs of the business, the timing can range from near real time to monthly, or even longer. A formula that can be used to describe data warehouse currency is

$$C = t_{dw} - t_s$$

where

C = currency of the data warehouse
t_{dw} = availability of data to the users
t_s = arrival of data to the source system

Let's walk through a simple example using this formula. A retail store is open from 8:00 A.M. to 7:00 P.M. On a nightly basis, the store creates the extract to be loaded into the data warehouse. The process, which also formats and checks the quality of the data, takes 12 hours. The extracted and transformed data is now loaded into the system and is available to the users 6 hours later, at 1:00 P.M. Tuesday. The currency of data is

$C = t_{dw} - t_s = $ 1:00 P.M. Tuesday – 7:00 P.M. Monday = 18 hours.

Customers of this data may be interested in having this information available sooner. Unfortunately the cost of improving data currency is an expensive proposition (see Figure 12.15). As the legend explains, as the data currency reaches real time, the cost goes up almost exponentially. This increase is due, in part, to the additional redundancy requirements to support and maintain such a data feed.

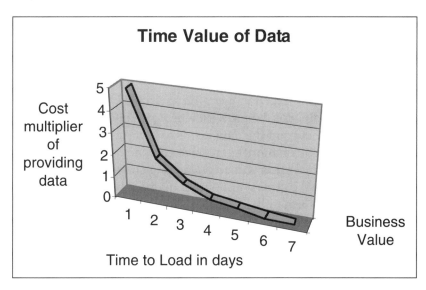

FIGURE 12.15
Time value of data.

Let's look at two additional examples of data currency requirements that approach real time. A telecommunications company uses real-time feeds that capture data from the telephone central offices to gauge the effectiveness of print, radio, and television ad campaigns. By linking their marketing campaigns through the data warehouse, this company evaluates the relative effectiveness of these mediums for changing the behavior of their target audience. As the behavior of the customers is better understood, more focused, effective, and ultimately more profitable campaigns can be waged. For example, soon after the advertisement is generated, a variety of call usage metrics are gathered. One metric may be calling patterns. Another measure may be the number of 800 calls. Whatever the measure, more sophisticated marketing programs are beginning to require real-time data feeds to assess the success of their programs.

At a retail company, the real-time feed also measures customer response to campaigns. Everything from in-store displays to flyers that have been distributed are evaluated for their relative effectiveness. In both examples, regional differences and other more subtle differences can be found and accounted for as customer preferences are stored and processed.

INCREASING DATA CURRENCY MAY ALSO INCREASE COSTS   Turning to the implications of data currency, as batch extracts move to trickle or real time, the costs and complexity can be enormous. If customer requirements call for accelerating data currency, the company must be willing to support the increased support and maintenance costs. Service management can help focus discussions between IT and customers of the service on the business value and benefit they expect to receive from having more current data. Often users will be able to determine for themselves, when presented with the associated costs, how current the data needs to be. Sometimes more critical areas will be on more aggressive currency schedules and less business-critical areas will be on lagging currency schedules.

As the data size grows, utilizing sequential batch processing techniques to perform bulk loads to the data warehouse eventually becomes an operations bottleneck. No matter how efficient the techniques, at a certain data size and application complexity, it is impossible to perform all of the required tasks within the available batch processing time window.

At this point it may become necessary to switch to a "trickle feed" update model; that is, remove the batch update time window and replace it with a continuous background update capability. Some in the industry refer to this model as an operational data store (ODS). The major difference between a data warehouse and an ODS is the latter is typically not a source of history for trending and, unlike the data warehouse, its mission in life is to capture individual transactional changes in operational systems. For ODSs, a large number of relatively small updates are performed versus a data warehouse that has a large load applied on an intermittent basis.

OPERATIONAL DATA STORES Creating an ODS is a major reengineering activity. For starters, new update routines must be written. The source systems must be "taught" to provide many small batches of updated records in a quick fashion rather than batch files at a pre-scribed time of the day. In addition, the operations team must be taught how to continuously apply the updates rather than queuing them to run overnight or over the weekend.

It may also affect user query response times. Depending on where the ODS is located in the platform and how often the up-dates are propagated to the data warehouse, user queries may now compete with update transactions. The update activity was con-fined to the defined batch update cycles when users were typically not active. They were able to run their queries with minimal inter-ference from other applications locking out the records they needed. Therefore the end users running the queries were used to relatively quick response time. Now, with the battle over locked records between the queries and update programs, both environ-ments may see diminished response times. What then is the attrac-tion with this approach?

Batch extractions are easy and nonobtrusive to the production reporting environment on the data warehouse. So why go to trickle mode update? The answer: increased currency. The data gets from the source system to an operational data store much more quickly—near real time, without the artificial time delay cre-ated by waiting for the next batch update process to run.

There is even a further step beyond ODS, that is, immediate feeds directly from the same source feeds. This is a practice most often seen around telecommunications call detail record (i.e., CDR)

A large U.S.-based telecommunications company wanted to analyze its equipment for service-level compliance. It wanted to monitor its major lines, hubs (places where their telephone lines interchange with other providers' phone lines), and telephony equipment to see if their operational uptime matched (contractually) promised service levels. Moreover, they wanted to do this in real time.

It was determined that the arrival rate of the telephone call information (call detail records, or CDRs) would be so high (millions per second) that it would be a major factor in the warehouse design. In fact the feed rates from the central office switches were so high, a decision had to be made: either reduce the feed rate by selectively targeting a subset of CDRs or increase the capacity of the feeding mechanism. Having an uncompromised feed was the most important aspect of the service-level compliance system, so changes to the feeding system were necessary. The solution to the problem was not hardware alone. Even the largest computer system could not keep pace with the millions of CDRs per second the system received and then cleanse, format, and load the records into the data warehouse. Since the original single-layer data warehouse using trickle update techniques could not keep up, a three-step system was devised.

The first step was to collect the data right off the central office switches and make the intermediate data available for limited query use. Data is then properly cleansed and ready to be loaded into the data warehouse. The new design took advantage of some degree of parallelism by introducing multiple loading layers into platform design. The new design has one system that's dedicated to collecting data right off the telephone central office switches. Its sole purpose is to outpace data arrival and pass it off to the next system. Because of the high CDR arrival rate, there is insufficient time to perform data standardization and cleansing.

The second step in the process stores the collected data for a 2-week rolling window, in a simplified third normal format with no associated aggregation. Although aggregates are often desirable, they are of limited use (and are often more trouble than they are worth) if the underlying data is rapidly changing because it requires similar updates to both the underlying fact and dimension tables and the aggregate tables. This collection of data is a highly volatile data staging area that, while in a relational database, keeps only 2 weeks' worth of data at any one time. This step allows limited queries. Most of the queries are for forecasting, to answer questions like, What does the entire population of data look like once it has been properly cleansed and loaded? What is the error rate for incoming CDRs?

The third step is to properly cleanse, dedupe, transform, and load data into the data warehouse. At the end of the second week, the data has been loaded onto the third node, the data warehouse node, and is deleted from the data store. Data is retained on the data warehouse for 13 months, but this can be expanded in the future.

The point of this example is that use of multiple layers or staging of data has handled currency for this application. The currency on the original system is real time, but the data accuracy and consistency is suspect. Queries run against this data are confined to a small number of record lookups (random I/Os). Queries involving a large date range, sorting activity, and "what if?" modeling are specifically disallowed because of the high demand they place on the system and the low refinement of the data.

Currency on the data warehouse tier is up to 14 days late. However, the data is now accurate, and the data is retained long enough to perform current month/last month and current year/last year comparisons. It is a very conventional data warehouse, but with substantially poorer data currency. In addition, the front ends must be smart enough to determine if the user's query is intended against this week's or last week's data (hence going to the data store), or against longer-term data found only in the data warehouse. A weakness of the design has been the need to "hardwire" the time boundary into the front end, thus limiting flexibility in the future.

feeds or financial institution ticker feeds. The data arrival rate becomes so overwhelming that additional hardware layers must be introduced to "buffer up" the data again.

Data Quality Dimension

According to many data warehouse industry experts, anywhere from 5% to 50% of the data in corporate databases is missing or inaccurate. Thus moving this data to a warehouse creates rather than solves reporting problems for companies. Therefore a large focus of the extraction and transformation process is on correcting these problems before they are loaded into the data warehouse (Figure 12.16).

Measuring and scoring the quality of data is vital. It enables SMCs to be created and used as a vehicle to know when a data quality problem exists and/or when a noteworthy trend has potentially been discovered. Unfortunately, early users of data warehouses sometimes assume that the data is inaccurate and consequently they have little or no confidence in the results of their analysis. Here again, the trumpet of acquiring user requirements must be sounded.

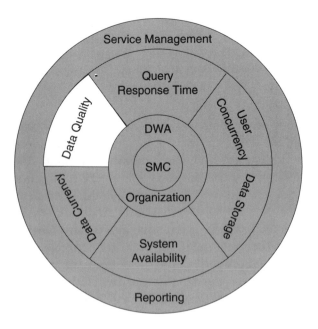

FIGURE 12.16
The data quality dimension.

USER REQUIREMENTS ARE ESSENTIAL   Having a discussion with the user community about their expectations for data quality will help facilitate the IT's understanding of what and how to measure data quality. The expectation must be set early that there will be areas of the data warehouse that may experience data quality issues. IT, as part of their assessment, must determine which areas are most prone to having inaccurate data and what measures can be reasonably taken to maintain or improve it. At a minimum, the user should expect quality safeguards that, for example, will inhibit the same data from being loaded twice into the data warehouse. In addition, users should be made aware of dimensions that have difficulty maintaining semantic consistency or which will from time to time have inaccurate or incomplete information.

There are many types of data quality issues within data warehouses. Let's take a moment and look at them in more detail. The most common quality issues fall into the category of referential integrity (RI). A simple definition of RI is the establishment and maintenance of data relationships in the database. The good news is that RI capabilities are included with all major RDBMSs. It enables a variety of sophisticated tests to be applied to the incoming data before it is inserted into the database to ensure it maintains the established relationships. By performing rudimentary RI tests, it ensures that the loaded data is of known quality. The most common RI check ensures that for every fact row, every foreign key has an associated and valid entry in a supporting dimension row. For example, before a new fact row for item movement can be inserted, a lookup is performed on the associated dimensions, ensuring that sufficient definition exists for the dimensional data model.

RI tests can be performed at the table or column level. Let's look at some examples of RI:

❑ Check incoming rows to ensure that the last name begins with a range of letters, from A–Z.
❑ Check to see if they have a valid two-character state abbreviation.
❑ Check to see if there is an M or F in the gender column.

There are many other checks that can be performed, with the only limitation being the amount of programming and processing time you are willing to invest.

MANAGING REFERENTIAL INTEGRITY   Typically RI is expensive in terms of processing resources. Using this capability can quickly tax the load/update process. However, if employed it can help data warehouse administrators ensure that the data warehouse has high-quality data. Thus far we have focused on identifying RI problems. The next step is to decide what should be done about an RI violation? There are four basic approaches to solving RI exceptions:

❏ Do nothing and ignore the exceptions. This is not recommended.

❏ Stop the load and manually correct the exceptions. Restart once the error is corrected. This is not recommended.

❏ Load the exceptions into a separate file to be processed later. This is recommended.

❏ Load the exceptions with available correct values and flag for correction later. This is recommended, but you must ensure the records are corrected.

As noted, there are only two satisfactory approaches to resolving RI exceptions. Of these, loading the exceptions into a separate file for subsequent correction is the most common approach. In this way, the data warehouse administrator can discuss source data quality with the appropriate persons. The fourth approach is also good, with the only issue being that if the data is loaded in the data warehouse to be reconciled later, it will be more difficult to address data quality problems. It will also be more difficult to track problems over time when the exception rows are loaded into the data warehouse and not kept separately for reprocessing.

CLEAN DATA IS VITAL TO DATA WAREHOUSE SUCCESS   One thing is certain: cleanliness of data is vital in data warehousing. But this area is often ignored by many involved in data warehousing. Perhaps this is because there is little in the way of tools and techniques to improve the quality of data, or maybe it is because many (wrongly) assume that the data in source systems is clean. Whatever the reason, not many tools exist to assist in the arduous process for creating and maintaining accurate data warehouse data. Few tools can comprehensively address the data quality issues customers have. Instead, most of the tools that help with data quality are relegated to improving mailing lists or data of that type. This type of semantic quality is important, but the industry's need for high-quality data is much broader than value standardization such as

❑ street = ST., Str., St., STr., etc.
❑ Robert = Bob, Bobby, Rob, etc.

Let's look at assessing and improving data quality in more detail. The first step in assessing the overall data quality of the data warehouse is to identify all critical attributes. A critical attribute is a data element which if wrong or missing will lead to erroneous reporting of the data warehouse. An example of this could be stock-keeping units (SKUs) for a product data warehouse. Having dimensions and facts disagreeing when it comes to SKUs would be disastrous. Similarly, there are other attributes in the data warehouse which if populated with missing or invalid data would be disastrous. Consequently, prioritizing attributes of the data warehouse is imperative to creating SLAs on data quality.

WHERE SHOULD THE DATA BE CLEANED?   Once the critical attributes have been prioritized, the next step is to see how accurate and complete these attributes are in their source systems. Once this is known, a plan can be devised to correct the data once extracted from the source systems. A common question at this point is, why not go back and correct the source systems? That is the right idea. Unfortunately many of these source systems are fragile and are not able to accommodate corrections like this. The reality of the situation is that while cleaning up the data after the fact is really a temporary fix, and one that will have to be used every time data is extracted from the source systems, it is the most common and widely used approach. The bottom line is that unless businesses are convinced that having dirty data in the source system is costing them money, there will be little interest in investing in improving the source systems.

So let's assume that properly correcting the source information is impractical. Service management can still help manage the process of data quality. First, given the situation, it must be understood that it's impossible to guarantee that 100% of all data in the data warehouse is accurate. If customer requirements are that no more than 5% of items stored in the data warehouse are in error, the data warehouse administrator should work with the source data provider to ensure this measure will be met. In fact, in many companies, the data warehouse administrator will have another SMC with the source data provider that ensures data provided is properly formatted, free of "known" errors, and otherwise fit to be loaded into the data warehouse.

We have now made the case that having missing or invalid data hampers the effectiveness of the data warehouse environment. Almost without exception, the most critical data elements in the data warehouse are numerical and are found in the fact tables. Depending on the application, recovery from unintended (I'll cover intended errors shortly) fact table errors is difficult. The good news is most data quality issues are not with the facts but are with the dimension attributes.

MANUFACTURING DATA FOR THE DATA WAREHOUSE   Turning to intended errors, why would any company intentionally introduce erroneous information into the warehouse? We briefly covered this concept earlier in this chapter. Consider the example of a single retail store out of 500 that is unable to post its sales results for a day. While the other 499 have posted their results, the one store is unable to (and for this example has lost the ability to post these results for good). Certainly this may have an effect on the reporting capability of the data warehouse. The district and region numbers will be artificially low. Commissions, promotions, and other activities may be affected. What can be done about this?

In this case, it is often considered appropriate to take an average day sales data for that store and input it into the data warehouse. In this way, reports that depend on this data being present will still be able to run. But isn't that introducing poor data quality into the data warehouse? Yes, it is. But in this case the users decided that it's best to manufacture the missing data rather than having weekly sales totals that may, because of the absence of data, be misleading. Finally, how should users be notified when data is missing or manufactured? The Web has certainly made notification, like status or currency of data, much simpler to manage.

It's clear that this example shows that there's no easy answer. The solution therefore is to spell out the quality the users expect of their data. Perhaps having up to two stores per month not reporting their data is acceptable.

HOW WILL CHANGING DIMENSIONS AFFECT DATA QUALITY?   Another area that should be spelled out for the user community is how the data mart is modeled to accommodate slowly changing dimensions. By explicitly explaining to the users how dimensions will represent changes, they can ensure they interpret the data correctly. For example, let's assume that a new box color has been created for a retail product. And let's also assume that the product dimension is our key dimension, meaning that this dimension is richly attributed. The vendor of the product does not create a new SKU, they simply continue to use the existing SKU. Sales of the product pick up noticeably. If the history of the previous SKU is not maintained, the analysis and subsequent conclusion may not be accurate as to why the product is all of a sudden selling so well. This example, while somewhat dramatic, is intended to show the complexity of dimension management. Having multiple product dimension entries for the same SKU is no easy answer either. This needs to be resolved with the users to ensure the warehouse supports accurate and complete reporting.

So after all of this discussion it comes down to, What should a service management contract for data quality cover? Ideally, discussions with users of data from a data warehouse should focus on the impact of data not being accurate, that is, associating a business impact of data quality. For most organizations, having a 5% lapse in source data quality is acceptable if the offending area is not business critical.

Bottom line, does the quality of data meet user expectations in terms of accuracy and completeness?

SUMMARY

In this chapter we've looked at how service management can assist the data warehouse administrator deliver a more predictable and manageable environment. In fact, use of the techniques outlined here will help ensure that all departments within an organization better understand each other's roles and responsibilities and are equipped to support the evolving nature of the data warehouse environment.

Looking back, we covered the many important aspects of service management, from starting with the right data warehouse and IT organization, through the components of the service itself.

We looked at the importance of measurable metrics and effective reporting of compliance. By following the guidelines found in this chapter, you will be well on your way to providing a predictable, efficient data warehouse environment. And remember, if this is your first SMC, start small. Do not try to cover every dimension. Instead, focus on one or two key areas that have a good chance of success and are currently of concern to your customer base. Then, once successful, look to expand the SMC to cover other important dimensions. In this way you'll reduce your risk and increase your chances of gaining and maintaining the confidence and expectations of the data warehouse community.

In the next chapter we look at how concepts and ideas presented from the usage, data, platform, and service management perspectives can be applied in arriving at a high-performance data warehouse environment.

Delivery and Performance

Chapter 13 "Delivering a High-Performance Data Warehouse Environment"

In the previous Parts, we talked about the four elements that comprise a high-performance data warehouse environment. Specifically, we talked about the elements that contribute to the delivery of services (usage, data and platform) as well as the element that ensures that the services delivered meet immediate and ongoing business needs (service management). In this section, we will use a case study to demonstrate how to combine these elements in delivering a high-performance data warehouse enviroment.

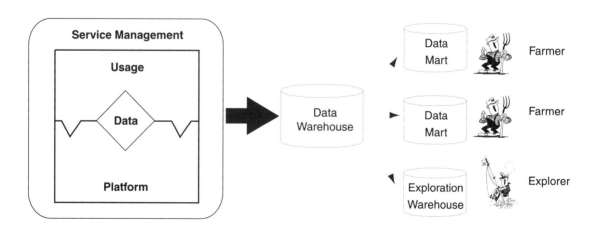

13

CHAPTER THIRTEEN

Delivering a High-Performance Data Warehouse Environment

Well there you have it. We have talked about what it means to have a high-performance data warehouse environment. Simply put, a high-performance data warehouse environment is one that supports the immediate expectations (i.e., needs) of the business and is an environment that will scale (i.e., grow) to support these needs as they evolve. In addition, we covered what it takes to build and maintain a high-performance data warehouse environment from several very important perspectives, as depicted in Figure 13.1 below.

FIGURE 13.1
Perspectives on building a high-performance data warehouse environment.

373

First we looked at building the high-performance data warehouse environment from the perspectives of usage and data, since these perspectives fundamentally shape the landscape of this environment. Next we focused our discussion on constructing the platform on which the usage and data reside. This was an important perspective because if the platform is not constructed properly, our high-performance data warehouse environment will not scale to support the evolving needs of the business.

Finally, we talked about the "pearl" of the high-performance data warehouse environment—service management. In contrast to the perspectives of data, usage, and platform which focus on the delivery of business capabilities, the perspective of service management focuses on ensuring that these capabilities meet customer expectations. More importantly, it ensures that as customer expectations evolve, the data warehouse environment adapts to meet these expectations. Suffice it to say, a data warehouse environment without service management would be like a cruise ship without a captain. Even though the ship (data, usage, and platform) is in port, passengers (users) are on board, and the destination (business need) is clear, it is highly unlikely that the ship will ever arrive at that destination or even leave port. The captain plays a crucial role in ensuring that the resources of the ship are directed to suit the needs of the passengers, that the passengers enjoy the cruise, and ultimately, that the passengers arrive safely at their destination. In a similar fashion, service management ensures that the data warehouse environment suits the needs of the users, that the users are happy with the level of service they receive, and that the environment is positioned to support the strategic destination of the business.

Now that we have covered building the high-performance data warehouse environment from these very important perspectives, this chapter will take a closer look at how the concepts and techniques presented can be applied in arriving at a high-performance data warehouse environment. To illustrate this we will use a case study. This case study uses concepts and techniques presented in the previous sections in arriving at a high-performance data warehouse environment that supports several key capabilities common to companies trying to better understand, market, and serve their customers. Though no single case study can cover all of the concepts and ideas presented in the previous chapters, or their variations, the sections that follow will provide the reader with a basis for applying these concepts and techniques in delivering a high-performance data warehouse environment.

CASE STUDY OVERVIEW

Although the company presented in this case study is fictitious, their environment and the applications being presented are very real and especially relevant to companies who compete in a deregulated marketplace and see their success (and viability) as being contingent on their ability to outpace the competition by identifying, acquiring, and retaining high-value customers.

Why is this model for doing business so important? For more than 30 years, the growth of many companies has been measured by their ability to market more products to more people cheaper than the competition. The most evident signs of this practice are the growing number of unsolicited telemarketing calls, direct mail packages, and e-mail messages we receive as consumers on a daily basis (sound familiar?). However, a significant change is afoot. These companies are no longer seeing long-term growth and viability as being measured by this process of product differentiation and discounting. Growing consumer dissatisfaction and expectations and global competition are demanding that these companies differentiate individual consumers so that relevant products and services can be offered to those customers who represent the most value to the business on their terms. And technology and new marketing channels (e.g., the Internet) are fueling this change. Excellent examples of this new marketing paradigm are the use of frequent flyer programs in the airline industry and MCI's Friends and Family program. This revolutionary new marketing model is referred to as one-to-one marketing and is quickly reshaping the business landscape in which we live.

We selected this business scenario because it touches nearly every industry across the globe. However, even if every aspect of this scenario isn't relevant to you, the concepts and ideas presented are relevant to anyone building a high-performance data warehouse environment.

Now let's take a look at the company, the team, and the three- to six-month deliverable before moving forward with the delivery of CCI's high-performance data warehouse environment.

Company Background

Customer Communications, Inc. (or CCI) is a phone company that provides local services similar to those services provided by the bigger (and better known) local exchange carriers such as Bell Atlantic, US West, Southwestern Bell, Pacific Bell, and Ameritech. These services include phone installation and maintenance, local and intra-LATA calling, yellow and white pages, call waiting, voice mail, e-mail, and pagers. CCI services roughly three million households and businesses (consisting of roughly four million accounts) and generates roughly $4 billion a year in revenue.

Changing Business Landscape

Until recently, CCI enjoyed the luxury of having a monopoly over local phone service (albeit regulated). The beauty of this arrangement was that CCI had no competition. Furthermore, CCI controlled phone-line access to its customers and received remuneration for this access. For example, when a customer used Sprint to make a long-distance phone call, a percent of the cost of the call would go to CCI (via Sprint) for the use of their local phone lines. In this environment, CCI had no competition for local phone access, and the customer had no choice.

However, CCI is facing a new business landscape. Under significant consumer pressure, and pressure from large national/ international communications companies (e.g., AT&T, Sprint, MCI, etc.), the government is deregulating local phone service. This deregulation will allow companies like AT&T, MCI, and Sprint to offer local phone service (along with a variety of other communication services such as long distance) in an area that has long been exclusive to CCI. As a result, CCI's customers will be offered more choices and lower rates, and CCI will be thrust into an unfamiliar business landscape where they will have to compete to survive.

In response to this business challenge, CCI decided that it had one of following three options:

❏ Grow the company by leveraging the current customer base and expanding into new product (e.g., long distance) and market (e.g., new regions) opportunities

❑ Sell the company to one of the larger communications companies (e.g., MCI, Sprint, AT&T, etc.) or local phone service providers (e.g., US West, Pacific Bell, etc.)

❑ Go out of business

After serious deliberation and consideration, CCI decided that they were ready to compete. They concluded that they could leverage their engineering and customer service prowess (which were well known to be the best in the industry) to protect their current customer base from the competition and to retain new customers as they were acquired from the competition. However, management knew that there were a few pieces missing from the puzzle if CCI was to succeed in their quest to become a dominate player in the market. They needed more robust order processing and billing capabilities and, more importantly, a marketing prowess comparable to that of customer service. In response, management created and staffed a marketing organization to begin formulating strategies to retain and acquire high-value customers.

Marketing Challenges

After several months, marketing arrived at their process for segmenting customers and for formulating strategies to acquire, retain, and increase the value of these customer segments. Unfortunately, much of the information gathering to support the marketing planning process was being done manually because needed data was dispersed across systems both internal and external to CCI.

Like many companies, CCI had developed a myriad of systems on mainframes, minis, and even PCs. They built and/or bought other communications companies as part of their strategy of growth which resulted in even more disparate systems and databases. Currently they have IBM 3090s, DEC VAXs, Tandems, Suns, and HPs, plus PCs and Macintoshes. Their data is spread out in DB2, VSAM, and Enscribe files, nonstop SQL, RDB, Oracle, Sybase, and Informix. End users have Paradox, RBase, Microsoft Access, Lotus Notes, etc. Needless to say, their data is spread out in dozens of databases throughout the company—most are in nonaccessible formats and are unintegrated. As a result, a marketing process that should have taken weeks was taking four to six months because of the work involved in identifying, sourcing, and integrating data. Not only was this manual process slowing down time to market (a key factor of success in a competitive industry), but it was expensive, and prone to errors and inconsistencies.

Justifying the Data Warehouse Environment

In response, marketing commissioned the creation of a data warehouse environment to automate the integration and use of information to support their market planning process. In addition, marketing envisioned that this data warehouse environment would be the vehicle for disseminating marketing intelligence throughout the different customer contact points (customer service, phone installation and maintenance, etc.) within the corporation. For example, if marketing developed a capability to predict if a customer was likely to leave, the data warehouse environment should be able to provide access to this capability to anyone in the corporation who could use this information to improve customer retention.

BUILDING THE TEAM

Once marketing received approval (and more importantly funding) to move forward with the data warehouse project, they met with the information services (IS) group. This was an important first step in the project because without a high-performance team, consisting of both marketing and IS personnel, marketing knew that they could not expect to arrive at a high-performance data warehouse environment. This is an important point. Although we have not talked much about selecting the right people, we need to reflect on the importance of this early decision in arriving at a high-performance data warehouse environment. Without the right skills and the right working relationship between IS and the user community, it is doubtful that you will ever get far enough in your project to apply the concepts and techniques presented in this book.

As a result of their joint efforts, marketing and IS arrived at the following list of roles on the project team:

End-user representatives. Given that the marketing group is organized around the major marketing segments (e.g., residential, small business, large business, and national accounts), it was agreed that there should be one end-user representative for each segment. This person was selected based on their ability to commit time to the project, their knowledge of the business and CCI, and their authority (formally or informally) to speak for the group they represent. As a result, four end-user representatives were identified: one representative for residential, one for small business, one for large business, and one for national accounts.

"Get data in" group. This group would consist of IS personnel responsible for sourcing, transforming, and integrating the needed data from both internal and external systems. In addition, this team would be responsible for the loading and managing of the data in the data warehouse. The roles identified to fulfill this responsibility included

❑ Data acquisition programmer/analyst
❑ Data analyst
❑ Data warehouse architect and DBA
❑ Metadata analyst

"Get information out" group. This group would consist of IS personnel responsible for creating capabilities (using the atomic data in the data warehouse) to support the different end-user needs. The roles identified to fulfill this responsibility included

❑ Business analyst
❑ End-user application specialist (i.e., someone who knows analytic tools and how to configure them)
❑ Data mart delivery programmer/analyst (i.e., someone who can use tools and/or write programs/processes to create data marts to support the different end-user applications using detail data from the data warehouse)
❑ Data mart DBA

Project Manager. This person would be responsible for coordinating the activities of the various IS team members to ensure that capabilities met the needs of the end-user representatives.

Once the roles were identified, marketing and IS assigned the appropriate resources to the defined roles. In some cases (with regard to the IS roles), several roles were assigned to a single person. For example, the project team was fortunate enough to find a single person with the skills to fulfill the roles of business analyst and end-user application specialist, and the work effort was small enough that this person could fulfill both roles.

SCOPING THE THREE- TO SIX-MONTH DELIVERABLE

With the formation of the high-performance project team came the need to define the high-level requirements for the data warehouse environment and, more specifically, those requirements to be delivered with the first iteration—building the data warehouse environment in three- to six-month iterations is critical to its success.

Like the creation of the high-performance project team, this subject was not covered in much detail in this book because so

---

THREE-TO SIX-MONTH ITERATIONS

The term "three to six months" is used throughout this chapter to describe the duration for each iteration of a high-performance data warehouse environment. Although this term implies that the duration for an iteration could be as long as six months, this is quite uncommon. High-performance data warehouse environments generally see new iterations every three to four months (or less). Six months is only used in the term to remind us that some iterations may take as long as six months because of the newness of the process and people, and/or the additional time needed to build the infrastructure (e.g., selecting, procuring, and configuring hardware, database, utilities, etc.). In general, only the first several iterations will ever take six months. All subsequent iterations should take no longer than three to four months (or less).

much has already been published on the subject. However, having a scoping process that can quickly identify the high-level requirements and, more importantly, help distill out of those requirements of the first/next three- to six-month deliverable is critical to the success of a high-performance data warehouse environment. Without such a high-performance scoping process, it would be difficult—if not impossible—to focus the high-performance project team on delivering a high-performance data warehouse environment. Many times you can recognize projects that have failed (or neglected) to employ a high-performance scoping process. What typically characterizes these types of projects is that they have been going on for more than a year without a deliverable or they have produced a deliverable that the business isn't sure how to use.

Now that we have taken a look at the importance of the scoping process, let's take a look at the process CCI used to quickly arrive at their high-performance requirements and, more importantly, their first three- to six-month deliverable. CCI's process consists of three workshops, as depicted in Figure 13.2.

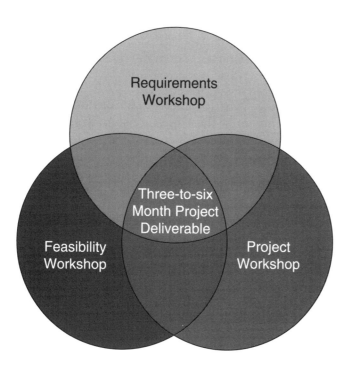

FIGURE 13.2
CCI's workshops conducted in arriving at a three- to six-month project deliverable.

As was previously stated, the objective of the workshops is to strive toward identifying the first (or next) three- to six-month deliverable. The requirements workshop tries to identify, categorize, and prioritize the high-level customer's (i.e., end-user) needs and requirements. The feasibility workshop tries to understand the level of effort and risk involved in delivering a data warehouse environment to support these needs. The final workshop, the project workshop, tries to arrive at the deliverables for the first/next three- to six-month project iteration based on the outputs of the requirements and the feasibility workshops. Now let's walk through CCI's high-performance requirements process step-by-step in scoping the deliverables to be included in their first project iteration.

To get the process started, the project manager conducted a requirement workshop to identify end-user needs in terms of key business questions. For example, key business questions (or needs/requirements) might be

❏ What are my customer segments?

❏ What is my revenue by customer segment by month for the last year?

❏ What are my profits by customer segment by month for the last year?

❏ What are the characteristics of my most profitable customers?

Once these questions were documented, the customers were asked to categorize and prioritize these questions. As a result, the following categories (i.e., capabilities) of analysis were identified in priority order:

1. **Customer segmentation.** This capability allows marketing to organize customers into meaningful groups. The primary segments are residential, small business, large business, and national accounts. Within each of these segments the customer is further differentiated (i.e., groups) into more granular subsegments (as defined by the respective marketing groups).

2. **Profitability analysis.** This capability allows marketing to analyze the profitability of customers by customer segment and subsegment.

3. **Customer churn analysis.** This capability allows marketing to analyze customer attrition and the characteristics of those customers who stay versus the characteristics of those customers who leave, by product.

4. **Lead list generation.** This capability allows marketing to generate a list of customers for a selected sales or service activity. For example, marketing could use this capability to generate a list of high-value customers who are likely to leave for competitive reasons and who would like stay if they were offered a 5% discount. In addition, this capability would also track the performance of these different lead lists and the campaign that the lead list supports. For example, a single campaign to improve retention for those residential customer who generate more that $300 of revenue per month may be supported by multiple lead lists.

5. **Campaign analysis.** This capability allows marketing to analyze the effectiveness of their various campaigns.

Following the requirements workshop, the IS group conducted a two-day workshop to assess the feasibility of delivering each capability. This feasibility included a high-level list of tasks to be performed in delivering each capability, along with the level of effort, degree of risk, dependencies, and capacity estimates.

Armed with the output from these workshops, the core team (end users and IS) conducted a project workshop to decide—given the business priority, level of effort, risk, dependencies, and capacity estimates—which capability(s) would be delivered as part of this first three- to six-month iteration of the data warehouse environment. The joint decision was that the deliverable for the first iteration would be the capabilities to support customer segmentation and profitability analysis.

DELIVERING THE DATA WAREHOUSE ENVIRONMENT

Having a high-performance project team, a high-performance scoping process, and a well-defined three- to six-month deliverable for the first/next iteration is a characteristic common to all high-performance data warehouse environments—the term successful is implied. CCI has followed this pattern of success. CCI has created a high-performance team and has used their high-performance scoping process to arrive at a project deliverable that is SMART (specific, measurable, achievable, realistic, and timely) and one that is of significant value to the end-user community and, subsequently, the business. All that is left to do is deliver. Sounds simple, right? Well, not exactly. If it were that simple then this book would not have been written. Now that CCI's project foundation is in place (project team and deliverable for the first iteration), let's put the concepts and techniques presented in this book to work in the delivery of CCI's high-performance data warehouse to support customer segmentation and customer profitability analysis.

Assess the Capabilities

Now that the scope is defined, it is time to assess the capabilities in terms of the type of user and the type of work to be performed (see Chapter 2 for a discussion on the types of users and their respective types of work). This is a critical next step in the delivery of a high-performance data warehouse environment in that it helps to ensure that the proper component of the platform (e.g., data warehouse, data mart, exploration warehouse, etc.) is being used to support the selected capability. For example, you probably wouldn't want the data warehouse to support a standard (highly repetitive) report that is run 300 times daily. It just wouldn't make sense because response times would be poor and the query cost would be high given the amount of detail data that would need to be scanned and aggregated. A better way to position this workload would be to use a data mart containing summary-level data to support end-users (i.e., farmers) requesting this report. In addition to positioning the workload correctly, this assessment process will also highlight situations where multiple components of the platform would be needed to support a single capability. By profiling and positioning the capabilities correctly on the platform, we can ensure that the appropriate design approach and technologies are used to optimize performance, minimize costs, and deliver on end-user expectations. With that said, let's assess CCI's two capabilities: segmentation and profitability analysis.

SEGMENTATION   Segmentation, as described previously, is clearly the type of activity that would be performed by an explorer. That is, the end user of this capability is looking for hidden patterns within the data for the purpose of trying to determine how customers cluster together. This is very much a discovery activity, and as such is very consistent with the type of work performed by an explorer.

Now that we have identified the type of user performing this activity as an explorer, let's take a look at the type of workload that is consistent with explorers doing these types of modeling activities. At this time we won't worry so much about the technique employed by the explorer (i.e., statistical techniques or machine learning techniques) but, rather, let's profile the types of work being performed in the segmentation process, as depicted in Figure 13.3.

As depicted in Figure 13.3, the first step in the customer segmentation process is for the explorer to profile the data in the data warehouse. This is an important predecessor step to modeling (segmentation or otherwise) in that it gives the explorer a good idea of what data is available for modeling and, given the level of

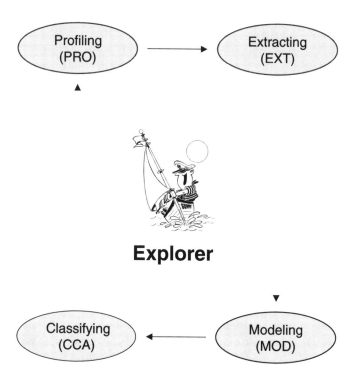

FIGURE 13.3

Types of work performed in the customer segmentation process.

quality, what data would be most appropriate for creating the customer segmentation model. For example, upon profiling the detail data in the data warehouse, the explorer may uncover that the column Household Income is very sparsely populated. This is unacceptable to the explorer. The explorer knows (based on experience) that this column will play a fundamental role in arriving at a useful segmentation model. As a result, the explorer may decide to use another column that can accurately predict household income range, or the explorer may decide to do nothing until additional sources of household income data can be identified and applied to the data warehouse. Once all the needed data has been identified and the level of quality is acceptable (as determined through profiling), it is time for the explorer to move onto the next step in the segmentation process—extracting.

Extracting performs the necessary selection and formatting of detail data from the data warehouse for loading into the exploration warehouse. The technology common to the exploration warehouse was an ideal fit for the explorer's needs, given that it allowed very large sample of customers to be loaded into the tokenized database (see Chapter 3 for more on the exploration warehouse and its technology). From the exploration data warehouse, the explorer models the data to determine how customers naturally cluster. Once the cluster definitions are defined, the explorer performs classifying against all customers in the data warehouse so as to assign each of them to a customer segment.

What we have learned from analyzing the segmentation capability can be summarized as follows:

❏ The user of this capability can be categorized as an explorer.

❏ There are four types of work being performed in the segmentation process: profiling, extracting, modeling, and classifying.

❏ Profiling will run against the data warehouse given the level of detail data needed and the unknown nature of how the explorer will want to access this data. This type of workload is very likely to be unpredictable in terms of time-of-day access and query complexity. The good news is that the result set produced by the queries should be fairly small. For example, many of the result sets will be simple counts. These outputs, which define the complexion of data in the data warehouse, can be reused (if documented in a metadata repository) to support future profiling activities.

❑ Extracting will extract desired detail data from the data warehouse for loading into the exploration data warehouse. This workload will require significant resources. However, this workload is very predictable and is not likely to run frequently. The query response time for this type of workload could be as much as six hours or more. This is not an issue for the explorer, who is more interested in data quality than query response time.

❑ Modeling will run against the exploration warehouse. This was an appropriate choice given that the token-based technology commonly employed within an exploration warehouse is appropriate for the segmentation modeling activity being performed by CCI. For some modeling activities, this technology may not be appropriate. As a result, other modeling activities (other than segmentation) may be better positioned to use a customized or "living sample" data mart. See Chapter 3 for more on the "living sample."

❑ Classifying will run against the data warehouse. This made sense because the data warehouse is the only place where all customers and all customer details exist. The output of the casting activity (i.e., customer segments) is stored and managed in the data warehouse.

PROFITABILITY ANALYSIS   After reviewing the questions (as defined in the requirements workshop) in arriving at this category of analysis, it seemed that the pattern of access was going to be predictable in terms of business dimensions (e.g., organization, customer segment, etc.) and metrics (e.g., revenue, number of customers, etc.). In addition, it also appeared that the time-of-day access was going to be fairly predictable. For example, it appears that most of the access will take place between the hours of 9:00 A.M. and 5:00 P.M. MST. As a result of this predictability and use of aggregated/summarized data, it seems very clear that the type of user we are looking at for profitability analysis is the farmer. Because of this, we can make the observation that there will be two types of workloads to support the farmers doing profitability analysis: extracting and multidimensional analysis.

Multidimensional analysis will be used to support the farmers' profitability questions. This workload will be positioned to run on a data mart. This makes sense, given the data mart can be optimized to provide excellent query performance given the predictability of access and level of summarization that is typical of a farmer.

Extracting will be performed to create the data mart. Very much like the extracting activity for segmentation, this workload will require significant resources. However, this workload is very predictable and is not likely to run infrequently.

As you can see, the process to support profitability analysis is going to be far less complicated than the process to support customer segmentation. However, the demands for query response time, availability, and freshness will grow as this capability is offered to farmers outside of marketing. For example, customer service representatives will have higher demands for query response time and availability given that they are using this information to assist in servicing a customer call. In some ways it is probably better to classify this type of user as an "operator." That is to say, they have similar needs to the farmer in terms of analytical functionality but have much higher expectations in terms of query response, data currency, and availability. Though this operator type of access is not a requirement for the first implementation of profitability analysis, some consideration should be given to this type of support so that the platform can scale to support such future needs.

Aligning the Users, Workload, and Capabilities

Now that we have assessed the types of users, types of workloads, and placement of these workloads by capability (i.e., segmentation and profitability analysis), let's take a look at how these aspects of the high-performance data warehouse environment align and shape the platform (see Figure 13.4).

As depicted in Figure 13.4, the CCI capabilities to be delivered in this first iteration of the data warehouse environment (segmentation and profitability analysis) live in both the data warehouse and the analytical components of the platform: the exploration warehouse and data mart. Based on this observation, we can make the following statements for use in subsequent iterations of CCI's data warehouse environment:

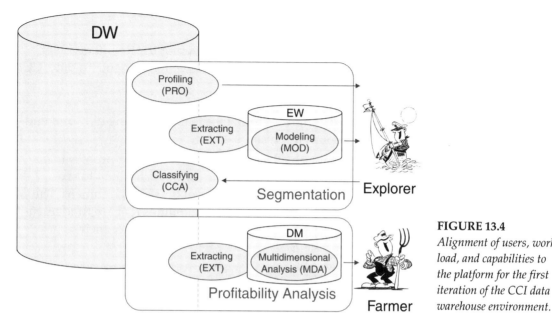

FIGURE 13.4
Alignment of users, work-load, and capabilities to the platform for the first iteration of the CCI data warehouse environment.

❏ The data warehouse will be used when a sample or aggregated view of the data warehouse will not suffice. For example, when a CCI explorer wants to access details about all customers versus just a sample of customers (which would be supported by a data mart). This type of need is very characteristic of the profiling, extracting and classifying activities of the explorer. As a result, you will generally find this type of workload in the data warehouse.

❏ The exploration warehouse and data mart will be used to off-load work from the data warehouse and provide a much more cost-effective environment tailored (though samples and summaries) to support the multidimensional analysis needs of the farmer and the modeling needs of the explorer.

Now that we have discussed placement of capabilities based on type of user and type of workload, let's take a look at the database design to support these capabilities.

Design the Databases

CCI has come along way toward delivering the first iteration of their high-performance data warehouse environment. To date, CCI has:

❑ Formed a high-performance team consisting of IS and end-user representatives.

❑ Gone through a high-performance scoping process to arrive at a focused deliverable for the first three- to six-month iteration of the data warehouse environment. The deliverable consists of two capabilities that are fundamental to helping CCI better market and service their customers:

❑ Customer segmentation and profitability analysis.

❑ Assessed the capabilities to identify the type of user and type of workload to expect. In addition, CCI has aligned the workload to the different platform components (i.e., data warehouse, data mart, and exploration warehouse–see Figure 13.4).

With this foundation in place, CCI now needs to focus on the database design for each of these platform components (i.e., data warehouse, data mart, and exploration warehouse). Specifically, CCI needs to

❑ Decide what database technology it is going to use for each platform component. That is, CCI needs to decide what database technology will be used to support the data warehouse, exploration warehouse, and data mart. It is possible that each component may need to exploit a different technology to address end-user needs.

❑ Design the different databases to support end-user access needs using techniques inherent to the selected database technology.

❑ Develop preliminary capacity estimates (number of disks, disk controllers, and CPUs) to support total disk storage and end-user throughput expectations for these databases. In addition, map the tables in the design to the disks using the appropriate database partitioning technique (e.g., range, hash, and round robin). This information will be used in subsequent activities to configure the hardware system.

Let's take a look at designing the three different databases that will support the first iteration of CCI's data warehouse environment starting with the discussion on selecting the database technology.

SELECTING THE DATABASE TECHNOLOGY   Before CCI could begin to design the database for the different platform components (i.e., data warehouse, data mart, and exploration warehouse), they needed to first assess which technologies would be most appropriate for each component. This decision was important given that the technology would influence the database design.

Selecting the most appropriate database technology is the easiest and at the same time, the most difficult step in delivering your high-performance data warehouse environment. On the one hand, selecting the technology to support the data warehouse and exploration warehouse is relatively simple given there are few options available. On the other hand, a variety of options exist for the data mart, making this technology decision very difficult.

Although the process of selecting the right database technology is a book in and of itself, let's take a look at what decisions CCI made and the rationale behind their decisions.

DATA WAREHOUSE DATABASE   To start the process, CCI went for the "low-hanging fruit." That is, they focused first on selecting the data warehouse database technology. Their decision was to use relational database technology and normalization techniques for arriving at the design for the database. Though there were many good reasons why CCI made this choice, several reasons stood out. This approach would result in a database implementation that would have little or no data redundancy. As a result, the database would optimize loading, minimize the amount of disk storage used, simplify data maintenance, and optimize data quality (given CCI would only have to worry about keeping a single data element updated in one place).

Second, it would organize data in a fashion that is independent of its usage, thus promoting flexibility in how the data is interpreted. In this fashion, the data could be used in a variety of

different ways over time with minimal impact on the database
design. For example, by using this technique, CCI could organize
data in such a way that it would not only support the capabilities
being implemented with this iteration (segmentation and profitability analysis) but also it could be used by new capabilities in
future iterations with little or no change to the design. Third, it was
built on a mature and scalable technology with a proven record of
success in the industry.

Exploration Warehouse Database The technology selection for the
exploration warehouse was relatively easy given that this component of the architecture evolved from the introduction of a new
technology that addressed the access needs of the explorer (i.e.,
token-based technology). As a result, the selection of token-based
technology was fairly straightforward. The challenge was finding a
vendor who could support it. For more on the exploration warehouse and related technology, see the section entitled "Exploration
Warehouse" in Chapter 3.

Data Mart Database Unlike the data warehouse and exploration
warehouse where the technology decision was clear and simple,
the database decision for the data mart was complex and at times
emotional. As it turns out, there are a number of technologies that
exist to support multidimensional analysis. At first the CCI team
thought the decision was going to be easy. Select a multidimensional database to support multidimensional analysis. That was
until several other vendors offered solutions that allowed multidimensionality to be represented using relational database technology. They accomplished this by using a new design technique
called the star-join schema. This approach allowed their clients
to leverage the maturity of relational technology to scale the number of business dimensions beyond that provided by the multidimensional database vendors. Immediately the multidimensional
database vendor responded by accurately stating that multidimensional structures in a relational database could never achieve the
query response time speed and consistency offered by a multidimensional database. By this time, another vendor who could provide multidimensionality in a relational database and deliver
query response times and consistency comparable to that provided
by a multidimensional database approached CCI. They accom-

plished this by providing query optimization techniques and indexing that were tailored toward navigating the star-join schema efficiently. This process went on for several months with other vendors coming forward with solutions that leveraged relational and multidimensional technologies in a single database and vendors who offered solutions using fractal technology. All of these technologies looked good, but which one should CCI select?

After several weeks of analyzing the profitability analysis capability and the available technologies to support multidimensional analysis, CCI decided to leverage the relational database technology (and vendor) used for the data warehouse. Working together IS and the end users decided that the need to scale dimensions was more important than speed or consistency of query response time and that the functionality supported by products that provide multidimensionality in a relational database was sufficient. In addition, the project also benefited from leveraging the investment in the data warehouse database product (e.g., training, licensing, etc.) and further minimizing project risks and costs.

It is important to note that this decision was made by the CCI project team to support this iteration of profitability analysis given their need to balance risks, costs, and delivered functionality. With each iteration the project team will need to reevaluate this decision and its appropriateness to support the capability and end user at hand. For example, this technology decision may not work to support the query response time or functional needs of the end user driving the next iteration. As a result, this farmer may need a different technology solution for his data mart.

Data Mart and Exploration Warehouse Designs

A good data warehouse design always begins with a good data mart and/or exploration warehouse design, and CCI's design was no exception. The CCI project team knew that modeling activities to support segmentation and the multidimensional analysis (MDA) activities to support profitability analysis would drive what data was needed in the data warehouse. As a result, they began the design process for their first iteration by focusing on the data mart and exploration warehouse designs first.

The project team began this design process by transforming the end-user requirements into an initial set of designs. Once these initial designs were complete, the project team proceeded to prototype these designs with the end users (using some real and some made-up data). This prototype process helped the project team refine the end-user requirements and ensure that the resulting design would support the functional needs of the end users. Following the completion of this prototype process the CCI project team had two designs which they were very confident would support the end-users needs for modeling activities to support segmentation and the MDA activities to support profitability analysis. Let's take a closer look at these resulting designs.

Data Mart Design

Let's begin this discussion by revisiting the role of the data mart and the selected database technology. Following this discussion, we will look at data mart design, the hardware capacity requirements to support the design, and mapping of the design to the hardware resources.

CCI positioned the data mart as the sole source of data to support farmers (i.e., marketing) doing profitability analysis. From this source of data, the farmers could view such metrics as revenue and cost across a combination of dimensions such as customer segment and time. The data mart is derived using data warehouse data and is built using relational technology. The design technique that was selected to design this database was star-join schema. This design technique, popularized by Ralph Kimball, enables (with the help of the right front-end tool) multidimensionality to be represented in a relational (i.e., two-dimensional) database. Ralph's book, *The Data Warehouse Toolkit,* provides a complete guide on how to design star-join schemas.

Let's take a look at the star-join schema design that resulted from the end-user requirements and subsequent prototyping efforts. The data mart design to support profitability analysis is depicted in Figure 13.5.

The star-join schema design to support profitability analysis consists of four logical tables. The fact table is in the center and the dimension tables surround it. The fact table is a roll-up (i.e., aggregation) of total revenue and total cost by the four dimensions shown. These dimensions are

> **M_Time.** This dimension allows the farmer to view profitability by year/month, year/quarter, etc.

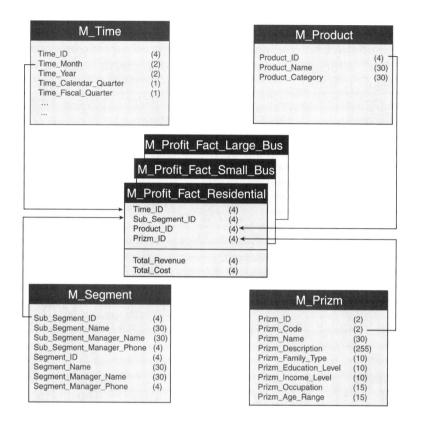

FIGURE 13.5
Data mart design to support profitability analysis.

M_Segment. This dimension allows the farmer to view profitability by customer segment or by the customer subsegment. In addition, the farmer can view profitability by manager name or phone number for each segment or subsegment.

M_Product. This dimension allows the farmer to view profitability by product or product category.

M_Prizm. This dimension allows the farmer to view profitability by prizm code or by some attribute of prizm code. Prizm code is an indicator that is used to characterize households within a defined demographic area by such attributes as family type, education level, income level, occupation, age, etc. There are sixty-two valid prizm codes.

Using any combination of these dimensions, the farmer can quickly view profitability (i.e., revenue – cost) in a variety of ways.

For example, the farmer could view profitability by customer segment, product, product and customer segment, or time by product.

In addition, the farmer can quickly navigate through the dimensions selecting only those occurrences within each dimension that she wants to view. For example, the farmer may decide that she only wants to view profitability for residential customers. To accomplish this, the farmer would simply navigate through the M_Segment dimension table and select Segment_Name. The resulting list would contain all valid customer segments. From this list, the farmer would select Residential and have a report generated that shows profitability by product for residential customers. As you can see, this design (with the right tool) provides the end user a significant degree of flexibility in how he views and reports on profitability. For more on the star-join schema, see Ralph Kimball's book, *The Data Warehouse Toolkit*.

Now that we know a little bit about the profitability analysis data mart, let's take a look at the physical design, the capacity estimates to support the design, and the mapping of the design to the disk.

THE DESIGN   A couple of interesting design techniques have been employed to optimize this star-join schema design. The product of the first technique is probably something that you have already noticed. Although the fact table appears as a single table to the farmer (as a result of their analysis tool), the reality is that it has been divided (i.e., partitioned) into three physical tables with each containing metrics and dimensions for a selected customer segment. To put it another way, the single large fact table has been divided into three smaller fact tables. As a result, when a farmer is doing analysis for a specific customer segment (e.g., small business), his query will run much faster because it need only go against the fact table containing residential data. Let's see how this would work by comparing the size of a single fact table versus the separate partitioned fact tables. Let's make some assumptions about the data in the profitability analysis data mart (by the way, this information was retrieved from CCI's metadata repository):

❑ There are 24 months of revenue in the fact table.

❑ There are three customer segments per month: residential, small business, and large business.

❏ There are five residential subsegments, two small business subsegments, and one large business subsegment. As a result, there are a total of eight subsegments across the three customer segments.

❏ There are 40 residential products, 10 small business products, and 10 large business products. As a result, there are a total of 60 products across the three customer segments.

❏ There are 62 prizm codes per residential segment. Given that prizm codes are a household classification, there are no prizm codes for small business or large accounts.

As a result of this information, we can conclude that the number of rows in the fact table can be computed as $24 \times 8 \times 50 \times 62 = 595{,}200$ rows (in the scheme of things, this a very small fact table). Taking into account that each row in the fact table is 24 bytes (4 bytes per column), we can compute the size of the single fact table to be 13.62MB. Now let's look at the computed size for the separate partitioned fact tables:

Residential fact table:	$24 \times 5 \times 40 \times 62 = 297{,}600$ rows $\times$ 24 bytes = 7MB
Small business fact table:	$24 \times 2 \times 10 \times 1 = 480$ rows $\times$ 20 bytes = 0.009MB
Large business fact table:	$24 \times 1 \times 10 \times 1 = 240$ rows $\times$ 20 bytes = 0.005MB

As is clearly demonstrated, the size of the individual fact tables is smaller than the single fact table. As a matter of fact, the small business fact table and large business fact table are substantially smaller. Though users of just residential segment data will gain benefits in this approach, users of small business data or large business data will gain significant benefits. For example, instead of scanning through a 14MB fact table to view profitability for the small business segment or large business segment, the farmer need only scan through 0.009MB or 0.005MB, respectively. This will result in a significant gain in performance. The only cost with this approach is when a farmer wants to see profitability across segments. In this scenario, all three fact tables would have to be joined. However, the database designer noticed during the prototyping activity that the users did most of their analysis (if not all) against one of the three customer segments (residential, small business, or large business). As a result, few joins are expected.

In addition to dividing the single fact table into three fact tables, you may have also noticed that redundancy has been introduced into the dimensions. For example, in the M_Segment dimension, you can expect that several subsegments will have the same segment name. In addition, in M_Product dimension, you can expect that several products will have the same product category. This denormalization was done to reduce the number of joins needed to access the fact table. For example, with the current implementation of M_Segment, one can expect a single join to the fact table upon selecting a customer segment. However, if M_Segment was normalized into M_Segment and M_Sub-Segment (as it is in the data warehouse), one would expect two joins to the fact table upon selecting a customer segment (M_Segment to M_Sub-Segment to F_Profit_Fact).

The final design decision (which isn't as apparent) was to index column Time_ID, Sub_Segment_ID, Product_ID, and Prizm_ID. Given the selectivity of queries executed against the fact table during the prototype, indexing these columns would provide significant improvements in performance. Bitmap was selected as the indexing technique, given the low cardinality of the columns to be indexed.

THE CAPACITY ESTIMATES   Using the guidelines detailed in Chapter 9, let's assess the total disk storage needed for the profitability analysis data mart and the number of disks, controller cards, and CPUs needed to support throughput. Let's start with several estimates that will drive the process.

Raw data size	7MB (three fact tables) + 0.5MB (four dimensions) = 7.5MB
Data scanned per query	4MB (This number is probably high given that the fact tables for small business and large business are much smaller than this, and given that a majority of the queries will be against the dimension tables. However, it is anticipated that several of the queries will require several passes through the fact table to generate a single report, for example, when calcu-

	lating profitability for a time period versus year to date.)
Desired response time	20 seconds
Number of concurrent queries	30 (Though outside the scope of this iteration, this number includes some anticipated customer service usage in addition to marketing.)

Using these numbers and the formula presented in Chapter 9, we can use the spreadsheet in Figures 13.6 and 13.7 to arrive at the estimates of hardware needed to support profitability analysis.

Arriving at the number of disks needed to house the raw data in the data mart was fairly straightforward. As shown in Figure 13.6, to calculate total disk storage is simply a matter of multiplying the raw data size by 3.5. This multiplier (3.5) is used to account for the additional disk storage to support such things as indexes, temporary tables, data staging areas, etc. This number is just an estimate. Over time, CCI will adjust this number to be more consistent with their experiences.

Arriving at the number of disks, controllers, and CPUs needed to support query throughput is a bit less exact than estimating total disk storage and requires a bit more planning and collaboration with the end users. The following steps were followed in arriving at the matrix in Figure 13.7 (for more details see Chapter 9):

Raw Data Size (MB)	Total Disk Storage (Raw x 3.5)	Disk Type (GB)	Number of Disks to Support Total Disk Storage
7.5	26	4	1

FIGURE 13.6
Number of disks needed to house the data mart design.

Data Scanned Per Query (GB)	Query Response (minutes)	Query Scan Rate (MB/sec)	# of Concurrent Queries	Target I/O Throughput (MB/sec)	# Disks to Support Throughput (5MB/sec/per)	# Controllers to Support Throughput (32MB/sec/per x 1.2)	# CPUs to Support Throughput (40B/sec/per)
4	20	0.20	30	6	1	1	1

FIGURE 13.7
Hardware needed to support query throughput.

1. Data scanned per query was divided by query response to arrive at the query scan rate.
2. Query scan rate was multiplied by the number of concurrent queries to arrive at a target I/O throughput rate.
3. The number of disks to support throughput was then calculated by dividing target I/O throughput by the disk I/O throughput.
4. The number of controllers to support throughput was calculated by dividing the total disk I/O throughput by the controller I/O throughput.
5. The number of CPUs to support throughput was calculated by dividing the total disk controller I/O throughput by the CPU throughput.

As a result of the above estimates for disk storage and query throughput, the CCI project team felt confident that a hardware system configured with one 4GB drive, 1 controller, 1 CPU, and 500MB of memory would easily meet end-user expectations (for profitability analysis) in terms of depth of history, query performance, and number of concurrent users.

It is important to note that the requirements that were used to create these hardware estimates will also be the foundation performance metrics for the service management contract.

THE DISK LAYOUT   The final step in the design process is to map the tables across the disks. Given that the number of disks needed to sustain needed throughput was one 4GB drive, the mapping of the tables was a fairly straightforward exercise, as depicted in Figure 13.8. As the figure illustrates, all of the tables in the profitability analysis design have been placed on a single 4GB drive.

Exploration Warehouse Design

Very much like the data mart, the exploration warehouse is a tailored view of the data warehouse designed to support the specific analytical needs of an explorer. For CCI, the exploration warehouse was positioned to support data mining activities used in developing a model to segment customers. Though this workload could have been done directly against the data warehouse, the demands of this workload would have made it difficult for the

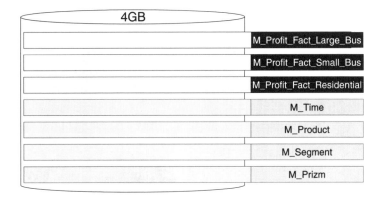

FIGURE 13.8

Table mapping across the disks.

data warehouse to support any other activity but modeling. In response, the CCI project team decided to create an exploration warehouse that contained a subset of the data warehouse tailored (using token-based technology) to support the specific needs related to developing a model to support the segmentation of customers. Once this model was developed and tested in the exploration warehouse, it would be used to classify (i.e., segment) all customers in the data warehouse. For more on the exploration warehouse, see Chapter 3. Now let's take a look at the design, the capacity estimates, and the disk layout in more detail.

THE DESIGN   Figure 13.9 depicts the exploration warehouse design that resulted from the scoping process and subsequent prototyping activities. As you have probably noticed, the design for the exploration warehouse is somewhat normalized. You are absolutely right. As a matter of fact, normalizing techniques are the recommended approach to use in arriving at exploration warehouse design. In many respects, creating an exploration warehouse using token-based technology is very much like creating any relational database. The only difference is in how token-based technologies store data on the disks. It is this difference that allows token-based technologies to achieve the compression and performance needed to make the exploration warehouse a reality.

Although the design for this exploration warehouse could have been more normalized, the explorer requested this organization of data to simplify navigation. If a more normalized model were used, it would have consisted of perhaps a dozen or so tables,

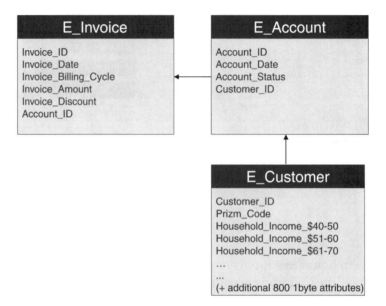

FIGURE 13.9

Exploration warehouse design to support modeling for segmentation.

which would have made navigation more difficult. It is important to note that this decision to denormalize was made for navigation purposes only. The reality is that by further normalizing the design, the explorer probably might have seen better response time (for complex queries) using token-based technology.

The design consists of three tables. The customer table (perhaps better termed the household table) contains 800+ pieces of demographic data that describe the characteristics of households in the neighborhood in which the customer's household resides. This demographic data includes such pieces of data as number of children, average income, etc. This table has been defined to contain a 25% sample or roughly one million of the customers in the data warehouse. For each customer table entry there will be an account table entry. At this time, a customer can only have one account, given the limitation inherit to the business process and supporting legacy systems. The invoice table will contain up to three months of invoice history for each entry in the account table. From this data contained in the exploration warehouse, the explorer will be able to create a meaningful segmentation model based on customer demographics and customer billing history.

A final important point to make before moving on is that this design will likely change shortly after being implemented. As the explorers begin to learn more about the data, it is highly likely that this exploration warehouse will need to be re-created several times before modeling activities to support segmentation are complete. However, this ability to build and rebuild data marts and exploration warehouses is of no worry to CCI, who built their data warehouse environment with this need for adaptability in mind. Now let's take a look at assessing the capacity for the exploration warehouse design.

THE CAPACITY ESTIMATES   Capacity estimates for the CCI exploration warehouse are fairly straightforward. After talking to the vendor, CCI decided to size their exploration warehouse to be one-third that of the raw data size. That's right, one-third not three times (which is common with traditional relational database technologies). Given the nature of the technology, the more sparse the data, the greater the degree of compression. For example, a column like Gender which has only two possible values will see a high degree of compression. On the other hand, a column like Zipcode will see a much smaller degree of compression. In the end, the token-based database will never be any larger than the raw data size and has seen compression in the thousands of percent.

Given the formula recommended by the vendor, CCI arrived at the following disk estimates.

Customer table	1,000,000 rows × 809 bytes/row 0.75GB
Account table	1,000,000 rows × 13 bytes/row 0.012GB
Invoice table	3,000,000 rows × 30 bytes/row 0.084GB
Total raw disk required	0.846GB
Total disk required (total raw disk/3)	0.282GB

THE DISK LAYOUT   Given the small amount of disk space required to support the exploration warehouse, the CCI project team had a very difficult decision. Do they place the database on the same disk as the data mart and leverage unused disk space at the risk of causing CPU and I/O contention, or do they place the database on a separate disk with a separate CPU? In the end the decision was easy. Given the unpredictable nature of the work being performed by the explorer and the demands being placed on the data mart for predictable query response time, it was decided to make a small investment and place the exploration warehouse on its own 4GB disk and CPU. This approach provided room for growth and made it easier for the data warehouse administrator to balance the workload to support the contrasting needs of the explorers and farmers.

Data Warehouse Design

With the completion of the data mart and exploration warehouse designs, CCI was ready to complete the third (and final) design in this iteration of their data warehouse environment, the data warehouse design itself. This design was important because it provided the basis for the database that would house data used in the creation of the data mart and exploration warehouse. In addition, this database would support profiling and classifying activities involved in the segmentation process. Finally, if designed correctly, this database would provide the foundation to support future (yet unplanned) data marts and exploration warehouses. The CCI design team followed the following steps in arriving at their data warehouse design:

1. Create the logical data model.
2. Transform the logical model into a design.
3. Estimate the capacity needed to support the design.
4. Layout the physical design onto the disks.

Let's take a look at what work was performed at each step by the CCI design team.

THE LOGICAL DATA MODEL   As stated above, one of the goals of the data warehouse design was to ensure that it not only supports the current iteration but that it organizes data in such a fashion that it can be used to create future data marts and exploration warehouses. Because of this need to organize data independent of its use, the CCI design team decided to employ entity relationship modeling techniques. By using this technique, the CCI team could arrive at a data model (and subsequent design) that organized data in a fashion that was independent of its use.

To further ensure the reuse of data structures in the data model, the design team solicited involvement from business representatives across the enterprise. By getting input from this cross section of future users, they were able to arrive at a design that not only supported the first iteration of users but one that represented data in a fashion that was consistent and usable by the rest of the enterprise.

After two weeks of interviews and workshops, the design team arrived at the following logical data model (Figure 13.10) for use in current and future design efforts. Although this model is not complete, it provided sufficient detail to support this iteration of the data warehouse environment. Very much like the data warehouse environment itself, the data model will evolve over time as needs are better understood.

Shaded in the figure are 11 entities that represent things of interest to CCI's enterprise. These entities are

Account. Represents a management and reporting entity for CCI products. For example, a CCI customer may have their products rolled up into two separate accounts (business and home) for discounting and reporting purposes.

Address. The smallest geographic location identified by either the conventional postal addressing system or by longitude and latitude measurement.

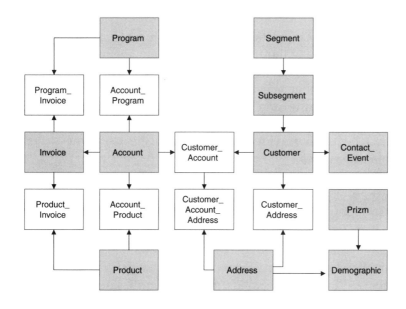

FIGURE 13.10
Logical data model for CCI.

Contact Event. A detailed list of contact events (direct mail, telemarketing, etc.) that are scheduled or have taken place with a customer.

Customer. Current or prospective subscriber to CCI. This could potentially include every person and organization in the world.

Demographic. Provides details that describe the characteristics of people living within a particular area as defined by ZIP+4.

Invoice. A detailed list of goods and services rendered with an account of all costs.

Prizm. A scheme for classifying people who live within a selected demographic area.

Product. A combination of goods and services offered and marketed by CCI.

Program. A plan or procedure for developing relationships with customers. Generally consists of something a customer enrolls into.

Segment and subsegment. A grouping of customers who have common characteristics. This grouping is organized into two levels of hierarchy. The highest level of hierarchy is the segment and within each segment there can be multiple subsegments.

In addition to these entities, there were a number of associative entities (depicted without shading) that show the many-to-many relationships between the core entities. For example, Customer_ Address shows that a customer may have many addresses (as shown by the arrow) and that an address may belong to many customers. In addition to the entities and their relationships, CCI has also begun to provide attribution to further detail the content within the entities.

THE DESIGN   With the logical data model in place, it was time for the CCI design team to transform this model into a data warehouse design. The first step in this process was to identify the entities in the model that were needed to support the data mart and exploration warehouse. After reviewing the data needs for these analytic databases, the design team identified the entities needed, as highlighted in Figure 13.11.

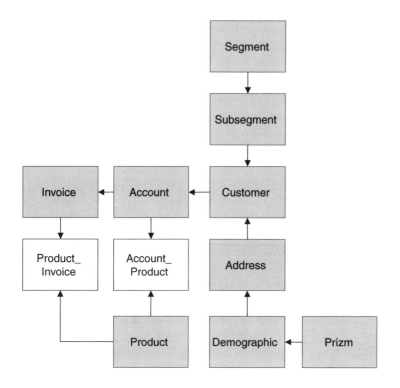

FIGURE 13.11
Entities needed to support the first iteration of the data warehouse.

As you may have noticed, several core entities and their associative entities have been removed because the data they define are not needed for this iteration. Specifically, Program, Program_Invoice, Account_Program, and Contact_Event have been removed. In addition, several other associative entities have been removed: Customer_Address, Customer_Account_Address, and Customer_Account. It was decided that for the purpose of this iteration, these entities would not be needed, given that a customer (given the current business process and supporting legacy) could only have one account and one address in the source system. These associative entities could have been included for use in the future, but they would have provided no added functionally and would have introduced costs and complexities in managing and navigating the resulting database. For example, if Customer_Address is included, not only will there be another table to manage, but to obtain customer address information, a three-table join would have to be performed instead of two.

With the needed entities selected, the next step in the process was to transform the logical model into a design based on usage.

There were three distinct types of workload that were expected to go against the data structures of the data warehouse:

- ❏ Profiling to support segmentation
- ❏ Extracting to support the creation of the exploration warehouse and data mart
- ❏ Classifying to support segmentation

After reviewing the workload, the CCI design team arrived at the following data warehouse design. To simply this design, it has been divided into two parts: design for account data and design for customer data. Let's take a closer look at each of these designs.

Design for Account Data The design in Figure 13.12 depicts the tables in the data warehouse design needed to house account-related data. As you may have noticed (good data warehouse people generally do), not every table contains an element of time. As a matter of fact, the only history being tracked is invoice history (W_Invoice and W_Invoice_Product). After close collaboration with user representatives, it was decided that this iteration would track invoice history. This approach would address immediate business needs

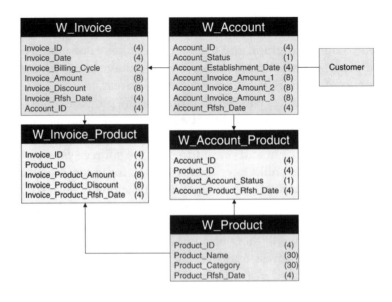

FIGURE 13.12
Design for account data.

and mitigate risk associated with complexities involved in managing history (i.e., time-stamped tables). As additional history is needed (and can be justified), it will be incorporated into the data warehouse.

Another point of interest about this part of the design is that there are no prejoin, column replication, or preaggregation denormalization techniques employed. This was deemed appropriate given the unpredictability of the profiling activities to be performed and the infrequency of extracting activities to create the data mart and exploration warehouse. The benefit of this approach is that data redundancy is kept to a minimum, resulting in less data management complexity and improved load performance. For example, if Account_Date changes, it need only be updated in one place.

The one denormalization technique being deployed was to create arrays of data in the W_Account table in the form of Account_Invoice_Amount_1, Account_Invoice_Amount_2, and Account_Invoice_Amount_3. These three columns provide invoice amounts for the last three months and were placed in the table to support profiling. Using these new columns, an explorer can easily do month-to-month comparisons of invoice amounts for an account (a task not easily performed using a standard profiling tool going against the W_Invoice table).

In a similar light to the above denormalization techniques, indexing was not pursued, given the unpredictability of profiling activities and the infrequency of extracting activities. It was decided to monitor usage to this environment and to incorporate indexing in the event a frequent pattern of access is observed. For example, if it is observed that Account_Invoice_Amount columns are frequently being compared, it probably makes sense to index them using bitmap (although you would probably have to group the discrete amount values into buckets in order to reduce cardinality).

The final point to make about the design is that each table does have a Rfsh_Date column. This column is used to track when a row is refreshed in the data warehouse. This date becomes very important when trying to research data quality issues that may have resulted from the timing of data refreshes.

Design for Customer Data The design in Figure 13.13 depicts the tables in the data warehouse design needed to house customer-

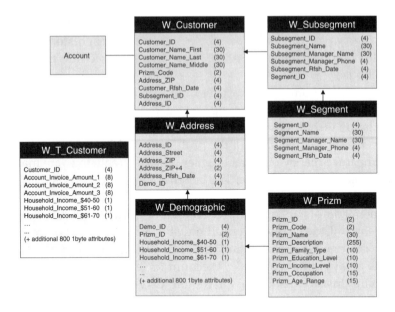

FIGURE 13.13
Design for customer data.

related data. In a similar fashion to the account-related data structures, there is no customer history being managed, although the marketing group thought that it would be nice to track customer segment (and subsegment) history to see the cause and effect of customers moving in and out of segments. The need did not as yet justify the cost. At this time, knowing revenue by current customer segment was a huge leap forward for marketing. Being able to trend the effect of customer movements in and of out these segments still required further thought and justification. It was felt that once the value of this iteration of the data warehouse environment was demonstrated, marketing could easily obtain the needed justification (and funding) to incorporate tracking of customer segment history in a subsequent iteration.

Probably the most interesting table in the design for customer data is the W_T_Customer table. This is a temporary table resulting from the prejoin of W_Account, W_Customer, W_Address, and W_Demographic. Even though this table is relatively expensive to build and refresh, it was justified in several ways:

❏ After reviewing the data needs in the exploration warehouse to support modeling, it was expected that this type of data would be needed together on a fairly regular basis to support profiling and classifying activities related to segmentation. By creating this table once, join activity

❏ involving these tables could be nearly eliminated, thus reducing I/O and CPU overhead in the data warehouse (at the cost of some additional disk), while improving query response time.

❏ After reviewing the business needs and the frequency of refreshment of the types of data in the W_T_Customer table, it became apparent that this table only needed to be refreshed monthly to capture account invoice data and quarterly to capture demographic data. This helped to minimize the overhead involved in building and maintaining this table, thus making it more attractive.

To summarize, this approach was pursued to improve query response time and reduce the costs associated with accessing account invoice and demographic data to support profiling, extracting, and classifying activities related to segmentation.

Another use of denormalization in the design for customer data is the use of column replication in the W_Customer table. As you may have noticed, CCI replicated the Prizm_Code and Address_ZIP column from the W_Demographic and W_Address tables, respectively. After interviewing and observing the explorers in the prototype environment, it became clear that these columns would be used on a regular basis with customer data to support profiling activities. By replicating these columns, frequent joins resulting from these profiling activities would be eliminated, thus improving query response time and reducing CPU and I/O overhead at the cost of some additional disk space.

THE CAPACITY ESTIMATES　　The steps to arrive at capacity estimates for the data warehouse are similar to those of the data mart; that is, we start the process by estimating the hardware needed to house the data. In some respects this step in the process is a bit easier given that all we need to know is the number of rows that will be loaded into the data warehouse by table and the size of each row. This is in contrast to the fact table in the data mart where the number of rows had to be determined based on the number of unique combinations of values across dimension columns.

After analyzing the input files to the data warehouse, the CCI project team identified the following row counts for the different tables, followed by anticipated growth for the remainder of the year (6 months). This is shown in Figure 13.14.

Table	#Rows	Bytes Per Row	6 Month Growth	Raw Data Size (GB)
W_Invoice (Start with 6 months of history)	24,000,000	34	100%	1.520
W_Invoice_Product (3 products per invoice)	72,000,000	28	100%	3.755
W_Account	4,000,000	37	5%	0.145
W_Account_Product (3 products per account)	12,000,000	13	15%	0.116
W_Product	60	68	1%	0.000
W_Customer	2,000,000	112	4%	0.325
W_Address	3,000,000	22	4%	0.064
W_Demographic	200,000	809	1%	0.152
W_Subsegment	8	76	1%	0.000
W_Segment	3	72	1%	0.000
W_Prizm	62	379	1%	0.000
W_T_Customer	3,000,000	831	4%	2.415
Total Raw Data Size (GB)				8.492

FIGURE 13.14
Raw data size for the data warehouse.

Following the process used in the data mart design, CCI arrived at the following hardware needed to house the data (Figure 13.15) and hardware needed to support query throughput (Figure 13.16).

As depicted in Figure 13.15 the data warehouse will need approximately 30GB of disk storage to support users' needs as defined for this iteration. This estimate includes space to support database indexes and temp tables as well as disk space to stage the data prior to loading. It is important to remember that these are only estimates and will be refined by CCI as they monitor actual disk allocation and growth in the data warehouse.

Hopefully by now you have come to appreciate why monitors are so important even in the early stages of data warehouse delivery. Just imagine what your implementation would be like with only your estimates and no way to track and steer your course. This would be synonymous to planning a trip from San Francisco to New York City and driving the trip blindfolded. You might get where you want to go but it will be a slow painful process.

As you have probably noticed, the matrix created for the data warehouse is slightly different than that created for the data mart. In the data mart we only had one workload to size (i.e., MDA to support profitability analysis), in the data warehouse we have four workloads to size.

The first workload involves profiling. It is expected that the explorer will average about 2.5GB per query on average given

Raw Data Size (GB)	Total Disk Storage (Raw x 3.5)	Disk Type (GB)	Number of Disks to Support Total Disk Storage
8.492	29.722	4	8

FIGURE 13.15
Number of disks needed to house the data warehouse design.

most queries are expected to go against the W_T_Customer table. These queries are expected to be the most frequent and unpredictable. At this time, the sizing has taken into account that only two explorers will be active at any one time.

The next two workloads involve the two extracting queries that create the exploration warehouse and data mart. Though these queries are fairly complex and require access to significant amounts of data, their query response time demands are fairly low, and they can be scheduled after hours so that they do not compete with profiling queries. It is expected that the extracting query to create the exploration warehouse will use the W_T_Customer table most of the time. However, the extracting query to create the data mart will likely need to access most of the tables in the data warehouse. Fortunately, the data mart will be created infrequently. Long-term, CCI plans to incorporate a refreshment process for the data mart that entails periodic updates versus a complete refresh. This will require a bit more programming but will free-up resources to support future iterations of the data warehouse.

The fourth and final workload involves the query to classify customers based on the segmentation model that the explorer developed using the exploration warehouse. This query is similar to the two extracting queries in that it is complex and requires access to significant amounts of data. Fortunately, this query is fairly infrequent and can be run after hours so that it does not compete with profiling queries. This query is expected to use the W_T_Customer table most of the time. Over time, CCI plans to enhance this process to support classifying using multiple models with a single

Workload	Data Scanned Per Query (GB)	Query Response (minutes)	Query Scan Rate (MB/sec)	Number of Concurrent Queries	Target I/O Throughput (MB/sec)	Number of Disks to Support Throughput (5MB/sec/per)	Number of Controllers to Support Throughput (32MB/sec/per x 1.2)	Number of CPUs to Support Throughput (40B/sec/per)
Profiling	2.5	2.5	17.07	2	34.13	6.8	1	1
Extracting (Exploration Warehouse)	2.5	180.0	0.237	1	0.24	0.1	0	0
Extracting (Data Mart)	5.4	180.0	0.512	1	0.51	0.1	0	0
Classifying	2.5	180.0	0.237	1	0.24	0.1	0	0
Total	2.5	542.30	19.54	5	38.09	7.1	1	1

FIGURE 13.16
Hardware needed to support query throughput.

pass through the data. Very much like the long-term changes to the extracting process to support updates to the data mart (see previous), this will require a bit more programming but will free-up resources to support future iterations of the data warehouse.

Given the throughput requirements, it was decided that this combined workload would only need one CPU, one controller card and data stripped across seven disks to support desired throughput. You might be wondering why seven disks and not eight? This is a very good question. If we expected all workloads to be running concurrently, you are absolutely correct. In this scenario we would need to stripe the data across eight disks to support desired throughput. However, given the nature of the extracting and classifying workloads, they can be scheduled to run when profiling queries are not running. As a result, we need only size the machine to support throughput requirements for profiling.

Hopefully by now, you have started to appreciate the importance of dividing the user workload into those workload types defined in Chapter 3. By doing so, you not only ensure that the workload is positioned to run on the right component of the platform (e.g., data warehouse, data mart, exploration warehouse, etc.) but that that component of the platform is optimized (e.g., being able to support throughput needs with seven disks instead of eight).

Now that we have seen how CCI sized the machine to support the data warehouse, let's take a quick look at the final stage in the design process, the disk layout.

THE DISK LAYOUT   As you can see, CCI decided to partition the larger tables across seven 4GB disks (to achieve throughput requirements) and the smaller (look-up) tables on a separate 4GB disk. This was done to help minimize contention between queries that are looking for "valid values" in the look-up tables (i.e., W_Prizm, W_Product, W_Segment, and W_Subsegment) from those queries scanning the larger tables. In addition, CCI also used this 4GB drive as the data staging area to help further reduce contention against queries scanning the larger tables.

The partitioning scheme used to stripe the data varied a bit. Given the serial nature of the key for all of the larger tables except W_Demographic (and therefore little concern for skewing), "hash" partitioning was used to stripe data across the seven drives. In this way, fragment elimination could be leveraged whenever possible. W_Demographic was striped using round-robin. In this way, CCI

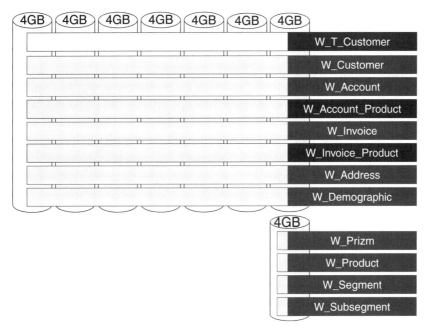

FIGURE 13.17
Table mapping across the disks.

could be ensured of an even distribution of data and maximum throughput when a query was requesting this data. Finally, no striping was performed on the four smaller look-up tables. These tables were all placed on a single drive.

Configure the Hardware

With the database technology decision and design in their pocket, CCI proceeded on to the next decision, the selection of the hardware technology. As it turned out, this decision was fairly easy as well, given their budget constraints for the first iteration. Their decision was (after talking to a number companies of similar size and business need) to start with SMP technology. This approach provided several benefits:

❑ Some degree of scalability
❑ Relatively low entry-level cost
❑ Access to fairly mature technology

This approach would allow CCI to get up and running quickly with minimal investment and risk. In addition, this approach would provide CCI needed scalability to support several iterations of the data warehouse platform. Once this SMP solution was outgrown, CCI would replace it with a more scalable MPP or NUMA solution and reallocate the SMP solution to support data marts and/or exploration warehouses. In this way, CCI would be able to scale their data warehouse platform and protect/leverage their SMP investment.

In addition to selecting SMP technology for this iteration, the CCI project team decided to implement the data warehouse, data mart, and exploration warehouse on the same tier (i.e., hardware) as depicted in Figure 13.18. As discussed in Chapter 9, this

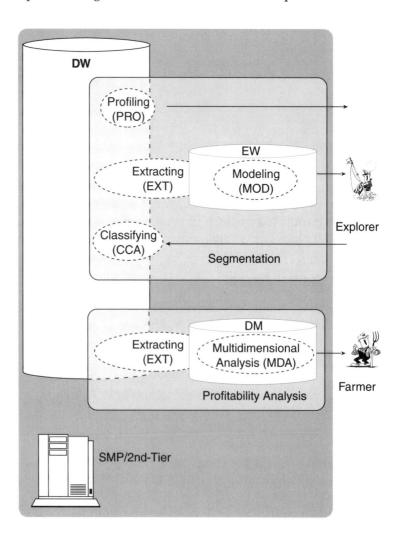

FIGURE 13.18
SMP 2-Tier Implementation.

approach helps to further minimize risk and complexity of the implementation. However, the data warehouse, data mart, and exploration warehouse will be logically separate so that as the second tier becomes constrained, the data mart and/or exploration warehouse can be migrated to a third tier as depicted in Figure 13.19. See Chapter 9 for more information on this scalable data mart approach to delivering your platform.

In addition to deciding on two-tier versus three-tier, CCI had to determine the actual configuration. As it turned out, this was a fairly straightforward exercise given the capacity estimates had

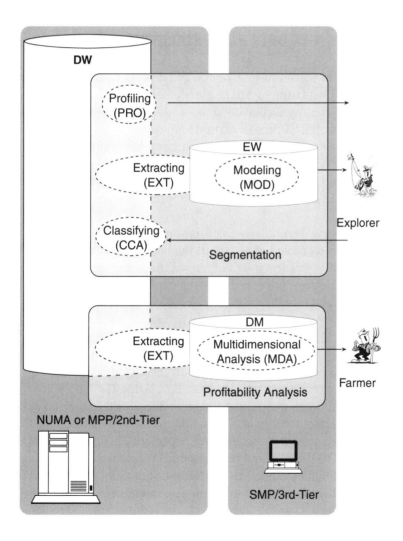

FIGURE 13.19
SMP Three-tier implementation.

already been done for the individual database designs (data warehouse, data mart, and exploration warehouse). All CCI had left to do was to compile the separate estimates into a final configuration. The final SMP configuration consisted of 3 CPUs, 2 controller cards and 10 4GB disks. You may be asking yourself, why two controller cards and not three? This seemed to make sense given only the data warehouse throughput needs even came close to using the full capacity of a controller card. As a result, it was decided to configure one controller card to support the data warehouse and to share a controller card between the data mart and exploration warehouse.

SERVICING THE DATA WAREHOUSE ENVIRONMENT

With the data warehouse environment designed, configured, and delivered, it was time to put in place a service management contract (SMC) that would be used to administer the environment going forward. CCI project team decided to take a conservative approach to the creation of this document. Rather than create the SMC based on the metrics used to size the environment, the project team decided to monitor the production environment for several weeks and use observations on query performance as a baseline for the SMC.

Following several weeks of use and tuning of the designs, the project team reconvened to layout the SMC for going forward. So as not to make this too much of a task, the team decided to focus measuring performance in three areas: query performance, availability, and data quality.

Deriving metrics for query performance was relatively easy. The project team assigned query performance metrics for each of the types of workload (e.g., profiling, MDA) based on observed query response-time. As it turned out, these query response times were fairly close to the estimates used in sizing the hardware for the different databases. The only exception was the query response time for the profitability analysis data mart. As it turned out, these queries were quite a bit faster than expected. This exception was largely due to the fact that the data mart was sized for more concurrent users than existed in marketing. Remember that this data mart was sized for limited customer service access as well. As a result, the project team agreed to stick with the query performance metrics as defined in the hardware throughput estimates rather than what was actually being observed. This made sense given these metrics were more realistic of what would be observed once customer service began accessing the data mart. Finally, the project team agreed that classifying and extracting queries would run over the weekend and complete by 8:00 A.M. Monday morning.

Deriving metrics for availability turned out to be fairly easy. The project team quickly agreed that the data warehouse environment would be available to support profiling and MDA from 8:00 A.M. to 6:00 P.M. 90% of the time.

Deriving metrics for data quality turned out to be a bit more difficult than expected. The project team quickly discovered that they knew less about the valid values for a particular data element than they expected. For example, they thought that an account could only have one of three statuses (A, Z, and Q). However, after monitoring the content of data and doing a bit of research, they discovered that an account could have one of seven statuses (A, Z, Q, C, D, R, and P). This process of discovery continued as they began to monitor the actual contents of data in the data warehouse. Given this process could continue for some time, the project team decided to incorporate the valid value rules they did know (and observed) into the SMC and refine the metrics as the contents of the data warehouse were better understood. In addition to these valid value tests, the project team also agreed to test that referential integrity was working as expected, that the daily integration and transformation process were working correctly, and that the data in the data warehouse reconciled back to the source system.

The above metrics may seem fairly simple, but that is exactly what the CCI project team set out to accomplish. That is, establish a handful of simple (and measurable) metrics that the service management group could use to assess whether the data warehouse environment was meeting user expectations. CCI would then enhance these metrics as the environment matured to account for other metrics that were of importance to the business. The biggest challenge that faced the CCI project team was that of monitoring usage and content of data such that performance could be measured objectively. The CCI project team knew that without this monitoring, the existence of an SMC would be of little value.

SUMMARY

Congratulations! You have been given a wealth of knowledge from which to begin your journey to delivering and servicing a high-performance data warehouse environment.

In the first section of this book, we introduced you to usage, data, and the monitors needed to effectively manage these two layers of a high-performance data warehouse environment. In addition we discussed the importance of understanding these two layers in that they shape the landscape of your data warehouse environment. That is, they provide the basis for assessing and positioning workload, the basis for assessing database design techniques and technology, and the basis for sizing the hardware on which the database(s) reside.

In the second section of this book, we talked about the components that comprise the platform layer used to support usage and data. In addition, we talked in detail about architecting, designing, sizing, and implementing these components into a balanced platform. Finally, we covered advanced topics to consider in evolving this platform.

In the third section, we talked in detail about the process for managing services being delivered. In particular, we talked about the importance of service management, the role of the service management contract, and steps for putting the service management contract in motion. This was a critical discussion given many data warehouse environments start out high-performing but quickly become sub-performing because steps were not taken to ensure they continued to meet user expectations.

Finally, we used a case study (Customer Communications, Inc.) to put many of the techniques and practices covered in the previous three sections to work. In addition, this case study introduced several building blocks (building the team and scoping the three-to-six month deliverable) critical to arriving at a solid foundation from which to deliver a high-performance data warehouse environment. Though no single case study could cover everything presented in this book, this case study provided a basis from which you can begin to apply the extensive knowledge and experience contained within.

We hope you find this book useful and that it becomes your handbook to designing, evolving, and nurturing your high-performance data warehouse environment.

Recommended Reading

ARTICLES

Adelman, Sid. "The Data Warehouse Database Explosion." *DMR* (December 1996). A very good discussion of why volumes of data are growing as fast as they are in the data warehouse environment and what can be done about it.

"An Architecture for a Business and Information System." *IBM Systems Journal* 17, no. 1 (1988). A description of IBM's understanding of the data warehouse.

Ashbrook, Jim. "Information Preservation." *CIO Magazine* (July 1993). An executive's view of the data warehouse.

Bair, John. "It's about Time! Supporting Temporal Data in a Warehouse." *INFODB* 10, no. 1 (February 1996). A good discussion of some of the aspects of time-variant data in the DSS/data warehouse environment.

Ballinger, Carrie. "TPC's Emerging Benchmark for Decision Support." *DBMS* (December 1993). A description of the extension of the TPC benchmark to include DSS.

Discount Store News. "Retail Technology Charges Up at KMart." (February 17, 1992). A description of the technology employed by KMart for its data warehouse, ODS environment.

Geiger, Jon. "Data Element Definition." *DMR* (December 1996). A good description of the definitions required in the system of record.

Geiger, Jon. "Information Management for Competitive Advantage." *Strategic Systems Journal* (June 1993). A discussion of how the data warehouse and the Zachman framework have advanced the state of the art.

Geiger, Jon. "What's in a Name." *Data Management Review* (June 1996). A discussion of the implications of naming structures in the data warehouse environment.

Gilbreath, Roy, Jill Schilp, and Robert Rickton. "Towards an Outcomes Management Informational Processing Architecture." *HealthCare Information Management* 10, no. 1 (Spring 1996). A discussion of the architected environment as it relates to health care.

Gilbreath, Roy. "Health Care Data Repositories: Components and a Model." *Journal of the Healthcare Information and Management Systems Society* 9, no. 1 (Spring 1995). An excellent description of information architecture as it relates to health care.

Gilbreath, Roy. "Informational Processing Architecture for Outcomes Management." A description of the data warehouse as it applies to health care and outcomes analysis. Under review.

Goldberg, Paula, Robert Lambert, and Katherine Powell. "Guidelines for Defining Requirements for Decision Support Systems." *Data Resource Management Journal* (October 1991). A good description of how to define end-user requirements before building the data warehouse.

Graham, Stephen. "The Financial Impact of Data Warehousing." *Data Management Review* (June 1996). A description of the cost-benefit analysis report done by IDC.

Graham, Stephen, analyst. "The Foundations of Wisdom." IDC Special Report (April 1996). International Data Corp. (Toronto, Canada). The definitive study on the return on investment for the data warehouse, as well as the measurement of cost effectiveness.

Hackney, Doug. "Vendors Are Our Friends." *Data Management Review* (June 1996). Doug Hackney talks about beneficial relationships with vendors.

Hufford, Duane. "A Conceptual Model for Documenting Data Synchronization Requirements." American Management Systems. Data synchronization and the data warehouse.

Hufford, Duane. "Data Administration Support for Business Process Improvement." American Management Systems. The data warehouse and data administration.

Hufford, Duane. "Data Warehouse Quality, Part I." *Data Management Review* (January 1996). A description of data warehouse quality.

Hufford, Duane. "Data Warehouse Quality—Part II." *Data Management Review* (March 1996). The second part of the discussion on data quality.

Imhoff, Claudia. "Data Steward." *ComputerWorld* (September 4, 1995). Provides an overview of the data steward's role in the data warehouse environment. Additionally, this role is contrasted to the traditional role of a data analyst.

Imhoff, Claudia. "End Users: Use 'em or Lose 'em." *DMR* (November 1996). An excellent discussion of the ways to manage the end-user data warehouse effort.

Imhoff, Claudia, and Jon Geiger. "Data Quality in the Data Warehouse." *Data Management Review* (April 1996). A description of the parameters used to gauge the quality of data warehouse data.

Imhoff, Claudia, and Ryan Sousa. "Information Ecosystem–Introduction." *Data Management Review* (January 1997). Introduction to the information ecosystem.

Imhoff, Claudia, and Ryan Sousa. "Information Ecosystem–Corporate Information Factory." *Data Management Review* (February 1997). Details the parts and pieces of the Corporate Information Factory as defined by Bill Inmon. In addition, reviews the business relevance of the capabilities produced.

Imhoff, Claudia, and Ryan Sousa. "Information Ecosystem–Administration." *Data Management Review* (March 1997). Details the components and techniques used in administering the information ecosystem.

Imhoff, Claudia, and Ryan Sousa. "Information Ecosystem–People & Process." *Data Management Review* (April 1997). Details suggested organizational structures and roles. Additionally reviews processes for building, using and managing the information ecosystem.

Imhoff, Claudia, and Ryan Sousa. "Information Ecosystem–Information Services." *Data Management Review* (May 1997). Discusses how Information Services is used to provide a common navigation interface to the information ecosystem (Metadata, Data Delivery, DSS tools, etc.), how this interface facilitates the coordination of People & Process and how it ultimately provides a common knowledge fabric.

"In the Words of Father Inmon." *MIS* (February 1996). An interview with Bill Inmon in November of 1995 in Australia.

Inmon, W. H. "The Anatomy of a Data Warehouse Record." *Data Management Review* (July 1995). A description of the internal structure of a data warehouse record.

Inmon, W. H. "At the Heart of the Matter." *Data Base Programming/Design* (July 1988). Primitive and derived data and what the differences are.

Inmon, W. H. "Building the Data Bridge." *Data Base Programming/Design* (April 1992). Ten critical success factors in building the data warehouse.

Inmon, W. H. "The Cabinet Effect." *Data base Programming/Design* (May 1991). A description of why the data warehouse-centered architecture does not degenerate into the spider web environment.

Inmon, W. H. "Chargeback in the Information Warehouse." *Data Management Review* (March 1993). Chargeback in the data warehouse can be both a blessing and a curse. This article addresses both sides of the issue.

Inmon, W. H. "Choosing the Correct Approach to Data Warehousing: 'Big Bang' vs Iterative." *Data Management Review* (March 1996). A discussion of the proper strategic approach to data warehousing.

Inmon, W. H. "Commentary: The Migration Path." *ComputerWorld* (July 29, 1996). A brief description of some of the issues of migrating to the data warehouse.

Inmon, W. H. "Cost Justification in the Data Warehouse." *Data Management Review* (June 1996). A discussion of how to justify DSS and data warehouse on the cost of reporting.

Inmon W. H. "Data Structures in the Information Warehouse." *Enterprise Systems Journal* (January 1992). A description of the common data structures found in the data warehouse.

Inmon, W. H. "Data Warehouse—A Perspective of Data over Time." *370/390 Data Base Management* (February 1992). A description of the relationship of the data warehouse and the management of data over time.

Inmon, W. H. "The Data Warehouse—All Your Data at Your Fingertips." *Communications Week* (August 29, 1994). An overview of the data warehouse.

Inmon, W. H. "Data Warehouse and Contextual Data: Pioneering a New Dimension." *Data Base Newsletter* 23, no. 4 (July/August 1995). A description of the need for contextual data over time, as found in the data warehouse.

Inmon, W. H. "The Data Warehouse and Data Mining." *CACM* 39, no. 11 (November 1996). A description of the relationship between data mining and data warehouse.

Inmon, W. H. "Data Warehouse Lays Foundation for Bringing Data Investment Forward." *Application Development Trends* (January 1994). A description of the data warehouse and the relation to legacy systems.

Inmon, W. H. "The Data Warehouse: Managing the Infrastructure." *Data Management Review* (December 1994). A description of the data warehouse infrastructure and the budget associated with it.

Inmon, W. H. "Data Warehouse Security: Encrypting Data." *Data Management Review* (November 1996). A description of some of the challenges of data warehouse security and industrial strength security.

Inmon, W. H. "EIS and Detail." *Data Management Review* (January 1995). A description of how much detail is needed to support EIS and the role of summarized data in the data warehouse environment.

Inmon, W. H. "EIS and the Data Warehouse." *Data Base Programming/Design* (November 1992). The relationship between EIS and the data warehouse.

Inmon, W. H. "From Transactions to the Operational Data Store." *INFO DB* (December 1995). A discussion about how quickly transactions in the operational environment go into the operational data store.

Inmon, W. H. "The Future in History." *DMR* (September 1996). A discussion of the value of historical information.

Inmon, W. H. "Going Against the Grain." *Data Base Programming/Design* (July 1990). A description of the granularity issue and how it relates to the data warehouse.

Inmon, W. H. "Growth in the Data Warehouse." *Data Management Review* (December 1995). A description of why the data warehouse grows so fast and the phenomenon of increasing amounts of storage while decreasing the percent utilization of storage.

Inmon, W. H. "Knowing Your DSS End-User: Tourists, Explorers, Farmers." *DMR* (October 1996). A description of the different categories of end users.

Inmon, W. H. "The Ladder of Success." *Data Management Review* (November 1995). Building and managing the data warehouse environment entails more than selecting a platform. This article outlines the many necessary steps required to achieve a successful data warehouse environment.

Inmon, W. H. "Managing the Data Warehouse Environment." *Data Management Review* (February 1996). Defining who the data warehouse administrator is.

Inmon, W. H. "Managing the Data Warehouse: The Data Content Card Catalog." *DMR* (December 1996). An introduction to the notion of a data content card catalog, i.e., stratification of data content.

Inmon, W. H. "Measuring Capacity in the Data Warehouse." *Enterprise Systems Journal* (August 1996). A discussion of how capacity should be measured in the data warehouse, DSS environment.

Inmon, W. H. "Metadata: A Checkered Past, A Bright Future." *370/390 Data Base Management* (July 1992). A conversation about metadata and how metadata relates to the data warehouse.

Inmon, W. H. "Monitoring the Data Warehouse Environment." *Data Management Review* (January 1996). What is a data monitor for the data warehouse environment and why would you need it?

Inmon, W. H. "Multidimensional Data Bases and Data Warehousing." *Data Management Review* (February 1995). A description of how current detailed data in the data warehouse fits with multidimensional DBMS.

Inmon, W. H. "Neat Little Packages." *Data Base Programming/Design* (August 1992). A description of how data relationships are treated in the data warehouse.

Inmon, W. H. "The Need for Reporting." *Data Base Programming/Design* (July 1992). The different kinds of reports found throughout the different parts of the architecture.

Inmon, W. H. "Now Which Is Data, Which Is Information." *Data base Programming/Design* (May 1993). The difference between data and information.

Inmon, W. H. "The Operational Data Store." *INFODB* 9, no. 1 (February 1995). A description of the ODS.

Inmon, W. H. "Performance in the Data Warehouse Environment." *Data Warehouse Report* Issue 3 (Autumn 1995). A description of the different aspects of performance in the data warehouse environment.

Inmon, W. H. "Performance in the Data Warehouse Environment— Part 2." *Data Warehouse Report* (Winter 1995). A continuation of the prior article on data warehouse performance.

Inmon, W. H. "Profile/Aggregate Records in the Data Warehouse." *Data management Review* (July 1995). A description of how profile/aggregate records are created and used in the data warehouse environment.

Inmon, W. H. "Profiling the DSS Analyst." *Data Management Review* (March 1995). A description of DSS analysts as farmers and explorers.

Inmon, W. H. "Rethinking Data Relationships for Warehouse Design." *Sybase Server* 5, no. 1 (Spring 1996). A discussion of the issues of data warehouse data relationships.

Inmon, W. H. "SAP and the Data Warehouse." *DMR* (July/Aug 1996). A description of why data warehouse is still needed in the face of SAP.

Inmon, W. H. "Security in the Data Warehouse: Data Privatization." *Enterprise Systems Journal* (March 1996). Data warehouse requires a very different approach to security than the traditional VIEW based approach offered by DBMS vendors.

Inmon, W. H. "The Structure of the Data Warehouse." *Data Management Review* (August 1993). This article addresses the different levels of data found in the data warehouse.

Inmon, W. H. "Summary Data: The New Frontier." *Data Management Review* (May 1996). A description of the different types of summary data including dynamic summary data and static summary data, lightly summarized data and highly summarized data, et al.

Inmon, W. H. "Transformation Complexity." *Data Management Review* (September 1995). Why automating the transformation process is a superior idea to manually programming the transformations that are required in order to build the data warehouse.

Inmon, W. H. "Untangling the Web." *Data Base Programming Design* (May 1993). Exploring the factors that turn data into information.

Inmon, W. H. "User Reaction to the Data Warehouse." *DMR* (December 1996). A description of the different user types in data warehousing.

Inmon, W. H. "Virtual Data Warehouse: The Snake Oil of the '90s." *Data Management Review* (April 1996). A discussion of the virtual data warehouse and how the concept tries to attach itself to the legitimacy of the data warehouse.

Inmon, W. H. "Winds of Change." *Data Base Programming/Design* (January 1992). Data administration and the data warehouse—a description of how data administration evolved to where it is today.

Inmon, W. H., and Chuck Kelley. "The 12 Rules of Data Warehouse." *Data Management Review* (May 1994). A description of the defining characteristics of the data warehouse.

Inmon, W. H., and Phyliss Koslow. "Commandeering Mainframe Database for Data Warehouse Use." *Application Development Trends* (August 1994). A discussion of optimal data warehouse use inside the mainframe.

Inmon, W. H., and Michael Loper. "The Unified Data Architecture: A Systems Integration Solution." Auerbach Publications (1992). The original paper (republished in a revised state) suggesting that a data architecture was in order for future systems development.

Inmon, W. H., and Sue Osterfelt. "Data Patterns Say the Darndest Things." *Computerworld* (February 3, 1992). A description of the usage of the data warehouse in the DSS community and how informational processing can be derived from a warehouse.

Jordan, Arthur. "Data Warehouse Integrity: How Long and Bumpy the Road?" *Data Management Review* (March 1996). A discussion of the issues of data quality inside the data warehouse.

Kador, John. "One on One." Interview with Bill Inmon, Midrange Systems (October 27, 1995). A discussion about data warehouse with Bill, including some of the history of how data warehouse came to be.

Kimball, Ralph. "Is ER Modelling Hazardous to DSS?" *Data Warehouse Report* (Winter 1995). A dialogue on dimensional modelling versus ER modelling.

Kimball, Ralph, and Kevin Strehlo. "Why Decision Support Fails and How To Fix It." *Datamation* (June 1994). A good description of fact tables and star joins, with a lengthy discussion about Ralph's approach to data warehouse and decision support.

Konrad, Walecia. "Smoking Out the Elusive Smoker." *BusinessWeek* (March 16, 1992). A description of database marketing in the advertising restricted marketing environment.

Lambert, Bob. "Break Old Habits to Define Data Warehousing Requirements." *Data Management Review.* A description of how the end user should be approached to determine DSS requirements.

Lambert, Bob. "Data Warehousing Fundamentals: What You Need to Know to Succeed." *Data Management Review* (March 1996). Several significant strategies for data warehousing to guide you through a successful implementation.

Laney, Doug. "Are OLAP and OLTP Like Twins?" *DMR* (December 1996). A comparison of the two environments.

"Liberate Your Data." *Forbes* (March 7, 1994). An interesting but naive article about the data warehouse as viewed from the uninformed businessperson.

Myer, Andrea. "An Interview with Bill Inmon." *Inside Decisions* (March 1996). An interview discussing the start of data warehousing, use of data warehousing for competitive advantage, the origins of Prism Solutions, building the first data warehouse, etc.

O'Mahoney, Michael. "Revolutionary Breakthrough in Client/Server Data Warehouse Development." *Data Management Review* (July 1995). A description of older legacy development methodologies versus modern iterative methodologies.

Rudin, Ken. "Parallelism in the Database Layer." *DMR* (December 1996). An excellent discussion of the differences between DSS parallelism and OLTP parallelism.

Rudin, Ken. "Who Needs Scalable Systems." *DMR* (November 1996). A good discussion of the issues of scalability in the data warehouse environment.

Sloan, Robert, and Hal Green. "An Information Architecture for the Global Manufacturing Enterprise." Auerbach Publications (1993). A description of information architecture in the large-scale manufacturing environment.

Swift, Ron. "Creating Value Through a Scalable Data Warehouse Framework." *DMR* (November 1996). A very nice discussion of the data warehousing issues scale.

Tanler, Richard. "Data Warehouses and Data Marts: Choose Your Weapon." *Data Management Review* (February 1996). A description of the differences between data marts and the current level detail of the data warehouse.

Tanler Richard. "Taking Your Data Warehouse to a New Dimension on the Intranet." *Data Management Review* (May 1996). A discussion of the different components of the data warehouse as they relate to the intranet.

"The Doctor of DSS." DBMS Interview. *DBMS magazine* (July 1994). An interview with Ralph Kimball.

Thiessen, Mark. "Proving the Data Warehouse to Management and Customers: Where Are the Savings?" A presentation given at the 1994 Data Warehouse Conference; for foils and handouts.

Verity, John W., and Russell Mitchell. "A Trillion Byte Weapon." *BusinessWeek* (July 31, 1995). A description of some of the larger data warehouses that have been built and how they play a role in business competition.

Wahl, Dan, and Duane Hufford. "A Case Study: Implementing and Operating an Atomic Database." *Data Resource Management Journal* (April 1992). A description of the U.S. Army DSS data architecture.

Welch, J. D. "Providing Customized Decision Support Capabilities: Defining Architectures." Auerbach Publications (1990). Discusses decision support systems and architecture (based on the PacTel Cellular DSS architecture).

Winsberg, Paul. "Modeling the Data Warehouse and the Data Mart." *INFODB* (June 1996). A description of architecture and modelling as it relates to different types of data warehouses.

Wright, George. "Developing a Data Warehouse." *DMR* (October 1996). A very good discussion of snapshots and the basic structures of data warehouse.

BOOKS

Berry, Michael, J.A., and Gordon Linoff, *Data Mining Techniques for Marketing, Sales and Customer Support.* New York: John Wiley & Sons, 1997.

Berson, Alex, and Stephen J. Smith. *Data Warehousing, Data Mining, and OLAP.* New York: McGraw-Hill, 1997.

Brackett, Mike. *The Data Warehouse Challenge.* New York: John Wiley & Sons, Inc., 1996.

Devlin, Barry. *Data Warehouse: From Architecture to Implementation.* Reading, Massachusetts: Addison Wesley, 1997.

Fleming, Candace C., and Barbara Von Halle. *Handbook of Relational Database Design.* New York: Addison-Wesley, 1989.

Inmon, W. H. *Building the Data Warehouse,* 2d ed. New York: John Wiley & Sons, Inc., 1996. (1st edition 1992)

Inmon, W. H. *Information Systems Architecture: Development in the '90s.* New York: John Wiley & Sons, Inc., 1992.

Inmon, W. H. *Rdb/VMS: Developing the Data Warehouse.* New York: John Wiley & Sons, Inc., 1993.

Inmon, W. H. *Third Wave Processing: Database Machines and Decision Support Systems.* New York: John Wiley & Sons, Inc., 1990.

Inmon, W. H., and R.D. Hackathorn. *Using the Data Warehouse.* New York: John Wiley & Sons, Inc., 1994.

Inmon, W. H., Claudia Imnoff, and Greg Battas. *Building the Operational Data Store.* New York: John Wiley & Sons, Inc., 1996.

Inmon, W.H., J.D. Welch, and Katherine L. Glassey. *Managing the Data Warehouse.* New York: John Wiley & Sons, Inc., 1997.

Inmon, W. H., John A. Zachman, and Jonathan G. Geiger. *Data Stores, Data Warehousing and the Zachman Framework.* New York: McGraw-Hill, 1997.

Kelly, Sean. *Data Warehousing—The Key to Mass Customization.* New York: John Wiley & Sons, Inc., 1994.

Kimball, Ralph. *The Data Warehouse Toolkit.* New York: John Wiley Sons, Inc., 1996.

Kimball, Ralph, Laura Reeves, Margy Ross, and Warren Thornthwaite. *The Data Warehouse Lifecycle Toolkit.* New York: John Wiley & Sons, Inc., 1998.

Love, Bruce. *Enterprise Information Technologies.* New York: John Wiley & Sons, Inc., 1993.

Parsaye, Kamran, and Marc Chignell. *Intelligent Database Tools and Applications.* New York: John Wiley & Sons, Inc., 1989.

BOOK REVIEWS

Information Systems Management (Winter 1997) Bookisms. Paul Gray, "Mining for Data Warehouse Gems." A review of several books on data warehousing.

Index